7/07

PALLADIO'S ROME

PUBLISHED WITH THE ASSISTANCE OF
THE GRAHAM FOUNDATION
FOR ADVANCED STUDIES IN THE FINE ARTS

ANDREAS PALLADIVS

ex eleganti antiqua tabella
apud March.ᵉ Capra Patricios Vicetinos

1   Palladio, engraved by Francesco Zucchi. Ashmolean Museum, Oxford.

PALLADIO'S ROME

A Translation of Andrea Palladio's
Two Guidebooks to Rome
by
VAUGHAN HART and PETER HICKS

YALE UNIVERSITY PRESS
NEW HAVEN AND LONDON

Designed by Gillian Malpass

Printed in China

Library of Congress Cataloging-in-Publication Data

Palladio, Andrea, 1508–1580.
[Antichità di Roma. English]
Palladio's Rome : a translation of Andrea Palladio's two guidebooks to Rome /
Vaughan Hart and Peter Hicks.
p. cm.
Includes bibliographical references and index.
ISBN 0-300-10909-1 (cloth : alk. paper)
1. Architecture–Italy–Rome–Guidebooks–Early works to 1800. 2. Rome
(Italy)–Buildings, structures, etc.–Guidebooks–Early works to 1800. 3. Rome
(Italy)–Guidebooks–Early works to 1800. I. Hart, Vaughan, 1960– II. Hicks, Peter,
1964– III. Title.
NA1120.P33 2006
720.945'6309031–dc22
2005028847

The photographs are the authors' own, except where otherwise indicated.

In memory of

Mary Hart

and

Augusto Da Prati

CONTENTS

2 (*facing page*)   View inside the Baths of Antoninus/Caracalla.

PREFACE

Andrea Palladio (1508–1580) is one of the most famous architects of all time. His pocket-sized guides to the churches and antiquities of Rome were, on their publication in 1554, enormously popular and almost immediately reprinted. Whilst some of the buildings that Palladio describes have now disappeared, and some of the churches have been rebuilt or lie within the confines of the Vatican City, a remarkable number have survived. The pilgrimage routes that the churches and their relics define make for hugely enjoyable walks across the city. With this book in hand modern visitors can quite literally follow in the footsteps of their Renaissance counterparts, rediscovering the charm of Rome's ancient and medieval wonders. Even the city's residents can discover a neglected – and sometimes hidden – aspect to their city in the form of its medieval churches, just as the Renaissance visitor had often to search for the half-buried ancient ruins that Palladio describes.

In these early guides to Rome Palladio sought to be both scholarly and popular, laying the ground for the success of his buildings. His guidebooks obviously appealed to a different audience from that of his more famous treatise on architecture and ancient buildings, the *Quattro libri*, which was aimed at princes and designers. Nevertheless, within the context of the recent English translations of such treatises this present translation fills a chronological gap. For it lies between Sebastiano Serlio's study of ancient buildings of 1540, translated by the present authors in 1996, and the *Quattro libri* of 1570, translated by Tavernor and Schofield in 1997. In much the same way, Raphael's letter to Pope Leo X concerning the monuments of ancient Rome, here translated in the appendix, fills a gap between Leon Battista Alberti's *Descriptio Urbis Romae*, translated by Hicks in 2003, and Serlio. This is the first ever full English translation of this famous letter, which is included for the light it throws on Renaissance interest in the ancient monuments of Rome.

This book is, like Palladio's originals, pocket-sized and therefore easily read on site – indeed the utility of the originals has been enhanced for the armchair visitor by the inclusion of illustrations and commentary. This new edition thus facilitates the same kind of enjoyment of Rome that Palladio intended almost exactly 450 years ago, when the preface to his guide to the city's ancient wonders urged the visitor to: 'Read carefully, then, this new work of mine if you wish fully to experience the huge pleasure and the wonder that can come from a detailed understanding of the great things in so noble and celebrated a city as that of Rome.'

ACKNOWLEDGEMENTS

We should like to thank the following for their help and support at various stages in the preparation of this translation: Dr Mario Carpo, Professor Ingrid Rowland, Dr Susan Russell, Professor Joseph Rykwert, Mark Wilson Jones, Philippa Baker, and Fathers Martin Draper and Matthew Harrison at St George's, Paris. In particular, Professor Robert Tavernor gave us valuable advice on the introduction. Librarians have given assistance at Bath University Library; the Warburg Institute, London; the Staatsbibliothek, Munich; The British School at Rome; The British Architectural Library, Royal Institute of British Architects, London; and the RIBA Drawings Collection. We thank also the Rare Books Departments at Cambridge University Library; the British Library, London; the Vatican Library, Rome; the Bibliothèque Nationale, Paris; and the Institut national d'histoire de l'art, Département de la Bibliothèque et de la Documentation Collections Jacques Doucet, Paris.

The Graham Foundation for Advanced Studies in the Fine Arts generously funded archive visits in Italy and a tour of the churches and ancient monuments in Rome described by Palladio. The Department of Architecture and Civil Engineering at the University of Bath also funded travel associated with the work. The British School at Rome provided us with accommodation and the use of their library during our visits to the city.

Finally, we thank Gillian Malpass at Yale University Press, Elisabetta Da Prati and Charlotte Hart for their invaluable support and efforts throughout this project.

Vaughan Hart and Peter Hicks
University of Bath

ABBREVIATIONS

Alberti   Alberti, L.B., *De re aedificatoria* (1452): references in square
brackets are to the English translation: *On the Art of Building in Ten Books*,
trans. J. Rykwert, N. Leach and R. Tavernor (1988).

Arte Antica   Bianchi Bandinelli, R. (ed.), *Arte Antica – Enciclopedia dell'arte
antica, classica e orientale*, 7 vols (1958–66).

Palladio, *Antiquities*   refers to the translation and original page numbers
cited in this volume in square brackets, *The Antiquities of Rome . . .
Succinctly Compiled From Authors both Ancient & Modern* (1554).

Palladio, *Churches*   refers to the translation and original page numbers
cited in this volume in square brackets, *Description of the Churches, Stations
of the Cross, Indulgences, and Relics of the Bodies of Saints, in the City of Rome*
(1554).

QL   Palladio, A., *I quattro libri dell'architettura* (1570); references in square
brackets are to the English translation: *The Four Books on Architecture*,
trans. R. Tavernor and R. Schofield (1977).

RIBA   indicates the catalogue number of a Palladio drawing held in the
Drawings Collection of the Royal Institute of British Architects, London.

Serlio   Serlio, S., *Il Terzo libro di Sabastiano Serlio Bolognese* (1540);
references in square brackets are to the English translation: *Sebastiano
Serlio on Architecture*, vol. 1: Books I–V of *Tutte l'opere d'architettura et
prospetiva*, trans. V. Hart, P. Hicks (1996).

4 (*facing page*)   The 'Temple of Pudicitia'.

INTRODUCTION

> Being aware of the great desire in everyone to acquire a
> thorough understanding of the antiquities in, and other worthy
> features of, so celebrated a city, I came up with the idea of
> compiling the present book, as succinctly as I could, from
> many completely reliable authors, both ancient and modern,
> who had written at length on the subject.
> Andrea Palladio, *L'antichità*, fol. 1.

This book brings together for the first time in translated form the
publications on Rome of one of the most famous figures of the Italian
Renaissance, whose influence was both immediate and long lasting.
Andrea Palladio's architecture is so well known that it seems surprising
that his works on the monuments of ancient and medieval Rome should
be relatively unfamiliar, and therefore be downplayed as sources for our
understanding of his concerns.[1] This is all the more so since the material
represents such an important record as to his understanding of
antiquity.

Palladio's *L'antichità di Roma di M. Andrea Palladio, raccolta brevemente da
gli auttori antichi, & moderni* first appeared in 1554 and by the middle of
the eighteenth century had run to more than thirty editions (the most
recent reprint was in 1988).[2] It was republished in Oxford in 1709 in a

---

1   See Puppi, L., *Andrea Palladio: Scritti sull'architettura (1554–1579)* (1988), in
which both guides are transcribed without commentary. Olivieri correctly treats
the guidebook to the churches as a statement of Palladio's utopian and spiritual
ideals. See Olivieri, A., *Palladio, le corte e le famiglie* (1981), pp. 99–104.

2   Puppi (1988). For a complete bibliography of editions, see Schudt, L.,
Le Guide di Roma; Materialien zu einer Geschichte der römischen Topographie (1930;
reprint 1971). See also E.D. Howe's translation of the *Descritione de le chiese*,
omitting the list of the stations: *Andrea Palladio: The Churches of Rome* (1991),
p. 139, n. 2. In the first edition of *L'antichità* held in the British School at Rome
(classmark 600 639, with the bookplate of Thomas Ashby), a pencil note in
English in the flyleaf claims that notes (and underlinings) throughout the book
are in Palladio's hand. These thus far unauthenticated notes, twelve in number,
are very brief and are truncated because the book has been trimmed.

Latin translation, and was translated into English (with omissions) and
appended to the third edition of James Leoni's translation of Palladio's
I quattro libri dell'architettura (1570) in 1742. In this position it enjoyed a
status as nothing less than Palladio's 'fifth' book.[3] The anachronistic
terminology of the eighteenth-century translation of *L'antichità* obscures
its original language in the same way that Leoni's *Quattro libri* had done
before the 1997 English translation of the 'Four Books'.[4]

Comprising about sixty pages in its pocket-sized (octavo) format, the
text is organized into brief descriptions of the appearance and history of
the ancient ruins, written for travellers who flocked to Rome to witness
its marvels at first hand. It includes sections on the bridges, hills, water
supply, aqueducts, baths, circuses, theatres, fora, arches, temples and
columns of the ancient city, as well as legendary buildings such as the
Golden House of Nero. Palladio avoids repeating earlier authors' censure
of buildings of vanity and luxury – the Golden House, for example,
which had been criticized by Pliny the Elder – describing their opulence
in the same matter-of-fact terms used for utilitarian structures of
unquestionable virtue such as aqueducts and cisterns, which Pliny had
praised. In this way the text offers a more neutral catalogue of ancient
archetypal structures, prefiguring modern methods of classification by
type used by scientific archaeology. In this approach Palladio followed his
peers – men such as Pirro Ligorio (*c.*1510–83), whose unillustrated *Libro
di M. Pyrrho Ligori napolitano, delle antichità di Roma, nel quale si tratta de'
circi, theatri, & anfitheatri* was published in Venice in 1553, with categorized
accounts of the circuses, theatres and amphitheatres of ancient Rome.[5]

Rome's monumental ruins were, together with its law and literature,
perhaps the most powerful legacy from pre-Christian times. This
realization is summed up by the inscription on the frontispiece of
another influential work on Rome, the third volume of Sebastiano
Serlio's treatise, published in Venice in 1540, which reads 'Roma qvanta
fvit ipsa rvina docet' – 'How great Rome was, the ruins themselves

---

3   See introduction in R. Tavernor and R. Schofield, *The Four Books on
Architecture* (1997), p. xvi (page references below in square brackets for *I quattro
libri dell'architettura* are to this translation). The translation is not present in the
1965 Dover facsimile reprint of the *Quattro libri*, based as it is on Isaac Ware's
edition of 1738.

4   Tavernor and Schofield (1997).

5   See Mandowsky, E., and C. Mitchell, *Pirro Ligorio's Roman Antiquities*
(1963); Palladio (1991), p. 10; Van Eck, C., *British Architectural Theory 1540–1750*,
(2003), p. 244, n. 24.

IL TERZO LIBRO
DI SABASTIANO SERLIO BOLO.
GNESE, NEL QVAL SI FIGVRANO, E DESCRIVONO LE
ANTIQVITA DI ROMA, E LE ALTRE CHE SO.
NO IN ITALIA, E FVORI D'ITALIA.

ROMA QVANTA FVIT IPSA RVINA DOCET

6   Frontispiece of the third volume of Sebastiano Serlio's
treatise *On Antiquities* (1540), woodcut.

reveal'. Serlio (1475–1554) took this inscription from Francesco Albertini's
Opusculum de mirabilibus novæ et veteris urbis Romæ of 1510. Albertini
(fl. 1510) relates that Cardinal Galeotto Franciotto della Rovere (d.1507),
the nephew of Pope Julius II, encouraged him to correct the 'fabulous
nonsense' in existing guidebooks to Rome. In trying to achieve this aim
he juxtaposed categorized descriptions of ancient and modern Rome just
as Palladio would do – albeit through two separate guides.[6]

   For in the same year as *L'antichità* first appeared, but slightly later (if his
own account is to be believed), Palladio published a companion volume
– a guide to Rome's churches entitled *Descritione de le chiese, stationi,*

6   Albertini, F., *Opusculum de mirabilibus novæ et veteris urbis Romæ* (1510),
p. 5. On Albertini see Palladio (1991), pp. 32–3.

indulgenze & reliquie de Corpi Sancti, che sono in la città de Roma.[7] For this guide he chose the same Rome publisher as before, Vincentio Lucrino. Lucrino was less prominent than the leading Rome publishers with whom Palladio later collaborated such as Antonio Blado and the Dorico brothers, Valerio and Luigi.[8] His office was at the Campo dei Fiori and, later, on Via del Pellegrino. Two views and one map of Rome, issued as prints and sold to tourists, can be credited to him during the 1550s and 1560s. He was no doubt drawn to publish Palladio's books through the expectation that they would generate similar financial gain to the maps. Palladio, on the other hand, may have chosen Lucrino because of his Church connections (in particular with the Jesuits), whose sanction was desirable for such works.[9] In contrast to *L'antichità*, *Le chiese* was never republished or translated in its original form with Palladio's name on the title page, although it was frequently reissued without the introductory letter and bound with other guides.[10]

Palladio's opening remarks in *Le chiese* emphasize the intended order of the two books and their relationship as a pair, dealing in turn with the secular and the sacred (or more accurately, with the pagan and the Christian – and, for the most part, with the ancient and the modern):

> Since I have described the antiquities of Rome, with as much care and brevity as I could manage, in another book of mine, I also wished to describe for your more complete satisfaction and pleasure the sacred things in that city and their current circumstances; because the accounts of them that have been written in the past do not in many respects correspond to the facts today, since being holy objects they

7 Both guides were reproduced in facsimile in Peter Murray's *Five Early Guides to Rome and Florence* (1972), and were transcribed by Puppi (1988) and on CD-ROM in the collection entitled 'Art Theories of the Italian Renaissance', published by Chadwyck-Healey in 1997 (the CD-ROM transcription of *L'antichità* is from the Venice edition of 1554). The *Descritione de le chiese* alone was translated by Eunice D. Howe in 1991 and published as a Medieval and Renaissance Texts and Studies volume, now out of print. There are frequent errors in Howe's translation, and Palladio's list of *Le Stationi, Indulgentie & Gratie spirituali* is omitted. A copy of the 1554 *Le chiese* survives in the library of the Royal Institute of British Architects, London. On other copies see Palladio (1991), pp. 32, 149, n. 3.

8 On Lucrino see Barberi, F., 'I Dorico, tipografi a Roma nel cinquecento', *La Bibliofilia*, vol. 67, (1965), pp. 221–61; Palladio (1991), pp. 26–9.

9 See Palladio (1991), p. 28.

10 See Palladio (1991), pp. xi–xii, 19, 38–46.

have become altered and moved from one place to another owing to the wars, fires and ruination to which they have been subjected, and to the building of new churches, hospitals and confraternities.[11]

In consequence the topical overlap between the two works is limited and concerns the consecration of ancient buildings such as the Pantheon. About the same length as *L'antichità*, *Le chiese* was written to provide pilgrims with a religious itinerary and on occasions includes Palladio's judgement as to the relative artistic value of the works being visited. Both were intended to be read as guidebooks and were consequently unillustrated, thereby allowing the visitor to appreciate the city's monuments through Palladio's words alone. Since both guides introduced structures later cited in the *Quattro libri* – for example, the bronze columns in St John Lateran and ancient Rome's senate houses – they should be seen as valuable if somewhat neglected precursors to that most famous and influential of Renaissance books on architecture.[12]

Palladio's Early Life and Visits to Rome

Palladio was born Andrea della Gondola, or di Pietro, in 1508, the son of a Paduan mill worker. He died on 19 August 1580 and was buried in the church of Santa Corona in Vicenza. Apprenticed to a stonemason at thirteen, he had broken his contract by 1524 and moved to Vicenza, where he joined the guild of masons and stone carvers. From 1524 to the 1540s he was associated with the Pedemuro workshop of Giacomo da Porlezza (fl. 1530s), which produced most of the decorative sculpture in Vicenza. Around 1537 Andrea met Gian Giorgio Trissino (1478–1550), a Vicentine humanist and diplomat who was rebuilding a villa at Cricoli, outside Vicenza, and it is thought possible that Trissino encountered Andrea during the villa's construction.[13] Here Trissino established a learned academy to enable the city's young noblemen to receive a classical education. He took Andrea into his academy to direct his

7

11   Palladio, *Churches*, [p. 1] (in reference to original page numbers, here and below).

12   See for example Tavernor, R., 'Palladio's 'Corpus': *I quattro libri dell'architettura*', in *Paper Palaces: The Rise of the Renaissance Architectural Treatise*, ed. V. Hart and P. Hicks (1998), pp. 233–46.

13   See Constant, C., *The Palladio Guide* (1985), p. iii; Tavernor, R., *Palladio and Palladianism* (1991), p. 17; but see also Puppi, L., *Andrea Palladio* (1975), p. 8. On Trissino's academy see Boucher, B., *Andrea Palladio, The Architect in his Time* (1994), pp. 23–4.

7 Vincenzo Catena, *Giangiorgio Trissino*, *c*.1525, oil on canvas. Musée du Louvre, Paris.

education, giving him the name 'Palladio', possibly after Palladius, the ancient author of an agricultural treatise, or after Pallas Athena and the Roman talisman in her image, the Palladium. According to the Vicentine Paolo Gualdo, canon of Padua Cathedral, who wrote a biography of the architect in 1616, 'Finding Palladio to be a young man of very spirited character and with a great aptitude for science and mathematics, Trissino encouraged his natural abilities by training him in the precepts of Vitruvius.'[14] Palladio's study of the treatise of the Roman author Vitruvius not surprisingly stimulated his interest in antiquity and its architecture during this formative period, and was naturally supplemented with the

14   Transcribed in Gualdo, P., 'La vita di Andrea Palladio', ed. G.G. Zorzi, *Saggi e Memorie di Storia dell'Arte*, vol. 2 (1958–59), pp. 91–104. See the English translation in Lewis, D., *The Drawings of Andrea Palladio* (1981), pp. 3–4. See also the biographical summary in Burns, H., L. Fairbairn and B. Boucher, *Andrea Palladio 1508–1580: The Portico and the Farmyard* (1975), pp. 69–72.

work of the Renaissance architectural master, Leon Battista Alberti
(1404–72).[15]

The probable year of Palladio and Trissino's meeting – 1537 – coincided
with the publication in Venice of the fourth volume of Serlio's treatise,   8
which was on the Orders of architecture, and Palladio would also closely
study this treatise (his copy of Serlio is the only book to survive from his
library).[16] Palladio's Basilica in Vicenza (1546–1617) was to be based on   9
Serlio's design, and it is thought probable that the two architects were on   10
familiar terms.[17] Palladio may well have been part of the intellectual
circle meeting in Serlio's house in Venice before 1541 (the year of Serlio's
departure to France), where he could have studied Serlio's collection of
drawings of Roman monuments, many by Baldassare Peruzzi
(1481–1536). And he attended the theatrical performance staged by
Serlio in 1539 in the courtyard of a *palazzo* in Vicenza belonging to
the Porto family.[18] Between 1538 and 1540 Trissino was in Padua,
accompanied at least part of the time by Palladio. Here Palladio was
influenced by the humanist and patron Alvise Cornaro (*c.*1484–1566),
whose Loggia had been built in 1524 and Odeon in 1530, both to the
all'antica designs of Cornaro and Giovanni Maria Falconetto (1468–1535),
although the Odeon was built under the supervision of Andrea della Valle
(d.1577).

During his first decade as an architect, Palladio concentrated on
building palaces and country villas for the nobility of Vicenza.[19] The
esteem in which his adopted city held him is indicated by the city
council's decision to give the architect the design of its most important
public building, namely the Basilica. During the 1560s Palladio travelled
extensively, eventually establishing his reputation as a leading architect in
Venice. In the same way that the publication in Rome of the guides to
that city was intended by Palladio as a means to further his reputation at
the very heart of the Catholic Church, so the publication of the second

---

15   *QL*, I, foreword, p. 5 [p. 5].

16   It is in the Kunsthistorisches Institut, Florence. See Burns, Fairbairn and
Boucher (1975), pp. 75–6, no. 141, although see note 2, above. See the English
translation of Serlio's text by V. Hart and P. Hicks, *Sebastiano Serlio on Architecture*,
vol. 1: Books I–V of *Tutte l'opere d'architettura et prospetiva* (1996) (page references
below in square brackets for Serlio's treatise are to this translation).

17   Serlio, Book I, fol. XXXIIr [p. 311].

18   On Serlio's influence on Palladio, see Puppi (1975), pp. 10, 14; Tavernor
(1991), pp. 21–2, 110–11.

19   Puppi (1975); Constant (1985).

8a (*above left*)   Frontispiece of the fourth volume of Sebastiano Serlio's treatise
On the Orders (1537), woodcut.

8b (*above right*)   Serlio's Composite Capitol, woodcut from his fourth volume.

edition of *L'antichità* in Venice by Matteo Pagan, in the same year as its
Rome printing, 1554, was no doubt intended to help establish its author's
reputation in Venetian circles (as would the Venetian publication of his
I Commentari di C. Giulio Cesare in 1575). After all, in publishing a work
on Roman antiquity in Venice he followed in the honourable footsteps
of fellow architects Ligorio and Serlio, and it is notable that in his short
account of Palladio's achievements, Gualdo singles out *L'antichità* but fails
to mention *Le chiese*, which had not been published in Venice.[20] Palladio
moved to Venice in 1570, taking advantage of the opportunity created by
the death of the prominent architect Jacopo Sansovino, and it is here that
much of his later work is situated. Through the influence of the humanist
scholar Daniele Barbaro (1514–70), he built a series of remarkable
churches there, notably San Giorgio Maggiore (1564–80) and the
Redentore (1576–80). He returned to Vicenza in 1579 to execute his last

20   Gualdo (1958–59); Lewis (1981), p. 3: 'he published a little guidebook to
the city's antiquities, which is commonly sold together with the book called
The Wonders of Rome.' See Palladio (1991), p. 1.

9 (*above left*)   The Basilica at Vicenza, designed by Palladio.

10 (*above right*)   A model façade, woodcut from the fourth volume of Sebastiano Serlio's treatise *On the Orders* (1537), which is thought to reflect his design for the Basilica in Vicenza.

public commission, the Teatro Olimpico (begun 1580), in a design that represents a perfect example of his combination of modern invention based on ancient precedent.   14

   With Padua the city of his birth and Vicenza the city of his youth, Palladio was first and foremost an architect of the Veneto and its neighbouring provinces. The modern-day fame enjoyed by the cities of Vicenza and Venice rests in no small part on his works there. Held to have been founded by refugees at the fall of the Roman Empire, Venice cultivated the myth of Roman origins without the ruins to prove it.[21] Palladio himself bought into this myth, describing the city in 1570 as 'the sole remaining exemplar of the grandeur and magnificence of the Romans'.[22] With its pointed windows, Venetian architecture was in fact as much Gothic or Byzantine as it was built *all'antica* (as John Ruskin would later demonstrate). But despite the relative splendour of Venice,

21   On the uniqueness of Venice among major Italian cities in having no classical past of its own, see Brown, P.F., *Venice and Antiquity* (1996).

22   *QL*, I, foreword, p. 5 [p. 5].

11 Paolo Veronese, *Daniele Barbaro*, oil on canvas. Rijksmuseum, Amsterdam.

12 (*above right*) San Giorgio Maggiore, Venice, designed by Palladio.

15 (*facing page*) The Temple of Vesta at Tivoli in plan, section and elevation, woodcut from the third volume of Sebastiano Serlio's treatise (1540).

13 (*above*) The Redentore, Venice, designed by Palladio.

14 (*right*) The Teatro Olimpico, Vicenza, designed by Palladio.

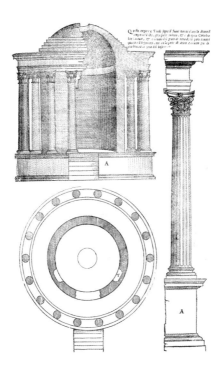

Rome was endowed like no other Italian city with monumental antique ruins in various states of preservation.

In early 1541, just after the outset of his architectural career and a year after the publication of the third volume of Serlio's treatise, on the antiquities of Rome, Palladio had first visited the city, accompanied by Trissino. Serlio's book, with its striking woodcuts of the most important monuments in plan, section and elevation, must surely have caught Palladio's imagination and, with Trissino's help, guided him on subsequent trips as to what buildings to study and how they should be drawn.[23] For here, according to Gualdo, 'Palladio measured and made drawings of many of those sublime and beautiful buildings which are the revered relics of Roman antiquity'.[24] Indeed, although these drawings

15

23   On Palladio's debt to Serlio in reconstructing the Mausoleum of Romulus, for example, see Tavernor (1991), p. 77. See also Lewis (1981), pp. 42–3, no. 21. See Serlio (1996).

24   Gualdo (1958–59); Lewis (1981), p. 3.

16   The ciborium in the church of Santo
Spirito in Sassia, Rome, of 1546–47,
engraving from Petrus Saulnier's *De capite
sacri ordinis Sancti Spiritus dissertatio* (1649).

were mostly produced from on-site measurements, some were copied
from studies by Serlio and Ligorio.[25] The influence of the city on
Palladio's intellectual development was immediate and marked, testified
by the pronounced Roman character of his design for the Palazzo Thiene
in Vicenza (*c*.1542–50) as but one example.[26] This short trip – Palladio
was back in Vicenza by the autumn – was to be the first of five visits to
Rome. He returned between September 1545 and February 1546 and
between March 1546 and July 1547 (both visits once again with Trissino,
as confirmed by Gualdo), then again in November–December 1549 and
finally in 1554.[27]

25   On Palladio's reliance on drawings by Serlio, see Puppi (1975), pp. 10, 13.

26   Ackerman, J., *Palladio* (1966), p. 95; Tavernor (1991), pp. 29–32; Boucher
(1994), pp. 29, 48–59.

27   See Puppi (1975), pp. 13, 23, n. 71, 276. In Palladio (1991), p. 4, E.D.
Howe assumes that Palladio made Rome his base between 1545 and 1547,
thereby counting only four trips (in contradiction of Gualdo).

17 Antonio da Sangallo the Younger, the wooden
model of the project for St Peter's built by Antonio
Labacco, 1539–46, Vatican, Fabbrica di S. Pietro,
cat. no. 346.

He undertook only relatively minor works in Rome. The ciborium in   16
the church of Santo Spirito in Sassia of 1546–47 is thought to be by him,
although it goes curiously unmentioned in the description of the church
in his guide.[28] His visit in November–December 1549 was possibly to
advise on the basilica of St Peter's, but once again he does not boast of
this in his guide.[29] He probably saw Sangallo the Younger's recently built   17
giant model for the building, with its 'quotation' of ancient wonders such
as the tomb of Lars Porsenna. Rome's principal merit was in offering
Palladio first-hand experience of its monuments and wonders and of

28   See Puppi (1975), pp. 27, 265, no. 24, 266, no. 25; Palladio (1991),
pp. 11–12. RIBA XVII 18V. Howe also mentions, although discounts, the
tradition that Palladio designed a two-storey loggia in the garden façade of the
palace of the dukes of Tuscany (Palladio (1991), pp. 13–14), and the façade of
Santa Maria at the Collegio Romano (p. 14).
29   See Gualdo (1958–59); Lewis (1981), p. 3. See also Puppi (1975), p. 276,
n. 30.

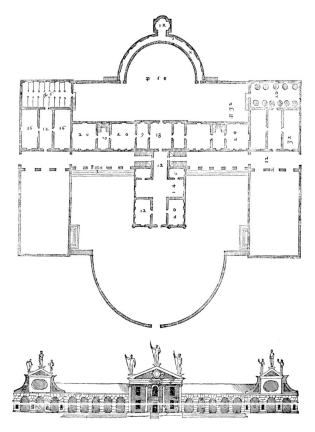

18a   The Villa Barbaro at Maser, woodcut from Palladio's *I quattro libri dell'architettura* (1570).

18b   The Villa Barbaro at Maser, designed by Palladio.

how architects were adapting these to imbue them with spiritual virtue in new works such as those of Donato Bramante, Peruzzi, Antonio da Sangallo, Raphael, Michelangelo and Giulio Romano. In consequence the city was of enormous importance for Palladio's study of *all'antica* architecture.

Palladio produced not only many detailed drawings of the ruins of Roman antiquities but also imaginative reconstructions, most of which were probably drawn between 1545 and 1547 and on his last visit, in the year of publication of both guidebooks, 1554.[30] Both books are thought to have been written on this last visit, when he was accompanied by Barbaro and Ligorio – *L'antichità* most likely between February and July and *Le chiese* thereafter.[31] Barbaro became Palladio's guiding light after the death of Trissino in 1550, most famously commissioning Palladio some time between 1549 and 1551 (finishing in 1558) to build him and his younger brother, Marc'Antonio, the Villa Barbaro at Maser. Barbaro served as Patriarch Elect of Aquileia and on the Council of Trent, convened for the second time by Pope Julius III in 1551. This involvement of Palladio's new mentor with the Catholic Church can only have helped focus his attention on its relics, indulgences, architecture and history, as outlined in *Le chiese*.

18

Palladio's Guidebooks, the Edition of Vitruvius and the *Quattro libri*

Palladio's early drawings of ancient Roman remains led via *L'antichità* to Barbaro's edition of Vitruvius' treatise published two years later in 1556, in an ongoing project to decipher the text of the Roman author, which was often confused or wanting in detail. The dissection of the ancient ruins to establish their original purposes was, for example, vital in understanding Vitruvius' theory of appropriateness of scale and decoration for particular building types and patrons, referred to by him as 'decorum'. Palladio was clearly much concerned with this principle, as, for example, his opening chapter in the *Quattro libri* – 'On the decorum or suitability that must be maintained in private buildings' – makes clear. From 1547 Palladio and Barbaro collaborated on the illustrations for the Vitruvius text; their interest in the 'wonders' of the ancient world led them to reconstruct the mausoleum at Halicarnassus, for example.[32] Also

30   See Lewis (1981), especially chapters 5–6, pp. 129–50.
31   Burns, Fairbairn and Boucher (1975), p. 91; Puppi (1975), p. 441. But see Palladio (1991), pp. 9, 143, n. 38.
32   Lewis (1981), pp. 122–3, no. 71.

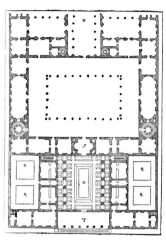

19   Palladio's reconstruction of the Roman house, woodcut from Daniele
Barbaro's Latin edition of Vitruvius's treatise (1567).

included were Palladio's illustrations of the Roman theatre and his

19   imaginative reconstruction of the Roman house with its pedimented
elevation. He also published studies of the latter in the *Quattro libri*,[33]

20   while his plan of the Venetian monastery of Santa Maria della Carità was
based on the ancient house.

Having described Nero's Golden House in *L'antichità* (based on
descriptions by Suetonius and Pliny), Palladio's section 'On other Houses,
notably those for Citizens' equally reflects this special interest in the
ancient house as described by Vitruvius, rather than being based on any
actual ancient remains, which lay as yet undiscovered. Palladio justified

21   his use of the temple pediment on domestic architecture by arguing in
the *Quattro libri* that the form of the ancient temple, as the house of the
gods, was derived from primitive dwelling types.[34] Indeed the same
origins are traced by him in *L'antichità* when discussing domestic
residences. Here he starts with the Palatine hut of Romulus as the
physical and symbolic origin of the city and its architecture, only then
progressing to more opulent residences, which are sourced, for the most
part, again in Pliny. In this way consistent lines of thought can be traced
across his works.

33   *QL*, II. vii, [pp. 109–11].
34   *QL*, I, foreword, p. 5 [p. 5], II, xvi, p. 69 [p. 147]. See Tavernor (1991),
pp. 44, 50–5.

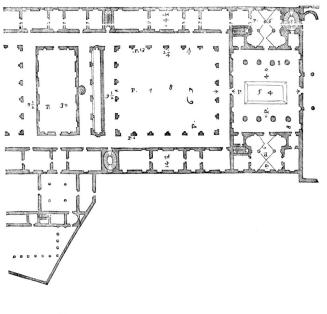

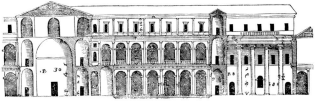

20   The monastery of Santa Maria della Carità, woodcut from Palladio's *I quattro libri dell'architettura* (1570).

21   The Villa Rotunda, near Vicenza, designed by Palladio, with its pediments.

22 Contemporary Mannerist ornamental 'abuses', two gates, engravings from Sebastiano Serlio's *Extraordinario libro di architettura* (1551).

Palladio's studies in Rome – of which *L'antichità* formed an important part – were the foundation of his and Barbaro's attempt to construct a 'true' *all'antica* architectural style in the wake of contemporary

22 Mannerist ornamental 'abuses' (as he termed them) with respect to ancient models.[35] It is significant that Bramante's Tempietto (1502–10) stands alone as the sole modern example of excellence in the *Quattro libri*, just as for the most part Palladio does not praise contemporary churches in *Le chiese* (although the Tempietto is mentioned in passing). In *Le chiese* his focus is mostly on liturgical artworks, relics and icons rather than on architects and architecture (aside, that is, from a church's foundation story, or legends such as Honorius I's use of the bronze tiles from the Capitoline temple of Jupiter to cover St Peter's). His reference to Giacomo Vignola's Sant'Andrea as a 'chapel built with great skill and beauty for His Holiness, Our Lord Pope Julius III', stands out as a notable exception in approving a modern *all'antica* work.[36]

His cautious, even conservative, attitude to the achievements of his age is underlined by the fact that, despite mentioning works by a number of the more celebrated Renaissance architects and artists – including

35   *QL*, I, xx, p. 51 [p. 55].
36   Palladio, *Churches*, [pp. 34–5].

Bramante, Raphael and Vignola – he does not cite them by name, apart from a single reference to Michelangelo when describing his tomb design for Julius II. His approach is similar in *L'antichità*, where he includes structures from the Middle Ages like the Tor de' Conti and Torre delle Milizie, but buildings from the more recent, early Renaissance are omitted – apart, that is, from a brief mention of the Belvedere and the Vatican and the paintings of Michelangelo.

But quite obviously the guidebooks were not architectural treatises intended to provide models of good practice along the lines of the *Quattro libri*.[37] Indeed, in *Le chiese* Palladio notes that Santa Costanza is 'circular in form', but not that it had become a celebrated 'model' for contemporary church design (as illustrated by Serlio in the third book of his treatise).[38] In the *Quattro libri*, in contrast, the circular church would be put forward as a model and lauded as the 'most beautiful and regular'.[39] Instead, in *Le chiese* Santa Costanza's virtues lie in its roots in early Christianity, alongside – but not in preference to – many other churches in the book's itinerary. The concluding churches on Palladio's routes are no more important than their predecessors. Guided by Palladio, the pilgrim is, after all, on a journey that does not end in any particular earthly church (not even St Peter's). Spiritual virtues were clearly more important here than physical ones.

Just as the text of Vitruvius was checked and deciphered through drawings of ancient monuments, so in the preparation of both guidebooks Palladio went beyond desk-bound reading in using the emerging techniques of antiquarians such as Ligorio and Serlio – namely direct on-site surveys.[40] For instance in *Le chiese* he tells his readers that he has taken information concerning the foundation of certain churches from ancient plaques to be found in the buildings themselves.[41] These plaques are, in many instances, still in existence. Good examples are the two long inscriptions on the façade of the church of Santa Maria del Popolo in the Piazza del Popolo. Following on from an opening source list of modern authors on Rome, Palladio continues in *L'antichità*: 'But

23

---

37 See Hart and Hicks (1998).

38 Palladio, *Churches*, [p. 57].

39 *QL*, IV, ii p. 6 [p. 216].

40 See Burns, Fairbairn and Boucher (1975), pp. 84–5; Mitrovic, B., 'Palladio's Canonical Corinthian Entablature and the Archaeological Surveys in the Fourth Book of *I quattro libri dell'architettura*', *Architectural History*, vol. 45 (2002), pp. 113–27.

41 Palladio, *Churches*, [p. 2].

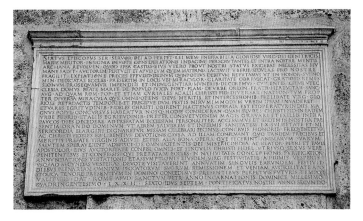

23   Inscription on the façade of the church of Santa Maria del Popolo in the Piazza del Popolo.

I did not rest there. I also wished to see and measure everything with my own hands in minute detail.'[42] Later, in his foreword to the readers in the *Quattro libri*, he notes that he has set himself 'the task of investigating the remains of the ancient buildings that have survived despite the ravages of time and the cruelty of the barbarians, and finding them much worthier of study than I had first thought, I began to measure all their parts minutely and with the greatest care. I became so assiduous an investigator of such things that, being unable to find anything that was not made with fine judgement and beautiful proportions, I repeatedly visited various parts of Italy and abroad in order to understand the totality of buildings from their parts and commit them to drawings.'[43] And in introducing his fourth book, on temples, he again emphasizes the 'scrupulous care' he has taken with his measurements.[44]

The accuracy of his study needed emphasis, since a great many of the monuments were half-buried under centuries of accumulated earth and debris. In his preface to *L'antichità*, Palladio echoes Raphael's concern for the state of the monuments expressed in the latter's famous letter to Pope Leo X (r.1513–21).[45] Palladio notes that

42   Palladio, *Antiquities*, fol. 1.

43   *QL*, I, foreword, p. 5 [p. 5].

44   *QL*, IV, p. 3 [p. 213].

45   See the appendix.

24   *The Roman Forum*, Maarten van Heemskerck, *c.*1532. Kupferstichkabinett, Staatliche Museen zu Berlin – Preussischer Kulturbesitz. Römische Skizzenbücher, inv. no. 79D2, I, fol.6r.

Many very noble and grand edifices were built in Rome – both as an eternal memorial to that people's valour and also as an exemplar to posterity – of which not much can be seen still standing today owing to the wars, fires and structural collapses that have occurred over the many years in that city and which have ruined, gutted and buried a large part of these remains.[46]

Even the Forum was deeply buried, with the famous Arch of Severus visible only above its pedestals.[47] Palladio comments in his section 'On the Campidoglio' that 'in the courtyard there are many antique marbles beautifully and ornamentally arranged, which were recently found in the Forum, beneath the Arch of Severus.'[48]

Given that Palladio wrote or completed *L'antichità* while on his last visit to the city in 1554, unsurprisingly there is a close correlation between the monuments he chose for the guide and those he had drawn or was drawing at this time. His descriptions in *L'antichità* can thus be

46   Palladio, *Antiquities*, fol. 1.

47   See the drawings of the mid-1530s by Maarten van Heemskerck; Filippi, E., *Maarten Van Heemskerck* (1990), nos 7, 8, 24 (fols. 6r, 9r, 12r). See also Burns, Fairbairn and Boucher (1975), pp. 84–5.

48   Palladio, *Antiquities*, fol. 17v.

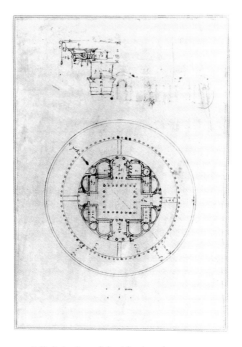

25   Palladio's plan of the Island enclosure at
Hadrian's Villa, *c.*1554, The British Architectural
Library, RIBA, London.

read as a neglected commentary to his surviving drawings of the same
structures. He produced drawings of Hadrian's villa, for example, in the
same year as the publication of the guide, which briefly cites the beauties
of the villa. In *L'antichità* he listed a multitude of building types that were
the subject of his measured drawings. For example, he produced many
drawings and reconstructions of the huge Roman bath complexes of
Nero, Agrippa, Trajan, Titus, Diocletian, Caracalla and Constantine, which
are also cited in the guide.[49] Equally common to both drawings and text
are porticoes (those of Octavia, Saturn/Concord, Antoninus and Faustina,
the Septizonium, and the Claudian), temples (of Peace, and the
Pantheon), mausoleums (of Augustus), columns (of Trajan), theatres
(those of Marcellus, Castrense and Balbus, and the Colosseum), villas

49   See Ackerman (1966), pp. 172–5. See also Palladio's *Fabbriche Antiche
Designate Da Andrea Palladio Vicentino E Date In Luce Da Riccardo Conte Di
Burlington* (inscribed 1730, but possibly printed as late as 1740).

(Hadrian's), fora (Boarium, of Nerva), arches (those of Constantine, Septimius Severus, Gallienus and Titus), basilicas (of Maxentius), gates (Maggiore) and palaces (Domus Augustana). Some of these structures – such as the Forum of Nerva, the portico of the Temple of Saturn/ Concord and that of the Pantheon – were later illustrated in the *Quattro libri*, further underlining the (neglected) role played by *L'antichità* in the eventual composition of the 'Four Books'.

Indeed, according to Giorgio Vasari (1511–74) in 1568, Palladio may well have made these drawings (especially his reconstructions) with a future publication in mind. Vasari notes that 'Since there is soon to come into the light of day a work of Palladio, in which will be printed two books of ancient edifices and one book of those that he himself has caused to be built, I shall say nothing more of him, because this will be enough to make him known as the excellent architect that he is held to be by all who see his beautiful works.'[50] In fact the *Quattro libri* comprised the Orders (Book I), private houses (Book II), roads, bridges, squares, basilicas and xysti (Book III), and ancient temples in Rome (Book IV). In his letter to the duke of Savoy, Emanuel Filiberto, which opens Book III, Palladio comments 'I must now send into the light a part of my work on architecture in which I have committed to drawing many of those superb and marvellous ancient buildings of which the remains are to be found in various parts of the world, but in Rome more than in any other place.'[51] However, he also refers to a forthcoming book on antiquities in the *Quattro libri*,[52] and Gualdo mentions Palladio's desire to publish his drawings of ancient buildings, prevented only by his death.[53]

That Palladio was greatly moved by his visits to Rome is shown by the opening letter to Giacomo Angarano, his patron for the first book of the *Quattro libri*, where he notes:

> For many years I have not only perused with great care the books of those who . . . have enriched this most lofty science with the most admirable principles, but have also travelled many times to Rome and other places in Italy and abroad where I have seen with my own eyes and measured with my own hands the fragments of many ancient

50 Vasari, G., *Lives of the Painters, Sculptors and Architects*, trans. G de Vere (1996), vol. 2, p. 828.

51 *QL*, III, letter, p. 3 [p. 161].

52 *QL*, I, ix, xx, pp. 12, 52, [pp. 14, 56].

53 Gualdo (1958–59); Lewis (1981), p. 3. See introduction in Tavernor and Schofield (1997), p. xvi.

26   Frontispiece of Palladio's *I quattro libri dell'architettura* (1570), woodcut depicting *Regina Virtus*.

buildings, which, having remained upright until our own age as astonishing testimony of the cruelty of the barbarians, provide, even as stupendous ruins, clear and powerful proof of the *virtù* and greatness of the Romans.[54]

26   The frontispiece of each of his four books on architecture depicts *Regina Virtus* – or 'Virtue the Queen' – as mother of the arts. In antiquity, virtue meant 'excellence' and 'good action', which the well-rounded individual was to direct for the benefit and enhancement of civic life.[55] Palladio continues that he has found himself 'moved and inflamed by my profound studies of *virtù* of this type'. Roman monuments thus provided

54   *QL*, I, letter, p. 3 [p. 3].
55   See the introduction in Tavernor and Schofield (1997), p. ix. See also Tavernor (1991), p. 20.

clear evidence of ancient *virtù* – a virtue that merged with early Christian virtues evident in Rome's churches. In this way, far from being unrelated as some commentators have maintained, both of Palladio's guidebooks can be seen to form part of a single Christian vision, emphasizing the compatibility of the ancient pagan city with the modern Christian one.[56] Both guides thereby formed two sides of the same coin. As if to underline this continuity of virtue, Palladio does not miss the opportunity in *Le chiese* to mention when a church has been converted from or built on the foundations of a Roman building, as with Sant'Adriano – 'in ancient times it was the Treasury' – or SS Cosma e Damiano – 'in ancient times it was the Temple of Romulus'.[57] Moreover in the *Quattro libri* he writes that temples are 'essential for religion, without which the maintenance of civilization of any kind is impossible'.[58] And he introduces his fourth book by announcing the intention 'to illustrate in this book the form and ornaments of many ancient temples of which one can still see the ruins and which I have recorded in drawings, so that anyone can understand the form and ornaments with which churches must be built'.[59]

Palladio's enduring interest in the greatness of the Romans (together with the wish to memorialize his two sons, Leonida and Orazio, following their untimely deaths) would lead him to publish *I Commentari di C. Giulio Cesare* in Venice in 1575.[60] In attempting to clarify and reveal guiding principles and virtues recommended by the ancients, this illustrated edition of Caesar's *Gallic Wars* was in line with Palladio's work on Vitruvius (and, following Serlio, on a lost edition of Polybius).[61] Palladio regarded Julius Caesar's reign as a golden age of Roman rule that was reflected in his encampments and famous bridge over the Rhine,

27

---

56 In Palladio (1991), p. 1, E.D. Howe notes, for example, that Palladio's 'motivations for publishing *Le chiese* are difficult to comprehend, as the production of a traditional guidebook for the Christian pilgrim to Rome appears an uncharacteristic and unusual undertaking'.

57 Palladio, *Churches*, [p. 49].

58 *QL*, III, foreword, p. 6 [p. 164].

59 *QL*, IV, foreword, p. 3 [p. 213].

60 Caesar's *Commentaries* are cited by Palladio in the *Quattro libri*: *QL*, III. xxi, p. 44, [p. 206]: see below. See Hale, J.R., 'Andrea Palladio, Polybius and Julius Caesar', *Journal of the Warburg and Courtauld Institutes*, vol. 40 (1977), pp. 240–55; Isermeyer, C.A., 'I Commentari di G. Cesare nell'edizione palladiana del 1575 e i suoi precedenti', *Bollettino del Centro Internazionale di Studi di Architettura A. Palladio*, vol. 21 (1979), pp. 253–71; Palladio (1991), p. xiii.

61 See Hale (1977).

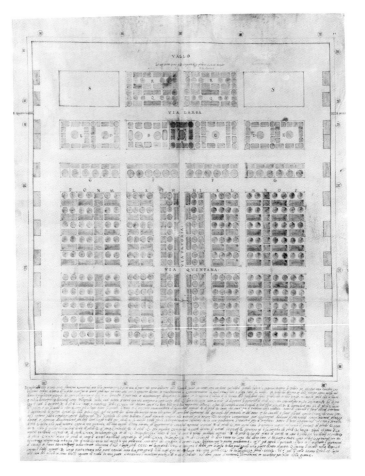

27 Hypothetical Roman encampment based on Polybius, from Sebastiano Serlio's unpublished manuscript 'Castrametation of the Romans' (the so-called Book Eight), *c*.1546–50, Staatsbibliothek Munich (Codex Icon. 190).

both illustrated in the engravings of Palladio's book. In the third book of the *Quattro libri* he notes:

> Caesar writes in his *Commentaries* that, when suddenly attacked by the Nervi and seeing that the seventh and the twelfth legions were so hemmed in that they could not fight, he gave orders that they should spread out and arrange themselves side by side so that they had the space to handle their weapons and could not be surrounded by the

enemy; when the soldiers jumped to it, they gave him victory and
themselves immortal fame and a reputation as brave and well
disciplined. So in the heat of battle, when things were dangerous and
absolutely chaotic, they were able to pull off something that seems
extraordinarily difficult to many people in our own times even when
the enemy are at a distance and one has the advantage of time and
place. Practically all the Greek and Latin histories are full of glorious
feats like this.[62]

Palladio's admiration for Caesar is equally evident in *L'antichità*, where
Caesar is presented as the object and conclusion of Roman development.
In the introduction Palladio enthusiastically notes that 'Julius Caesar with
the title of Perpetual Dictator took control of the imperium and liberty
simultaneously.' And later, writing about a commemorative column to
Caesar in the Forum, he observes that 'The people of Rome had carved
into it homage to Julius Caesar: AL PADRE DE LA PATRIA.'[63]

Palladio's Sources:
Early Guidebooks to the City of Wonders

In serving to highlight the magnificence of the ancient, pre-Christian era
alongside the Christian splendours of his own, modern age, both
Palladio's guidebooks had a topographical antecedence in the works of
Alberti and Raphael and in the many medieval guidebooks to the city.
Alberti's *Descriptio Urbis Romae* was written around 1444.[64] It is very
short, about 1,200 words, with tables of references relating to the
locations of ancient monuments. Alberti notes:

> Using mathematical instruments, I have recorded as carefully as I could
> the passage and *lineamenta* of the walls, the river and the streets of the
> city of Rome, as well as the sites and locations of the temples, public
> works, gates and commemorative monuments, and the outlines of the
> hills, not to mention the area which is occupied by habitable buildings,
> all as we know them to be in our time. Furthermore, I have invented a

---

62 *QL*, III. xxi, p. 44 [p. 206].

63 Palladio, *Antiquities*, fols 2*v*, 11*v*.

64 It was translated by Giovanni Orlandi into Italian in 1968 (then again
with changes in 1974) and into French by Martine Furno in 2000. For the first
full English translation, see Alberti, L.B., 'Leon Battista Alberti's Delineation of
the City of Rome', trans. P. Hicks, in 'Leonis Baptistae Alberti Descriptio urbis
Romae', *Albertiana*, vol. 6 (2003), pp. 125–215.

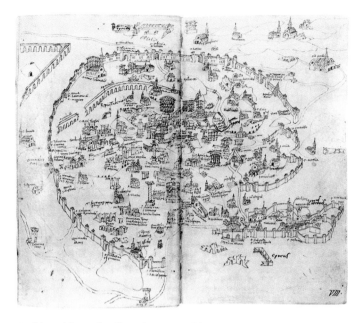

28   Map of Rome by Alessandro Strozzi, fifteenth century, Florence, Biblioteca
Medicea Laurenziana. MS Laur. Redi 77, CC.

method by which anyone, even a man endowed with only an average
intellect, may make both exceptionally easily, and also very accurately,
depictions on any surface, however large. It was some intellectuals,
friends of mine, who moved me to do this, and I thought it good to
assist their studies.[65]

Alberti continues by describing a method for drawing to scale a plan of
Rome, taking the Capitol, the seat of law and government of the city, as
its approximate centre.[66] He makes clear that 'from the centre of the city,
that is, from the Capitol, the distance to any one of the gates nowhere
exceeds 6,140 cubits; and finally that the circumference of the built walls
is about 75 stades'.[67] Despite Alberti's claims to accuracy, he echoed
fifteenth and sixteenth-century views of Rome such as those by
Alessandro Strozzi, Taddeo di Bartolo and Fabio Calvo, which idealized

65   Alberti (2003), p. 197.
66   See Tavernor, R., *On Alberti and the Art of Building* (1998), pp. 13–14.
67   Alberti (2003), p. 197.

29 Map of Rome by Taddeo di Bartolo, 1406–14, Siena, Palazzo Pubblico, Anticappella.

the city as a circular form enclosed by its walls and centred on the Capitol.

28, 29,
32, 35

Alberti's more precise plan is in fact an orthogonal projection – a type of drawing that is subsequently recommended by Raphael in his famous letter to Leo X appealing for the preservation of the ancient monuments of Rome in the wake of recent and earlier destruction.[68] Leo X had appointed Raphael inspector of Rome's ancient ruins and Raphael set about reconstructing the plan of the ancient city by means of surveys and excavations. His letter was drafted around 1519 with the assistance of the Mantuan diplomat and author Baldassare Castiglione (1478–1529) and the collector and epigraphist Angelo Colocci (1474–1544). It sets out the method for recording the ancient monuments in plan, elevation and cross-section. The letter to the pope may well have also been intended to

68   See the appendix.

serve as a preface to an Italian translation of Vitruvius that Raphael is known to have promoted.[69] The letter has one of the first recorded uses of the word 'ordine' in reference to the combinations of elements, first described by Vitruvius, that characterize what are today called the 'Orders' (Doric, Ionic, Corinthian). A manuscript of Raphael's letter is in Munich and another is in Mantua, while a variant version appeared in Castiglione's *Opere volgari e latine*, published in Padua in 1733. Of these versions, the Munich manuscript is the last and most 'complete' in having additional, concluding comments on the use of perspective, and it is this version that is translated in the appendix.[70] Raphael's letter set the tone for subsequent interest in Rome's monuments and for Palladio's researches and orthogonal scale drawings in particular.

Palladio follows the promise of his title – *Antichità raccolta brevemente da gli auttori antichi, & moderni* – and lists his sources in *L'antichità*, citing the ancient authors 'Dionysus of Halicarnassus, Livy, Pliny, Plutarch, Appian of Alexandria, Valerius Maximus, Eutropius', and the moderns 'Biondo, Fulvio, Fauno and Marliani'.[71] Unsurprisingly, his list includes some of the main authorities on ancient Rome. Dionysius of Halicarnassus was a Greek historian who had lived and taught rhetoric in Rome during the time of Augustus. His *Roman Antiquities* was originally in twenty books, of which the first eleven survive, dealing with the origins of the city and going through to the outbreak of the First Punic War. Here Palladio would have seen celebrated such Roman virtues as oratory and rhetoric,

---

69   See Rowland, I., 'Raphael, Angelo Colocci, and the Genesis of the Architectural Orders', *Art Bulletin*, vol. 76, (March 1994), pp. 81–104.

70   Two English translations have been published: one in Elizabeth Holt's *A Documentary History of Art* (1957), vol. 1, pp. 289–96. This was, however, made using a text that is a conflation of the printed (1733) and the 'Munich' versions (but without specifying the differences), and it omits both the long middle section, in which Raphael describes how he mapped the city using an astrolabe, and the final (Munich) section on perspective. Moreover, inaccurate terminology is used, there are mistakes in the translation and there is no commentary despite the wealth of recent scholarship concerning the letter. The second translation is in Carlo Pedretti's *A Chronology of Leonardo da Vinci's Architectural Studies After 1500: In Appendix: A letter to Pope Leo X on the Architecture of Ancient Rome* (1962), pp. 157–71. This is a translation of the printed version of 1733. A translation of the final section of the Munich manuscript is added as an appendix, but the source texts used were the inaccurate transcriptions in Vogel, J., *Bramante und Raffael* (1910), pp. 103–14, and Golzio, V., *Raffaello, nei documenti e nelle testimonianze del suo secolo* (1936), pp. 78–92.

71   Palladio, *Antiquities*, fol. 1.

which must have underlined the important links between these and
Roman architectural theory – particularly 'decorum' – as outlined by
Vitruvius and reiterated by Barbaro.[72] (Indeed, his quotation of Cicero's
On the Laws in *L'antichità* shows his study of the rhetorician.)[73] Livy's
Ab urbe condita libri (*Books from the Foundation of the City*) covered Roman
history from the origins of Rome to 9 BC. Pliny the Elder's *Natural
History* was one of the most widely studied texts in the Renaissance since
in Book Thirty-Six it recorded details of the lost monuments of ancient
Rome. Here Palladio would have read of the caryatids that had once
stood in the Pantheon, the magnificent but destroyed Temple of Peace
and an obelisk once used as the gnomon for Augustus' sundial. Indeed his
entries in *L'antichità* on the ancient colossi and the houses of Roman
citizens are taken directly from Pliny.

Palladio's citation of Plutarch probably refers to the ancient
philosopher's *Parallel Lives*, which included the heroic deeds of
Coriolanus, Brutus and Mark Antony. Appian of Alexandria was a Greek
who became a Roman citizen and whose work (particularly Book One
of his *Civil Wars*) preserves much valuable material, although the details
concerning republican institutions and conditions are often unreliable.
Valerius Maximus' nine books of illustrative examples of memorable
Greek and Roman deeds and sayings are divided under headings mostly
moral or philosophical in character (omens, gratitude, chastity, cruelty
and so on). And the last in Palladio's list of ancient sources, Eutropius,
published a survey of Roman history from the time of Romulus in ten
books entitled *Breviarium ab urbe condita* (*Abridgement of Roman History*).

Palladio's list does not include all his ancient sources, however. He also
makes passing reference to Sextus Julius Frontinus, whose *De aquis urbis
Romae* was a Roman work on the aqueducts of the city from about
AD 100. And the brief description of Hadrian's villa is taken almost word
for word from the anonymous imperial biographies (from 117 through to

---

72   John Onians has pointed out that Cicero's three types of oratory
provided 'a close model for Vitruvius' classification of Doric and Corinthian as
extremes of "severity" and "softness", with Ionic embodying *mediocritas* in
between'; *Bearers of Meaning: The Classical Orders in Antiquity, the Middle Ages and
the Renaissance* (1988), p. 38. On Barbaro and rhetoric see Tavernor (1991), p. 49.
On the links between rhetoric and architecture, see Van Eck, C., '"The Splendid
Effects of Architecture, and its Power to Affect the Mind": the Workings of
Picturesque Association', in *Landscapes of Memory and Experience*, ed. J. Birksted
(2000), pp. 245–58.

73   Palladio, *Antiquities*, fol. 31v.

284) entitled the *Historia Augusta* (*Scriptores historiae augustae*), written around the fourth century.

These ancient sources were less concerned with Rome's monuments than they were with the people who built them and the deeds they celebrated, and were of particular relevance in Palladio's retelling of the legendary foundation of Rome at the outset of *L'antichità*. On the other hand, his modern sources were for the most part concerned with the city's built fabric. Flavio Biondo's *De Roma instaurata* was written in Rome in 1446 and republished in Italian translation in Venice in 1542. Biondo (1392–1463) was one of the earliest humanist writers on ancient Rome, and a manuscript copy of his work was in the library of Frederico da Montefeltro, duke of Urbino. True to humanist methods, Biondo's consideration of sources went beyond the ancient texts to include the Roman ruins, their inscriptions, coins and statues. Indeed Biondo protests that, despite their beauty, these monuments suffer continual decay.

The first work by Andrea Fulvio (fl. 1510–43) on the antiquities of Rome was the *Antiquaria urbis* of 1513, a poem dedicated to Pope Leo X. His subsequent work, *Antiquitates urbis*, is a eulogy on Rome's antiquity and appeared in Rome in 1527, ironically just before the city was sacked by the troops of the Holy Roman emperor, Charles V (1500–58). In describing the monuments of Rome, it was of great appeal to the visitor to the city and appeared in Italian translation (by Paolo del Rosso) in 1543. A further study of the antiquities of Rome was brought out by Lucio Fauno (fl. 1540s). His *Delle antichità della città di Roma* was published in Venice in 1548 and the Latin translation came out the following year. Bartolomeo Marliani's popular *Antiquae Romae topographia* was first published in Rome in 1534 and issued a further six times before 1554. These editions included an Italian translation (entitled *L'antichità di Roma* and published in Rome in 1548) and a revised Latin version of 1544 with woodcut illustrations – notably a map of antique Rome prepared by Giovanni Battista Palatino, and elevations, sections and plans 'borrowed' from Serlio. Marliani (1488?–1560 or 1566) boasts that he measured the Aurelian walls of Rome himself, step by step. These modern sources paved the way for Palladio's own works on the city, in their subject matter, methodology and popularity.

As a relatively frequent visitor to Rome in the 1540s, Palladio had first-hand experience of the guidebook genre – no doubt stimulated by the fact that Trissino had an interest in this.[74] Through such guides he could not have helped but be inspired to explore the marvellous nature

74   Palladio (1991), p. 20.

of the city. Indeed he says in his preface to *L'antichità* that he was particularly spurred on to write his own guide after reading *Le cose maravigliose di Roma* (*The Marvels of Rome*) – that is, the *Mirabilia urbis Romae*. This was a popular guide of thirty-two short chapters describing the ancient sites or wonders (*mirabilia*) of the city, for which the earliest existing manuscripts date from the twelfth century and which was republished in different versions many times.[75] Pliny the Elder had initiated this tradition through his famous descriptions of Rome's marvellous marble buildings, or *mirabilia*, in the *Natural History*.

Alongside this medieval *Mirabilia* guide there existed the tradition of indulgence books, or *Libri indulgentiarum*, which were initially lists of the indulgences available to pilgrims visiting the seven principal churches but later became full-blown guides to a great number of the churches in Rome.[76] While the early *Mirabilia* concentrated on ancient monuments and fables, referring to churches only to locate a presumed site, the later, expanded indulgence books appended histories and descriptions of a total of eighty-four churches, short histories of the Roman emperors up to Constantine and a brief history of the city.[77]

Having examined the ruins at first hand, however, Palladio's research methods were, as noted, more compatible with those of modern scientific archaeology and, echoing Albertini, he came to see the *Mirabilia* as 'packed full of astounding lies' ('tutto pieno di strane bugie' as he puts it in *L'antichità*).[78] For example, the *Mirabilia* describes the Colosseum as a Roman temple of the sun.[79] But although Palladio's emphasis on his scholarship in consulting authorities both ancient and modern underlines his originality in the guidebook tradition, he still relied on this tradition for sections of his guidebooks' text (on the life of Constantine, for

---

75 Anonymous, *Mirabilia urbis Romae: The Marvels of Rome, or a Picture of the Golden City*, trans. F.M. Nichols (1889). See Krautheimer, R., *Rome, Profile of a City, 312–1308* (1980), pp. 198, 355. The authorship of the *Mirabilia* is unknown, although Krautheimer credits Benedict the Canon.

76 Indulgence books included the *Indulgentiae, Mirabilia et indulgentiae, Indulgentiae ecclesiarum urbis Romae* and *Mirabilia urbis Romae nova*. See Palladio (1991), p. 35.

77 See, for example, the confusingly titled *Mirabilia romae*, published by Antonio Blades in Rome in 1516 (in fact an indulgence book) and its Italian translation *Le cose maravigliose della citta di Roma*, published by Guglielmo da Fontaneto in Venice in 1544.

78 Palladio, *Antiquities*, fol. 1.

79 Nichols (1889), p. 62.

example), and he himself was not immune from making mistakes (such as with the Pons Aemilius, mentioned under two separate names),[80] perhaps because he did not come from Rome. Nevertheless, these mistakes are not due to his lack of dedication. Far from being disengaged from the material as some commentators have maintained, Palladio's total commitment to his works is made clear from the outset in both his prefaces.[81]

Palladio's Narrative Structures and Four Pilgrimage Routes

Palladio's *L'antichità* followed the works of Serlio and Ligorio in emphasizing the civic importance and virtue of the ancient monuments of Rome. However, the structure of *Le chiese* differs in that, being organized into four sections, the work highlights four preferred or ideal routes through the city (and consequently, unlike *L'antichità*, has no index). The effect of these routes was to divide the modern city into quadrants. In his introduction to *Le chiese* Palladio highlights the novelty and utility of his pilgrimage routes when compared to earlier guides, and the effort involved in arranging them by ordering 121 churches. He observes, 'And because these holy things are scattered among many churches and cemeteries in Rome, I thought that in order to allow everyone the possibility of visiting them easily in their current locations without long meanderings, I would describe them in a new order and sequence – and all who follow this will be led to give no little praise for this my effort.'[82]

Where earlier guidebook routes in the *Mirabilia* tradition followed a haphazard order, Palladio's text takes the tourist on four logical journeys covering most of the main churches of the city. Beginning, naturally enough, with Rome's seven principal churches, the first route links the two churches on the Tiber Island to nine in Trastevere and nine in the Vatican Borgo (ending at Santa Maria in Traspontina). The next sequence, the longest, begins at the Porta del Popolo, the northern entrance to Rome, and includes fifty-two churches, ending at the Capitoline Hill. The third and fourth itineraries both begin at the Capitol, one heading north towards the mountains and the other south

80   See Palladio, *Antiquities*, fol. 4r, n. 65.
81   On arguments in favour of Palladio's disengagement, see Puppi (1988).
82   Palladio, *Churches*, [pp. 1–2].

towards the ancient city. Where the city's wonders had been revealed to the medieval tourist through a degree of hunting and, as Palladio puts it, 'meanderings', now they were to be laid out in a logical sequence compatible with a more rational age.

Palladio's arrangement of the ancient monuments by 'type' in *L'antichità* followed the example of the *Mirabilia*. He begins, logically enough and again reflecting the *Mirabilia*, with the walls of the city, turning next to the Roman gates through which his readers 'enter' the city, moving on to the principal streets and roads, and crossing the Tiber via its bridges to view the legendary seven hills. The essential physical features and monumental structures within the city are then each dealt with in an encyclopaedic manner, starting with the water supply, sewer, aqueducts and cisterns. It is as if Palladio – ever the architect – is rehearsing the original laying-out of the great city. Then come the necessary public buildings for pleasure – hot baths, lakes for naumachias or mock naval battles, racetracks, theatres and amphitheatres – after which are those for utility, namely the markets. These are followed by military monuments in the city, starting with triumphal arches.

As with Alberti's map of Rome and traditional topographical views of the city, Palladio's city has an implied circularity, to the extent that he begins with its 'circumference' (*del circuito*), while in the physical centre of the book (on page 16 out of 32) he describes the Capitol – the city's symbolic centre and the physical centre of Alberti's map. (This is curiously reflected in the 1742 English translation, now arranged under chapters, where the Capitol ends up as chapter 41 out of 80.) Despite its fundamental difference in structure, *Le chiese* also uses the Capitoline as the hub of the system of routes leading to and from the outer walls in the different quadrants of the city.[83] In his concluding remarks Palladio deals with temples, villas and pastures outside the ancient city boundary – a boundary emphasized by the final part, on 'How many times the City of Rome was Taken'.

Conclusion:
From Books to Buildings

Both guidebooks provide valuable and rare clues as to Palladio's interests associated with, but in some ways lying outside, those normally linked to

---

83   See Palladio (1991), p. 37.

architecture.[84] In *L'antichità* he is concerned with the rituals and priesthood of the ancient Romans, for example. And in *Le chiese* his enthusiastic recital of the fables of magical phenomena associated with the various churches testifies not only to his strong Christian faith but also to his (unrecognized) belief in – or, at the very least, his interest in and knowledge of – the supernatural. Here, in preference to any architectural or artistic details but reflecting the fantastical tales of the *Mirabilia* tradition, there is the story of fabulous events such as the spring at San Lorenzo in Fonte and the three fountains at Sant'Anastasio that 'miraculously sprang up' at the points where St Paul's head bounced.[85] Equally strong, evidently, was his faith in the famous – although much disputed – relics of the Catholic Church, which are listed throughout, and in the indulgences that a penitent could gain through specific prayer. Indeed Palladio's *Le chiese* underlines the importance to him of the liturgical calendar, reflected in his own Christian name, Andrea, which celebrated his birth on St Andrew's Day (30 November).

Just as Palladio's guide to Rome's churches for the most part eschewed describing their physical details in favour of long lists of inspirational relics, so his guide to its antiquities went beyond their physical remains – a normal guidebook topic – to include information on Roman society – the rearing of its children, its military victories and losses and so on. Moreover, of the monuments cited by Palladio in *L'antichità*, some had disappeared for good (the demolished column in the Forum in honour of Caesar, for example), some were described only in ancient sources (Roman houses in Pliny), and some were never even part of the city fabric (the column of Constantine erected in Constantinople in AD 330). This underlines the fact that Palladio saw his guide to the ancient Roman city as less to do with its surviving physical attributes, as would be expected from a standard guidebook, than with its invisible ones of virtue and 'history'. For, with its emphasis on Roman culture and lost buildings, *L'antichità* was not just a pocketbook as has often been maintained, but was also a work of antiquarian scholarship.[86] As such it

84   Burns notes that 'There is disappointingly little information about his personality or beliefs and feelings about anything other than architecture'; Burns, Fairbairn and Boucher (1975), p. 69.

85   Palladio, *Churches*, [pp. 53, 64].

86   Most commentators describe the books as 'guides'. E.D. Howe concludes by emphasizing that *Le chiese* 'was a book which never was intended to reside in a library, but rather to remain in the pockets of travellers'; Palladio (1991), p. 46. Boucher (1994), p. 24, describes *L'antichità* as a 'checklist of famous Roman monuments' and fails to mention *Le chiese*.

should be read as intending to inspire a wider civic – that is, not just architectural – virtue and grandeur, which his buildings were also attempting to restore.[87] (The act of binding illustrations of these buildings with those of Roman monuments in the *Quattro libri* makes this relationship clear.)

Ultimately Palladio's guides represent two types of history (and indeed guidebook): namely a medieval one comprising myths and legends, and a more rational, modern one founded on site analysis, written evidence and classification by 'type'.[88] The books are thus 'transitional' in character, reflecting in some ways their author's own transformation from 'di Pietro' the stonemason, whose training was rooted in medieval craft legends, to 'Palladio' the architect, whose training was rooted in Renaissance humanism and the study of Vitruvius.[89]

In his guide to ancient Rome, Palladio's narrative begins with the city's foundation, progresses through its principal civic and architectural achievements and ends with its fall. This cycle was destined to recur in his own lifetime. The sack of the city by Charles V in 1527, when Palladio was nineteen, closely followed the apparent 'rebirth' of antique architecture under the High Renaissance masters. Echoing Serlio's praise for Bramante, Palladio makes clear that the Tempietto features in *Le chiese* and in the *Quattro libri*, 'since Bramante was the first to make known that good and beautiful architecture which had been hidden from the time of the ancients till now'.[90] And in relating 'How many times the City of Rome was taken', Palladio's list in *L'antichità* concludes: 'finally, in the year 1527 on 6 May, at the hands of the imperial army. It was thus that Rome, conqueror of the world, was despoiled and derided by barbarians.'[91] The 'cruelty' of the barbarians quoted earlier was the exact opposite of Roman *virtù* and magnanimity (or 'Greatness of Soul') – in the 1527 sack even the Vatican was despoiled.

Trissino's epic poem *L'Italia liberata dai Gotthi* (*Italy Freed from the Goths*) of 1547 had described an archangel called 'Palladio' who was an expert on architecture and instrumental in expelling the 'barbarians' from

87   See Tavernor (1991), p. 9.

88   On Palladio's tendency to collect 'types', see Puppi (1975), p. 20.

89   The 'latter' Palladio was most famously studied in Wittkower, R., *Architectural Principles in the Age of Humanism* (1949).

90   *QL*, IV, xvii, p. 64 [p. 276]. Here closely echoing Serlio's Book Three, p. XXXVI [p. 127], where Bramante was said to have 'brought back to life (you might say) the fine architecture which, from the ancients to this time, had lain buried'.

91   Palladio, *Antiquities*, fol. 32r.

Italy.[92] There can be little doubt that his architect namesake – in
reflecting the Palladium, the ancient protector of Rome – saw the
publication of both his guides seven years later as helping to revive the
city in the wake of the uncertainties insinuated by the Protestant
Reformation in general and this most recent sack in particular. After all,
the indulgences and relics that were central to the city's vitality as a
pilgrim centre and that Palladio celebrates in *Le chiese* lay at the heart of
the Reformers' animosity to Rome's practices.[93] The *Quattro libri* would
express the same spirit of revival, from Bramante's revelation of true
Roman architecture 'hidden from the time of the ancients till now', to
the correction of abuses 'imported by the barbarians'.[94]

Palladio's fame rests in no small part on the series of remarkable villas
he built in the countryside of the Veneto and adjacent provinces, but the
countryside is not the 'site' of history – the city is. And in later life
Palladio became preoccupied with the renewal of the *imago urbis* not of
Rome but of another city – Venice.[95] His guidebooks to Rome show
that he saw the purpose and meaning of a city – defined as in ancient
times by walls and lagoons – as dependent on its function as a repository
of civic order, military glory and ecclesiastical piety. These virtues were
conveyed through a city's monuments which, rather like books, told the
story of its origins and subsequent glory – in the *Quattro libri* Palladio
notes that the wisdom and courage of the 'ancient Roman heroes . . .
one reads about with awe in the histories' and 'one can observe in part in
the ancient ruins themselves'.[96] It follows that Palladio's guidebooks to
Rome can also be read as 'guides' to the meaning behind his own civic
buildings. For they underline why he sought to fuse pagan and Christian
forms in his Venetian churches, with their temple fronts and domes, and
to adapt Roman archetypes in his Basilica and Teatro Olimpico at
Vicenza – two designs at the opposite chronological poles of his career.

Read together, Palladio's guides tell the story of Rome as the
archetypal 'eternal city'. Through witnessing its marvels, the pilgrim
visitor was to be inspired by the actions of its early heroic citizens and
the piety of its later, medieval saints. Just as the antique ruins 'revealed'
past glory, so for Palladio the churches and their relics bore vital witness

---

92   See Tavernor (1991), p. 18; introduction in Tavernor and Schofield (1997),
p. xi.
93   See Palladio (1991), pp. 22–4.
94   *QL*, I, xx, p. 51 [p. 55].
95   See Puppi (1975), p. 38.
96   *QL*, IV, letter, p. 3 [p. 161].

to the legends of martyrdom and magic associated with the early
Church. And just as Rome had been the centre of the ancient world, so
it was perfectly fitting that – with a little help from his guides – it should
be nudged into the centre of the modern, Christian one. 'Palladio's
Rome' is thus a union of ancient glory and modern *virtù*, as his final
words in *L'antichità* on the 'eternal' nature of the city make clear: 'And
even though she was taken and destroyed many times, nevertheless the
glory and majesty of Rome still stands, not as widely spread but founded
upon a stronger stone, namely Christ. She is the head of religion and is
the seat of His Vicar, upon which worthily sits Julius III, an honour and
glory to the pontifical name.'[97]

97   Palladio, *Antiquities*, fol. 32r.

NOTE ON THE TRANSLATION

The names of saints have been translated in cases where they are in
current English usage; in all other cases, the names are given in modern
Italian. The names of churches, chapels, piazzas and gates are also given
in modern Italian, with the exceptions of 'St Peter's' and the 'Sistine
Chapel' which are in current English usage. We have retained Palladio's
inconsistent style in the citation of numbers, for example '88' and 'eighty-
eight', and followed his use of capital letters. As for names of monuments,
we have retained Palladio's Italian in the text. Where the monument in
question has a common equivalent in English, that version is retained in
the commentary. We have aimed for consistency in style and a translation
that conveys Palladio's meaning as literally or simply as possible. We did
not wish to modernize Palladio's texts since, after all, he was not a writer
of our time. It might be noted in passing that the sentence structure and,
in places, the clarity of these texts (not to mention their emphasis on
magical myths and legends) betray a mind much less rational than the
'metrical' Palladio of Rudolf Wittkower.[1]

1.   Wittkower (1949). Recent analysis of Palladio's buildings has shown them
not to have followed his rules in the *Quattro libri*. See Rybczynski, W., *The
Perfect House: A Journey with the Renaissance Master Andrea Palladio* (2002).

N

PORTA

S. Ma
Miracul

P.d.
Piazza Cesari
Giulia

Ponte Margherita

Ponte S. Angelo

TEVE

Piazza
sorgimento

S. Martini de Post

Piazza
Cavour

POSTERULA

S. Aegidii

PORTA VIRIDARIA

POSTER
DE PI

POSTERULA
IV. PORTARUM

PORTA CASTELLI

CASTELS Ango

PARS · SANCTI

3

POSTERULA
DIMIZIA

PORTA
S. PETRI

S. Celsi

PALATIOLUM.

S. Mariae
in Saxia

S. Marine de
O[r]

29

31

28

PORTA S. SPIRITUS

RO

MONS · IO
RONZONIS

S. Sal is de Lauro

34

S. Nic

27

36

S. Pantaleonis iuxta Flumen

33

S. Caecinae
de Turre Campi

 ·S. Eus

S. Leonardi de Sitignano

RION

S. Blasii de Capuiseculare
de Panetta

35

Agnetis de Agone

32

26

37

38

S. Mariae

39

Uicella

S. Thomae in Parione

ARI

43

RE

S. EV

S. Pantaleo

40

S. Iohannis in
Agina

S. Laurentii in Damaso

REGIO

S. Iacobi in Septiniano

41

42

OVH

rpitatis Angli

44

S. Mariae in Catherina

45

46

ARS · SANCTI · THO

S. Salvatoris
de Unda

47

S. Pan   Arenula

S. Tho

0   100   200   300   METRES

S. Iohannis
de Portas
(de Malva)

S. Joh

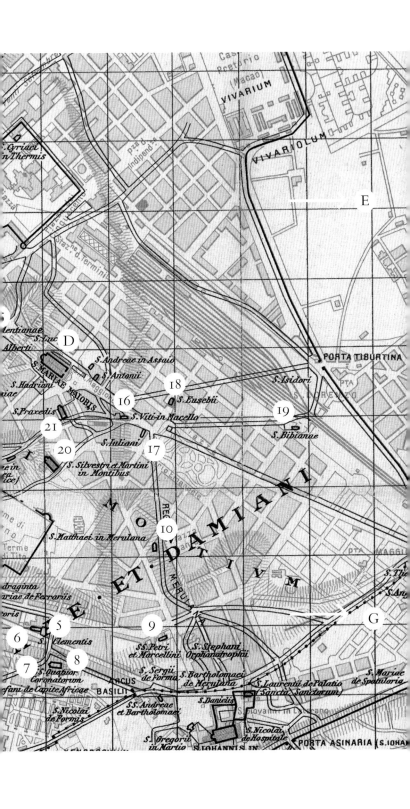

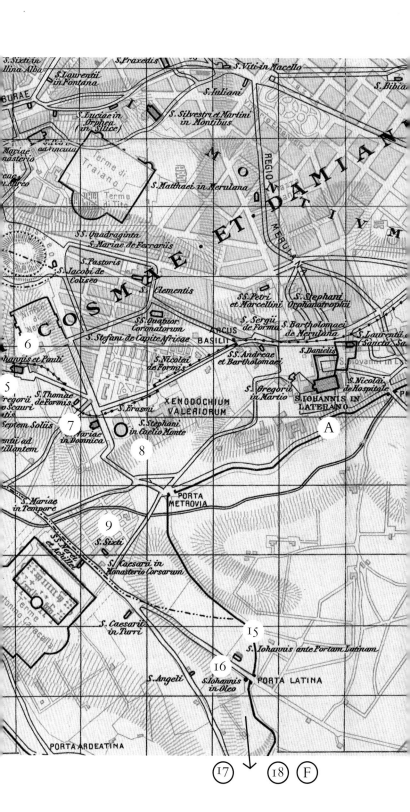

Gazetteer

THE ANTIQUITIES
OF ROME

BY MESSER ANDREA PALLADIO.

SUCCINCTLY COMPILED

From Authors both Ancient & Modern.

Here published for the first time.

With Grace and Privilege for ten years

FORTES, FORTÁ VNÁ ADIVVAT,

IN ROME

At the Press of Vincentio Lucrino.[1]

1554.

TO THE READERS

As the whole world has known for a long time, the ancient Romans performed many more military deeds than are recorded in books. And many very noble and grand edifices were built in Rome – both as an eternal memorial to that people's valour and also as an exemplar to posterity – of which not much can be seen still standing today owing to the wars, fires and structural collapses that have occurred over the many years in that city and which have ruined, gutted and buried a large part of these remains. After meditating upon this a great deal, and particularly since there came into my hands (completely by chance) a certain short book entitled *Le cose maravigliose di Roma*,[3] packed full of astounding lies,[4] and being aware of the great desire in everyone to acquire a thorough understanding of the antiquities in, and other worthy features of, so celebrated a city, I came up with the idea of compiling the present book, as succinctly as I could, from many completely reliable authors, both ancient and modern, who had written at length on the subject – such as Dionysus of Halicarnassus, Livy, Pliny, Plutarch, Appian of Alexandria, Valerius Maximus, Eutropius,[5] and such as Biondo, Fulvio, Fauno and Marliani, and many others.[6] But I did not rest there. I also wished to see and measure everything with my own hands in minute detail.[7] Read carefully, then, this new work of mine if you wish **[fol.[2]]** fully to experience the huge pleasure and the wonder that can come from a detailed understanding of the great things in so noble and celebrated a city as that of Rome.

CONTENTS

ON THE ANTIQUITIES OF
THE CITY OF ROME
BOOK ONE

On the Building of Rome

Rome is situated in Latium on the banks of the Tiber, 15 miles from the Tyrrhenian Sea. It was built by Romulus and Remus in world year 5550, 4333 years after the destruction of Troy, on 21 April.[9] Romulus and Remus were the sons of Ilia, that is, Silvia, daughter of Numitor, king of Alba. Amulius, Numitor's brother, had driven Numitor out of the kingdom so as to accede in his place, and in order to make quite sure that Numitor would have no descendants, he placed Silvia, Numitor's daughter, as a priestess in the temple of the goddess Vesta.

But it was in vain. For in a few days Silvia became pregnant – people say either by Mars or the *genius loci*, or indeed by a man – and she produced two sons in the same birth. When he learnt of this, King Amulius had them carried off to be thrown into the Tiber, far from Alba. It was at this point, many say, that a she-wolf who had just given birth heard their cries and came to them. She suckled them as if they had been her own cubs. A shepherd called **[fol. 1*v*]** Faustulus just happened to be passing. He shouted at the wolf to scare her off, picked up the boys and took them home, giving them to his wife, called Acca Larentia, to rear. And so they grew up among shepherds, becoming big and strong, full of the magnanimity of their ancestors and eager to participate in the conflicts between shepherds. It so happened that Remus was taken prisoner, brought before King Amulius and falsely accused of having stolen Numitor's sheep. The king ordered that Remus be handed over to Numitor who could then punish the man who had wronged him. When Numitor saw that the young man had such a noble aspect, he was deeply moved and became convinced that this man was his grandson. While he was reflecting on this, Faustulus the shepherd arrived with Romulus. Numitor learnt from them the origin of the boys and, discovering that they were his grandsons, he had Remus set free. Together the boys killed Amulius and returned the kingdom (since it rightfully belonged to him) to Numitor, their grandfather. And under his rule they chose to build a new city, square in form,[10] on the most commodious site on the banks of

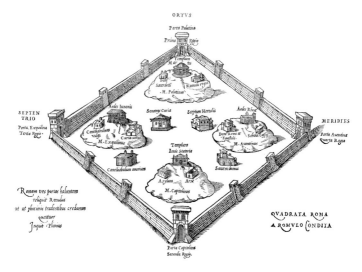

30   Ancient Rome as a square form, woodcut from M. Fabio Calvo's *Antiquae urbis Romae simulachrum* (1532).

the Tiber,[11] in the place where the two had been reared. Thereupon, they started to argue about the name of the city and who should rule, since each wished to glorify his own name. Moving beyond words to deeds, Romulus slew Remus and had this city called Roma after his own name – he was 18 years old.

Four months later, with the city built but having no women, this Romulus sent ambassadors to the nearby cities to ask for some in marriage. On being refused, he commanded the celebration of a festival called the Consualia, on 18 September.[12] To this festival came a great **[fol. 2r]** multitude of Sabines, both men and women, and at a certain signal, Romulus had all the young girls – of which there were 683 – seized, giving them as brides to the worthiest. He also chose as his advisers one hundred men from among the chief families. Because of their age, these were called Senators, and for their qualities they were called Fathers; their assembly was called the Senate and their descendants were called Patricians.[13] He divided the youth up into military ranks. From these he selected three centuries of horsemen as his guard. They were very strong young men, from the best-born families, and they were called Celeres. He also made the most powerful the Patrons of the poor – and as for these poor, the rest of the multitude of the people, he called

31   Roman Senators, from an engraving by Giovanni Antonio da Brescia (after
Andrea Mantegna), *c.*1500, Graphische Sammlung Albertina, Vienna, 1951–396.

them Clients.[14] He divided this Plebs into 35 Curias, and he passed many
laws, among which was the following: that no Roman should exercise a
sedentary occupation but should restrict himself to military or
agricultural matters. Subsequently, when the troops were gathered for a
review near the marsh at Capraea,[15] he vanished, never to be seen again
here or elsewhere. He was 56 years old and had reigned for 38 of them
without leaving behind him an heir. In the city he left 46 thousand foot
soldiers and nearly one thousand cavalrymen, having begun with only
three thousand foot and 300 horse, which had come from Alba.
Romulus, then, was the founder of the city and of the Roman
imperium, and he was the city's first king. After him there were six other
kings, of whom the last was Tarquinius Superbus,[16] who was driven out

of Rome because his son, Sextus, came at night and raped Lucretia, the wife of Collatinus. These seven kings ruled for 243 years; their imperium did not exceed 15 miles. When the kings had been driven out, **[fol. 2*v*]** political and civil life was put in order, and this form of government lasted 465 years. In this time, they won by means of 43 battles dominion over nearly the whole world. There were 877 Consuls, two years of government by the Decemviri, 43 Military Tribunes with Consular Power, and there were 4 years without governors. After that, Julius Caesar with the title of Perpetual Dictator took control of the imperium and liberty simultaneously.[17]

On the Circumference of Rome

32 At the time of Romulus, Rome comprised the Capitoline and the Palatine hills with the valleys between them, and it had three gates. The first was called the Porta Trigonia because of the triangle it formed at the foot of the Palatine Hill. The second was called Pandana[18] because it was permanently open; it was also known as the Porta Libera because of the ease of entry. The third was called the Porta Carmentalis, from Carmenta, the mother of Evander, who lived there.[19] It became known as the Porta

32 Idealised plan view of ancient Rome, showing the early gates, woodcut from M. Fabio Calvo's *Antiquae urbis Romae simulachrum* (1532).

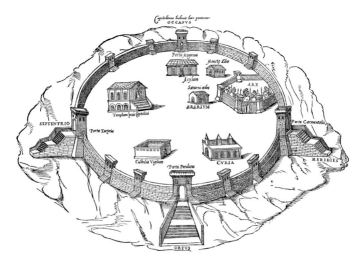

Scelerata as a result of the deaths of the 300 Fabii. They left with their Clients via that gate and were cut to pieces beside the Aronne river. Subsequently, with the ruin of Alba and peace between the Romans and the Sabines, the circumference of the city grew, as did the numbers of Citizens and the People, who kept arriving. They girded the city with rough walls.[20] Tarquinius Superbus was the first to build with large, magnificently carved marble blocks. And the walls continued to move ever further out so as to encompass the seven hills of today, indeed to such an extent that at the time of the Emperor Claudius there were 630 towers and 22 thousand porticoes.[21] However, because of the varying accounts of authors, it is not possible to be [fol. 3r] certain concerning the circumference of the walls, for some say that it was 50 miles, others 32, yet others 18. Nevertheless, from as much as can be seen today, including Trastevere and the Borgo of Saint Peter's, it is not more than 15.[22]

33, 34

33 (*above*) The city walls (between the Porta San Sebastiano and the Porta Latina).

34 (*right*) The city walls near the Porta Tiburtina.

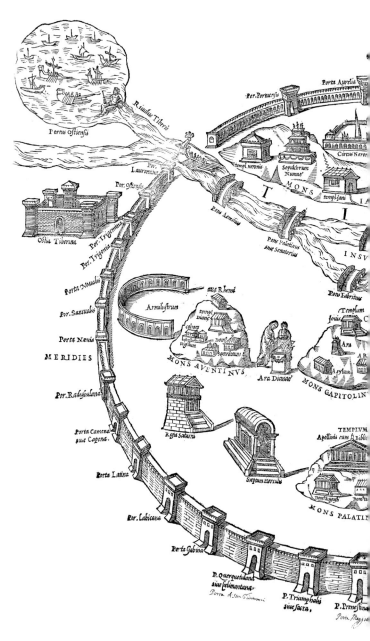

35   Idealised plan view of the principal monuments of ancient Rome, woodcut from M. Fabio Calvo's *Antiquae urbis Romae simulachrum* (1532).

S

Porta Septimiana

Porta Valeria

templ Apollinis

templ.
Carment.

ET VATICANVS

E
R
I
S

Pons Hadriani

Pons Vaticanus

Domus Pastorum

DOMVS
Aurea Neronis

Porta Salaria

Porta Flumentana siue
Flaminia

Porta Rhutumenasiue
Veientana.

Porta Rhomanula

Porta Collatina

Porta Collina

Porta Catullaria

Porta Quirinalis

SEPTEN
TRIO

Castra Mesonatuum

templ.Isaraialis templ.Isidis

MONS EXQVILINVS

META
Veneris
siue ludas

Nympheum publ.

templ. quirini

M.QVIRINALIS

Porta Viminalis

Porta Lauernalis

AMPHITHEATRVM

Castra pretoria

Porta Piacularis

castra peregrina

templ Claudiæ

Porta Salutaris

Curia
hostilia   Armamentum publ.

MONS CELIVS

Porta Exquilina

Porta Minutia

Porta Mutia

Porta Tiburtina

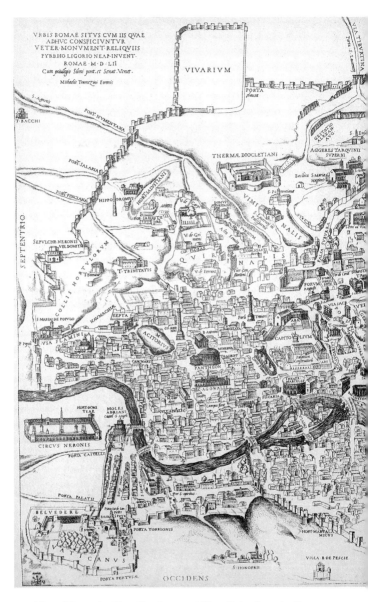

36   Map of Rome by Pirro Ligorio, 1552, Milan, Civica Raccolta Stampe
Achille Bertarelli.

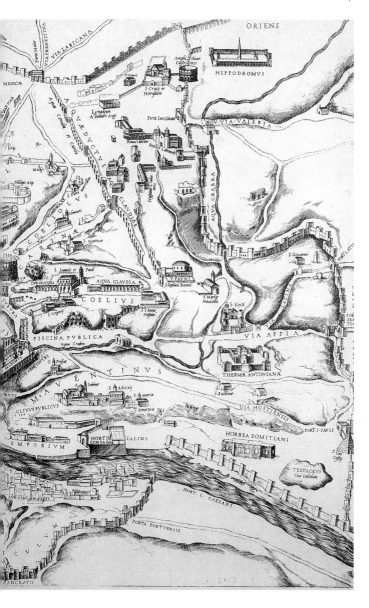

37   Porta Tiburtina.   38   Porta Maggiore.

On the Gates

In the profusion of alterations to the city, some of the walls and also the
gates lost their names and others retained them. They were all built with
quadrate stones in the ancient manner. The roads were all paved and
called Consolare, Censoriale, Praetoria or Trionfale after the person who
built the road, whether Consul, Censor or Praetor.

Triumphal gates and roads were built with much greater magnificence
than the others. No expense was spared in their making – whether in the
cutting of slopes, the levelling of hills, the infilling of valleys, the building
of bridges, the matching of levels and ditches – and they were made
straight and true in most excellent order, commodiously endowed with
fountains, posts marking the distance between places, and very solid
paving stones, as can be seen still surviving today. There is a difference of
opinion among the various authors as to the number and names of the
gates, for some say 36, others 24.[23] However, from what can be seen
today, the city has only 18, which are open and enclose the seven hills –
and the whole city was divided into fourteen *Rioni*.[24]

39 Porta Latina.

40 Porta San Sebastiano.

The principal gate is the Porta del Popolo, called the Porta Flumentana and the Porta Flaminia in ancient times.[25]

The Porta Pinciana, previously called the Porta Collatina.[26]

The Porta Salaria, previously called the Porta Quirinale, the Porta Agonale and the Porta Collina.[27] **[fol. 3v]** The Galli Senones entered the city through this gate when they sacked Rome, and Hannibal camped on the banks of the Teverone[28] three miles from this spot.

The Porta di Sant'Agnese, previously called the Porta Nomentana, the Porta Figulense and the Porta Viminale.[29]

The Porta di San Lorenzo, previously called the Porta Tiburtina and the Porta Taurina.[30]

37

The Porta Maggiore, previously called the Porta Labicana, the Porta Prenestina and the Porta Nevia.[31]

38

The Porta di San Giovanni, previously called the Porta Coelimontana, the Porta Settimia and the Porta Asinaria.[32]

The Porta Latina, previously called the Porta Forentina.[33]

39

40   The Porta di San Sebastiano, previously called the Porta Appia, the
Porta Fontinale and the Porta Capena.[34] One of the three Horatii who
overcame the Curiatii entered by this gate, as have the majority of those
that ever held a Triumph.[35]

The Porta di San Paolo, previously called the Porta Ostiense and the
Porta Trigemina. The three Horatii left the city via this gate.[36]

The Porta Ripa, previously called the Porta Portuense.[37]

The Porta di San Pancrazio, previously called the Porta Aurelia and the
Porta Pancratiana.[38]

The Porta Settimiana, previously called the Porta Fostinale.[39]

The Porta Torrione, previously called the Porta Posterula.[40]

The Porta Pertusa.[41] The Porta di Santo Spirito.[42] The Porta di
Belvedere[43] and the Porta di Castello, previously called the Porta
Enea.[44]

On the Roads

There were twenty-nine principal roads.[45] Even though each gate had its
own road – and C. Gracchus straightened and paved them[46] – the most
celebrated were, however:

The Via Appia[47] – Appius Claudius, when he was Censor, had this road
paved from the Porta di San Sebastiano[48] as far as Capua.[49] On its
becoming ruined, **[fol. 4r]** Trajan restored it as far as Brindisi. It was
called the 'Queen of Roads'[50] because nearly all the Triumphs passed
along it.

The Via Flaminia[51] – C. Flaminius, when he was Consul, had it paved
from the Porta del Popolo[52] as far as Rimini. It was also known as the Via
Larga because it extended as far as the Campidoglio.

The Via Emilia[53] – this was paved as far as Bologna by the Consuls
Lepidus and C. Flaminius.

The Via Alta Semita[54] began on Montecavallo and went as far as the
Porta di Sant'Agnese.[55]

The Via Suburra[56] began at the Colosseum and went as far as the
church of Santa Lucia in Orfea.

The Via Sacra[57] began near the Arch of Constantine and went to
the Arch of Titus, and also passed via the Forum Romanum to the
Campidoglio.

The Via Nova[58] went via the Palazzo Maggiore[59] to the Septizonium,[60]
continuing as far as the Baths of Antoninus.[61]

The Via Triumphalis[62] went from the Vatican to the Campidoglio.

When many of these roads became ruined, Vespasian had them

restored, as can be seen in a marble inscription that is in the Campidoglio on the Palazzo de' Conservatori.

The Via Vitellia[63] went from the Janiculum Hill to the sea.

The Via Re[c]ta[64] was in the Campus Martius.

On the Bridges over the Tiber
and their Builders

There were eight bridges over the Tiber.[65] Two of these are ruined, namely the Pons Sublicius and the Pons Triumphalis or **[fol. 4v]** Vaticanus. The Pons Sublicius was at the foot of the Aventine Hill, near the Porta Ripa. Remains of it can still be seen in the middle of the river, and it was built of wood by Ancus Marcius.[66] On its becoming damaged when Horatius Cocles withstood the attack of the Etruscans, Aemilius Lepidus had it built in stone and called it the Pons Aemilius.[67] When a flood of the Tiber destroyed it, the Emperor Tiberius had it restored. In the end, Antoninus Pius had it built of marble. It was of a great height and malefactors were cast down from it. It was the first bridge ever built over the Tiber. The Pons Triumphalis, or Vaticanus,[68] was near the Ospitale di Santo Spirito.[69] Its foundations can still be seen in the middle of the Tiber. It was so-called because all the Triumphs used to pass over it.

The Ponte di Santa Maria used to be called the Pons Senatorius and Pons Palatinus.[70] The Ponte de' Quattro Capi was called the Pons

41, 42

41 The so-called Ponte Rotto, a fragment of the Pons Aemilius (142 BC).

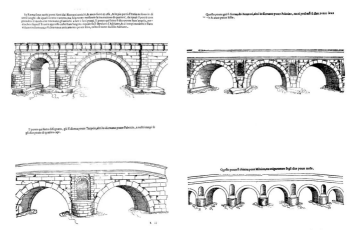

42   Rome's bridges, woodcuts from the third volume of Sebastiano Serlio's
treatise *On Antiquities* (1540): top left – Ponte Sant'Angelo; bottom left – Ponte
de' Quattro Capi, or Pons Fabricius; top right – Pons Aemilius, or Ponte di
Santa Maria; bottom right – Ponte Molle, or Pons Milvius.

Tarpeius and then Pons Fabricius after L. Fabricius, who had it built
when he was Master of Roads.[71] The Ponte di San Bartolomeo was
called the Pons Cestius and the Pons Esquilinus.[72] It was restored by the
Emperors Valens and Valentinianus.

The Ponte Sisto was previously called the Pons Aurelius and the Pons
Janiculensis.[73] Antoninus Pius had it built of marble. On its becoming
ruined, Sixtus IV had it rebuilt in 1475.

The Ponte Sant'Angelo used to be called the Pons Aelius after the
Emperor Aelius Hadrianus who built it.[74] Nicholas V arranged it in the
form which can be seen today.

The Ponte Molle, or Pons Milvius, is about two miles beyond the
Porta del Popolo.[75] It was built by Aemilius Scaurus. Today, its only
remaining antique parts are the foundations. Near this **[fol. 5r]** bridge,
Constantine the Great overcame the tyrant Maxentius and had him
drowned in the river. He saw a cross in the air and heard a voice that said
to him, 'You shall conquer in this sign'.

Three miles from the city stands the Ponte Salario, so-called from the
name of the road.[76] It is a very ancient bridge, and under this passes
the river Anio that demarcates the boundary between the Sabines and
the Romans – the water is good to drink. Narses, in the time of the

43   The Tiber Island, woodcut from Bernardo Gamucci's *Libri Quattro dell'antichità della città di Roma* (1569).

Emperor Justinian, restored it after his victory over the Goths[77] – the bridge had previously been destroyed by Totila.[78]

The Ponte Mam[m]olo is named after Mamaea, mother of the Emperor Severus Alexander.[79] Before its restoration by Severus it had been built by the Emperor Antoninus Pius – it is an exceedingly ancient bridge. It is about three miles from the city, over the River Anio, now called the Teverone.

On the Tiber Island

When Tarquinius Superbus was driven out of Rome, the Romans thought it abhorrent to eat his corn, some of which had been harvested and some of which, on the Tiber plain, had yet to be cut. They threw it and the straw into the Tiber. Since it was the hot season and since the river was low, this, along with other rubbish, formed a mass that became an island.[80] Through the industry and assistance of men, this became so large that, as can be seen, it was filled with houses, temples[81] and other buildings. In shape it is similar to a ship, with one end like the prow and the other the **[fol. 5v]** stern. It is about a quarter of a mile in length and about fifty paces wide.

43

44 The Palatine Hill overlooking the Forum.

On the Hills

The main hills upon which Rome was built are seven in number.[82] The most celebrated is the Capitoline, also known as the Tarpeian or Saturnian Hill, which today is called the Campidoglio.[83] Upon this, among the 60 temples, shrines[84] and holy houses, the most famous was the Temple of Jupiter Optimus Maximus.[85] At the end of a Triumph it was into this place that those celebrating would come to give thanks for their victory.

44   The Palatine, today called the Palazzo Maggiore, is uninhabited, covered in vineyards and a mile in perimeter.[86] Romulus began the city on this hill because it was here that he was suckled.[87] Heliogabalus had it paved with porphyry.[88]

The Aventine, or rather Querquetulanus, has a perimeter of more than two miles. It is the hill upon which stands the church of Santa Sabina.[89]

The Celian goes from where the church of SS Giovanni e Paolo stands to San Giovanni in Laterano.[90]

The Esquiline, or rather the Cespian, is the hill upon which stand the churches of Santa Maria Maggiore and San Pietro in Vincoli.[91]

The Viminal is the hill upon which stand the churches of San Lorenzo in Panisperna and Santa Pudenziana.[92]

The Quirinal, or rather the Egonius, is today called Montecavallo.[93]

The Pincian is the hill upon which stands the church of the Trinità.[94]

The Janiculum is the hill upon which stands San Pietro in Montorio.[95]

[fol. 6r]

There are also other, smaller hills, such as: the Janiculum, today called Monte Auro;[96] the Vatican, where stands the church of Saint Peter and the Papal Palace;[97] the Citorium, once called the Citatorium because this was the place to which the tribes were summoned when they came together to create their magistrates;[98] the Hortuli, or Pincian Hill, begins at the Porta Salaria and goes as far as the Porta del Popolo, and from that hill the Candidati would descend in the direction of the Campus Martius in order to present before the people their candidature for the office of magistrate;[99] Monte Giordano, so-called because members of the most illustrious Orsini family lived there, and to this day they have their palaces in this place.[100]

On Monte Testaccio

This hill is near the Porta di San Paolo and it grew as a result of the huge number of terracotta vase fragments dumped here (and not, as people believe, because of the broken vases in which tributes were once brought to Rome).[101] This fact is not remarkable given that in this neighbourhood there were innumerable potters, and statues of the gods, ornaments for temples and all vases were in those days made of terracotta, and the ashes of the dead were also stored in terracotta vases. Corebos the Athenian was the first to discover the technique of making terracotta.[102]

On the Aquae
and those who built them, bringing them into Rome

There used to be nineteen aquae that were brought into Rome.[103] However, the most famous were the Marcia, the Claudia **[fol. 6v]**, the Appia – which was the first to be brought into Rome – the Tepula, the Julia, the Anio Vetus, the Anio Novus, and the Virgo. As for the Marcia, or rather Aufeia, Q. Martius when he was Praetor took the water for it from Lake Fucinus, 37 miles outside Rome.[104] As for the Claudia, the Emperor Claudius took the water for it from two large springs on the Via Subiaco, one called the Ceruleus and the other the Curtius, 36 miles outside Rome.[105] Since Claudius' waterway was very frequently damaged, it was restored by Vespasian, Titus, Aurelian and Antoninus Pius, as can be seen from the inscriptions that are above the Porta Maggiore. As for the Appia, Appius Claudius when he was Censor took the water for it from a place in the Tusculanum countryside eight miles outside Rome.[106] As for

38

45   The Aqua Claudia.

the Tepula, Servilius Caepio and D. Cassius Longinus, Censors, took the
water for it from a place in the Tusculanum countryside 11 miles outside
Rome and brought it to the Campidoglio.[107] As for the Julia, Agrippa[108]
took the water for it from the Tepula.[109] As for the Anio Vetus, Marcus
Curtius and L. Pupinius, Censors, took the water for it from twenty miles
beyond Tivoli and brought it into Rome using the spoils from Albania.[110]
As for the Anio Novus, Julius Frontinus, Master of the Roads, took the
water for it down the Via Subiaco from a place about 24 miles outside
Rome.[111] As for the Virgo, Agrippa, when he was Aedile, took the water
for it down the Via Prenestina from a place about 8 miles outside
Rome.[112] This is the waterway that today feeds what is called the Trevi
Fountain.[113] As for the Alsietina, Augustus took the water for it down the
Via Claudia from Lake Alsietina, 14 miles outside Rome.[114] It also served

Trastevere. The Juturna is the waterway that can be seen today next to San Giorgio, where the women go to do their laundry.[115] There were still further aquae **[fol. 7r]**, named after those who founded them or who built the waterway itself, such as the Traiana after Trajan,[116] the Septimia after Septimius,[117] the Drusa after Drusus[118] and the Alexandrina after Alexander.[119]

On the Cloaca

The Cloaca, or what we call the main sewer, was near the Pons Senatorius, now called the Ponte di Santa Maria.[120] It was built by Tarquinius Priscus and its great size was recorded with wonder by writers, in that inside it was large enough for a cart to pass comfortably through.[121] As for myself, I have measured it and find that it is 16 feet wide. All the other sewers in Rome drained into this one, and hence it was said that the fish called Lupi caught between the Pons Sublicius[122] and the Pons Senatorius were better than all the rest because they fed on the filth that came out of this sewer.

On the Aqueducts

There were seven aqueducts in Rome.[123] The most famous was that for the Aqua Marcia, the remains of which can be seen in the road that goes to San Lorenzo fuori le mura.[124] That for the Aqua Claudia used to go from the Porta Maggiore to the church of San Giovanni in Laterano.[125] This aqueduct went via the Celian Hill to the Aventine, and today its half-collapsed arches can still be seen rising to a height of 109 feet. This work was begun by Caesar and finished **[fol. 7v]** by Claudius, and it cost one million, 385 thousand and 50 gold scudi. Caracalla later brought it to the Campidoglio, and some of its arches are still standing in the Ospedale di San Tommaso. As for the aqueduct for the Aqua Appia, there are still some remains at the foot of Monte Testaccio and others near the Arch of Titus Vespasian.[126] The Aqua Virgine is what they call in the vernacular the Trevi Fountain.[127] The Aqua Juturna rises in the Velabrum[128] near the church of San Giorgio.[129] It once made a lake[130] in the piazza near the temple of the goddess Vesta, where today stands the church of San Silvestro nel Laco. The Aqua Sabattina was originally named after the Lago di Sabate.[131] Today the lake is called the Lago dell'Angillare; it is the one that makes the fountain that can be seen today in the Piazza di San Pietro.

La conserua delle acque delle Therme di Tito è mirabile, e di grande artificio : percioche gli archi di queste
conserue sono posti con tal ordine , che stando una persona nel mezo di uno gli uede tutti per traguardo. Questo è quel luogo che'l uulgo lo dice le sette sale: perche in effetto i spatii sono di numero settenario, e così se por
te per traguardo sono sette per ogni uerso . La grossezza de i muri è piedi quattro e mezo . La latitudine de gli
archi è piedi sei, dall'uno all'altro arco è piedi uentisette . La latitudine da un muro all'altro è circa piedi xv, e
sono uoltati a botte di una conueniente altezza. I muri, e le uolte sono smaltate d'una durissima materia,

46   The 'Seven Halls' near the Baths of Titus,
woodcut from the third volume of Sebastiano
Serlio's treatise *On Antiquities* (1540).

On the Seven Halls

Near the Baths of Titus there are nine underground cisterns, these days
46 called the 'Seven Halls'.[132] Each one is 17 and a half feet wide,[133] 12 feet
tall, and more than 137 feet long. They were built by Vespasian for use by
the College of Pontiffs, as a marble inscription that was found in this
place a long time ago reveals. The inscription reads:

IMP. VESPESIANVS AVG.

PER COLLEGIVM PONTIFICVM

FECIT.

[fol. 8r]

On the Thermae,
that is Baths, and who built them

The Baths were very grand, exceptionally sumptuous and exceedingly
spacious places built to wash in.[134] They had huge porticoes, the

pavements were of marble, the walls whitewashed or set with very
beautiful marbles, and with very imposing columns supporting arches of
a tremendous size. There were many in Rome, but the most famous were
the Baths of Alexander and Nero, built by Nero and Alexander
Severus.[135] They were behind the church of Sant'Eustachio, where their
ruins can be seen. The Baths of Agrippa, built by Marcus Agrippa, stood
between the Rotonda and the Minerva in the place that is called the
Ciambella.[136] Their remains can still be seen. The Baths of Antoninus,   2, 47,
begun by Antoninus Caracalla and completed by Alexander, were on the   48
Aventine Hill.[137] They are still standing, though half ruined, and are of a
remarkable size, ornamented with beautiful marbles and huge columns.
The Baths of Aurelian, built by the Emperor Valerius Aurelian, stood in
Trastevere.[138] Their remains can still be seen. The Baths of Constantine
were on Montecavallo.[139] Their ruins can be seen on the estate of that
most illustrious family, the d'Ivrea. The Baths of Diocletian, built by   49, 50,
Diocletian and for the most part still standing, are near the church of   51
Santa Susanna and of a stupendous size.[140] In order to build them,
Diocletian kept 140,000 Christians for many years in the buildings there.
The Baths of Domitian, built by Domitian, were on the site where now
stands the monastery of San **[fol. 8v]** Silvestro; some of their remains can
still be seen.[141] The Baths of Gordian were adorned with two hundred of

47   The Baths of Antoninus/Caracalla (AD 212–16), woodcut from the third
volume of Sebastiano Serlio's treatise *On Antiquities* (1540).

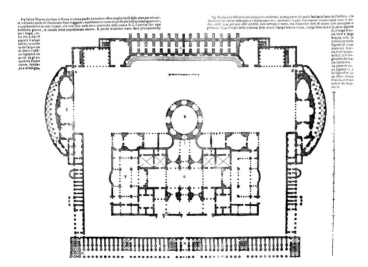

48   The Baths of Antoninus/Caracalla.

49   The Baths of Diocletian (AD 305–06), woodcut from the third volume of Sebastiano Serlio's treatise *On Antiquities* (1540).

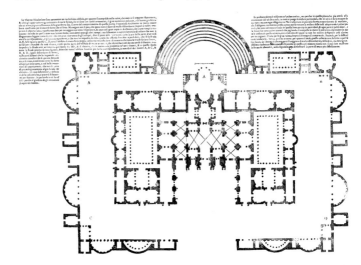

50 (*above*) The Baths of Diocletian.

51 The Baths of Diocletian, woodcut from Bernardo Gamucci, *Libri Quattro dell' antichità della città di Roma* (1569).

the most beautiful columns and they stood close to the church of Sant'Eusebio.[142] The Baths of Novatianus stood on the site of the church of Santa Pudenziana.[143] The Baths of Severus, built by the Emperor Severus, stood in Trastevere.[144] They were ornamented with very beautiful marbles and columns, some of which are in the churches of Santa Cecilia and San Crisogono. The Baths of Trajan were on the Esquiline Hill near the church of San Martino.[145] On the other side of this hill were the Baths of the Emperor Philip, and some remains of them can still be seen near the church of San Matteo.[146] The Baths of

Le Therme di Tito sono minori delle altre, e però dal uulgo sono dette le Therme minori: nódimeno per mio parere elle sono bene ordinate. La pianta di quelle Therme è misurata col palmo antico, ilquale è qui adietro e faccie lxxxv. e prima, il diametro della forma roronda segnata A, e circa cl. palmi. La parte B, e in longitudine da palmi lxxx. e la latitudine palmi cinquant'uno. La parte C, e palmi lxxx. in longitudine, & in latitudine palmi lx. la forma D, e in longitudine palmi cento per diametro, & il uestibulo E, e circa palmi cinquanta. La parte F, e lunga da cxx. palmi. La sua larghezza q da palmi lxx. La parte G, di netto faccie e circa palmi cento. La parte ro- tonda H, e da palmi cl. per diametro, la parte I, e cento piedi, & e di due quadri in circa. Le due parti K, sono pal- mi xxx per ogni laro. la parte L, e in longhezza da palmi cxxv. la sua larghezza e palmi xxx. la rotondità M, e per diametro circa palmi cxv. la parte N, e lunga palmi calviii. e larga palmi lviii. la parte O, e il medesimo. la con- serua delle acque sara qui a canto.

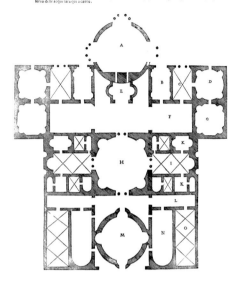

52   The Baths of Titus (*c.*AD 80), woodcut from
the third volume of Sebastiano Serlio's treatise
On Antiquities (1540).

52   Titus were in what are now the gardens of the monastery of San Pietro
in Vincoli, and their ruins can be seen.[147] The Baths of Olympias stood
on the site of the monastery of San Lorenzo in Panisperna.[148]

On Naumachias,
where they staged Naval Battles,
and what they were for

Naumachias were certain places excavated by hand to form a kind of
lake in which young people would fight in a combat of ships.[149] One
naumachia stood before the church of the Trinità, built by Augustus.
Another stood before San Pietro in Montorio, built by Nero, filled with
sea water. The third was in Trastevere, built by Julius Caesar.

On the Circuses
and what they were for

Whilst there used to be many circuses, the principal ones were four in number:[150] the Circus Maximus, **[fol. 9r]** the Circus of Nero, the Circus Flaminius and the Circus Agonius. These were places where they used to stage bullfights and races with horses yoked to chariots; and around these circuses there were places banked up above ground level upon which people could sit to watch the said events. The Circus Maximus was between the Palatine and the Aventine on the site that they call Cerchi.[151] It was three stadia long, one stadium wide, and ornamented with very beautiful gilt columns. It was built by Tarquinius Priscus and enlarged by Caesar, Octavian, Trajan and Elagabalus. Two hundred and sixty thousand people could sit there. The Circus of Nero was on the Vatican Hill behind the church of Saint Peter's, where the 'needle' stands.[152] The Circus Flaminius was where the church of Santa Caterina de' Funari now stands.[153] The Circus Agonius stood where Piazza d'Agone now is, called in the vernacular the Piazza Navona.[154] There were yet other circuses, inside and outside the city, one of which being outside the Porta Maggiore, and its ruins can be seen in the vineyard and monastery of Santa Croce in Gerusalemme.[155] There was another on the hill of the Hortuli below the Trinità.[156] And between the church of San Sebastiano and Capo di Bove[157] there is another, half ruined, built by Antoninus Caracalla, in which they used to celebrate the Olympic Games.[158] It was in this place that Saint Sebastian was shot through with arrows.

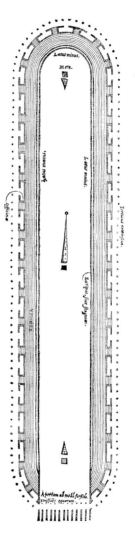

53

53 Plan of the Circus Maximus, woodcut from Bartolomeo Marliani's *Urbis Romae topographia* (1544).

On the Theatres,
what they were for, and who built them

There were three principal theatres in Rome: the Theatre of Pompey
[fol. 9v] – this was the first to be built in stone – the Theatre of
Marcellus and the third was the Theatre of Cornelius Balbus. These were
places in which they used to celebrate festivals, with plays and other like
performances, and each one of them had a capacity of eighty thousand
people.[159] The Theatre of Pompey was in the Campo dei Fiori, on the
site where the palazzo of the exceedingly illustrious Orsini family
stands.[160] The Theatre of Marcellus was begun by Caesar and finished by
Augustus and named after Marcellus, the son of Augustus' sister.[161] It was
on the site where the palazzo of the exceedingly illustrious Savelli family
stands. The Theatre of Cornelius Balbus, dedicated to the Emperor
Claudius, was close to the Circus Flaminius.[162]

56,
57

On the Amphitheatres,
who built them, and what they were for

The amphitheatres were places in which they held gladiatorial contests
and wild animal bating.[163] Only two still stand today, and they are half
ruined. One is today called the Colosseum, after the colossus of Nero
that used to be there in antiquity.[164] The other was called the
Amphitheatre of Statilius. The Colosseum was built by the Emperor
Vespasian and dedicated to Titus.[165] At this dedication five thousand wild
animals of different sorts were
slaughtered. What can be seen of
the Colosseum at present is less
than half of what it was. On the
outside it is built of travertine
marble and round in shape. On the
inside it is oval. It is so tall that it
almost reaches to the top of the
Celian Hill. Inside, 85 thousand
people could sit. The amphitheatre
of Statilius was made of brick, not
very large, and used to be where the
monastery of Santa Croce in
Gerusalemme stands, and its ruins
can still be seen.[166]

54,
55

54   The Colosseum, woodcut from
the third volume of Sebastiano
Serlio's treatise *On Antiquities* (1540).   55 *(facing page)*   The Colosseum.

56   The Theatre of Marcellus.

57   The Theatre of Marcellus, woodcut from the third volume of Sebastiano Serlio's treatise *On Antiquities* (1540).

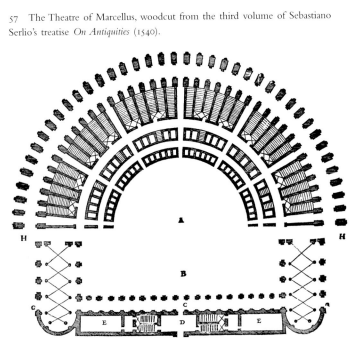

58   The Roman Forum.

On the Fora, that is, Piazzas

There were seventeen principal fora in Rome: the fora Romanum, Boarium, Holitorium, Piscarium, Suarium, of the Sallustii, Archimonium, Pistorium, of Diocletian, Paladium, Esquilinium, of Oeneobarbus, of Caesar, of Augustus, of Nerva, of Trajan, of Cupid, and of the Rustics.[167] But the most famous were the Forum Romanum, the Forum of Caesar, the Forum of Augustus, the Forum of Nerva and the Forum of Trajan. The Forum Romanum began at the foot of the Campidoglio, at the Arch of Septimius Severus, and went as far as the church of SS Cosma e Damiano.[168] Its ornamentation was exceedingly beautiful, and there was a raised part called the Rostra from which they would speak to the people.[169] In that place stood the Temple of Vesta,[170] near the church of Santa Maria Liberatrice, and a marble walkway built by C. Caligula – supported by eighty huge fluted marbled columns, three of which are still standing – that went from the Campidoglio to the Palatine Hill. The Forum of Caesar was behind the Portico of Faustina, and Caesar spent one hundred thousand sestertii on the paving.[171] The Forum of Augustus was where the church of Sant'Adriano stands, and it extended towards the Tor de' Conti.[172] The Forum of Nerva was between the church of Sant'Adriano and that of San Basilio, where these half-ruined columns stand.[173] The Forum of Trajan was where his [fol. 10v] column stands, near the church of Santa Maria di Loreto.[174] The Forum Boarium was in those days between San Giorgio and Sant'Anastasia.[175] The Forum Holitorium was where the Piazza Montanara is today; it was so-called because they used to sell horticultural produce there.[176] The Forum

24, 58, 59

97

60

62, 63

61

59   The Roman Forum, woodcut from Bernardo Gamucci's *Libri Quattro dell'antichità della città di Roma* (1569).
A – Arch of Septimius Severus; B – 'Temple of Concord'; C – The Temple of Antoninus and Faustina; D – The 'Three columns'; E – Temple of SS Cosma e Damiano; F – Temple of Peace; G – Santa Maria Nuova; H – Arch of Titus.

60   Edge of the Forum of Augustus with the temple of Mars Ultor, woodcut from Palladio's *I quattro libri dell'architettura* (1570).

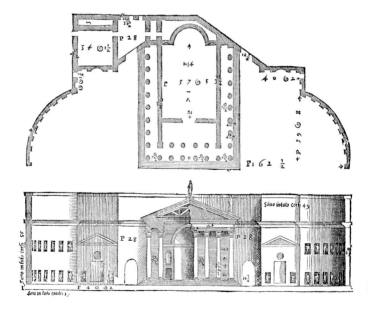

61   The Forum and column of Trajan [photo: Mark Wilson Jones].

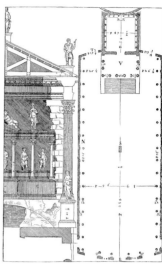

62   The Forum of Nerva, or Forum Transitorium, with the Temple of
Minerva, woodcut from Palladio's *I quattro libri dell'architettura* (1570).

Piscarium was between the church of Santa Maria in Porticu and Santa
Maria Egiziaca, and here they used to sell fish.[177] The Forum Suarium,
so-called because it was the place where they sold swine, was close to
Santo Apostolo, where the church of San Nicolao in Porcilibus stands.[178]

63   The Forum of Nerva, woodcut from Bernardo Gamucci's *Libri Quattro
dell'antichità della città di Roma* (1569).

The Forum Archimonium was where the church of San Nicolao degli Archimonii stands.[179] The Forum Sallustianum was between the church of Santa Susanna and the Porta Salara.[180] Of the others, only the names remain, nor is it known where they stood.

On the Triumphal Arches
and who built them

There were thirty-six triumphal arches in Rome, and they were built in honour of those who placed foreign cities, provinces and nations under Roman imperium. However, today there are only six still standing. That of Septimius Severus (which is at the foot of the Campidoglio) was built in his honour because he overcame the factions;[181] carved into both ends are winged victories bearing the trophies of land and sea battles, with representations of the places stormed by him. That near the Colosseum

64, 65

64   The Arch of Septimius Severus (AD 203), woodcut from the third volume of Sebastiano Serlio's treatise *On Antiquities* (1540).

65   The Arch of Septimius Severus.

66,   was built in honour of Constantine the Great for having beaten the
67   tyrant Maxentius at the Milvian Bridge, and it is very beautiful.[182] That
68,   which stands beside Santa Maria was built by Vespasian and by Titus in
69   honour of the victory in Jerusalem.[183] **[fol. 11r]** On one side is sculpted a
      carriage drawn by four horses with the Triumphator and Victory
      preceded by fasces and other consular insignia. And on the other side
      there are carved the spoils that he brought back from Jerusalem. The arch
      that is near San Giorgio in Velabro was built by the goldsmiths and

66   The Arch of Constantine.

67 Detail of the Arch of Constantine [photo: Mark Wilson Jones].

68 The Arch of Titus (AD 81), woodcut from the third volume of Sebastiano Serlio's treatise *On Antiquities* (1540).

O detto qui adietro de le latitudini, e de le grossezze , hora trattarò de le altezze, e prima: l'altezza de la luce de l'arco è dupla a la larghezza . le piedi del piedestalo è minuti quattro o meno di due piedi . la cornice d'esso piedestalo e alia minuti trentacinque . l'altezza de la base de la colonna col zocco, che ui è sotto, e circa un piede; e tutti questi membri, et anchò il capitello de la colonna ben proportionati di misure sono nel principio de l'ordine Composito nel mio quarto libro . il netto del piedestalo e piedi quattro e mezo.l'altezza de la colonna senza la base e'l capitello è piedi.xvii.e minuti.xiii. l'altezza del capitello è piede uno , e minuti uentisette . l'architraue è piede uno , e minuti dicinoue . l'altezza del fregio è piede uno , e minuti dicisette . l'altezza de la cornice è piedi due e minuti sei . il basamento del'epitaffio è quarto il fregio . l'altezza d'esso epitaffio è piedi noue , e minuti dodici . la sua latitudine e piedi uentitre : i quali membri saranno piu diffusamente disegnati , e descritti ne le carte seguenti .

SENATVS
POPVLVSQVEROMANVS
DIVO TITO DIVI VESPA-
SIANI. F. VESPASIANO
AVGVSTO.

Setto quest'arco cè sono.vv.quadri molto ornati , e nel mezo e un maggior quadro con un Gioue sculpito .

69 The Arch of Titus.

cattle[184] merchants in honour of Septimius.[185] The arch that is called the Arco di Portogallo was built by Domitian.[186] The arch that is called the Arco di San Vito is made of travertine and was built by Gallienus.[187]

On the Porticoes

Caesar Augustus built one on the Palatine, ornamented with diverse marbles and painting.[188] Gordian built another in the Campus Martius, a thousand feet long, ornamented with a double row of remarkable columns.[189] There was also the Portico of Mercurius, which is still standing, half in ruins, near Sant'Angelo di Pescheria.[190] The Portico of Livia was once on the site where now stand the ruins of the Temple of Peace.[191] The Portico of Octavia, sister of Augustus, was beside the

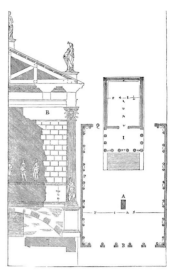

70   The Temple of Antoninus and Faustina, woodcut from Palladio's *I quattro libri dell'architettura* (1570).

71   Portico of the Temple of Antoninus and Faustina, with the church of San Lorenzo in Miranda.

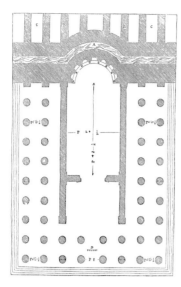

72 (*left*) Palladio's reconstruction of the Temple of Vespasian, three columns of which remained, woodcut from the *I quattro libri dell'architettura* (1570).

73 (*below left*) The so-called Temple of Concord (Saturn), woodcut from Palladio's *I quattro libri dell'architettura* (1570).

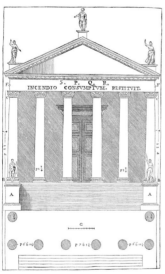

74 (*above*) Portico of the so-called Temple of Concord (Saturn).

70, Theatre of Marcellus.[192] A great deal of the Portico of Faustina is still
71 there on the site where today stands the church of San Lorenzo in
73, Miranda.[193] The Portico of Concord, with its eight columns, stands
74 completely intact on the small hill of the Campidoglio.[194] Next to this
72 there once stood another much larger portico, built as ornament for the
  Campidoglio; all that remains are three columns.[195] The Portico of

Agrippa still stands almost completely intact on the front of the church of Santa Maria Rotonda.[196]

[fol. 11*v*]

On the Trophies and Commemorative Columns

The trophies that are next to Sant'Eusebio were put there in honour of   75, 76
C. Mario, when he triumphed over Jugurtha and the Cimbri.[197] The
'winding' column that stands beside Santa Maria di Loreto was dedicated   61, 77
by the Senate in honour of Trajan when he was fighting against the
Parthians.[198] He never saw it, however, because he died in Soria in the
city of Seleucia when he was returning from this campaign. His bones
were brought back to Rome in a golden urn and placed in the top of
the column, which is 128 feet tall. And the staircase inside for ascending
has 123 steps and forty-four small windows. All around the outside wind
marble sculptures recounting the deeds performed by him, in particular

75   The 'Trophies of Marius', woodcut from Bernardo Gamucci's *Libri Quattro
dell'antichità della città di Roma* (1569).

those in Dacia. The column that is on the Montecitorio is the Column   78,
of Antoninus Pius.[199] It is 165 feet tall, the staircase inside has 206 steps,   89
and it has 56 small windows. All around the outside wind sculptures of
the deeds performed by him. Additionally, there is a porphyry column,
also 'winding', that Constantine the Great had brought to Constantinople
and placed in the piazza.[200] In the Forum there is one of smooth
Numidian marble, twenty feet tall. The people of Rome had carved into
it homage to Julius Caesar: AL PADRE DE LA PATRIA.[201]

76 (*above*) The Trophies of Marius, in their present location on the Campidoglio.

77 (*left*) Detail of Trajan's column, woodcut from the third volume of Sebastiano Serlio's treatise *On Antiquities* (1540).

78 (*facing page*) Column of Marcus Aurelius (Colonna Antonina), Montecitorio.

On the Colossi

On the Campidoglio there stood the Colossus of Apollo, thirty **[fol. 12r]** cubits tall, which cost one hundred and forty talents. Lucullus had it brought from Apollonia in Pontus to Rome.[202] In the Library of Augustus there was another made of bronze which was fifty feet tall.[203] In the vicinity of the Temple of Peace there was a colossus that was 102 feet tall.[204] On its head it had seven rays and each ray was twelve and a half feet long. In the Campus Martius there was another of a similar height, dedicated by Claudius to Jupiter.[205] There used also to be the Colossus of Commodus, made of bronze, which was 300 cubits tall.[206] Furthermore, there was another in the vestibule to Nero's Golden House, which was 120 feet tall.[207]

On the Pyramids

79 Near to the Porta di San Paolo there is a pyramid that is the tomb of C. Cestius.[208] He was one of the seven men whom they used to choose as stewards of the solemn banquet during sacrifices, and the pyramid is not the tomb of Romulus, as the people believe. This remarkable work was built in 330 days, as appears in the inscription upon it.

ne pecuniam succefforibus, aut æmulis insidiantibus præberent, aut ne plebs effet ociofa. Sed hæc mo-lem, de qua loquimur, fuisse Sepulcrum C. Cestij. VII. uiri epulonum, offendit titulus in exteriori, & interiori latere eius incisus. Ab exteriore tantum latere, & litteris longe minoribus subijcitur.
OPVS. APSOLVTVM. EX. TESTAMENTO. DIEBVS. CCC. XXX.
ARBITRATV
PONTI. P. F. CLAMELAE. HAEREDIS. ET. PONTHI. L.

C. CESTIVS. L. F. POB. EPVLO PR. TR. PL.
VII. VIR. EPVLONVM.

79 (*left*) The pyramid of Cestius, woodcut from Bartolomeo Marliani's *Urbis Romae topographia* (1544).

80 (*facing page*) The tomb of Caecilia Metella, or the 'Capo di Bove', *c.*20 BC [photo: Mark Wilson Jones].

On the Mete

The small piece of masonry that can be seen standing near to the Colosseum is a semicircle of the meta called the Meta Sudans,[209] on top of which stood a bronze statue of Jupiter.[210] It was so-called because on the days when they celebrated the festivals in the Colosseum, it used to shoot out water in **[fol. 12v]** great quantities so as to quench the thirst of the people who came to watch. Near San Sebastiano there was another made in travertine called the Capo di Bove.[211] People think that it was the tomb of Metella, wife of Crassus, as appears in some lettering that is cut into it.

On the Obelisks, or 'Needles'

There used to be seven large 'needles' in Rome, two of which were in the Circus Maximus.[212] The large one was 132 feet tall, and the ship that brought it carried 120 thousand modi[213] of lentils as ballast.[214] The small one was 88 feet. There was one in the Campus Martius that was 72 feet,[215] and there were two in the Mausoleum of Augustus, of 42 feet – one was on the site where San Rocco stands today.[216] And there was one, still standing today, behind the church of Saint Peter which is 72 feet tall, and in the top of it there are the mortal remains of Julius Caesar.[217] As for small ones, there used to be 42 of them, and on most of these there were Egyptian characters. Today, however, only two still stand, one in the Aracoeli[218] and the other at San Mauto.[219] Six years ago another was found in a small house behind the Minerva,[220] while they were digging a cantina.

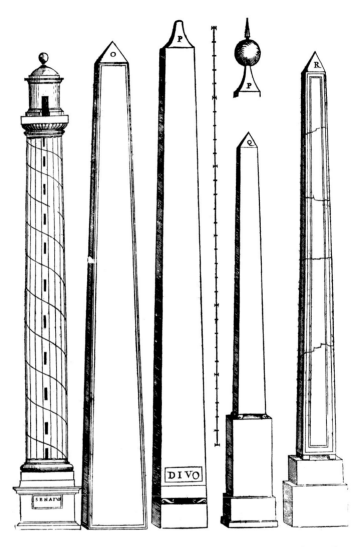

81 Rome's obelisks and Trajan's column, woodcut from the third volume of
Sebastiano Serlio's treatise *On Antiquities* (1540): from left to right – Trajan's
column; the smaller of the two Circus Maximus obelisks, now in the Piazza del
Popolo (O); the St Peter's obelisk (P); one of the Mausoleum of Augustus
obelisks, found near San Rocco (Q); the Campus Martius obelisk, now in the
Piazza Montecitorio (R).

84 *(facing page bottom)*   The statue of Marcus Aurelius on the
Campidoglio.

On the Statues

There were in Rome an infinite number of statues, both standing and equestrian, of all types of materials, particularly marble. While some of these are still standing today, most of them are ruined. And as for equestrian statues, there is only **[fol. 13r]** one, and that is in the piazza of the Campidoglio.[221] It is of the Emperor Marcus Aurelius. It was the Greek custom to erect nude statues, and the Roman custom to erect clothed ones.[222]

84

82 (*above left*)   The St Peter's obelisk, woodcut from Bernardo Gamucci's *Libri Quattro dell'antichità della città di Roma* (1569).
A   Porta del Campo Santo
B   St Peter's sacristy
C   St Peter's basilica
D   obelisk

83 (*above right*)   Obelisk in the Piazza Montecitorio (formerly in the Campus Martius).

On the Marforio

As for the statue that is at the foot of the Campidoglio, called today the Marforio, it is believed that it was of Jupiter Panarius, made in commemoration of the loaves that the guards of the Campidoglio, when they were under siege there, threw into the camp of the Gauls. Others say that it is a representation of the river Rhine,[223] and that above its head was once a foot of the bronze horse of the Emperor Domitian.[224]

On the Horses

There used to be twenty-four gilt horses and 94 of ivory. As for the two half-destroyed marble ones that are on Montecavallo – this hill is named after them – one by Pheidias and the other by Praxiteles, both exceedingly excellent sculptors, Tiridates, King of Armenia,[225] brought those horses to Rome and gave them to Nero.[226]

On the Libraries

There were thirty-seven libraries in Rome, ornamented with diverse marbles and painting.[227] However, the best known were the Augusta, the Gordiana, and the Ulpia. The Augusta was built by Augustus from the spoils from Dalmatia and in it there were innumerable books in Latin and Greek.[228] As for the Gordiana, built by the Emperor Gordian **[fol. 13v]**, the emperor placed 62 thousand volumes there.[229] As for the Ulpia, built by Hadrian near to the Baths of Diocletian, in it were the books in which were written the acts of the Senate.[230] The originator of these libraries in Rome was Asinius Pollio.[231]

On the Timepieces

The first sort of timepiece the Romans used was the sundial brought by M. Valerius Messalla from Catania, a city in Sicily.[232] Messalla conquered Sicily in the year of his Consulate, 377 years after the building of Rome. They used the sundial for 99 years. 219 years later, Scipio Nasica invented a timepiece – not one like ours with sand but with water.[233] The dripping of this water differentiated in great detail the hours and was much better than the sundial, in that sundials could only work when the sun was out, while the former was useful all of the time.

On the Palaces

The Palace of Augustus was in a corner of the Roman Forum,[234] ornamented with various marbles and very beautiful columns.[235] The Palace of Claudius was between the Colosseum and San Pietro in Vinculi, very beautiful and grand. The Palace of Vespasian and Titus was close to San Pietro in Vinculi. The Palace of Nerva was between the Tor de' Conti and the Torre delle Milizie.[236] The Palace of Antoninus was close to his column. It was ornamented with marbles and exceedingly beautiful porphyry. The Palace of Caracalla was near to his **[fol. 14r]** Baths and was ornamented with huge columns and very beautiful marbles. The Palace of Decius was on the Viminal, on the site where the church of San Lorenzo in Panisperna stands today.[237] The Palace of Constantine the Great was at San Giovanni in Laterano.[238] There were very many others, all ornamented exceedingly sumptuously, which I shall leave to one side for brevity's sake.

85 (*facing page*)   *The Horsetamers* or *The Dioscuri*, now in the Piazza del Quirinale.

On Nero's Golden House

86 Nero built a house with one end between the Celian and Palatine hills
and the other at the very end of the Esquiline (that is, from the church
of SS Giovanni e Paolo almost as far as Termine).[239] The entrance was so
large that it was able to contain a
bronze colossus 120 feet tall.[240]
It had a portico with three rows
of columns, a mile in length,
which surrounded a lake and
buildings in the manner of a city.
Here there were vineyards,
pastures, and woods, with a large
number of domestic and wild
animals of every sort. The whole
house was gilded and set with
diverse gems and precious stones.
The ceilings of the *sale* were of
richly carved ivory and made in
such a way as to allow the guests
when dining to be sprinkled with
flowers or precious odours, sent
down through certain tubes. The
principal *sala* was domed and
rotated continuously like the
world. This house was burnt
down in the time of Trajan,
when, without warning, it caught
fire.

86   Ruins of Nero's 'Golden House',
or Domus Aurea, woodcut from
Bernardo Gamucci's *Libri Quattro
dell'antichità della città di Roma* (1569).

[fol. 14*v*]

On other Houses,
notably those for Citizens

There were one thousand, seven hundred and ninety-seven very
opulently ornamented Citizens' houses in Rome.[241] However, the best
known are the following. That of Romulus, which used to be on the
Palatine;[242] with neither columns nor marbles, it stood for many centuries
because men were appointed to repair it when parts fell down, and they

were not allowed to add anything new. That of Scipio Africanus used to be beside the church of San Giorgio.[243] Those of the family of the Flavii and the Cornelii[244] and that of Pomponius Anaeus were on the Quirinal, most sumptuously built. Those of M. Crassus, Q. Catulus and C. Auguilius used to be on the Viminal and were ornamented with diverse marbles and very beautiful columns – the ruins of these can still be seen in the vineyards near Santa Susanna – and Crassus was the first in Rome to have imported columns in his house.[245] That of Scaurus was near the Arch of Titus on the ridge of the Palatine. In its loggia there were marble columns 34 feet tall.[246] That of Mamurra was on the Celian Hill. He was the first in Rome to face his house entirely with marble.[247] That of Gordian, Emperor, was near the church of Sant'Eusebio. It was ornamented with two hundred exceedingly opulant columns. Those of Catiline, Catullus and Cicero were on the Palatine. That of Virgil was on the Esquiline and that of Ovid was near the church of the Consolazione.[248] And P. Clodius bought his house for one hundred and forty-seven thousand sestertii.

[fol. 15r]

On the Public Halls[249]
and what they were for

There were thirty-five public halls in Rome, and they were of two sorts – one where priests attended to sacred matters, and the other where Senators dealt with public matters.[250] The most famous were the

87

87 Plan and section of a Senatorial curia, woodcuts from Cosimo Bartoli's *L'architettura di Leon Battista Alberti* (1550).

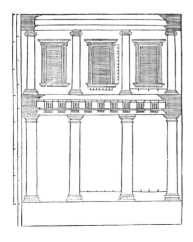
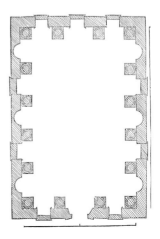

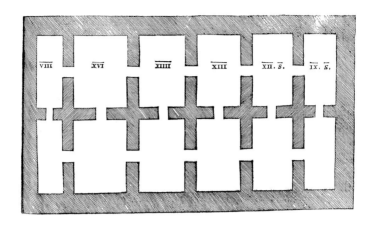

VIII   XVI   XIIII   XIII   XII. S.   IX. S.

88   Plan of the Curia Hostilia, woodcut from Bartolomeo Marliani's *Urbis Romae topographia* (1544).

following. The Curia Vecchia was once where the church of San Pietro in Vincoli stands today.[251] In it they used to perform the auguries. There were two called Hostiliae. One was near the Forum and the other was where the monastery of SS Giovanni e Paolo now stands.[252] The Curia Calabra was on the Campidoglio in the place where the salt pits and the prisons now stand. Here the Pontifex Minor used to inform the people of the dates for the feast days. The Curia Pompeiana was in the Campo dei Fiori behind the Orsini Palace, and since this was where Caesar was murdered, it was destroyed, never to be rebuilt.

On the small Senate Houses, and what they were for

There were three small Senate houses.[253] These were places where Senators would gather to deliberate. One was in the Temple of Concord,[254] the second was at the Porta di San Sebastiano,[255] and the third was in the Temple of Bellona,[256] where they used to receive ambassadors from enemy provinces who had been refused entry into the city.

On the Magistrates

In the beginning Rome had seven kings.[257] After this there were Consuls who governed **[fol. 15v]** with royal power, but their mandate was only for one year. The Praetor Urbanus was the Curator of laws and judged in private cases. The Praetor Peregrinus judged matters for foreigners. The Tribuni Plebis, of which there were 14, had authority to block the decrees of the Senate, the Consuls and other magistrates. Indeed a single Tribune could have a Consul put in prison. The Quaestores Urbani were in charge of the money in the treasury, malefactors, and the reading of letters in the Senate. Aediles were in charge of the city, food supplies and solemn public games.[258] There were two sorts of Aedile – Curulis and Plebeius. There were two Censors. Their authority lasted five years. They surveyed the people and their possessions, and divided them up into their different Tribes. They were in charge of temples and common revenues. They kept guard over mores in the city and punished vices. There were three sorts of Triumvirs: Criminales, Mensarii and Nocturnes. The Criminales were in charge of prisons, and no malefactors could be punished without them. The Mensarii governed the bankers and those who minted coins. The Nocturnes were in charge of the nightwatchmen of the city, particularly firemen. There were four types of Prefect: Urbanus, Annonum, Vigilum and Praetorius. The Praefectus Urbanus had authority to give judgement in place of a magistrate who had, for a particular reason, left the city. The Praefectus Vigilum[259] pursued arsonists, housebreakers, thieves and those harbouring malefactors. The Praefectus Praetorius had full authority to correct **[fol. 16r]** public discipline, and there could be no appeal against his sentences. There were also other magistrates, such as the Centumviri and others – whom I shall omit for brevity's sake – and they were appointed on the first day of January, March or September.

On the General Assemblies, and what they were for

There were many General Assemblies,[260] and they were roofless places where the Equites[261] and the people would gather in order to organize the voting in the creation of magistrates. The Universal General Assembly was near the Roman Forum, at the site where today stands the church of San Teodoro.[262] The Setri[263] were close to the Montecitorio, on the site where today stands the Antonine Column.[264]

On the Tribes

There were thirty-five tribes in Rome:[265] the Titienses, the Ramnenses, the Luceres, the Suburruna, the Palatina, the Esquilia, the Collina,

the Claudia, the Crustannia, the Lemonia, the Metia, the Uffinteia, the
Pupinia, the Popilia, the Romulia, the Scaptia, the Sabatina, the
Tormentina, the Stellatina, the Arniense, the Pontia, the Publia, the Matia,
the Scatia, the Anienses, the Terentina, the Sergia, the Quirina, the
Trinitica, the Voltiana, the Valentiniana, the Fatiana, the Scapienses, the
Voltinea and the Narnienses.

[fol. 16v]

On the Wards,
that is, the *Rioni* and their Symbols

In ancient times, Rome had fourteen *Rioni*, but today there are only
thirteen.[266] They are: the Monti *rione*, which has three hills[267] as its
89 symbol; the Colonna *rione*, which has a column; the Trevi *rione* has three
swords; the Sant'Eustachio *rione* has Our Saviour between two horns; the
Ponte *rione* has a bridge; the Regola *rione* has a stag; the Ripa *rione* has a
wheel; the Trastevere *rione* has a lion's head; the Campidoglio *rione* has a
dragon's head; the Parione[268] *rione* has a griffon; the Pigna *rione* has a pine
cone; the Campomarzio *rione* has the moon; and the Sant'Angelo *rione*
has an angel.

89 Piazza Colonna with the Column of Marcus Aurelius (*colonna Antonina*) in
the Colonna *rione* at the time of Sixtus V, sixteenth century, Vatican, Biblioteca
Apostolica Vaticana.

On the Basilicas
and what they were for

There were twelve basilicas in Rome. They were places where the   90
Romans pursued litigation, and they were ornamented with statues and
beautiful columns, with two storeys of portico. The principal basilicas
were the Paulus, the Argentaria and the Alexandrina.[269]

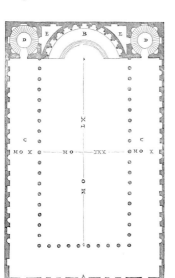

90   Palladio's reconstruction of the
ancient Basilica, woodcut from the
I quattro libri dell'architettura (1570).

On the Campidoglio

Tarquinius Superbus began building the Campidoglio[270] using the booty   91, 92
from Dometia,[271] a city of the Latins. It was named after the man's
head[272] that was found while the foundations were being laid.
M. Horatius Pulvillus, when he was Consul, finished it, and Q. Catulus
dedicated it to Jupiter Capitolinus and had it covered with gilded bronze
tiles. On the ascent to it from the Forum there were **[fol. 17r]** one
hundred steps. There used also to be gold and silver statues, gold, silver
and crystal vases of inestimable worth, and three thousand bronze tablets
in which the laws were inscribed.[273] The Campidoglio burnt down four
times. The first fire occurred 415 years after it was built, the second was

91   The Campidoglio, woodcut from Bernardo Gamucci's *Libri Quattro dell'antichità della città di Roma* (1569).

92   The Campidoglio.

in the time of Sulla and it was rebuilt by Vespasian. The third was in the time of Domitian, who rebuilt it and made it more magnificent than it had been before – it cost him more than twelve thousand talents. The fourth was in the time of Commodus. Of all the buildings that were once here, the only one that can be seen today is the half-ruined Campidoglio, restored by Boniface VIII and given by him as a place of

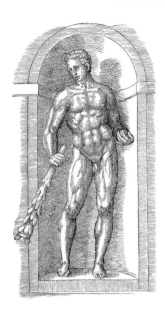

93   Statue of Hercules in the
Palazzo de' Conservatori on the
Capitol, woodcut from Bartolomeo
Marliani's *Urbis Romae topographia*
(1544).

meeting for the Senate.[274] There is no
doubt that the ornaments that used to
be there outdid the marvels of Egypt.
And since it was exceedingly
ornamented, today it is filled with
ruins, although they are once again
restoring it.[275] The only antiquities
that can be seen there are the bronze
she-wolf[276] that was in the General
Assembly,[277] and that was made with
the fines imposed upon certain
money lenders. It is in the Palazzo de'
Conservatori,[278] where, in the
antechamber, there is a gilded bronze   93
statue of Hercules, holding in his
right hand his club and in his left a
golden apple.[279] This statue was found
during the time of Sixtus IV in the
ruins of the Temple of Hercules,
which was in the Forum Boarium.
And in the audience chamber there
are bronze statues of two young men.
One is standing and wearing the
clothes of a slave.[280] The other is
naked and appears to be a shepherd; with a needle he is taking a splinter
out of the sole of his foot.[281] In the courtyard there is a head, foot and   95
other fragments of the colossus that was near the Temple of Peace.[282]
In the façade near the stairs there are certain **[fol. 17v]** marble panels
in which is sculpted the Triumph of M. Aurelius when he conquered
Dacia.[283] In the courtyard there are many antique marbles beautifully
and ornamentally arranged, which were recently found in the Forum,
beneath the Arch of Severus. Here are carved the names of all the
Roman Consuls, Dictators and Censors.[284] The great bronze head that is
under the portico is of Commodus; there is also a hand and a foot from
the said colossus.[285] Above, in the *sala*, there is a statue of Leo X taken
from life.[286] In the *sala* where they dispense justice there is the statue of
Paul III and that of King Charles, who was a senator.[287] The two statues   94, 96
that are at the foot of the steps up to the Senate represent the Tigris and
the Nile, rivers of Egypt.[288] The eight columns that can be seen towards
the Forum were once in the portico of the Temple of Concord.[289]

95   Fragments of a gigantic statue of Constantine, discovered in the Basilica of
Maxentius ('Temple of Peace') in 1487, in the courtyard of the Palazzo de'
Conservatori.

On the Treasury,
that is, the Chamber of the Commune,
and the money that people used in Rome in those times

The first treasury in which they stored the money of the Roman People,
built by Valeria Publicola, was on the site where the church of San
Salvatore in Erario stands today, near the Tarpeian Rock towards the

94 and 96   The Nile (*facing page top*) and the Tigris/Tiber (*above*) in the
Palazzo de' Conservatori on the Capitol.

Piazza Montanara.[290] From this treasury, Julius Caesar, having broken
down the doors, took 4,135 libbre of gold and nine hundred thousand
libbre of silver, and in their place he put the same quantity of gilt bronze.
Seven years before the Punic War, in the Consulate of Sextus Julius and
L. Aurelius, it contained 726 libbre of gold, 92 thousand libbre of silver,
and 375 thousand libbre of extraordinary moneys. The second treasury
was where **[fol. 18r]** the church of Sant'Adriano stands today.[291] The first
coin ever spent in Rome was made of bronze without any markings on
it whatsoever.[292] Servius Tullius[293] was the first to mark a coin and he put
the image of a *pecora*[294] on it, hence it was called *pecunia*.[295] During the
consulate of Q. Fabius, 585 years after the founding of Rome, a silver
coin was minted with two-wheeled carriages [on one side] and on the
other, the prow of a ship. Gold coins were minted 62 years later. The first
to reintroduce bronze coins was Saturnus.[296]

<h2 style="text-align:center">On the Graecostasis
and what it was</h2>

The Graecostasis was a place where they used to receive the ambassadors
who came to Rome.[297] It was on the corner of the Palatine, on the site
where the ruins can be seen above Santa Maria Liberatrice.[298]

97   The Rostra in the Roman Forum.

On the Secretariat of the Roman People

Near to the statue of the Marforio[299] stood the Secretariat of the Roman People.[300] It was rebuilt in the time of emperors Honorius and Theodosius, since it had accidentally been burnt down.

On the Asilo

In the piazza on the Campidoglio where today can be seen the horse of Antoninus[301] stood a site called the Asilo.[302] It was built by Romulus for the encouragement of his new city, giving rights and sanctuary to anyone, whether free or slave, local or foreigner. **[fol. 18v]** Caesar Augustus stopped this because he thought it served only to give people the chance to perform wicked deeds.

On the Rostra
and what they were

97   The Rostra was a speaker's platform that stood in the Roman Forum, adorned with metal.[303] From here judgements were passed and laws

published. They also used to recite here orations to the people. Before this speaker's platform there were innumerable statues. When seeking greatness in the republic, the ancients used to carry here the heads of those they had conquered and killed.

On the column known as the Columna Miliaria

Facing the Arch of Septimius Severus in the Roman Forum there stood a column that the ancients called the Miliarium Aureum.[304] Here, using this column, people could manage to find their way to the city gates and go on whatever journey they wished to undertake.

On the Temple of Carmenta

At the foot of the Campidoglio where the now ruined church of Santa Caterina stands there was once the Temple to Carmenta, Evander's mother.[305] It was built by the women of Rome in her honour because she had allowed women to travel in carriages, whereas the Senate had for many years forbidden women to use them.

[fol. 19r]

On the Colonna Bellica

Below the Campidoglio near the Piazza Montanara[306] was the Temple of Bellona.[307] Before the door stood a column that the ancients called the Colonna Bellica because from it they used to hurl a spear towards the region against which they were to make war.[308] This was because, since the Roman Empire had grown to such an extent, it would have been too fatiguing to go to the frontiers of those against whom they were to make war.

On the Columna Lactaria

In the Forum Holitorium, now called the Piazza Montanara, there was a column called the Columna Lactaria.[309] To this 'milk' column, babies born out of wedlock were brought in secrecy. When found, they were taken away to be fed in places arranged by the public.

On the Aequimelium

Near the church of San Giorgio there was a place called Aequimelium,[310] after M. Sp. Maelius[311] – a man who, having wished to take control of

Rome, was killed and his property confiscated and given to the public. The Censors had his house razed to the ground, and as a memorial they made a piazza which was called Aequimelium after the name of Maelius (as we have said).

[fol. 19*v*]

On the Campus Martius

The Campus Martius was made by Tarquinius Superbus.[312] After his expulsion it was dedicated to Mars, hence it was called the Campus Martius. Here they used to have musters and other military events.

On the Tigillum Sororium

Close to the Temple of Peace, today called Santa Maria Nuova,[313] there was a place built with two walls, one facing the other, and upon these two walls they laid a large beam. Under this passed one of the three Horatii because he had killed his sister.[314] He did it as a sign of justice and to purge his sin.

On the Castra Peregrina

On the site of the church of Santi Quattro[315] used to be stationed those soldiers of the Roman army based at Misenum. Hence this was called the Castra Peregrina[316] or also the Castra Pelegrina.[317]

On the Villa Publica

The Villa Publica was a magnificent building near the saepta of the Campus Martius.[318] Here they would receive the ambassadors of provinces who were hostile to the Roman people and whom it was not permitted to lodge within the city walls. These ambassadors were lodged in this place by the public, who also fed them.

[fol. 20*r*]

On the Taberna Meritoria

On the site where Santa Maria in Trastevere stands there was a habitation called the Taberna Meritoria, in which lived the old and invalid soldiers who had served the Roman people, and they were maintained at public expense for the whole of their lives. As a result of this good deed of charity, our Lord Jesus Christ honoured this place with a great mystery at His birth, whereupon for a whole day and night an exceedingly abundant spring of oil came out of the ground in a great flood that ran down to the Tiber, thus signifying His grace which had come upon the earth.[319]

On the Vivarium

Between the Porta di San Lorenzo and Sant'Agnese, behind the Botte di Termine, the ancient Romans had a special place in which they kept diverse sorts of animals that were subsequently used in the public games, for the delight of the people.[320]

On the Horti

The ancient Romans had very famous horti or pleasure gardens.[321] But for the sake of brevity we shall mention only the principal ones. There were the Horti Sallustiani and the Horti Maecenati. Those of the Sallustii were on the Quirinal Hill near the church of Santa Susanna;[322] the place is still today called 'Sallustico'. In the centre of this place **[fol. 20v]** there is an obelisk stretched out upon the ground inscribed with Egyptian

98

98   Idealised reconstruction of the Horti Maecenati on the Esquiline Hill and other monuments, woodcut from M. Fabio Calvo's *Antiquae urbis Romae simulachrum* (1527).

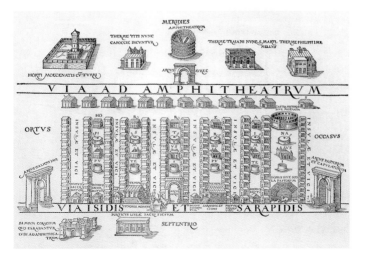

letters.[323] It was so pleasant here that many wished to leave the Palatine
Hill to come and live in this place. It was the house and piazza of the
Sallustii mentioned above. The Horti Maecenati were on the Esquiline
Hill near the tower of the said Maecenas.[324] Previously it had been a field
in which they used to bury the dead, putting the bodies into certain
wells that the ancients used to call 'puticoli', since the bodies would
putrefy in them. This was a most ancient style of burial. Subsequently,
the custom of cremation was introduced and this went on in the same
place. But because the smoke damaged and irritated both the Senate and
the people of Rome, Augustus gave this field to Maecenas, who made it
into the gardens so celebrated by writers. In the tower mentioned above,
Nero stood to watch Rome burn, enjoying the fact that it was on fire.[325]
The Colle degli Horti[326] began at the Porta del Popolo and went beyond
the Trinità church.[327] It was named after the valley below it, in which
were exceedingly fertile vegetable gardens. But today the amount of
housing is increasing so much that this place has the appearance of a new
city.

On the Velabrum

Between the church of San Giorgio and Sant'Anastasia e Scuola Grecha
an expanse of water would occasionally collect when the river was in
spate such that it was impossible to cross without a boat, and anyone in
this part of the city who wished to come or go had to pay a certain
fee.[328] **[fol. 21r]** Because of this crossing, the place was called
'Velabrum'.[329] When over time the place became filled with earth, it was
called the Forum Boarium after a bronze statue of an ox placed there by
Romulus.[330] Others hold that it was called the Forum Boarium from the
buying and selling of oxen that took place there.[331] The gladiatorial
games were staged for the first time in this forum.

On the Carinae

The Carinae began near the Colosseum at the foot of the Esquiline Hill,
followed the Via Labicana near the church of SS Marcellino e Pietro,
then joined the road opposite San Giuliano, before travelling up via the
Arch of Gallienus (today called San Vito), through the area of the
Suburra, finally returning to the Colosseum, passing below San Pietro in
Vincoli.[332] The Carinae were so-called because of the buildings which
were constructed in the form of ships. The majority of the nobility of
Rome lived in this area.

On the Steep Slopes

There were many steep slopes throughout the city, but the most celebrated were those that rose towards the Campidoglio. The oldest of these was that beside the church of the Consolazione,[333] and in the time of the Censors it was paved. The next was below the Palazzo del Senatore. It started at the Temple of Concord, at the place where eight very tall columns can be seen,[334] **[fol. 21v]** and rose via 100 steps to the Campidoglio fortress. After this, there was the other steep slope that began at the Arch of Septimius Severus, and it is quite possible that it was very highly honoured, both because it was matched to the arch and also because of the pavement of thick stone that was discovered several years ago during excavations. The fourth steep slope was on the other side of the hill at the flight of steps of the Aracoeli,[335] which people still climb today and where, also in our time, a door of the finest marble was discovered.

142

On the Meadows

In the Campus Vaticanus were the Quinctian Meadows, named after L. Quinctius Cincinnatus. They are near to the Castel Sant'Angelo and in the vernacular they are called 'Prati'.[336] Here can be seen the remains of a circus – what we mean is a place in which to exercise horses. And following the line of the river bank there were the meadows of Mucius Scaevola,[337] which were given to him by the people after he valued his native land's safety more than his own when fighting against King Porsenna.

On the Public Granaries and the Salt Stores

On the plain that lies behind the Aventine Hill near the Tiber there used to be 160 huge public granaries in which the grain of the people of Rome was kept.[338] In addition to these there were another 29 throughout the city. The salt stores, built by Ancus Marcius,[339] were close to the said granaries. Livius Salinator invented the salt tax.[340]

[fol. 22r]

On the Public Prisons

The prison that used to be at the foot of the Campidoglio, on the site where Saint Peter and Saint Paul were imprisoned, was called the Tullian

Prison, and it was built by Ancus Marcius and King Tullus.[341] The prison
that was close to the church of San Nicola in Carcere was built by
Claudius, one of the Decemviri, and he was the first person to die
therein.[342]

On some Festivals and Games
that they used to celebrate in Rome

The ancient Romans used to celebrate the Agonium festival in honour
of Janus on 9 January.[343] On the last two days of February they used to
make sacrifices to Mars. On 3 April they celebrated the Florales in
memory of Flora, a much-loved courtesan of Pompey's who made the
people of Rome the sole heir of everything she possessed. Her house was
once in the place where now stands the piazza, the Campo dei Fiori,
which was named after her. The Ludi Florales used to take place below
the estate of the Cardinal of Naples, at the foot of the Quirinal Hill –
these days called Montecavallo – where the valley is enclosed with walls.
These games were performed by naked courtesans, who were totally
licentious in their words and lascivious in their movements. On the sixth
of the said month, in memory of the victory over the Latins, nobly
dressed horsemen used to ride with great pomp, carrying olive branches
in their right hands, from the Temple of Mars[344] (which was about
4 miles outside Rome on the Via Appia) to the Temple of Castor and
Pollux.[345] On 26 **[fol. 22v]** May they held the Lustri. These were festival
days celebrated in honour of Mars, on which they used to display
trumpets, eagles and other military insignia. In the autumn they would

celebrate festivals in honour of Bacchus. In the month of December they used to celebrate the Saturnalia in honour of Saturn. They would also celebrate the Trajan Games, the Capitoline Games, the Scenic Games, the Apolline Games, the Ludi Seculari, the Roman Games, the Lebean Games, the Circus Games and others that I shall omit for the sake of brevity.

On the Tombs of Augustus, of Hadrian and of Septimius

The Tomb of Augustus was in the Valle Martia, and the remains of it can still be seen near to the church of San Rocco.[346] It was decorated with white marble, porphyry, huge columns, obelisks and beautiful statues. It had 12 doors, three rings of walls and was circular in form. It was 250 cubits tall and at the top there was a statue of Augustus in bronze. And he did not just make it for himself, but also for the other emperors. The Tomb of Hadrian was on the site of the Castel Sant'Angelo.[347]

99

100,
101

100   Fanciful reconstruction of Hadrian's mausoleum, engraving from Antonio Labacco's *Libro appartenente a l'architettura* (1552).

101 (*below*)   Castel Sant'Angelo, woodcut from Bernardo Gamucci's *Libri Quattro dell'antichità della città di Roma* (1569).

99 (*facing page*)   Mausoleum of Augustus.

Gran cofe,& in diuerfe forme faceuano i Romani : dalle quali per le ruine loro non fi puo comprendere a che cofa elle feruiffero , e maffimamente que ſto prefente edificio,ilquale fi addimanda le fette zone di Seuero . Dell'edifi cio fe ne uede ancora un'angolo in piede,& e di,tre ordini tutto di opera Co rinthia: ma fi comprende ch'ei fuffe fatto d'fpoglie d'altri edificii,percioche ci fono delle colonne canellate,e delle fchiette,& anco i capitelli , & altre ope re,che non fono tutte d'una maniera . Le altezze di quefto edificio io non le mifurai,ma la pianta fi bene,e le groffezze delle cafe : e per quanto io cōpren do gli ordini diminuifcono la quarta parte l'un fopra l'altro , come dice Vi truuio nei theatri . La figura qui forto rapprefenta la pianta dell'edificio, & anco rapprefenta il cielo de i lacunari fopra le colonne, e fu mifurata col pie de,col quale e mifurato il theatro di Pola : e prima la groffezza del muro e piedi tre e mezo . Fra l'un muro e l'altro e piedi quattro e mezo,fra il muro,e le colonne e piedi cinque e tre quarti,e cofi e lo interuallo da colonna a colō na . La groffezza di una colonna e piedi due,& un quarto : In quefto edificio non ci fi uede habitatione alcuna,ne anco ueftigio di fcale per falire ad alto : ma ben fi comprende che continuaua in maggior grandezza , doue in altro luogo ci poteuano effere fcale , & habitationi , e ueramente quefto edificio integro douea hauere prefentia grande per il gran numero delle colonne che ui erano, e per i ricchiffimi ornamenti .

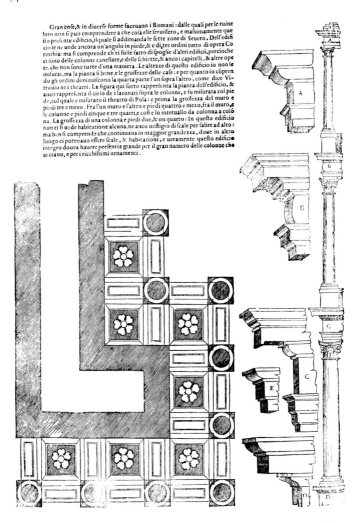

102   The Septizonium of Septimius Severus in the Domus Severiana on the south-east corner of the Palatine, woodcut from the third volume of Sebastiano Serlio's treatise *On Antiquities* (1540).

It was ornamented with beautiful marbles and statues of men, horses and carriages, skilfully carved. These things were destroyed by Belisarius's soldiers in the war with the Goths.[348] Boniface VIII built the castle, and Alexander VI surrounded it with moats and bastions, arranged the guardrooms and built the passageway, both covered and uncovered, that

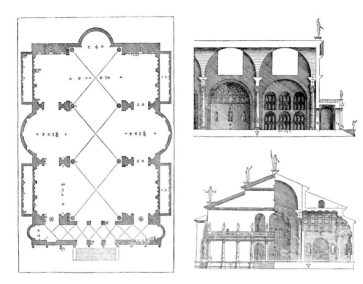

103   The so-called 'Templum Pacis' (Temple of Peace), woodcut from Palladio's
I quattro libri dell'architettura (1570).

goes to the Papal Palace.[349] Paul III ornamented it with beautiful rooms.
The Tomb of the Emperor Septimius Severus[350] **[fol. 23r]** was close to
the church of San Gregorio in the place where the three orders of
columns can be seen, one on top of the other like porticoes, and this is
called the Septizonium after the seven ceilings it had, one on top of the   102
other.[351]

104   The 'Temple of Peace'/Basilica of Maxentius.

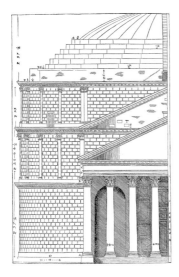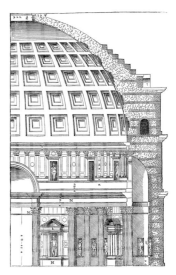

105   The Pantheon, woodcuts from Palladio's *I quattro libri dell'architettura* (1570).

On the Temples

There were many temples in Rome, but the most celebrated were the
Temple of Jupiter Optimus Maximus, the Temple of Peace and the
Pantheon. The Temple of Jupiter Optimus Maximus was in the
Campidoglio;[352] Tarquinius Priscus vowed to built it, but it was built by
Tarquinius Superbus. It was square in form and each of its faces was two
hundred feet long. It had three storeys of columns, and 40 thousand
libbre of silver were spent on the foundations. In addition to the other
ornaments, there was a ten-foot gold statue, and there were six emerald
cups brought to Rome by Pompey. The Temple of Peace was a great deal
bigger than all the others, rectangular in shape, and ornamented with vast
and very beautiful columns and statues.[353] It was built by Vespasian
80 years after the coming of Christ and it burnt down without warning
during the reign of Commodus[354] – its ruins can still be seen near the
church of Santa Maria Nuova – and it did not fall into ruin on Christmas
Eve (as people believe). The Pantheon still stands and is circular in
shape.[355] Both in height and width it is one hundred and forty-four feet.
On the outside it is made of brick and on the inside it is ornamented
with various marbles. All around it there are highly decorated small
chapels, in which used to be placed **[fol. 23v]** statues of the gods. Its
doors are made of bronze and are of a remarkable height.[356] It used to be

103,
104

105,
106,
133

106   The Pantheon [photo: Mark Wilson Jones].

dedicated to Avenging Jupiter, Ceres and all the gods. Boniface IV dedicated it to the Blessed Virgin and all the saints.[357] It is called 'the Ritonda'. It was also covered with sheets of silver, which the Emperor Constantine III removed and took to Syracuse, along with all the bronze

107   Drawing by Maarten van Heemskerck of two lions placed either side of a sarcophagus in front of the Pantheon, *c.*1532. Kupferstichkabinett, Staatliche Museen zu Berlin – Preussischer Kulturbesitz. Römische Skizzenbücher, inv. no. 79D2, I, fol.10*r*.

and marble statues that were in Rome.[358] He did more damage in the
seven days that he was here than the barbarians had done in 258 years.
It was not (as people believe) Saint Gregory who, for religious reasons,
had the most beautiful statues thrown into the Tiber, thus ravaging
antiquity.[359] On the contrary, he repaired many aqueducts that were
falling into ruin. But time – the consumer of all things – and men have
also worn them away, as we have seen equally in our time. The Pantheon
still has a very beautiful portico, built by M. Agrippa, ornamented with
13 exceedingly large columns, and its roof was supported by beams of
107   gilded bronze.[360] The two lions and the two porphyry vases that are in
the piazza were once in the Baths of Agrippa.[361]

On the Priests, on the Vestal Virgins, on the Vestments, Vases and other Instruments made for use during Sacrifices, and on those who instituted the Sacrifices

Once he had seized power, Numa Pompilius[362] introduced religion and
the worship of the gods to the city **[fol. 24r]** in order to tame that rough
and violent people. He instituted many things in honour of those gods.
He built the Temple of Vesta, which was a rotunda;[363] men were
forbidden to enter, and he selected the number of virgins to serve that
goddess.[364] The virgins had to be born of free men, no part of their
bodies could be missing, nor could they be weak in the head. They were
accepted from the age of six to a maximum of ten years old. For the first
ten years they learnt the rites for the sacrifices, for the same number of
years they performed the sacrifices, and for the last ten they taught the
young girls who had been newly recruited. Once these 30 years were
over they were allowed to marry, although those who did were without
good fortune. The principal, that is, the abbess, was called 'Massima', and
these virgins were held in great devotion and much revered by the
people of Rome. They guarded the eternal flame and the Palladium –
that is, the statue of Minerva – and other things sacred to the Romans.[365]
When the virgins were found in adultery, as were Porphyria, Minutia,
Sextilia, Emilia with her two companions, and many others, they were
put to death in the following way. They were stripped of their office and
then carried away, tied to a beam with their faces covered amidst total
silence (the entire city was in mourning on that day), through the city as
far as the Porta Salaria, near to which there was a place called the
'Campo Scelerato'.[366] Here there was a hand-built, vaulted sepulchre that
had a small hole and two small windows. In one of the windows was

placed a lighted lantern and in the other water, milk and honey. Once they reached this place, the principal priest recited some private prayers **[fol. 24v]** with his hands lifted up to the heavens. They would then send those virgins into the sepulchre through the small hole while the people averted their gaze. As soon as the ladder had been removed and the tomb had been covered with a stone, as for a sepulchre, the people would throw earth upon the tomb and spend the whole day in continuous lamentation.

Numa Pompilius created three priests – that is, the Flamines – one in honour of Jupiter, the other in honour of Mars and the third in honour of Romulus.[367] These priests went about wearing specific vestments and on their heads a white hat, which was called an 'Albus Gallerus'. He also instituted the office of Pontifex Maximus[368] and the twelve priests called the Salians in honour of Mars.[369] They wore special painted tunics and on their breasts a pectoral decorated with gold, silver and precious stones. When religion and the worship of the gods – of which the Romans had more than 30 thousand – later grew, the number of priests also increased, such as the Pater Patratus, the Feciales, the Epulones and the Augurs.[370] The latter had so much power that the Senate could not meet without their permission. They went about dressed in diverse vestments, but when they performed the sacrifices they all dressed identically, wearing the same baggy and long white linen shirt girded around the middle with a belt. This way of dressing was called 'Cinctus Gabinus'. They also had many instruments and vases made for use in the sacrifices, such as the Praefericulum,[371] which was a bronze dish without handles that was open like a ramina dish. The Patena was a small open dish. The Achamus was a small dish fashioned like **[fol. 25r]** a cup; in this they would taste the wine for the sacrifices. The Infula was a woollen cloth with which they used to cover the priest and the victim. The Inarculum[372] was a small gilded pomegranite branch, which priests used to put on their heads when they were performing sacrifices. The Acerra[373] was the boat in which they kept the incense. Anclabris[374] was the name for the table upon which the sacred things were placed, and the dishes that the priests had for their use were also called Anclabria. The Secespita[375] was an iron knife – in fact it was quite long, with a round ivory handle, garnished with gold and silver at the end and stuck with diverse bronze tacks. The Struppi[376] were bunches of verbena that they used to put in the cushions beneath the heads of the gods. The Suffibulum[377] was a white woven robe, fairly long and rectangular, that the vestal virgins used to place over their heads when they were performing sacrifices. They also used many other things, which I pass over for brevity's sake.

On the Armamentaria
and what it was

The Armamentaria stood near to the Temple of Peace, and it was a place where they held public arms.[378] Since the Romans did not have private arms, whenever they went to war they took their arms from this place – and when they returned they would bring them back here. The people of Rome went to war with no pay whatsoever, for more than two hundred years.

[fol. 25v]

On the Roman Army and Navy
and their Ensigns

In the time of the emperors, the Romans (as Appian writes)[379] had two hundred thousand foot soldiers, forty thousand cavalrymen, three hundred elephants, two thousand chariots and an additional three hundred thousand armed men if required. The navy had two thousand ships and one thousand, five hundred galleys, from biremes to quinqueremes. They had many military ensigns, but that specific to the Romans showed the eagle.

On Triumphs
and to whom they were granted,
and who was the first to receive a Triumph,
and how many different sorts there were

The Triumph was granted to the Dictator, Consul or Praetor who in a military exploit had beaten more than fifty thousand enemy soldiers and had placed provinces and cities under Roman imperium.[380] The most sumptuous and magnificent Triumphs were those of Pompey and of Caesar. Another type of Triumph was the 'ovatio', which was granted to a Captain who had routed the enemy.[381] He would enter the city on foot, with the Senate behind him and without the army. The first to have a Triumph of this sort were Postumius Tubertus,[382] Consul, when he was victorious over the Sabines, and Marcellus[383] for the taking of Sicily, and many others. However, the first to have a Triumph in Rome was Romulus and the last was the Emperor Probus. There were 320 Triumphs celebrated. And the first to lead enemies in chains **[fol. 26r]** in the city of Rome was Cincinnatus.[384] Those receiving a Triumph rode in a two-wheeled chariot drawn by horses or other animals, followed by the army

108   Elephants in the *Triumphs of Caesar*, detail from an engraving by Giovanni Antonio da Brescia (after Andrea Mantegna), *c*.1500, Musée du Petit Palais, Paris.

crowned with laurels. Once they reached the Campidoglio they would dismount from the chariot and enter the temple of Jupiter Optimus Maximus, where they would give thanks to him for granting them the victory, and on sacrificing a white bull they would go to their quarters.

On the Crowns
and to whom they were given

There used to be many sorts of crowns and they were given to soldiers as rewards for bravery.[385] The Triumphalis (made of bay) was given to Captains. The Obsidionalis (made of couch grass) was given to those who freed the city from a siege – the first to receive one was Sicius Dentatus. The Civica (made of oak or ilex) was given to those who saved a citizen from a great danger. The Muralis was given by Captains to the first soldier to climb upon the enemies' walls. The Castrensis was given to those who were the first to enter enemy quarters and who had passed over the bastions. The Navalis was given to those who first boarded an enemy ship. These three crowns were all made of gold: the Muralis was made to look like the crenellations on city walls, the Castrensis took the form of a bastion, and the Navalis looked like the beak of a galley. The Ovalis, made of myrtle, was given to Captains who had routed their enemies. The first crown ever used in Rome was made of ears of corn, and it was given to Romulus. Armillae **[fol. 26v]** were a sort of bracelet of gold and silver that soldiers wore on their left arm near the shoulder as ornament.

On the Total given for the Population of Rome

According to the census of Servius Tullius,[386] there were 84 thousand people in Rome including its surroundings.[387] After the death of the 306 Fabii, they took a review and there were one million, one hundred and seven thousand, three hundred and eighteen people in Rome. When they took a review during the First Punic War, there were two hundred and ninety thousand, three hundred and thirty men therein. Under Augustus there were one million, three hundred and one thousand and thirty-seven, and under Tiberius there were one million, six hundred thousand, nine hundred and forty-one.

On the Wealth of the Roman People

There was a great deal of wealth in ancient Rome, to judge from the splendid edifices, great theatres and other wonderful things there.[388] No citizen was considered wealthy unless he could personally finance the army for one year. One of the richest was Lucullus – when actors asked him to loan them one hundred cloaks, he said that he had five thousand to lend them. On his death, the fish in his fishpond were sold for thirty thousand sestertii and he was worth more than 20,000 citizens.

[fol. 27r]

On the Generosity of the Ancient Romans

The histories are full of tales of the generosity of the ancient Romans. I shall, however, submit only these few. The Senate, when the Carthaginian ambassadors had brought them a great sum of money to ransom 2,744 young prisoners, let the prisoners go without taking anything at all. In their agreement on the exchange of prisoners, Fabius Maximus and Hannibal established that he who received the greater number of prisoners would pay the other two and a half libbre of silver for each prisoner. Having received 247 more prisoners than Hannibal and seeing that the Senate never reached any conclusion (even though they had debated the matter many times), Fabius sent his son to Rome and had him sell one of his estates in order to pay off the debt that he had undertaken on behalf of the republic, preferring to compromise his wealth rather than his word. And the sum he paid was six thousand, two hundred ducats. Aware that Quintilian was too poor to be able to marry off one of his daughters, Pliny the Younger gave him five thousand ducats for her dowry.

On the Marriages of the Ancients and their Customs

When a woman went to her husband, it was the custom of the ancient Romans to adorn her in the way that follows.[389] Firstly they would give her a key to hold in her hand, next they would decorate her head with a lance that had killed a gladiator. They would gird her with a belt of sheep's wool, which her husband would later remove when she was on the bed. **[fol. 27v]** On her head and underneath her veil (which they called a 'flammeum') she would wear a garland of verbena mixed with other herbs, and she would be made to sit on a sheepskin. When she went to her husband's house she was accompanied by three boys whose mother and father were still alive. One of them carried before them a lighted torch made of hawthorn (since these ceremonies were held at night) and the other two went either side. They also had a distaff with flax on it and a spindle covered in thread carried in front of her. They would also make her touch fire and water. At marriages they never lit more than five torches, and these were usually lit by the Aediles.

On the good Upbringing which they gave to their Children

The ancient Romans were exceedingly diligent in giving their children a good upbringing.[390] First, the children were never allowed to eat away from the home, they were never permitted to use bad language, and they were sent to Tuscany, Athens or Rhodes to learn the worthy arts and disciplines. They were never allowed to go very far from home, and they never appeared in public before they were ten years old, at which age they went to the Treasury to have their names written in the books of their tribe. The next time they appeared was at seventeen years old; at that age they put aside the praetextus and started to wear the toga virilis.

Once they were so clothed, each young man would always accompany his father, showing him great honour and **[fol. 28r]** reverence. On the day when the Senate met, they would accompany a Senator – either a relation or a friend of their father's – to the Court and wait for them until the Senate broke up, and then accompany them back home again.

On the Dissolution of Marriages

The ancient Romans had three ways of dissolving marriages.[391] The first was called 'repudiation' and this was when the man performed it against the will of the woman. The first person to do this was Spurius Carvilius,[392] one hundred years after the building of Rome, because his wife did not have children. Caius Sulpitius repudiated his wife because she went out of the house cloaked but without a veil on her head, Q. Antistius[393] because he saw his speaking privately with a woman of free morals, and P. Sempronius[394] because his went to the public shows without his knowledge. C. Caesar[395] repudiated Pompeia[396] simply because of the suspicion he had concerning Clodius,[397] who was discovered dressed as a woman at the celebrations that Pompey held in honour of the Bona Dea. The second was called 'divorce' and this was performed when both were in agreement. The third was called 'diremption' and this was performed with the arbitration of the Princeps.

On the Funerals of the Ancients and their Ceremonies

The ancient Romans had two ways of burying their dead.[398] The first was placing them in the ground and covering them over with **[fol. 28v]** earth. The second was to cremate the bodies, but this practice did not last long. The first Senator to have his body cremated after his death was Sylla. Numa Pompilius[399] was the inventor of the funeral rites, and he instituted a Pontifex to be in charge of them. The first honour performed at the funerals of great men was the praise of those men in an oration; Caesar did this, aged 12, at the funeral of his grandfather, as did Tiberius, aged 9, at that of his father. The second honour was the performance of gladiatorial games; Marcus and Decimus, sons of Junius Brutus, were the first to do this when they held games in honour of their father. The third was an exceedingly sumptuous banquet. The fourth was the dispensing of meat to the whole populace; the first to do this were the undertakers for the funeral of P. Lucinius – a very rich and highly honoured citizen. Also, after the funeral they sometimes used to scatter diverse flowers and odours upon the grave, as the people of Rome did for Scipio. In the temples and public places they also used to set certain ornaments, such as shields, wreaths and suchlike. And those who could not be buried with such pomp (because the expenses were too great) used to be buried in the evening by certain people given the task, called Vespillones. The corpse when sent to the tomb was dressed in a white garment. The nearest relation closed the deceased's eyes. Shortly afterwards, they opened the chamber and allowed all the servants and neighbours to enter. Three or four of them would call his name out loud three times, and they would then wash the body with warm water. The heir swept the whole house with certain brooms set aside for the purpose, and above the door they put branches of **[fol. 29r]** cypress. And if the deceased was a person of importance, the citizens were invited to the funeral by a man charged with the task. The womenfolk of the deceased wore white clothing. And when a widow died who had only had one husband, they bore her to the grave with the crown of chastity upon her head.

On the Towers

The Tor de' Conti was built by Innocent III in memory of his family, whose name was Conti.[400] This family had 4 Pontiffs, all succeeding in close proximity: Innocent III, Gregory IX, Alexander IV and Boniface VIII. It was the latter who built the Torre delle Milizie, so-called because the soldiers of Trajan lived in that neighbourhood.[401]

109   Torre delle Milizie.

On the Tiber

This river [was] in the beginning called Albula and then Tiburinus after Tiburinus, king of the Albani, who drowned in it – or as some others would have it, after Tiberi, Captain of the Etruscans, a brigand who once operated on its banks.[402] It springs in the Appennines slightly higher than the Arno, and is at first a small stream. Later on it gets much bigger since forty-two rivers flow into it – the main rivers are the Nera and the Teverone – and it runs 150 miles to flow into the Tyrrhenian Sea via a single mouth near Ostia. It can accommodate every sort of large vessel, and it separates Tuscany from Umbria. **[fol. 29v]** It once flowed alongside the Campidoglio up to the Palazzo Maggiore,[403] where Romulus and Remus were found on the site where the church of San Teodoro stands today. Tarquinius Priscus straightened the river. Augustus widened its course so that it did not flood Rome,[404] and Marcus Agrippa, when he was an Aedile, changed its course and made it flow slower. Aurelian restrained it with a wall of bricks, built on both sides right down to the sea – some remains of this can still be seen today in certain places. In Rome, upon the said river, there are many mills built on pontoons; the instigator of these was Belisarius.[405]

On the Pope's Palace
and on the Belvedere

Symmachus, or as others would have it, Nicholas III, began the papal palace.[406] It was augmented by other Pontiffs, particularly Nicholas V, who fortified the Vatican with very high walls.[407] Sixtus IV built the Chapel,[408] the Conclave, the Library and began the Rota.[409] Innocent VIII finished it, and he had the fountain that is in the piazza built, as well as the Belvedere.[410] Julius II then added to the palace two very fine arcades, one on top of the other, and he planted there a garden with orange trees.[411] In the middle of this he placed representations of the Nile and the Tiber,[412] Romulus and Remus playing with the dugs of the she-wolf, Apollo[413] and Laocoön with his two sons in a single piece of marble executed by Agesander, Polydorus and Artemidorus[414] – men of Rhodes and excellent sculptors. This work was found in 1506 beneath the ruins of the palace **[fol. 30r]** of Titus.[415] There was also the statue of Venus with Cupid,[416] that of Cleopatra[417] and that of Antinous[418] – a boy much loved by the Emperor Hadrian – all found near San Martino ai Monti. Recently, Paul III had the divine Michelangelo paint the Universal Judgement above the altar in the Sistine Chapel. The Pope also

110,
112,
113

111

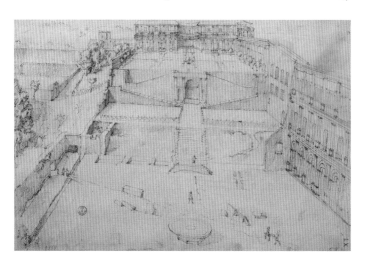

110   View of the Belvedere Court by Giovanni Antonio Dosio, Uffizi, Florence, Gabinetto Disegni e Stampe, Uff. 2559A, cat. no. 131.c.

111 (*left*)   The Laocoön in the Belvedere statue court, woodcut from Bartolomeo Marliani's *Urbis romae topographia* (1544).

had the *sala* of the Conclave worked in gilded stucco, and at one end of this he had a very beautiful chapel built, this too painted by Michelangelo.[419] He had the upper arcade that leads to the Belvedere covered.[420]

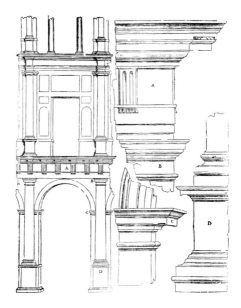

112   Bramante's 'Cortile del Belvedere', lower
court begun in 1505, woodcuts from the third
volume of Sebastiano Serlio's treatise *On Antiquities*
(1540).

On Trastevere

Trastevere was first called the Janiculum after the hill that stands behind
it.[421] It was also called the 'City of the men from Ravenna' because this
was the public place given as billets to the soldiers from Ravenna who
were for Augustus Caesar but against Mark Antony and Cleopatra. The
temple that is now called Santa Maria[422] was also named after these men.
Because of the unhealthiness of the winds, this neighbourhood was
inhabited only by artisans and men of little worth, hence there is not
much there worthy of note apart from the thermae of Severus and the
Emperor Aurelian, as well as the gardens and the naumachia of Caesar.[423]

Summary of the Antiquities

It was the custom of the ancient Romans to be friendly to foreigners and
to invite them into their houses to ensure that the visitors would
[fol. 30v] be able to watch the celebration of the festivals and similarly to

Auendo io trattato di tante cose antiche, e dimostratole in disegno uisibile, e cosa ragioneuole ch'io tratti, e dimostri qualch'una de le moderne, e massimamente di quelle di Bramante archi, tetto, benche però non l'ho lasciato adietro hauendo dimostrato il stupendo edificio di san Pietro, & altre cose trattando de i tempij sacri, e ueramettte si puo dire ch'egli habbia suscitata la buona Ar, chitettura col mezo però di Giulio. II. Pontefice massimo: come fanno fede tante, e così belle opere da lui fatte in Roma, de lequali la figura qui sotto ne e una. Questa e una loggia fatta a Beluedere ne i giardini del Papa, ne laquale si comprendono due belle cose : una la fortezza sua, che accenna a la perpetuita per essere i pi lastroni di tanta latitudine, e grossezza. l'altra tanti belli accompagnamenti, e così bene ornata, & oltra la bella inuentione ella e anchor molto ben proportionata. l'opera qui sotto e misurata a palmo antico, cioe a palmo, & a minuti il quale e a faccie. vi. La latitudine de ghiarchi e palmi diciotto, & altrettanto sono li pilastri, cioe tanto il pieno, quanto il uoto. la fronte del pilastro e diuisa in parti undici : una parte sara la pilastrata, che toglie su l'arco, che sono due parti : due parti si daranno a una colonna, che e quattro parti : due parti a le pilastrate del nic chio, e tre parti si daranno al nicchio, e così saranno distribuite le undici parti. l'altezza del piedestalo sara per la metà de la latitudine del pilastro. l'altezza de la base d'esso piedestalo sara quanto e la pilastrata de l'arco. l'al tezza de la cornice del piedestalo sia la nona parte manco de la base. l'altezza de la colonna con la base e'l ca pitello sia noue grossezze d'essa, e la settima parte di piu. la base sara per mezagrossezza di colonna, e'l capitello sara per una grossezza, & hauera la settima parte di piu per l'abaco. l'altezza de l'architraue, del fregio, e de la cornice sia quanto e il piedestalo senza la sua base, e quest'altezza sia diuisa in parti undici : quattro parti saran no per l'architraue : tre parti si daranno al fregio, perche e senza intaglio : le quattro parti restanti saranno per la cornice, e si poi tirato il mezo circolo a la grossezza de 'a pilastrata; l'altitudine del uano sara duplicata a la sua larghezza, e tirata l'imposta de l'arco al suo loco; l'altezza de laquale sia per meza grossezza di colonna; li nicchi & i quadri sopra esti haueranno la sua proportione.

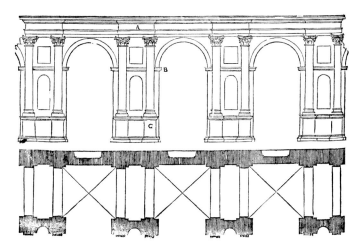

113 (*above*)   Bramante's 'Cortile del Belvedere', upper court begun in 1505, woodcut from the third volume of Sebastiano Serlio's treatise *On Antiquities* (1540).

go about viewing the city. This was why they built many temples and exceedingly beautiful habitations. Octavius[424] Augustus gloried in this: namely, that he had inherited a city of brick and left it entirely of marble.[425] He set about providing for Rome's needs: he created the Prefects of the Guard and the Street Watchmen – this office was initially filled by three men – and he placed them in various parts of the city, both for the lighting of fires and also for the paving of the streets and keeping them clean all day long. As for the height of buildings, he gave the order that no person living near to a public building was allowed to build higher than seventy feet. He repaired many temples and shored up bridges that were about to collapse. He provided a protection from Tiber floods using huge marble walls, and also extended roads, making them beautifully straight. He bequeathed a city divided into 14 *Rioni*.[426] It comprises seven hills and as many plains or 'campi', upon which were built 20 gates, two campidoglios, three theatres, two amphitheatres, three small senates, two large colossi, two large 'winding' columns, statues, busts, tablets without number, and the many other things scattered throughout this book, which I shall pass over for brevity's sake.

On the Temples of the Ancients, outside Rome

Outside Rome, in addition to that temple which I have mentioned, there were the temples dedicated to gods who people thought could be harmful.[427] For example, the temple of Venus Erycina[428] outside the Porta Collina[429] and the statue of Venus Verticordia,[430] meaning Venus who changed hearts – that is, she discouraged men from libidinousness **[fol. 31r]** and turned them towards chastity. Similarly, in the month of August, they would have a solemn and grand procession with the sacred objects during which they would carry a phallus into the temple of Venus outside the walls. And even though such a festival was suitable and appropriate only for prostitutes, nevertheless the sole person who was permitted to lay hands on that sacred relic was an honest and chaste gentlewoman, who would place it on Venus' bosom. There was in addition to this, outside the Porta Viminale,[431] the Temple of Nenia,[432] dedicated to the goddess so that she would bring her gloomy presence and mournful song to funerals. There was likewise, on the Via Labicana, the Temple of Quiet.[433] Furthermore, on the Via Latina there was the Temple of Womanly Fortune,[434] and beyond the Porta Capena two miles out of Rome there was the Temple of Ridicule – since Hannibal camped here, was made a fool of and so retreated, a temple to this god was consecrated in this place.[435] On the same road there was a Temple of Mars, as I have already said.[436] Similarly, beyond the Porta Carmentalis[437] there was the Temple of Janus.[438] On the Isola Tiberina there was a Temple of Jupiter, of Aesculapius and of Faunus.[439] In Trastevere there was the Temple of Fortuna.[440] There were some who removed far from Rome the temples of Fear and Pallor, of Poverty and of Old Age, since these gods were unpleasant and harmful – indeed these gods have their seat in the vestibule to Hell. There were, in addition to these, the god Liber and the goddess Libera, to whom they would make very holy and very chaste sacrifices in favour of the vintage.[441] Today, throughout the whole of the region of Rome, there are small chapels, both ancient and ruined, and ancient country habitations, marvellously wrought, of rough work but very beautiful to view, **[fol. 31v]** and it is thought that such habitations were built in honour of the Lares.[442] This belief comes from the words of Cicero in the second book of *On Laws*, when he says: 'There must be sacred woods and residences for the Lares throughout the region.'[443] The fact is that wealthy Romans built more opulently in the countryside than in the city, also building places for keeping birds and fish, parks and other like things for their pleasure and delight. They used to channel the sea into areas so they could bathe, and they made very beautiful and delightful places full of greenery and trees, as well as having gardens and hanging gardens. Outside Rome there were the Horti Terentii on the Via Appia, which occupied twenty iugera,[444] and those of Ovid on the Via Claudia.[445] Furthermore, there were very popular and fine estates, called 'Suburbani' since they were close to Rome, such as the Lucullanum, the Tusculanum and the Formianum and many others that today have become the property and estates of private individuals.[446] I do not wish to pass over in silence the Emperor Hadrian's Villa Tiburtina, which was very magnificently built by that emperor,[447] such that there were in it places named after provinces and other exceedingly famous sites – for example, the Lyceum, the Academia, the Prytaneum, Canopus, Poecile and Tempe.[448] In the region surrounding Rome there were many small castles or country estates that are now ruined and have become the land, possession and pasturage of Rome. Here today there are kitchen gardens, and people plant crops and pasture their animals. Indeed, the herds and flocks are fed and prosper greatly, since the land is grassy and water abundant, the hills sunny and the valleys pleasant.[449]

25, 114

[fol. 32r]

How many times the City of Rome was taken

Rome was taken seven times, by various nations. The first time was 364 years after the founding of the city, at the hands of the Galli Senones under their Captain, Brennus.[450] The second time was 800 years later, at the hands of the Visigoths.[451] The third time was 44 years later, at the hands of the Vandals.[452] The fourth time was 18 years later, at the hands of the Heruli. The fifth time was 14 years later, at the hands of the

114   Hadrian's Villa, the rear court and eastern section of the Larger Baths.

Ostrogoths.[453] The sixth time was 12 years later, at the hands of Totila;[454] and finally, in the year 1527 on 6 May, at the hands of the imperial army.[455] It was thus that Rome, conqueror of the world, was despoiled and derided by barbarians. And even though she was taken and destroyed many times, nevertheless the glory and majesty of Rome still stands, not as widely spread but founded upon a stronger stone, namely Christ. She is the head of religion and is the seat of His Vicar, upon which worthily sits Julius III, an honour and glory to the pontifical name.

THE END

DESCRIPTION
OF THE CHURCHES,

Stations of the Cross, Indulgences, and Relics
of the Bodies of Saints, in the
City of Rome.

SUCCINCTLY COMPILED
by Messer Andrea Palladio & here published
for the first time,
With Grace and Privilege for ten years.

IN ROME
At the Press of Vincentio Lucrino.[1]
1554.

TO THE READERS³

Since I have described the antiquities of Rome, with as much care and
brevity as I could manage, in another book of mine, I also wished to
describe for your more complete satisfaction and pleasure the sacred
things in that city and their current circumstances; because the accounts
of them that have been written in the past do not in many respects
correspond to the facts today, since being holy objects they have become
altered and moved from one place to another owing to the wars, fires
and ruination to which they have been subjected, and to the building of
new churches, hospitals and confraternities. And because these holy
things are scattered among many churches and cemeteries in Rome,
I thought that in order to allow everyone the possibility of visiting them
easily in their current locations without long meanderings, I would
describe them in a new order and sequence – and all who follow this
will be led to give no little praise for **[page [2]]** this my effort. First of
all, then, in this book I shall write of the things in the seven principal
churches of Rome, beginning on the Isola and going straight through
Trastevere and then the Borgo, which are all one part.⁴ And then I shall
go in order from the Porta del Popolo, once called the Porta Flaminia,
straight through the Città, which is now populated down to the Tiber,
curving round to end at the Campidoglio. Finally, I shall go from the
Campidoglio out towards the seven hills and old Rome.⁵ As for these
churches, you will discover who first founded them, how many relics of
saints adorn them, which High Pontiffs gave them privileges, and how
many indulgences and celebrations of Stations of the Cross they have
been endowed with, both in Lent and on every other day of the year. I
have taken all this from the bulls that can be consulted in many of these
churches, either near the choir or affixed in other places, from sacred
histories and from very ancient marble inscriptions. Please note that
there were once more than three thousand churches in Rome, four
hundred of which were consecrated to the Virgin Mary. Most are
[page [3]] ruined, although some were entirely rebuilt and in others
many hospitals and confraternities were founded that are assiduous in
performing a great deal of holy works for virgins, paupers and pilgrims,
as can be easily discovered in study. From this you will learn that even
though the world once held Rome in awe and respect for the great

things that the ancients did there, it is much more worthy of reverence for the many sacred things that are there and for which it became the capital and rightful seat of the true Christian religion. I wish you gladness therein. Live happily.

[page [4]]

ON THE BUILDING
of Rome and thereafter up to the conversion of the Emperor Constantine the Great and the donation made to the High Pontiffs of the Holy Roman Church

Romulus was the first king and founder of the city of Rome.[6] He built it in the world year 4333 on 21 April on the banks of the Tiber, 15 miles from the Tyrrhenian Sea. After him there were six other Kings, of whom the last was Tarquinius Superbus, who was driven out of Rome because his son Sextus came at night and raped Lucretia, the wife of Collatinus. These seven Kings ruled for 243 years; their imperium did not exceed fifteen miles. When the Kings had been driven out, political and civil life was then put in order, and this form of government lasted 465 years. In this time they fought 43 battles to win dominion over nearly the whole world. There were 877 Consuls, two years of government by the Decemviri, 43 Military Tribunes with Consular Power, and **[page [5]]** there were four years without governors. After that, Julius Caesar, with the title of Perpetual Dictator, took control of the imperium and liberty simultaneously,[7] such that from the Emperor Caesar to the high Christian Pontiffs the imperium in Rome lasted for 360 years. Constantine the Great then brought Rome to faith in Christ, as is written in the chronicles.[8]

The said Constantine was persecuting Christians just as his ancestors had done, as a result of which the Blessed Sylvester, Pope at that time, was hiding with some of his clergy on Mount Sorato, about 20 miles outside Rome. God then smote Constantine with incurable leprosy and, since medicines could do nothing for him, as a last remedy doctors advised him to wash in the warm blood of boys who were not yet weaned. However, when everything was prepared and he saw before him more than 20,000 young boys and their mothers with their hair let down, weeping and lamenting wretchedly, he was moved to pity at the sight of these women so afflicted and said to them 'Be not afraid, because I would rather die myself than live through the killing of so many innocent boys'. Having thus spoken, he ordered that all the children should be provided with gifts and returned to their mothers. As a result of this act of mercy, the following night the glorious Apostles, Peter and Paul, appeared to him **[page [6]]** and said 'Since the spilling of the blood of innocent children was abhorrent to you, our Lord, Jesus Christ, will send to you Pope Sylvester, who is hiding on Mount Sorato, instructing him that he should see to your health.' And so, having been advised by the vision, the Emperor sent for Saint Sylvester. Allowing himself to be persuaded by the saint, Constantine immediately put on the whitest of clothes and for seven days, morning, noon and night, he ordered celebrations in honour of Jesus Christ and all Christians. On the eighth day, he came to holy confession: laying aside all the imperial insignia, with his arms hanging low and with much weeping he threw himself to the ground for most holy baptism. And no sooner was he placed in the most sacred font than he saw with his own eyes a hand come from heaven that cleansed him of his leprosy. As soon as he had been baptized, he ordered by public proclamation that throughout the whole of the Roman Empire the temples dedicated to idols should be shut, that churches of Christ should be built, and that the sepulchres and reliquaries of martyrs should be venerated and revered with the greatest respect.

At this time Helena, the mother of Constantine, who was living in Britannia, was persuaded by the Jews that she should take up their ceremonies, abandon the worship of idols, and not follow the Christian religion. Because **[page [7]]** of this she sent a letter to her son in Rome. Constantine replied to her that he wished Jewish and Christian priests to have a debate in their presence. All the wise men of the Roman Empire came for this debate, and there met in Rome 75 Christian bishops and 290 Jewish priests, not including the 12 scribes that Isacar, their high priest, had sent, all men deeply learned in Hebrew, Greek and Latin. And the judges and arbiters of this contest were two philosophers, neither of whom were Christian or Jew. One was called Crato; no one had ever managed to persuade him either to receive their gift or to have any personal property – nor did he ever wish to save anything for himself for the morrow – and he said that because he possessed nothing he enjoyed the greatest safety. The other was Zenophilus, a trustworthy and wise man. These two men were so venerated that, without a shadow of a doubt, it was held by everyone that whatever they said would be the absolute truth and should be considered as binding. Once everyone had congregated before the Emperor Constantine and his mother, Helena, there was a mighty confrontation between Sylvester and the scribes. In the end, the Most Holy Pontiff convinced them so thoroughly that the whole populace cried out with one voice **[page [8]]** that those who did not confess Christ as the son of the true God should be cast out from Rome. At this, even many of the Jews who had come to impugn the holy faith were converted, and as for the philosopher judges of the dispute, they too were baptized. One of the scribes, wishing to show the power of his faith, had brought before everyone a bull of such ferocity that scarcely one hundred men could lead it. He spoke certain words into the bull's ear and it immediately dropped down dead. The scribe was not able to resuscitate the animal by force of words, whence all the Jews promised that they would receive baptism if someone managed to bring it back to life using the name of Jesus Christ. Saint Sylvester accomplished this, and at the same time with the sign of the † he removed the noxious power from a dragon that was contaminating the whole of Rome with an incurable plague. As a result, Helena, mother of Constantine, and all the people then kissed the feet of the Blessed Sylvester. Being confirmed in the faith by these miracles, Constantine spoke so wisely to the Roman Senate that all received baptism, and of their own volition and love they decided to exalt the seat of the Blessed Peter, Prince of Apostles, such that the See of Rome should have primacy over all the churches in the world. Constantine ordered that every **[page [9]]** successive Pontiff in this church should be the highest prince in the world and that his will and judgement should govern divine worship and the Christian faith, since he occupied the principate and stool of the apostolate that Jesus Christ had bid the Blessed Peter to hold and where that Apostle had drunk his cup of martyrdom. And in order to ensure that pontifical dignity was not compromised by poverty but rather should increase through the glory and dignity of the Roman See, Constantine gave to Blessed Sylvester and to all his successors his Lateran Palace, the City of Rome, all of Italy, and the western provinces, regions, places, cities and islands around Italy. And he himself left Rome, transferring the Empire to the East, to the city of Byzantium, which he subsequently had called Constantinople after his own name. He left behind him in his Lateran Palace in Rome a gold and silver church garnished with precious stones in honour of our Saviour Jesus Christ, and he also built the church of the Blessed Apostles Peter and Paul and other churches. And through the agency of Pope Saint Sylvester he had the relics of the martyrs collected and set in certain places, as shall be told in this book in praise of Jesus Christ, our Lord and Saviour.

115   The Seven Principal Churches of Rome, engraved by Antonio Lafréry (1575), Berlin, Kunstbibliothek.

[page [10]]

ON THE SEVEN PRINCIPAL CHURCHES[9]

The first church – which is also the Pontiff's seat – is that of
SAN GIOVANNI IN LATERANO on the Celian Hill.[10] It was built by
Constantine the Great within his palace and given enormous entrances.
After it was damaged and ruined by the heretics, Nicholas IV repaired it
and Martin V began having it painted and the paving stones laid.
Eugenius IV finished it, and it was consecrated in honour of the Saviour
and Saint John the Baptist and Saint John the Evangelist by Saint
Sylvester on 9 November. During the consecration an image of the
Saviour appeared that can still be seen today above the tribune of the
high altar; even though the church was damaged by fire twice, this image
was not burnt. They hold a Stations of the Cross here on the first Sunday
in Lent, Palm Sunday, Maundy Thursday and Holy Saturday, the Saturday
within the octave[11] of Easter and on the vigil of Pentecost. On the feast
of Saint John before the Latin Gate they have plenary remission of sins
and the liberation of a soul from Purgatory, and from the feast of Saint
Bernardino, which is on 20 May, until 1 August, every day there is
plenary remission of sins. On the feasts of Saint John the Baptist, the
Transfiguration of the Lord, the Beheading **[page [11]]** of Saint John
and the Dedication of the Saviour,[12] there is plenary remission of sins.
On the feast of Saint John the Evangelist there are 28 thousand years of
indulgence, the same number of quarantines,[13] and plenary remission of
sins. And every day there are 6,048 years of indulgence, the same number
of quarantines, remission of a third of all sins, and he who celebrates mass
or who has mass celebrated in the chapel next to the sacristy frees a soul
from the pains of Purgatory. There are also infinite indulgences – anyone
who received every single one would never need to go to the Holy
Sepulchre of Christ or to Saint James of Compostella! In this church
there are the following relics, and they are exhibited on Easter Day after
vespers in the tabernacle that is above the altar dedicated to Mary
Magdalene: the crown with which Constantine performed the
coronation of Saint Sylvester; the head of Saint Zacharias, the father of
Saint John the Baptist; the head of Saint Pancras, Martyr, from which
blood flowed continuously for three days when this church was burnt by
the heretics; certain relics of Saint Mary Magdalene; a shoulder blade of

115

Saint Lawrence; a tooth from Saint Peter Apostle; the cup from which
Saint John Apostle and Evangelist drank the poison ordered by the
Emperor Domitian but which could not harm him; the chain
[page [12]] with which he was bound when he was brought from
Ephesus to Rome, and one of his small tunics – when this was laid upon
three corpses they immediately came back to life; some of the mortal
remains and hair shirt of Saint John the Baptist; some milk, hair and
clothes belonging to the glorious Virgin Mary; the tunic that she made
for Jesus Christ; the small cloth with which our Redeemer dried the feet
of His disciples; the cane with which our Saviour's head was struck; the
red cloak that Pilate put upon Him, tinged with His most precious
blood; some wood from the Cross; the veil of the Glorious Virgin, with
which Jesus Christ's loins were covered when He was on the Cross; the
sudarium that was placed on His face when in the tomb; and the water
and blood that came out of His side. Above the Papal altar, behind the
iron gratings, there are the heads of the most glorious Apostles Peter and
Paul,[14] and every time they are displayed there are three thousand years
of indulgence for the inhabitants of Rome who are present, six thousand
for those from the surrounding countryside and twelve thousand for
those who come from afar; there is also the same number of quarantines
and the remission of a third of all sins. Below this altar is the Oratorio of
Saint John the Evangelist, when he was brought to Rome as a prisoner.[15]
The four bronze columns here, railed off, which face the said altar, are
[page [13]] full of holy earth brought from Jerusalem, and they were
made by Augustus from the beaks of the galleys that he took during the
naval battle for Egypt and he placed them in the Comitium.[16] In the
chapel next to the great door there is the altar that John the Baptist had
with him in the desert, the Arc of the Covenant, Aaron's and Moses' rod,
and the table upon which our Saviour had the last supper with His
disciples. These things were brought from Jerusalem to Rome by Titus.
Above, at one end of the *sala* that was used for the last Lateran Council,[17]
upon four columns there is the stone upon which they diced for our
Saviour's tunic. From the stone downwards is said to be equal to His
height. At the other end of the *sala* there are three marble doorways that
used to be in Pilate's palace in Jerusalem and they say that our Saviour
was brought through them to Pilate. The two porphyry seats here, which
stand outside the Capella di San Silvestro, are said to have been made
after that woman became Pope so as to be able to touch the testicles of
the new Pontiffs – the most recent Deacon performs this duty.[18] But
Platina in his 'Life' of the Pontiffs says otherwise.[19] The marble window
that is above the door of the said chapel was in the house of the Virgin

Mary in Judea, and they say that it was through **[page [14]]** this that the
Angel Gabriel entered so as to announce to the maid the incarnation of
the son of God. The flight of 28 steps that is next to this chapel was in
Pilate's palace, and our Saviour fell upon it and spilled some of his most
precious blood, the mark of which can still be seen today. And whoever
piously climbs this staircase on their knees will receive nine years of
indulgence for each step and the same number of quarantines, as well as
remission of a third of their sins. The column split in two used to be in
Jerusalem and it broke on the death of our Redeemer. In the chapel
called the Sancta Sanctorum,[20] which women may never enter and
which was dedicated by Nicholas III to Saint Lawrence Martyr, there is
in addition to the other relics an image of the Saviour aged 12, decorated
with silver and gems, which (people believe) was drawn by Saint Luke
and finished by the angel.[21] By order of Leo IV, after vespers on
14 August almost every year the most honourable citizens take turns in
carrying the picture on their shoulders, as if in an antique Triumph, to
Santa Maria Maggiore. All of Rome and nearby cities come to watch.
On the following day after mass has been sung, the picture is carried
back to the Lateran with equal pomp. On **[page [15]]** the same day they
free from prison 14 men held there for life. The washing of the Saviour's
feet at Santa Maria Nuova is done in remembrance of the washing the
priests used to do every year on the first day of April, on the feast of the
goddess Cybele, in the stream outside the Porta di San Sebastiano. Near
the said church,[22] towards the hospital, there is still standing a circular

116,
117

116   San Giovanni in Laterano, Baptistry.

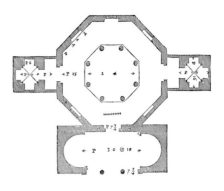

117   The Baptistry, woodcut from Palladio's
I quattro libri dell'architettura (1570).

form covered with lead and with porphyry columns around it; this place
is where Constantine the Great was baptized.[23] It used to be decorated in
the following way: the holy font was of porphyry, the part that held the
water was silver, and in the centre there used to be a porphyry column
upon which there hung a gold lamp weighing 50 libbre. In this, at the
Easter Vigil, instead of oil they used to burn balsam. At the end of the
font there was once a golden angel, and also a silver statue of the Saviour
weighing ten libbre which bore the inscription 'Behold the lamb of God,
behold he who takes away the sins of the world'. There were also seven
deer that used to scatter water, and each one of them weighed 80 libbre.
As for the three chapels that adjoin this place, Hilary III consecrated
them. One was dedicated to the Cross and wood from the Cross was
placed in it covered in gems,[24] and the two small columns clad in wood
that are in this chapel **[page [16]]** used to be in the house of the Blessed
Virgin. The next chapel, which women are forbidden to enter, was once
Constantine's *camera*. Hilary consecrated it to Saint John the Baptist and
placed many relics there.[25] The third is dedicated to Saint John the

Evangelist.[26] The Ospedale del Salvatore, today called the Ospedale di San Giovanni in Laterano,[27] was built by the most illustrious Colonna family and enlarged by various Roman Barons, Cardinals and others. The following objects were once in this church but they are not here today: Constantine the Great placed a statue of the Saviour here that weighed 330 libbre, 12 Apostles each of five feet and weighing 90 libbre, another Saviour weighing 140 libbre, and 4 angels that weighed 105 libbre. These were all made of silver. He also placed here 4 crowns with dolphins, each weighing 20 libbre, and seven altars, each weighing two hundred libbre. Hormisdas, Pope, offered a silver crown of 20 libbre and six vases.

SAINT PETER'S IN THE VATICAN.[28] This church was built and endowed by Constantine the Great. It was consecrated by Saint Sylvester on 18 November. There are Stations of the Cross here on the feast of the Epiphany, the 1st and 5th Sundays in Lent, the Saturday after the above-mentioned 1st Sunday, Easter Monday, the feast of our Lord's Ascension, the feast of Pentecost, the Saturday after Pentecost, and all the Saturdays **[page [17]]** that are Ember Days,[29] the 3rd Sunday in Advent, the feast of Saint Mark, the 1st and 4th Sundays in Advent, and the feast of

118,
119,
120,
121

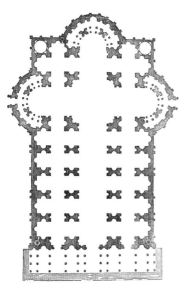

118   Raphael's plan for St Peter's, wood-cut from the third volume of Sebastiano Serlio's treatise *On Antiquities* (1540).

Corpus Christi. From the throne of Saint Peter's there is plenary indulgence. On Quinquagesima Sunday there are 28 thousand years of plenary indulgence and the same number of quarantines. On the feast of Saint Gregory there is plenary indulgence. On the feast of the Annunciation to Our Lady there are one thousand years of indulgence, and from that day until 1 August, every day there are 12 thousand years of indulgence and the same number of quarantines, and remission of a third of all sins. On the day before the feast of Saint Peter, and on the day itself, the 2nd Sunday in July, the feast of Saint Simon and Saint Jude, the feast

119   View of St Peter's by Maarten van Heemskerck, Kupferstichkabinett,
Staatliche Museen zu Berlin – Preussischer Kulturbesitz. Römische
Skizzenbücher, inv. no. 79D2, 1, fols 52r, 54r.

of the dedication of this church, the feast of Saint Martin and the feast of
Saint Andrew, there is plenary remission of sins. Every day there are
6,048 years of indulgence, the same number of quarantines and remission
of a third of all sins. During the festivities for Saint Peter, for the seven
principal altars in the church, and for all the double festivals, the above-
mentioned indulgences are doubled. And every day in the Sistine Chapel
there is plenary indulgence. Anyone who piously climbs the steps up to
the said church and up to the Capella di San Pietro will receive
[page [18]] 7 years of indulgence for each step. On the Fridays in March
there are innumerable indulgences. In this church there are the bodies of
Saints Simon and Jude, Apostles, John Chrysostom, Processus and
Martinian, Gregory Pope, and Petronilla; the head of Saint Andrew,
which was brought to Rome by the Principe della Marca in the time of
Pius II – indeed, Pius went out as far as the Ponte Molle to meet him –
the heads of Saints Luke the Evangelist, Sebastian, James the Lesser,

120   View of St Peter's from the southeast, 1580–81, by an
unknown artist, Frankfurt, Städtliches Kunstinstitut 814, cat.
no. 377.

Thomas Bishop of Conturba and Martyr, and Amand; one of Saint
Christopher's shoulders, one of Saint Stephen's shoulders, and other
Saints' bodies and relics, the names of whom are written in the book of
life. Beneath the high altar there is half of the body of Saint Peter and
half of that of Saint Paul. And in the tabernacle to the right of the great
door there is the veronica, or rather the true face, of our Saviour, and the
blade of the lance that pierced the rib of our Redeemer and that was
sent by the Grand Turk to Innocent VIII. Every time this lance is
displayed there are three thousand years of indulgence for the inhabitants
of Rome who are present, six thousand for those from the surrounding
countryside and 12 thousand for those who come from afar, the same
number of quarantines, and remission of a third of all sins. There is also
a small painting **[page [19]]** that on feast days in the said church is
exhibited above the high altar; in that work are painted Saint Peter and
Saint Paul. The picture once belonged to Saint Sylvester, and it was that

121   Foundation medal for the new St Peter's, 1505,
by (?)Caradosso (Cristoforo Foppa), Milan, Civiche
Raccolte Archeologiche e Numismatiche,
cat. no. 284.

which he showed to Constantine when the Emperor asked the Saint
who these two men, Peter and Paul, were who had appeared to him. If
you want this story, read the life of Saint Sylvester.[30] The columns that
are in the Capella di San Pietro and the column clad in iron that is in
the church (against which our Saviour used to lean when he was
preaching and to which they take those possessed by devils, and they are
immediately relieved), were once in Jerusalem in the Temple of
Solomon.[31] Honorius I covered this church with bronze tiles that had
been taken from the Temple of Jupiter Capitolinus.[32] Eugenius IV
had Antonio the Florentine[33] make the bronze doors here in
commemoration of the nations who in his time were reconciled with the
Church, and the bronze Saint Peter that is below the organ was formerly
the statue of Jupiter Capitolinus. The pine cone in the courtyard – made
of bronze and five braccia and two quinti tall – was once, they say, on the
dome of the Rotonda but a lightning bolt knocked it off and it was then
taken to Saint Peter's.[34] The peacocks were previously ornament to the
Tomb of the Scipios; Otto II, Holy Roman Emperor, who brought the
body of Saint **[page [20]]** Bartholomew from Beneventum to Rome, is
buried in that porphyry sepulchre.

In the said church there used also to be the ornaments mentioned
below, but malignant time has worn them away. First, Constantine the

Great placed a gold cross weighing 150 libbre upon the sepulchre of
Saint Peter, 4 silver candelabra engraved with the years of the Apostles, 3
gold chalices each of 12 libbre and 20 silver chalices each 10 libbre,
4 silver vases each 50 libbre and a paten and gold censer weighing
30 libbre ornamented with a jacinth dove. And he made an enclosure of
gold and silver for the altar of Saint Peter's, ornamented with many
precious stones. Pope Hormisdas donated 10 vases and three silver holy
water vats. The Emperor Justin the Elder gave a golden chalice,
weighing 5 libbre and ornamented with gems, and his paten, which
weighed 20 libbre. The Emperor Justinian donated a golden vase
weighing six libbre bordered with gems, two silver vases each of
12 libbre and two silver chalices each of 15 libbre. Charlemagne gave a
silver tablet incised with the city of Constantinople. King Theodoric
decorated the sepulchre with a beam made of silver weighing one
thousand and twenty libbre, and two silver candle holders, each
weighing 35 libbre. From the spoils of the Vitiges, Belisarius donated a
gold cross weighing one hundred libbre, ornamented with precious
stones, and two very valuable candle holders. And Michael
[page [21]], son of Theophilus the Emperor of Constantinople, gave a
chalice and a gold paten ornamented with gems of enormous worth.

SAN PAOLO.[35] This church is on the Via Ostiense, about a mile outside
Rome, and like Saint Peter's it was built, endowed and ornamented by
Constantine the Great in the place where the head of the Apostle Paul
was miraculously found. It was ornamented with huge columns, very tall
architraves, and subsequently with various marbles, wonderfully carved,
by Honorius IV. It was consecrated by Saint Sylvester and there is a
Stations of the Cross here on the Wednesday after the 4th Sunday in
Lent, the third feast of Easter, Sexagesima Sunday, and the feast of Holy
Innocents. On the feast of the Conversion of Saint Paul, then, there are
one hundred years of indulgence, the same number of quarantines and
plenary remission of sins. And on the feast of Saint Paul there is plenary
remission of sins. On the feast of the dedication of this church there are
one thousand years of indulgence, the same number of quarantines and
plenary remission of sins. And anyone who visits the said church on all
the Sundays of the year will receive the same number of indulgences as if
they had visited the Holy Sepulchre of Christ, or the church of Saint
James of Galicia. And every day there are **[page [22]]** 6,048 years of
indulgence and the same number of quarantines, and the remission of a
third of all sins. In the church there are the bodies of Saint Paul's disciple,
Saint Timothy, Saints Celso, Julian and Basilissa, and of many of the Holy

Innocents. There is one of the arms of Saint Anna, mother of the Virgin
Mary, the chain with which Saint Paul was bound, the head of the
Samaritan woman, one of the fingers of Saint Nicholas and many other
relics. And under the High Altar there is half of the body of Saint Peter
and half of that of Saint Paul, and to the right-hand side of this altar
there is a picture of the crucifix that spoke to Saint Bridget, Queen of
Sweden, when she was praying in that place.

SANTA MARIA MAGGIORE.[36] This church was the first in Rome to be
dedicated to the Virgin Mary and was built at the time of Pope Liberius
by Giovanni, a Roman Patrician, and his wife – since they had no
children they wished to spend their fortune in the Virgin's honour.
During the night of 5 August they saw a vision that required them to go
to the Esquiline the following morning and build a temple where they
saw the ground covered with snow. The Pope also had the same vision,
and the following morning he went with his whole court to the said
place, and finding the snow he began to dig with his own hands. The
church was subsequently built there. **[page [23]]** In this church there is a
Stations of the Cross on every Wednesday that is an Ember Day, Holy
Wednesday, Easter Day, the 1st Sunday in Advent, Christmas Eve and
Christmas Day, New Year's Day, and the feast of our Lady of the Snow.
On the feast of Saint Jerome and his translation (which is celebrated the
day before Ascension Day) there is plenary remission of sins. On the feast
of the Purification, Ascension, Nativity, Presentation and Conception of
the Virgin Mary, there are one thousand years of indulgence, and plenary
remission of sins. From the feast of her Assumption to that of her
Nativity, excluding the daily indulgences, there are 12 thousand years of
indulgence, and every day there are 6,048 years of indulgence, the same
number of quarantines, and remission of a third of all sins. And whoever
celebrates mass or has mass celebrated in the Capella del Presepio will
free one soul from the pains of Purgatory. In this church there are the
bodies of Saints Matthew, Apostle, Romula and Redenta, and Jerome, the
manger in which Christ lay in Bethlehem, the swaddling clothes in
which the Blessed Virgin wrapped Him, the stole of Saint Jerome, the
small tunic, the stole and maniple of Saint Thomas, Bishop of Conturbia,
stained with his blood; the head of Saint Vibiana, the head of
Saint Marcellinus, Pope, one of the arms of Saint Matthew, Apostle and
Evangelist, one of the arms of Saint Luke the Evangelist, one of the arms
of Saint Thomas, Bishop, and of Saint **[page [24]]** Vibiana, and many
other relics, which they display on Easter Day after vespers.
The following ornaments were once held here: Sixtus III donated a silver

altar weighing 400 libbre, three silver patens each weighing 40 libbre, five silver vases, 28 silver crowns, 3 silver candelabra, a censer weighing 15 libbre, and a silver stag above the baptistery. Symmachus had a silver arch made for this place weighing 15 libbre, and Gregory III gave a gold image of the Virgin Mary embracing the Saviour.

SAN LORENZO FUORI LE MURA.[37] This church is about a mile outside Rome on the Via Tiberina. It was built by Constantine the Great, and he donated to it one golden lamp weighing 20 libbre and ten silver lamps, each weighing 15 libbre. Cardinal Olivieri Caraffa later ornamented the church with various marbles and a very beautiful gilt ceiling. There is a Stations of the Cross here on Septuagesima Sunday, the third Sunday in Lent, the Wednesday in the octave of Easter, and the Thursday after Pentecost. Then on the feast of Saint Lawrence and on the feast of Saint Stephen and for the whole of that octave there are [?1]00 years of indulgence and the same number of quarantine, and the remission of a third of all sins. On the feast of the Invention of Saint Stephen and the festivities related to it and to the Stations of the Cross in this church, in addition to the above-mentioned indulgences there is plenary remission of sins. And everyone who **[page [25]]** enters through the courtyard door of this church – having first confessed, and being contrite – and then goes from the crucifix below the portico to that above the altar facing the said door, will receive plenary remission of sins. And everyone who visits this church each Wednesday in the year will free a soul from the pains of Purgatory, as will someone who celebrates mass or has mass celebrated in the small underground chapel in the cemetery of Cyriaca.[38] Every day there are 6,048 years of indulgence, the same number of quarantines, and the remission of a third of all sins. There are the bodies of Saint Lawrence and Saint Stephen, Protomartyr, and one of the rocks with which Saint Stephen was stoned. There is also the stone upon which Saint Lawrence was laid upon his death, stained with his body fat and blood, the vase that he used when in prison to baptize Saint Lucillo, a piece of the griddle upon which he was roasted, and many other relics.

SAN SEBASTIANO.[39] This church is outside Rome on the Via Appia and was built by the Blessed Lucina. On the feast of Saint Sebastian and on all the Sundays in May there is plenary remission of sins. Going via the well here into the catacombs where once the bodies of Saint Peter and Saint Paul were hidden gives as many indulgences as going to the **[page [26]]** churches of Saint Peter's and San Paolo. Every day there are 6,048 years of indulgence and the same number of quarantines, and remission of a third of all sins. And whoever celebrates mass or has mass celebrated at the altar of Saint Sebastian will free a soul from the pains of Purgatory. In the cemetery of Calisto, which is below the said church,[40] there is plenary remission of sins. There are one hundred and seventy-four thousand martyrs here, including 18 Pontiffs. In the church there is the body of Saint Sebastian, that of Saint Lucina, Virgin, and the stone upon which Christ left his footprint when He appeared to Saint Peter as the Saint was fleeing Rome, and which used to be in the Capella di Domine quo vadis.[41]

SANTA CROCE IN GERUSALEMME.[42] This church was built by Constantine, son of Constantine the Great, at the bidding of Saint Helena. It was consecrated by the Blessed Sylvester on 27 March.[43] Upon its falling into ruin, it was restored by Gregory II, and Cardinal Pietro di Mendoza renovated it. During the work the inscription from the Cross was rediscovered above the tribune of the high altar. It is a Cardinal's titular church.[44] There are Stations of the Cross here on the 4th Sunday in Lent, Good Friday, and on the 2nd Sunday in Advent. On the feast of the Invention and Exaltation of the Holy Cross, and its octave, there is **[page [27]]** plenary remission of sins. On the feast of the consecration of the said church, in the chapel under the high altar (into which women may enter only on that day) there is plenary remission of sins. Every Sunday in the year there are three hundred years of indulgence, the same number of quarantines, and the remission of a third of all sins. And so, every day there are 6,048 years[45] of indulgence, the same number of quarantines, and remission of a third of all sins. Here there are the bodies of Saint Anastasius and Saint Caesarius, an ampulla full of Our Saviour's most precious blood, the sponge with which He was given vinegar and gall to drink, two thorns from the crown of thorns that was placed upon His head, one of the nails with which the inscription set there by Pilate was fixed to the top of the Cross, some wood from the Most Holy Cross, placed there by Saint Helena, covered in silver and ornamented with gold and gems, one of the thirty pieces of silver [for] which Christ was sold, half of the cross of the good thief, and many other relics. These are all displayed on Good Friday. The ornaments described below used to be in the church: Constantine gave 4 silver candelabra, 4 vases, ten gold chalices, a silver gilt paten weighing 50 libbre, and a silver paten weighing 250 libbre.

[page [28]]

On the Island

SAN GIOVANNI NELL'Isola.[46] In this church there is an image of the Virgin Mary that, when the Tiber overflowed, suffered no damage whatsoever, nor did the water extinguish the lamps burning in front of it.

SAN BARTOLOMEO NELL'ISOLA.[47] This church was built by Pope Gelasius II,[48] and on the feast of Saint Bartholomew there is plenary remission of sins. On Palm Sunday there are two hundred years of indulgence. Here there are the bodies of Saint Paulinus, Saint Superante, Saint Albert and Saint Marcellus, which were found in the well situated in front of the high altar, and that of Saint Bartholomew, which was brought from Beneventum to Rome by the Emperor Otto II, not to mention many other relics. These are displayed on the feast of Saint Bartholomew and Palm Sunday.

In Trastevere

SANTA MARIA DE L'ORTO, near the Ripa, is a hospital for sick mariners.[49] The Madonna here is an object of great devotion and grants plenary indulgence **[page [29]]** to the salami butchers, greengrocers and artisans of Rome who have their company here.

SANTA CECILIA, also in Trastevere.[50] This church was the house and habitation of Saint Cecilia herself, and Pope Paschal consecrated it in honour of God, Saint Mary, the Saints and Apostles Peter and Paul, and Saint Cecilia. It is a Cardinal's titular church. They have a Stations of the Cross here on the Wednesday after the 2nd Sunday in Lent, and on the feast of Saint Cecilia there is plenary indulgence. Here there are the bodies of Saint Cecilia and Saint Valerian her husband, Saint Tiburtius, Saint Lucius I, Pope, and Saint Maximus, not to mention many other relics.

SANTA MARIA IN TRASTEVERE.[51] The site of the present church was once the Taberna Meritoria Transtiberina, in which Roman soldiers who were too old to fight received victuals from the Senate, right up to the end of their lives. On this site, near the choir, in the place where today there are two iron-grated windows, an abundant fountain of oil sprang

122   Santa Maria in Trastevere (the portico was added by Carlo Fontana in 1702).

miraculously from the ground on the night when our Saviour was born, and in a day it had flowed in a great stream as far as the Tiber. When Calixtus I saw this **[page [30]]** miracle, he had a small church built there. When the church later fell into ruin, Gregory III had it rebuilt from the foundations up, enlarged it and had the painted decoration executed in its entirety.[52] This is a Cardinal's titular church. There is a Stations of the Cross here on the Thursday after the 2nd Sunday in Lent. And in the octave of the Assumption of Our Lady there is plenary remission of sins. On the first day of the year there is an indulgence of 25,000 years and plenary remission of sins. Here there are the bodies of Saint Calixtus I, Innocent and Julius, Popes and Martyrs, and Saint Quirino, Bishop.

SAN CRISOGONO.[53] This church is also in Trastevere and it is a Cardinal's titular church. They have a Stations of the Cross here on the Monday after the fifth Sunday in Lent, and in it there are the following relics: one of the arms of Saint James the Great, one of Saint Andrew's shoulders,

123   San Cosimato.

the head and an arm of Saint Chrysogonus, some wood from the Cross, some of Christ's hair, a rib of Saint Stephen, some relics of Saints Sebastian, Cosmas and Damian, Julian, Martyr, Peter, Paul and Matthew Apostles, Urban, Pope, Lawrence, Primus and Felician, George, Cecilia, Prisca, Ninfa, and Dionisio, and some relics from the Holy Sepulchre, Mount Sion and some holy earth from Jerusalem.

SAN FRANCESCO.[54] On that saint's day and for the whole of the octave, there is plenary remission **[page [31]]** of sins, and in the church there is a chapel in which is buried the body of the Blessed Lodovica Romana, which performs miracles.[55]

SAN COSIMATO is on the site of what used to be Caesar's naumachia.[56] It is a monastery for venerable Roman women of the closed Order of Observant Franciscans. There are many indulgences and pardons for sins.

123

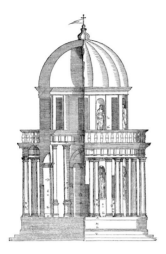

124 Bramante's Tempietto, woodcut from Palladio's *I quattro libri dell'architettura* (1570).

125 San Pietro in Montorio.

125 SAN PIETRO IN MONTORIO.[57] This church is on the Janiculum and was restored by King Ferdinand of Spain, and Clement VII, when he was a Cardinal, commissioned the altarpiece for the high altar and the tabernacle. On the right of the main door there is a picture of 'Christ at the Pillar' painted by brother Sebastiano from Venice, a very excellent

124 painter.[58] The ground upon which the circular chapel outside the above church was built is where the Apostle Saint Peter was crucified.[59] Paul III granted many indulgences to this place, as is clear from the marble tablet above the door that opens into the said chapel. These days there is a very beautiful sepulchre made by His Holiness Pope Julius III for his uncle Cardinal del Monte.[60]

126 SAN PANCRAZIO.[61] This church is outside the Porta Aurea[62] in the Via Aurelia and was built by Honorius I. It is ornamented with the most beautiful porphyry. It is a Cardinal's titular church. They have a Stations of the Cross here on the Apostles' Sunday.[63] Here there are the bodies of Saints Pancras, Bishop and Martyr, Pancras, Knight and Martyr, Victor, Malco, Madiano and **[page [32]]** Gotteria. In the cemetery of San Calipodio, Priest and Martyr, which is below the said church,[64] there are an infinite number of martyrs that people can touch and see but not carry without the permission of the Pope, on pain of Major Excommunication.

126 San Pancrazio.

SANT'ONOFRIO.[65] This church stands between the Porta Settimiana[66] and the Porta Santo Spirito on a delightful hill. Here there are many relics and pardons for sins.

In the Borgo

SANTO SPIRITO IN SASSIA.[67] This hospital was built by Innocent III and handsomely endowed.[68] Sixtus IV restored it and increased its income. It was called 'in Sassia' because at one time people from Saxony lived here. They give a great deal of alms and they have permanent care of many invalids and orphans. Recently, Reverend P. N. Lando, the Commendatore of this hospital, built a very beautiful church here from the foundations up.[69] Pardon can be had on the Sunday closest to the feast of Saint Anthony and on the feast of Pentecost. There is the arm of Saint Andrew, one of Saint Catherine's fingers and many other saints' relics.

SANT'ANGELO.[70] This church was built by the Very Blessed Pope Gregory after he had gone out in a procession with the Roman clergy and people singing the litany, and above the keep of the fortress the angel Michael **[page [33]]** was seen placing a bloody sword back into its scabbard.[71]

127　San Lazzaro e Marta e
Maddalena.

128　Santa Maria di Campo Santo.

Here there are many relics and plenary indulgence for remission of sins, and this lasts for the whole octave of the patronal festival. And here there is a company of noble Roman persons who every year marry off poor spinsters.

128　SANTA MARIA DI CAMPO SANTO.[72] In this place there is a cemetery made with holy earth brought from Jerusalem. Here they bury pilgrims and poor people of every nationality. It is said that the bodies are completely consumed in three days. And here there are many indulgences and relics.

SANTO STEFANO DEGLI INDIANI, behind the church of Saint Peter's in the Vatican.[73] This is where the Indians live and the divine offices are celebrated in their language. Here there are many indulgences granted by the Pontiffs.

SANT'EGIDIO ABBATE.[74] This church stands outside the Porta di San Pietro in Vaticano. It is held in great devotion by the Roman people; on the first of September they go there to receive protection from the plague, and there is plenary indulgence.

127　SAN LAZZARO E MARTA E MADDALENA is outside the Porta di San Pietro at the foot of Monte Mario.[75] On 22 July there are many indulgences and much forgiveness of sins. This church is set outside Rome because it contains the hospital for the poor who have the disease,[76] and they are well looked after here.

SANTA CATERINA.[77] This church is in the Piazza **[page [34]]** di San Pietro, and on the feast of Saint Catherine there is plenary remission of sins. And here they have some of the milk that, instead of blood, came from the neck of Saint Catherine when she was beheaded, and some of the oil that comes from her tomb.

SAN GIACOMO SCOSSACAVALLO.[78] This church stands in the piazza of the Very Reverend Cardinal Salviati. Here there is the stone upon which our Saviour was offered up in the temple on the day of His circumcision, and the stone upon which Abraham would have sacrificed his son. Both were brought by Saint Helena to Rome to be placed in Saint Peter's. When the horses bearing these stones reached the spot where this church stands today, they died. The stones could never be taken anywhere else, so they built this church and placed the stones within.

SANTA MARIA IN TRASPONTINA.[79] In this church there are two columns against which the Most Blessed Apostles, Peter and Paul, were scourged.

FROM THE PORTA FLAMINIA

now the Porta del Popolo to the foot
of the Campidoglio

129   SANT'ANDREA FUORI DELLA PORTA DEL POPOLO,[80] on the Via Flaminia,
is a circular chapel built with great skill and beauty for His Holiness
[page [35]] Our Lord Pope Julius III, who granted to this place plenary
indulgence for the living and the dead on the feast of Saint Andrew, on
the last day of November. And on that day they have a solemn procession
of all the companies and fraternities in Rome, which goes from San
Lorenzo in Damaso to Saint Peter's in the Vatican.

129   Sant'Andrea fuori della Porta del Popolo.

23.   SANTA MARIA DEL POPOLO.[81] In the place where the high altar of this
130   church stands, there used to be a walnut tree under which were buried
the bones of the Emperor Nero. These were guarded by demons who
used to attack those who passed by that place. And Pope Paschal, as a
result of a vision of the Most Blessed Virgin, dug the bones up and threw
them into the Tiber, building an altar there. Sixtus IV rebuilt this church
from the foundations up. From mid-Lent up to and including the octave
of Easter, every day there are one thousand years of indulgence and the
same number of quarantines. On the feast of the Nativity, the

130   Santa Maria del Popolo.

Purification, the Annunciation, the Visitation, the Assumption and Conception of the Virgin Mary, on their octaves and on all the Saturdays in Lent, there is plenary remission of sins. And there are many relics here, including one of the images of Our Lady that Saint Luke painted.

131   San Lorenzo in Lucina.

SANTA MARIA DEI MIRACOLI,[82] next to the walls of the Porta del Popolo, is a church that is much frequented and blessed with many miracles. Here there is plenary indulgence and remission of sins.

SANTA TRINITÀ. This church is on the Monte Pincio and was built by King Louis XI of France as a result of the prayers of Saint Francesco da Paola.[83]

[page [36]]

SAN GIACOMO IN AUGUSTA.[84] In this place there is a hospital where a great deal of charity is distributed and where those suffering from incurable diseases are looked after. On the feast of the Annunciation of the Blessed Virgin Mary, on the first day of May, and on All Souls day there is plenary remission of sins, and on all the Saturdays in the year there is remission of a third of all sins.

SANT'AMBROGIO at the foot of the Monte della Trinità.[85] This church was built by the men of Milan, with a hospice for the poor of that place. Pope Clement VII granted them many indulgences and privileges.

SAN ROCCO ON THE RIPETTA.[86] Here was where the mausoleum of the Emperor Augustus once stood.[87] This church was built recently by the Company of Saint Martin, with a very beautiful hospice for the men of Lombardy. Every day there is plenary indulgence granted by many great Pontiffs.

SAN GIROLAMO DEGLI SCHIAVONI, also on the Ripetta, is a very holy church.[88] And there is a hospice for Slavs where they receive board and lodging.

SAN LORENZO IN LUCINA.[89] This church was in ancient times the Temple of Juno Lucina. Celestine III dedicated it to Saint Lawrence, Martyr. It is a Cardinal's titular church. They have a Stations of the Cross here on the Friday after the third Sunday in Lent. Here there are the bodies of Saints Alexander, Eventio, Teodolo, Severinus, **[page [37]]** Pontiano, Eusebius, Vicentio, Peregrine and Gordian. There are two ampullas containing the body fat and blood of Saint Lawrence, a vessel full of his burnt flesh, a part of the griddle upon which he was roasted, a piece of cloth with which the angel cleaned his most holy body, and many other relics. [131]

SAN SILVESTRO.[90] This church was built by Symmachus I. It is a Cardinal's titular church. They hold a Stations of the Cross here on the Thursday after the 4th Sunday in Lent. On the feast of Saint Chiara and that of Saint Sylvester there is plenary remission of sins. Here they have the head [132]

of Saint John the Baptist, that of Saint Stephen, Pope, and that of the Blessed Margareta of the Colonna family, who was a nun in this place; they have a piece of the mantle of Saint Francis, some relics of Saint Francis and of many others.

LE CONVERTITE.[91] This is a convent, dedicated to the Blessed Mary Magdalene, for reformed prostitutes. They give many plenary indulgences here by concession of Popes Clement VII and Paul III.

SANTI APOSTOLI.[92] This church was built by Constantine the Great in honour of the 12 Apostles. When it was destroyed by heretics, the High Pontiffs Pelagius and John restored it. It is a Cardinal's titular church. They hold a Stations of the Cross here on every Friday that is an Ember Day, the Thursday in the octave of Easter and on the 4th Sunday in Advent. On the first day of May there is plenary remission of sins. Here they have the bodies of Saint Philip **[page [38]]** and Saint James, Apostles, of Saint John and Saint Pelagius, Popes[93] and Martyrs, of Saints Theodore, Cyril, Honorato, Colofio, Buono, Fausto, Protus and Hyacinth, Giovino, Maurus, Nazario, Superantio, Basilio, Primitivo, Eugenio, Claudia, Sabino, most of the body of Saint Crisante and of Saint Daria, a rib of Saint Lawrence, a knee of Saint Andrew, a shoulder and arm of Saint Blaise, some wood of the Cross, a sleeveless robe of Saint Thomas, Apostle, and the scapular of Saint Francis.

SAN MARCELLO.[94] This church was built by a noblewoman of Rome in honour of Saint Marcellus, Pope. Marcellus was put in this place (which was at the time a stable) on the orders of Maxentius, and he died there as a result of the great stench in it. It is a Cardinal's titular church. They hold a Stations of the Cross here on the Wednesday after the 3rd Sunday in Lent, and on the feast of Saint Marcellus there is plenary indulgence. Here there are the bodies of Saints Degna, Merita, Marcellus, Feda, John the Priest, Blaise, Diogene, Longinus, and Felicity with her seven sons. There are the heads of Saints Cosmas and Damian, a jawbone of Saint Lawrence, an arm of Saint Matthew, Apostle and Evangelist, and many other relics.

SANTA MARIA IN VIA LATA.[95] This is a Cardinal's titular church, and on the feast of the Purification and of the Nativity of the Virgin Mary there is plenary remission of sins. Here there is also the oratory dedicated to Saint Paul, Apostle, and Saint Luke; here Saint Luke wrote the Acts **[page [39]]** of the Apostles and painted the image of the Virgin Mary

132 (*facing page*) The twelfth- to thirteenth-century campanile of San Silvestro.

that is in this church. She is shown in the condition in which Saint Luke first learnt of her; thus he painted her with the ring on her finger. This picture can still be seen today in this oratory, and in this form the glorious Virgin performed many miracles, and many Christians who came to her for grace returned home happy, their prayers answered. The church was first called the 'Oratorio di San Paolo e San Luca'.

SAN MARCO.[96] This church was built by the Blessed Mark, Pope. On its becoming ruined, it was restored by Paul II. It is a Cardinal's titular church. They have a Stations of the Cross here on the Monday after the third Sunday in Lent. And on the first day of the year, on the feast of Saint Mark the Evangelist, in the octave of Corpus Christi and of Epiphany, on the feast of Saint Abdon and Saint Sennen, and from Holy Monday to Easter Tuesday there is plenary remission of sins. They have many relics here that they place on the high altar in that church on feast days.

SANTA MARIA DI LORETO.[97] This church stands in the Forum near the Antonine Column.[98] It is a highly revered church and is built with excellent order. On the eighth of September there is plenary indulgence for the living and the dead.

SANTA MARTA, in the Rione della Pigna, is a convent for destitute holy women.[99] There are many privileges to be had and plenary indulgence for any who visit the church. Nearby there is another convent called the Malmaritate.[100]

[page [40]]

SANTA MARIA DELLA STRADA, also in the Rione della Pigna, is in Piazza Altieri.[101] Here, every day, there is great indulgence given by the fathers of the Company of Jesus, called Reformed Priests, who selflessly perform many holy works – notably preaching, hearing confessions and celebrating communion – and they have formed colleges where 'human' letters – Hebrew, Greek and Latin – can be learnt in every faculty, gratis, for the benefit of the people of Rome.

SANTA MARIA SOPRA MINERVA.[102] This church is on the site of what was once the Temple of Minerva Calcidica. There is a company here that every year marries off many spinsters. And on the feast of Saint Dominic there is plenary remission of sins. He who celebrates mass or has mass celebrated at the high altar of this church will free a soul from the pains of Purgatory. Here they have the clothes and hair of the Virgin Mary and many other relics.

SANTA MARIA DELLA ROTONDA.[103] This church was in ancient times the Temple of all the Gods. Boniface IV received it from the Emperor Phocas, and on 12 May he consecrated it to the Virgin Mary and to all the Saints. They hold a Stations of the Cross here on the Friday in the octave of Easter. And on the feast of the Invention of the Holy Cross, the feasts of the Assumption, the Nativity and Conception of the Virgin Mary, and on All Saints' Day – and for the whole of its octave – there is plenary remission of sins. Here there are the bodies of Saints Rasio, Anastasius[104] and many others.

105,
106,
133

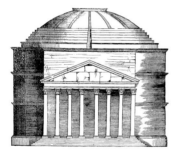 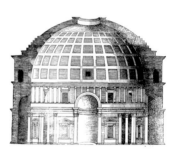

133   The Pantheon, woodcuts from the third volume of Sebastiano Serlio's treatise *On Antiquities* (1540).

[page [41]]

SANTA MARIA MADDALENA.[105] In this church on the feast of the Madeleine there is plenary remission of sins.

SANTA MARIA DE CAMPO MARZO.[106] In this church there are nuns – their founders came from Greece 300 years ago. Here there is a much-venerated image of the Saviour called 'The Pietà'. They have the head of

Quirino, Martyr, and the body of Saint Gregory of Nazianzus. Near this convent there are two other monasteries of the Order of Saint Francis. They are called the 'Monasteri di Montecitorio'.

Santa Elisabetta in the Piazza Capranica is a church with many relics and pardons granted by the High Pontiffs, especially most recently by Pope Paul III to pauper boys and girls.[107] In this place, the maintenance of these children comes from alms-giving and they are tutored in letters and virtues.

San Mauto.[108] In this church there are many relics of saints, and privileges are granted in the name of Saint Bartholomew and Saint Alexander for the company and people of [B]ergamo on 25 August.

134 Sant'Eustachio.[109] This church was built by Celestine III and it is a Cardinal's titular church. Here they have Christ's blood, clothes, crown of thorns and wood from His Cross, the cross of Saint Andrew, some of the coals upon which Saint Lawrence was roasted, relics of Saint Eustace, Teopista his wife, Teopisto and Agapitus his sons, and many others.

San Luigi, in the *rione* of Sant'Eustachio.[110] This **[page [42]]** church was built by the French. It is a very beautiful building and excellently appointed. In the said church there are many privileges, there is plenary indulgence every day in the Capella del Salvatore, and they have some relics of Saint Apollonia and many other saints.

135 Sant'Agostino.[111] This church was rebuilt from the foundation up by the Reverend Cardinal William of Rouen, and on the feast of Saint Nicholas of Tolentino there is plenary remission of sins. Here they have the body of Saint Monica and one of the images of the Virgin Mary painted by Saint Luke. During the time of Innocent VIII this work was the source of a great deal of grace. In the church of San Trifone, which adjoins this church,[112] they hold a Stations of the Cross here on the first Saturday in Lent. Here they have the head of Saint Ruffina.

San Trifone.[113] This church adjoins the church of Sant'Agostino. There are many relics here, and they hold a Stations of the Cross here on the first Saturday in Lent.

Sant'Antonio de' Portoghesi,[114] near the place they call the 'Scrofa'. Pope Gelasius dedicated this church to Saint Anthony and Saint Vincent.

134   Sant'Eustachio.

135   Sant'Agostino.

He endowed it with many indulgences and privileges for the Portuguese people, who in this place have their hospice which offers lodging and board to poor strangers from their country who come to Rome.

SANT'APOLLINARE.[115] This church was once the temple of Apollo. Hadrian I dedicated it to Saint Apollinaris and it is a Cardinal's titular church. They hold a Stations of the Cross here on the **[page [43]]** Thursday after the 5th Sunday in Lent. They have here the bodies of Saints Eustratio, Nardario, Eugenio, Oreste and Ausentio.

SAN GIACOMO DEGLI SPAGNOLI.[116] This church was built by Alfonso de Paradinas, a Spaniard and Bishop of Ciudad Rodrigo. There is plenary remission of sins on 25 July. In this place is the hospice for Spaniards.   136

SANTA MARIA DELL'ANIMA.[117] In this place there is a hospice in which any German can receive three nights' lodging.   137

SANTA MARIA DELLA PACE.[118] This church was built by Sixtus IV, and on the feasts of the Purification, the Annunciation, the Visitation, Our Lady

136   San Giacomo degli Spagnoli.

of the Snow,[119] the Assumption, the Nativity, the Presentation and
Conception of the Virgin Mary, and all the Saturdays in Lent, there is
plenary remission of sins. And from mid-Lent up until the end of the
octave of Easter, there are one thousand years of indulgence and the same
number of quarantines. There are many relics here, which on the holy
days celebrated in this church they place on the high altar.

SAN TOMMASO IN PARIONE.[120] This is a Cardinal's titular church and was
consecrated by Innocent II on 21 December in the year 1139. He placed
in the high altar an arm of Saints Damasus, Calixtus, Cornelius, Urban,
Stephen, Sylvester and Gregory, Popes, some of the clothes of the Virgin
Mary, some of the barley loaves, some of the rocks with which Saint
Stephen was stoned, some of Saint Lucy's blood, and some relics of Saints
Nicholas, **[page [44]]** Valentine, Sebastian, Tranquilino, Phocas, of the
Four Crowned Martyrs, Saints John and Paul, Crisante and Daria,
Cosmas and Damian, Ninfa, Sofia, Balbina, Martha and Petronilla. These
relics were hidden until the year 1546, the twelfth year of Paul III's
reign,[121] when the Very Reverend Messer Giuliano Gallo was rector of

137 *(facing page)*   Santa Maria dell'Anima.

138   San Salvatore in Lauro, in the Ponte Rione
(rebuilt 1857–62).

this church. The relics were discovered by the Reverend Messer
Ambrosio Maggio, Doctor in both secular and religious law, vice-rector
of this church.

138 SAN SALVATORE IN LAURO, in the Ponte Rione.[122] This church was built
by Cardinal Latino Orsini. It is adorned with the most beautiful work
and privileges. It is a monastery for brothers of the Order of Saint
George of Alega.

SAN GIOVANNI DEI FIORENTINI, on the Via Giulia, was begun in great
haste and the aim was to build a beautiful church.[123] On 24 June there is
plenary indulgence.

SAN BIAGIO DELLA PAGNOTTA.[124] This church was built in the time of
Alexander II. In it there is some wood from the Cross, a piece of the
robe of the Virgin Mary, some relics of Saints Andrew, Blaise, Crisante
and Daria, and Sofia. It is on the Via Giulia on the site where Pope Julius
II wanted to build the Palazzo della Ragione of Rome.[125]

139 San Giovanni in Agina, in the Corte Savella.

140 San Lorenzo in Damaso.

SANTA LUCIA, known as 'La Chiavica', in the Ponte Rione.[126] Every day in this church there is plenary indulgence granted by many exalted Pontiffs for the venerable Company of the Gonfalonier. **[page [45]]** In this church, that company has its oratory, which is excellently appointed.

SAN GIOVANNI IN AGINA, in the Corte Savella.[127] In this church there is the huge company known as the Company of Prayer or the Company of Death. Through their good works and their holy lives they have plenary indulgence on the second Sunday of every month.

SAN GIROLAMO near the Palazzo Farnese.[128] Every day in this church there is plenary indulgence for remission of sins. And here they also distribute a great deal of alms to the poor and needy of Rome, given via the Company of Charity, which meets in this church.

THE CASA SANTA.[129] This church is a convent for nuns of a holy life. They are teachers of excellent learning who instruct young girls in the virtues. And on 8 December there is forgiveness of sins.

140　SAN LORENZO IN DAMASO.[130] This church was built and endowed by
Blessed Damasus, Pope. He donated a silver paten weighing 20 libbre, a
vase weighing 10 libbre, five chalices and five crowns. On the church's
becoming semi-ruined, the Reverend Cardinal of San Giorgio rebuilt it
from the foundations up, and instituted a chapel choir there. It is a
Cardinal's titular church. They have a Stations of the Cross here on the
Tuesday after the 4th Sunday in Lent. In this church there are the bodies
of Saints Buono, Maurus, Faustinus, Giovino, Eutirio and his brother, the
head of Saint Barbara, some of the body fat from Saint Lawrence, a foot
of Saint Damasus, and many other relics. **[page [46]]** There are also two
companies here. One is the Company of the Most Blessed Sacrament,
which is very generous in alms-giving and which was the first to be
founded in Italy. The other is the Company of the Conception of Our
Lady, which every year on the feast of Immaculate Conception marries
off many spinsters.

SANTA BARBARA.[131] This church is between the Piazza Giudea and the
Campo dei Fiori. Here they have some of Mary Magdalene's hair, some
of the Virgin Mary's clothing, the veil and cape of Saint Barbara, some
relics of Saints Bartholomew, Philip and James, Apostles, Saints Margaret,
Felix, Ioricio, Christopher, Sebastian, Alexis, Mario, Martha, Lawrence,
Petronilla and many others.

SAN MARTINELLO in the Regola Rione.[132] This church was built by
a certain monk, Gualtiero of San Salvatore, in the time of Pope
Honorius III.[133] Here they have the tunic and garment that the Blessed
Virgin Mary made for her son, Jesus Christ, which increased in size as
the child grew.

SAN SALVATORE IN CAMPO, in the Regola Rione.[134] In this church, every
day, there is a great pardon. The Company of the Most Blessed Trinity is
here. Through a great deal of alms-giving, they see to the needs of poor
pilgrims who come to Rome, and they look after the infirm poor who,
on leaving the hospices, are not yet fully cured but who can build up
their strength here.

SANTA MARIA IN MONTICELLI.[135] This church is in the Regola Rione, and
here they have the bodies of Saint Ninfa, **[page [47]]** Virgin, and Saint
Manciliano, Bishop, not to mention other relics.

SAN BIAGIO.[136] This church is also in the Regola Rione. Here they have
the ring of Saint Blaise and many other relics.

Santa Maria del Pianto.[137] This church was previously called
Santo Salvatore. Because of the miracles that her glorious image has
performed recently and continues to perform, there is plenary
indulgence every day.

Santa Caterina dei Funari.[138] In this church there is the monastery for
poor spinsters. The women are nourished with a holy life and good
morals until they are of marriageable age. They then either marry or
become nuns in this place. Every day there is pardon, and on the feast of
Saint Andrew there is a plenary jubilee granted by Our Lord's Holiness,
Pope Julius III.

Sant'Angelo.[139] This church is in the Pescheria Rione, and it was once
the Temple of Juno. It is a Cardinal's titular church. Here there are the
bodies of Saint Symphorian and his companions, and many other relics.
Every year the senator offers a chalice.

San Nicola in Carcere.[140] The site where this church stands was once   141
occupied by ancient prisons. At the time of the Consuls C. Quintius and
M. Attilius they built the Temple of Piety here. The reason for this was as
follows. A man had been condemned to die of hunger in prison. One of
his daughters came every day and, on the pretext of visiting him, gave
him milk. When the guards noticed this **[page [48]]**, they referred the
case to the Senate. And for such an act of piety, the Senate pardoned the
father and gave food to both for the rest of their lives. This is a Cardinal's

141   San Nicola in Carcere.

142   Santa Maria in Aracoeli.

titular church. They hold a Stations of the Cross here on the Saturday
after the 4th Sunday in Lent. And on the feast of Saint Nicholas there is
plenary remission of sins. They have a rib of Saint Matthew, Apostle, a
hand of Saint Nicholas, and an arm of Saint Alexis.

142   SANTA MARIA IN ARACOELI.[141] This church is on the Capitoline Hill and is
ornamented with beautiful columns and various types of marble. It was
built on the ruins of the Temple of Jupiter Feretrius and of the Palace of
Augustus. On the feasts of Saint Anthony of Padua, of Saint Bernardino,
of the Assumption, Nativity and Conception of the Virgin Mary, of Saint
Louis, Bishop, and on the Nativity of our Lord, there is plenary remission
of sins. And they have here the bodies of Saints Artemio, Abondio and
Abondantio. In front of the choir there is a round stone with an iron
grill around it, in which there are the footprints of an angel that were left
there when Pope Gregory consecrated the church. There is an image of
the Virgin Mary, standing in the pose she took at the foot of the Cross,
painted by Saint Luke. On the slope up to the said church there is a very
broad flight of one hundred and twenty-eight marble steps that were
made from the ornaments of the Temple of Quirinus, which once stood
on Montecavallo.[142]

[page [49]]

FROM THE CAMPIDOGLIO
to the left-hand side, into the hills

SAN PIETRO IN CARCERE TULLIANO.[143] This church is at the foot of
the Campidoglio. Saint Sylvester consecrated it, and this was where
Saint Peter and Saint Paul were imprisoned. When they wanted to
baptize Processus and Martinian, guards in the said prison, a fountain
miraculously sprang up. Every day there are one thousand, two hundred
years of indulgence and remission of a third of all sins. On feast days
these are doubled. Here they have the bodies of Saints Processus and
Martinian.

SANT'ADRIANO.[144] This church is also in the Roman Forum and in
ancient times it was the Treasury.[145] Honorius I consecrated it to Saint
Adrian. It is a Cardinal's titular church. Here they have the bodies of
Saints Mario and Martha, as well as relics of Saint Adrian and many other
saints.

SS COSMA E DAMIANO.[146] This church is in the Roman Forum, and in
ancient times it was the Temple of Romulus. Felix IV dedicated it to
Saints Cosmas and Damian. On its becoming ruined it was restored by
Blessed Gregory. It is a Cardinal's titular church and they hold a Stations
of the Cross here on the Thursday after the 3rd Sunday in Lent. Every
day there are a thousand years of indulgence. Here they have the bodies
of Saints Cosmas and Damian and many other relics. The church doors
here, which are made of bronze, are ancient.

[page [50]]

SANTA MARIA NUOVA.[147] This church is near the Arch of Titus and was
built by Leo IV. On its becoming ruined, it was restored by Nicholas V.
It is a Cardinal's titular church, and here they have the bodies of Saints
Nemesio, Justin, Sinsoriano, Olimpio, Essemperio and Lucilla.[148] Before
the high altar, in the tomb with the iron railings around it, lies the body
of Francesca Romana, who was canonized by Alexander VI. Here in a
marble tabernacle there is one of the pictures that Saint Luke painted.
It used to be in Greece in the city of Troy and was brought to Rome by
the illustrious knight Angelo Freapani. When there was a fire in this

143   The entrance to San
Clemente.

144   View of the interior of San Clemente in
the early seventeenth century, before internal
alterations.

church in the time of Honorius III, the said picture suffered no damage
whatsoever.

143,   SAN CLEMENTE.[149] This church is between the Colosseum and San
144   Giovanni in Laterano. It is a Cardinal's titular church. There is a
Stations of the Cross here on the Monday after the 2nd Sunday in Lent,
plenary remission of sins, and every day there are 40 years of indulgence
and the same number of quarantines. In Lent these are doubled. Here
they have the bodies of Saints Clement and Ignatius, and in the chapel
outside the church there is the body of Saint Servolo. There are also
many relics that on the day of the Stations of the Cross can be viewed on
the high altar. The Capelletta del Salvatore outside the said church, in the
direction of the Colosseum, is on the site where the woman who was
made Pope gave birth.[150] This is why when the Pontiff goes to
San Giovanni in Laterano he does not go down this street but travels by
[page [51]] that which leads to the Seven Halls.[151] In the small chapel
called the Capella di Santa Maria Imperatrice,[152] on the way towards
San Giovanni in Laterano, there is an image of the Virgin Mary that

145   SS. Quattro Coronati.

spoke to Gregory and granted him, and to anyone who says the Pater
Noster and the Ave Maria three times, 15 [thousand][153] years of
indulgence for each recitation.

SS Quattro Coronati.[154] This church is on the Celian Hill and was   3, 145
built by Honorius I. On its becoming ruined, it was rebuilt by Leo IV,
and Paschal II restored it. It is a Cardinal's titular church, and they have a
Stations of the Cross here on the Monday after the 4th Sunday in Lent.
Here they have the bodies of Saints Claudio, Nicostrato, Semproniano,[155]
Castorio, Severo, Severiano, Carposoro, Vittorino,[156] Mario, Felicissimo,
Agapitus, Hippolytus, Aquila, Priscus, Aquinio, Narciso, Marcellus,
Marcellinus, Felix, Apolline, Benedict, Venantius, Diogene, Liberale and
Festo. They have the heads of Saints Protus, Cecilia, Alexander, Sixtus,
Sebastian and Praxedes.

SS Marcellino e Pietro.[157] This church is also between the Colosseum
and San Giovanni in Laterano. It was built by Constantine the Great, and
he donated a gold paten weighing 35 libbre, four gilt candelabra each

146 San Pietro in Vincoli.

12 feet tall, three gold chalices studded with precious stones, a silver altar weighing 200 libbre, and a gold vase weighing 20 libbre. When the church later fell into ruin, Alexander IV restored it in the year 1260, on 10 April. It is a Cardinal's titular church. They hold a Stations of the Cross here on the Saturday after the second Sunday **[page [52]]** in Lent. They have the relics of the above-mentioned Saints Marcellinus and Peter, and of many others, as can be seen from the marble plaque set into the outside wall of this church.

SAN MATTEO IN MERULANA.[158] This church is on the road that leads from San Giovanni in Laterano to Santa Maria Maggiore, and on the feast of Saint Matthew there is plenary remission of sins. Every day there are one thousand years of indulgence, the same number of quarantines and remission of a seventh of all sins.

146 SAN PIETRO IN VINCOLI.[159] This church was built upon the ruins of the Curia Vecchia by Eudossa, wife of the Emperor Arcadius.[160] Sixtus III consecrated it, and when it fell into ruin Pope Pelagius restored it. It is a Cardinal's titular church. They hold a Stations of the Cross here on the first Monday in Lent, and on the first day in August there is plenary remission of sins. In this church there are the bodies of the Maccabean Saints[161] and the chains with which Saint Peter was bound in prison in Jerusalem, a part of the cross of Saint Andrew, and many other relics.

There is also a marble Moses below the sepulchre of Julius II, carved with wonderful skill by the consummately divine Michelangelo.[162]

San Lorenzo in Panisperna.[163] This church is on the Viminal Hill in the place where Saint Lawrence was martyred. It was built by Pius I upon the ruins of the palace of the Emperor Decius. It is a Cardinal's titular church, and they hold a Stations of the Cross here on the Thursday after the first Sunday **[page [53]]** in Lent. In this church there is the body of Saint Bridget, an arm of Saint Lawrence, part of his griddle, some of the coals with which he was burnt, and many other relics.

Sant'Agata.[164] This church was Saint Gregory's maternal house, and he consecrated it to Saint Agatha. It is decorated with various marbles.[165]

San Lorenzo in Fonte.[166] This church is between Santa Pudenziana and San Pietro in Vincoli, and it was the prison of Saint Lawrence. When he wished to baptize Saints Hippolytus and Lucillo, a wellspring burst forth that can still be seen today.

Santa Pudenziana.[167] This church had previously been the saint's paternal house. It is on the site of what used to be the Novatian Baths, and Pius I consecrated it. On its falling into ruin, it was restored by Simplicius. It is a Cardinal's titular church. They hold a Stations of the Cross here on the Tuesday after the third Sunday in Lent. Every day there are three thousand years of indulgence and the same number of quarantines and remission of a third of all sins. Here they have the cemetery of Priscilla, in which are the bones of three thousand martyrs, and in the chapel near the high altar the Apostle Saint Peter celebrated his first mass. For the person who celebrates mass or has mass celebrated in the said chapel, there is the liberation of one soul from the pains of Purgatory. In the Capella di San Pastore there is a well in which there is the blood of three thousand martyrs, gathered and placed there by Saint Pudentiana. Once a priest celebrating in the said chapel doubted **[page [54]]** whether the true body of Christ was in the consecrated host, and as he was having these doubts the host left his hand and fell to the ground, making a mark of blood that can still be seen today. It is protected by a small iron grill.

San Vito in Macello.[168] This church is near the Arch of Gallienus. It is a Cardinal's titular church. And on the feast of Saint Vitus there are

six thousand years of indulgence and the same number of quarantines.
Every day there are six thousand years [of indulgence]. Here they have
the relics of Saint Vitus and with them they make an oil that cures the
bites of rabid dogs. Upon the marble stone with an iron grill over it were
slaughtered innumerable martyrs.[169]

SAN GIULIANO.[170] This church is also near the above-mentioned
Trophies.[171] Here they have the relics of Saints Julian and Albert, and
with these they make a water that cures all fevers and other infirmities.

SANT'EUSEBIO.[172] This church is also not far from the said Trophies, and it
is a Cardinal's titular church. They hold a Stations of the Cross here on
the Friday after the fourth Sunday in Lent. Every day there are 7,800
years of indulgence and the same number of quarantines. They have here
the bodies of Saints Eusebius, Vicentio, Romanus, Orosio, Gregory of
Nazianzus and Paulo Confessore, they have the bit from Constantine's
horse made from a nail that pinned Our Saviour to the Cross, they have
some of **[page [55]]** the column against which He was scourged, they
have some of His tomb, and relics of Saint Stephen, Pope, and Saints
Bartholomew, Matthew, Helena, Andrew and many others.

SANTA BIBIANA.[173] This church is beyond the Trophies of Mario in the
Via Labicana and it was built by Pope Simplicius. On its becoming
ruined it was restored by Honorius III. On All Saints' Day there are six
hundred thousand years of indulgence, and every day there are nine
thousand years of indulgence. Here there is the cemetery between the
two laurel trees, where lie the bones of five thousand martyrs. Here there
is a herb planted by Saint Bibiana that cures epilepsy.

SAN MARTINO.[174] This church is on the Esquiline Hill and was dedicated
by Sergius I. Symmachus had a silver tabernacle weighing 120 libbre
made to go on the high altar here. It is a Cardinal's titular church. Here
there are the bodies of Saints Sylvester, Martin, Fabian, Stephen and
Soter, Popes, Asterio, Cyricus and many others, as can be seen from the
inscription on a stone in the right-hand part of the choir in this church.

147   SANTA PRASSEDE.[175] This church is close to Santa Maria Maggiore and was
consecrated by Paschal I. It is a Cardinal's titular church. They hold a
Stations of the Cross here on the Monday in Holy Week, and every day
there are twelve thousand years of indulgence and the same number of
quarantines, as well as remission of a third of all sins. Below the high altar

147 (facing page)   Santa Prassede.

lies the body of Saint Praxedes. In the chapel called 'Horto del Paradiso'[176] – into which women may never enter – there are the bodies of Saint Valentine **[page [56]]** and Zeno, above the column against which our Redeemer was scourged and which was brought to Rome by the Reverend Cardinal Colonna, whose name was Giovanni. In the centre of this chapel, below the circular stone that is here, 40 martyrs are buried, of whom eleven were High Pontiffs. Whoever celebrates mass or has mass celebrated in this chapel will free a soul from the pains of Purgatory. In the centre of this church, in the place where stands the circular stone with the iron railing around it, there is a well in which is the blood of an infinite number of martyrs (the railing was put here by Leo X after having seen the blood mentioned). It was this blood that the Blessed Praxedes went about collecting with a sponge, putting it into the well. There are also many relics that they exhibit on Easter Day after vespers.

SAN QUIRICO.[177] This church is near the Tor de' Conti. It is a Cardinal's titular church. They hold a Stations of the Cross here on the Tuesday after the 5th Sunday in Lent. There are many relics here.

SANTA SUSANNA.[178] This church is on Montecavallo, and it is a Cardinal's titular church. They hold a Stations of the Cross here on the Saturday after the 3rd Sunday in Lent. Here they have the bodies of Saint Susanna, Sabino her father, and Felice her sister, they have some of her clothing, wood from the Cross and from the sepulchre of Christ, some of the Virgin Mary's clothing and hair, some relics of Saints Luke, Thomas, Lawrence, Marcellus, Simon, Sylvester, Boniface, **[page [57]]** Clement, Anthony the Abbot, Leo, Blaise, Sernin, Agapitus, Linus, Lucian, Crisante and Daria, Protus and Hyacinth, Vitalis, Stephen, Pope, Gregory of Nazianzus, Catherine, Dalmatio, Martin, Tecla, Praxedes, Copio, Martina and of many others.

SAN VITALE.[179] This church is in the valley near Montecavallo. On its becoming ruined, it was restored by Sixtus IV. It is a Cardinal's titular church. They hold a Stations of the Cross here on the Friday after the 2nd Sunday in Lent.

148 SANTA COSTANZA.[180] This church is outside the Porta di Sant'Agnese and is circular in form. In ancient times it was the Temple of Bacchus, and Alexander IV dedicated it to the virgin Saint Costanza, daughter of Constantine the Great. Costanza was buried in the said church in an

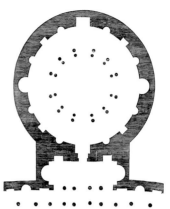

148a, b c Santa Costanza, woodcut from Palladio's *I quattro libri dell' architettura* (1570) and (*right and below*) from the third volume of Sebastiano Serlio's treatise *On Antiquities* (1540).

Ho dimostrato qui adietro la pianta con le sue misure, e qui sotto si vedrà lo diritto nella parte di dentro, per che da fuori non é ornato. L'altezza sua dal pauimento fin sotto il cielo é palmi ottantasei. La grossezza delle colonne é palmi due, e minuti quattordici, & la sua altezza é palmi uentuno, e minuti undici L'altezza delle basi é palmo uno, e minuti sette. L'altezza dei capitelli é palmi due & un quarto, l'altezza de l'architraue é palmo uno & un quarto, e così il fregio. L'altezza della cornice é palmi due e mezo. I membri piu particolari si possono uedere qui sotto, perche sono proportionati a i grandi, e questo tempio é fuori di Roma dedicato a Santa Agnese.

exceedingly beautiful porphyry tomb. There is also in this place the church of Sant'Agnese,[181] built by the said Saint Costanza in honour of Saint Agnes because she cured Costanza of leprosy. It has bronze doors and is ornamented with various stones, and they have a ring that was sent down from the heavens to Saint Agnes.

FROM THE CAMPIDOGLIO

to the right-hand side

SANTA MARIA LIBERATRICE.[182] This church is also in the Roman Forum. Saint Sylvester consecrated it after having bound the mouth of a dragon that lived there in a very deep cave and was polluting the air of Rome with his breath. He sealed its **[page [58]]** mouth with the impression of the Holy Cross and the dragon no longer caused any harm. He granted that every day there would be eleven thousand years of indulgence.

SANTA MARIA DELLA CONSOLAZIONE.[183] In this church there is an image of the Virgin Mary that is the source of a great deal of grace,[184] and on the 2nd Sunday in June between first and second vespers there is plenary remission of sins, granted by Sixtus IV. In the Capella di Santa Maria di Grazia there is one of the images that Saint Luke painted. Here there is a hospice in which they give a great deal of alms and always take in the infirm who flock there.

149 SANT'ANASTASIA.[185] This is a Cardinal's titular church. It was once the living of Saint Jerome. They hold a Stations of the Cross here on the Tuesday after the 1st Sunday in Lent, at dawn on the feast of the Nativity of our Lord, and on the Tuesday in the octave of Pentecost. Here they have the chalice of Saint Jerome and many other relics.

149   Sant'Anastasia (centre), *c.*1534–36, Kupferstichkabinett, Staatliche Museen zu Berlin, 72 D2A, fols 91*v*, 92*r*.

Santa Maria in Porticu.[186] This is a Cardinal's titular church. It was once the house of Galla, a saintly woman who was the daughter of the Roman Patrician Symmachus. When she was at table, angels brought her a sapphire of remarkable splendour, in which was impressed the image of the Virgin Mary with our Saviour in her arms, and placed it on her credenza. This was during the pontificate of John I. Moved by this miracle, Gregory VII consecrated the place as this church, and he placed the said image upon the high altar in a tabernacle behind an iron grill **[page [59]]**. It can still be seen today. The circular temple at the Ponte di Santa Maria was in ancient times the Temple of Pudicitia.[187]

4, 150

San Gregorio.[188] This church was the paternal house of Saint Gregory, Pope. In the second year of his pontificate, he consecrated it to Saint Andrew, Apostle, and beseeched almighty God to grant eternal life to whoever chose that place for their tomb, provided they were a faithful Christian. When he had finished his prayer, an angel appeared to him and said, 'O Gregory, your prayer has been answered'. On All Souls' Day, and for the whole of its octave, there is plenary remission of sins, and whoever celebrates mass or has mass celebrated in the chapel that is next to the sacristy will free a soul from the pains of Purgatory. Here they have an arm of Saint Gregory and a leg of Saint Pantaleon.

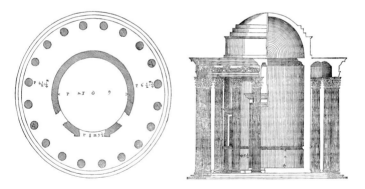

150   The 'Temple of Pudicitia', woodcuts from Palladio's *I quattro libri dell'architettura* (1570).

SS Giovanni e Paolo.[189] This is on the Celian Hill and it is a Cardinal's titular church. They hold a Stations of the Cross here on the first Friday in Lent. They have the bodies of Saints John and Paul, Sernin, Prestina, Donata and Secunda. They have some relics of Saints Stephen, Sylvester,

151

151   SS. Giovanni e Paolo.

Nicholas, Crisante and Daria, Cefas, Sernin, Sebastian, Mamiliano,
Alexander, Praxedes, Lucy, Matthew, Constantine, Secundo and Peregrine.
They have some of the clothing, Cross and tomb of Christ and the stone
upon which Saints John and Paul were beheaded – that stone is
[page [60]] the one on the altar in the centre of the church. Their
bodies are in the wall opposite the said altar.

152   SANTA MARIA DELLA NAVICELLA.[190] This is a Cardinal's titular church.
They hold a Stations of the Cross here on the 2nd Sunday in Lent.
It is called 'Navicella' because of the small stone ship that is in front of
the said church. This church is also on the Celian Hill.

153   SANTO STEFANO ROTONDO.[191] This church is on the Celian Hill. It was
once the Temple of Faunus, and Simplicius I dedicated it to Saint
Stephen, Protomartyr. On its becoming ruined, the church was restored
by Nicholas V. It is a Cardinal's titular church. They hold a Stations of the
Cross here on the Friday after the 5th Sunday in Lent and on the feast of
Saint Stephen. Here they have the bodies of Saints Primus and Felician,
and some relics of Saints Domicilla, Augustine and Ladislao, not to
mention many others.

SAN SISTO.[192] This church is near San Gregorio and was endowed by
Innocent IV. It is a Cardinal's titular church. They hold a Stations of the

152 Santa Maria della Navicella.

153 Santo Stefano Rotondo.

Cross here on the Wednesday after the third Sunday in Lent. Here they have the bodies of Saints Sixtus, Zephyrinus, Lucius I, Lucius II, Lucian, Felix, Antero, Maximus, Julius, Soter I, Soter II, Partenio and Calocerio. They have some of the milk and hair of the Virgin Mary, some of the clothing of Saint Dominic, some of the veil and nipple of Saint Agatha,

154   Santa Sabina.

and some relics of Saints Martin, Agapitus, Andrew, Peter, Lawrence and
Stephen, not to mention many others. They have an image of the Virgin
Mary painted by Saint Luke.[193] **[page [61]]**

154   SANTA SABINA.[194] In ancient times this church was the Temple of Diana,
and it is on the Aventine Hill. It is a Cardinal's titular church. They have a
Stations of the Cross here on the first day of Lent. On its becoming
ruined, it was rebuilt by a Slav bishop during the pontificate of Sixtus III.
It used to be the house of Saint Sabina and in the time of Honorius III it
was the pontifical palace. Honorius donated it to Saint Dominic and
confirmed his order in the year 1216. Here they have the bodies of Saints
Sabina, Sarafia, Peregrina, Eventio, Teodolo and of Saint Alexander, Pope;
they have a thorn from our Redeemer's crown, a piece of the reed with
which His head was struck, some of the clothing of Saint Dominic, some
of the Virgin Mary's tomb, some holy earth from Jerusalem, a piece of
Saint Andrew's cross, a rib of one of the Innocents, some relics of Saints
Peter, Paul, Bartholomew, Matthew, Philip and James, John Chrysostom,

155   Sant'Alessio.

Cosmas and Damian, Apollinaris, Stephen, Protomartyr, Lawrence, Ursula, Margaret, Christopher, Jerome, Julian, Gregory, Pope, Martin, Sebastian, Cecilia and Mary of Egypt. Here they have a silver cross full of relics, in the middle of which there is a small cross made from the wood of the Cross. The black stone affixed to the high altar was thrown at Saint Dominic in an attempt to kill him while he was praying in this place, but **[page [62]]** the stone miraculously shattered and he was completely unharmed.[195]

SANT'ALESSIO.[196] This church is on the Aventine Hill and was once the   155 house of Saint Alexis. On the right-hand side of the high altar can still be seen some large wooden steps where, on returning from a pilgrimage, Alexis did penance until the end of his life (this penance lasted seventeen years). Neither his father nor anyone else knew anything about this. In this church on the feast of Saint Alexis there is plenary remission of sins and every day there is an indulgence of one hundred years and the same number of quarantines. Below the high altar are the bodies of Saints

156   Santa Prisca.

Alexis, Boniface and Hermes, Martyrs, and many other relics. The image of the Most Blessed Virgin in the high tabernacle was once in a church in the city of Edessa. When he was in that city, the Most Blessed Alexis would often pray before it. When one day he went to this church to pray he found the doors locked. The said image spoke twice to the doorkeeper, telling him to admit Alexis, man of God, because he was worthy of heaven.

156 SANTA PRISCA.[197] This church is also on the Aventine Hill. It was once the Temple of Hercules. It was built by Evander, and Saint Peter the Apostle lived here. On its becoming ruined, it was restored by Calixtus III.[198] It is a Cardinal's titular church and they have a Stations of the Cross here on the Tuesday in Holy Week. Here they have the bodies of Saints Prisca, [A]quila her mother, and Aquilo, Priest and Martyr, and they have the stole **[page [63]]** of Saint Peter, a marble basin that he used for baptisms, and other relics.

157 SANTA SABA ABBATE.[199] This church is also on the said hill, and here there is a fountain in which is the scapular of Saint Saba. The water from this has a remarkable power to cure many infirmities, most notably haemorrhages. In a marble tomb near the choir there are the bodies of the Emperors Vespasian and Titus.

157   Santa Saba Abbate (restored in 1943).

158   Santa Balbina.

SANTA BALBINA.[200] This church is on the same hill and was consecrated   158
by Saint Gregory. It is a Cardinal's titular church and they have a
Stations of the Cross here on the Tuesday after the 2nd Sunday in Lent.
Every day there are seven years of indulgence, and they have the bodies
of Saints Balbina, Quirino and five others, whose names are written in
the book of life.

159   San Giovanni a Porta Latina.

159   SAN GIOVANNI A PORTA LATINA.[201] This is at the Porta Latina and is a
    Cardinal's titular church. They have a Stations of the Cross here on the
    Saturday after the 5th Sunday in Lent. On 6 May there is plenary
160   remission of sins. The small chapel before the said church is the place
    where Saint John, Apostle, was put in boiling oil on the order of the
    Emperor Domitian, and from which he emerged without any harm
    whatsoever.[202]

160   San Giovanni in Oleo.

Sant'Anastasio.[203] This church is outside Rome on the Via Ostiense. It was consecrated by Honorius I in the year 1201, at which ceremony there were 21 Cardinals present. They have a pillar against which Saint Paul, Apostle, **[page [64]]** was beheaded. Once his head was separated from his body, it bounced three times, from which points the three fountains that can still be seen today miraculously sprang. On the feast of Saint Anastasius there is plenary indulgence and every day six thousand years of indulgence.

Santa Maria Annunciata.[204] This church is on the same street and was consecrated in the year 1220, on 9 August. On the feast of the Annunciation there is plenary remission of sins, and every day there are ten thousand years of indulgence. Midway between this church and San Sebastiano, at the site of the cross, there are the bodies of ten thousand soldier martyrs.

THE END

THE STATIONS OF THE CROSS,

Indulgences and Spiritual Graces that can be had
At the churches in Rome, both for the whole of
Lent and for the whole of
The year, here
Published for the first time.
By Messer Andrea Palladio

[page [66]]

The month of January

On the first day of the year, that is, the Circumcision of Our Lord, there is a Stations of the Cross at Santa Maria in Trastevere 'ad fontes olei',[205] and there are 25 thousand years of true indulgence and plenary remission of all sins.

On the same day, there is a Stations of the Cross at Santa Maria Maggiore and at Santa Maria in Aracoeli and there is plenary indulgence for all sins.

On the 6th, the feast of the Lord's Epiphany, there is a Stations of the Cross at Saint Peter's and there are 28 thousand years of indulgence, the same number of quarantines and plenary remission of all sins for the whole of the octave.

On the 7th, the feast of Saint Julian,[206] plenary indulgence.

On the 10th, at the church of the Trinità, the feast of Saint Paul the first hermit, plenary indulgence.

On the 13th, in the octave, there is a Stations of the Cross at Saint Peter's and there is plenary indulgence for all sins.

On the 16th, the feast of Saint Marcellus, Pope, there is plenary indulgence.

On the 17th, the feast of Saint Anthony, Abbot, there is plenary indulgence.

On the 18th, the feast of Saint Prisca, plenary indulgence.

On the 20th, the feast of Saint Sebastian, there is plenary indulgence.

On the 21st, the feast of Saint Agnes, there is plenary indulgence.

On the 22nd, the feast of Saint Vincent and Saint Anastasius, there is plenary indulgence.

[page [67]]

On the 25th, the feast of the Conversion of Saint Paul, Apostle, at San Paolo, there is plenary indulgence.

On the 27th, the feast of Saint John Chrysostom, there is plenary indulgence for all sins.

On the 31st, the feast of Saints Ciro and Giovanni, there is a Stations of the Cross at Santa Croce, and there is plenary indulgence. There is plenary indulgence in the church of Saints Ciro and Giovanni.

The month of February

On the 1st, the feast of Saint Bridget, plenary indulgence.

On the 2nd, the feast of the Purification of the Virgin Mary, there is a Stations of the Cross at Santa Maria Maggiore and plenary indulgence for all sins. On the same day, there is a Stations of the Cross at Santa Maria Inviolata and at Santa Maria della Pace and there is plenary indulgence for all sins.

On the 3rd, the feast of Saint Blaise, plenary indulgence.

On the 5th, the feast of Saint Agatha, plenary indulgence.

On the 9th, the feast of Saint Apollonia, at the church of San Luigi, plenary indulgence.

On the 22nd, the feast of the cathedral of Saint Peter, there is plenary indulgence.

On the 24th, the feast of Saint Matthew, Apostle, there is plenary indulgence.

On the 26th, the feast of Saint Costanza, at the church of Sant'Agnese, plenary indulgence.

† On Septuagesima Sunday, there is a Stations of the Cross at San Lorenzo fuori le mura, plenary **[page [68]]** indulgence, 11 thousand years of indulgence and 48 of quarantines and the remission of a third of all sins; also the liberation of a soul from the pains of Purgatory.

On Sexagesima Sunday, there is a Stations of the Cross at San Paolo, plenary indulgence, 12 thousand years of indulgence, 18 of quarantines and the remission of a third of all sins.

On Quinquagesima Sunday, there is a Stations of the Cross at Saint Peter's, plenary indulgence, 28 thousand years of indulgence and the same number of quarantines.

The month of March

On the 7th, the feast of Saint Thomas Aquinas, there is plenary indulgence.

On the 12th, the feast of Saint Gregory, Pope, there is a Stations of the Cross at Saint Peter's and there is plenary indulgence for all sins.

On the 20th, the vigil of the feast of Saint Benedict, in the Capella di San Silvestro there is plenary indulgence for all sins.

On the 25th, the feast of the Annunciation of the Virgin Mary, there are infinite indulgences. There is a Stations of the Cross with plenary indulgence for all sins on this day and for the whole octave.

From the day of the above-mentioned Annunciation until the Kalends of August at the church **[page [69]]** of the Annunciata, every day there are 12 thousand years of true indulgence.[207]

The Stations of the Cross in Lent

On the first day of Lent, there is a Stations of the Cross at Santa Sabina, and there are three thousand years of indulgence and plenary remission of all sins.

On Thursday, there is a Stations of the Cross at San Giorgio, and there are ten thousand years of indulgence.

On Friday, there is a Stations of the Cross at SS Giovanni e Paolo, and there are 10 thousand years of indulgence.

On Saturday, there is a Stations of the Cross at San Trifone, and there are 10 thousand years of indulgence and plenary remission of all sins.

On the first Sunday in Lent, there is a Stations of the Cross at San Giovanni in Laterano, and there are 18 thousand years of indulgence and plenary remission of all sins, and in addition to this there are an infinite number of other indulgences.

On Monday, there is a Stations of the Cross at San Pietro in Vincoli, and there are 10 thousand years of indulgence and plenary remission of all sins.

† On Tuesday, there is a Stations of the Cross at Sant'Anastasia, and there are 28 thousand [years of indulgence], the same number of quarantines and the liberation of one soul from Purgatory.

On Wednesday, there is a Stations of the Cross at Santa Maria Maggiore, and there are 28 thousand years of indulgence, the same number of quarantines and remission of **[page [70]]** a third of all sins.

On Thursday, there is a Stations of the Cross at San Lorenzo in Panisperna, and there are 10 thousand years of indulgence and plenary remission of all sins.

On Friday, there is a Stations of the Cross at Santi Apostoli, and there are 12 thousand years of indulgence and plenary remission of all sins.

On Saturday, there is a Stations of the Cross at Saint Peter's, and there are 18 thousand years of indulgence, the same number of quarantines and plenary remission of all sins.

On the second Sunday, there is a Stations of the Cross at Santa Maria della Navicella, and there are 28 thousand years of indulgence and the same number of quarantines.

On Monday, there is a Stations of the Cross at San Clemente, and there are 11 thousand years of indulgence and remission of a third of all sins.

On Tuesday, there is a Stations of the Cross at Santa Balbina, and there are 10 thousand years of indulgence.

On Wednesday, there is a Stations of the Cross at Santa Cecilia, and there are 10 thousand years of indulgence.

On Thursday, there is a Stations of the Cross at Santa Maria in Trastevere, and there are 10 thousand years of indulgence.

On Friday, there is a Stations of the Cross at San Vitale, and there are 10 thousand years of indulgence.

On Saturday, there is a Stations of the Cross at SS Marcellino e Pietro, and there are ten thousand years of indulgence and plenary remission of all **[page [71]]** sins.

† On the third Sunday, there is a Stations of the Cross at San Lorenzo fuori le mura, and there are 10 thousand years of indulgence, 48 of quarantines and the liberation of a soul from Purgatory.

On Monday, there is a Stations of the Cross at San Marco, and there are ten thousand years of indulgence.

On Tuesday, there is a Stations of the Cross at Santa Pudenziana, and there are ten thousand years of indulgence.

On Wednesday, there is a Stations of the Cross at San Sisto, and there are ten thousand years of indulgence.

On Thursday, there is a Stations of the Cross at SS Cosma e Damiano, and there are ten thousand years of indulgence.

On Friday, there is a Stations of the Cross at San Lorenzo in Lucina, and there are ten thousand years of indulgence.

On Saturday, there is a Stations of the Cross at Santa Susanna, and there are 13 thousand years of indulgence.

† On the fourth Sunday, there is a Stations of the Cross at Santa Croce in Gerusalemme. Here there is plenary remission of all sins and the liberation of a soul from the pains of Purgatory.

On Monday, there is a Stations of the Cross at Santi Quattro Coronati, and there are ten thousand years of indulgence.

On Tuesday, there is a Stations of the Cross at San Lorenzo in Damaso, and there are ten thousand years of indulgence and the remission of a third of all sins.

On Wednesday, there is a Stations of the Cross at San Paolo, and there are ten thousand years of indulgence and the remission **[page [72]]** of a third of all sins.

On Thursday, there is a Stations of the Cross at San Silvestro, and there are ten thousand years of indulgence.

On Friday, there is a Stations of the Cross at Sant'Eusebio, and there are ten thousand years of indulgence.

On Saturday, there is a Stations of the Cross at San Nicola in Carcere, and there are ten thousand years of indulgence and plenary remission of all sins.

† On the fifth Sunday, there is a Stations of the Cross at Saint Peter's, and there are 28 thousand years of indulgence, the same number of quarantines and remission of a third of all sins.

On Monday, there is a Stations of the Cross at San Crisogono, and there are 10 thousand years of indulgence.

On Tuesday, there is a Stations of the Cross at San Quirico, and there are 10 thousand years of indulgence.

On Wednesday, there is a Stations of the Cross at San Marcello, and there are 10 thousand years of indulgence.

On Thursday, there is a Stations of the Cross at Sant'Apollinare, and there are 10 thousand years of indulgence.

† On Friday, there is a Stations of the Cross at Santo Stefano on the Celian Hill, and there is the liberation of one soul from the pains of Purgatory.

† On Saturday, there is a Stations of the Cross at San Giovanni a Porta Latina, and there are 13 thousand years of indulgence and the liberation of a soul from the pains of Purgatory.

On Palm Sunday, there is a Stations of the Cross at San **[page [73]]** Giovanni in Laterano, and there are 25 thousand years of indulgence, the same number of quarantines and plenary remission of sins.

On Holy Monday, there is a Stations of the Cross at Santa Prassede, and there are 15 thousand years of indulgence, plenary remission of a quarter of all sins and also plenary remission of sins.

On Holy Tuesday, there is a Stations of the Cross at Santa Prisca, and there are 18 thousand years of indulgence and plenary remission of all sins.

On Holy Wednesday, there is a Stations of the Cross at Santa Maria Maggiore, and there are 28 thousand years of indulgence and there is plenary remission of all sins.

On Maundy Thursday, there is a Stations of the Cross at San Giovanni in Laterano, and there are 12 thousand years of indulgence, 48 of quarantines, and also double the plenary remission of all sins.

On Good Friday, there is a Stations of the Cross at Santa Croce in Gerusalemme and there is plenary remission of all sins.

On Holy Saturday, there is a Stations of the Cross at San Giovanni in

Laterano, and there are 12 thousand years of indulgence, 48 of quarantines and plenary remission of all sins.

On Easter Sunday, the Resurrection of the Lord Jesus Christ, there is a Stations of the Cross at Santa Maria Maggiore, and there are 28 thousand years of indulgence, **[page [74]]** the same number of quarantines and plenary remission of all sins.

On Monday, there is a Stations of the Cross at Saint Peter's, and there are 28 thousand years of indulgence and plenary remission of all sins.

On Tuesday, there is a Stations of the Cross at San Paolo, and there are 20 thousand years of indulgence, 28 of quarantines and plenary remission of all sins.

On Wednesday, there is a Stations of the Cross at San Lorenzo fuori le mura, and there are 18 thousand years of indulgence, the same number of quarantines and the liberation of a soul from the pains of Purgatory.

On Thursday, there is a Stations of the Cross at Santi Apostoli, and there are 15 thousand years of indulgence and plenary remission of all sins.

On Friday, there is a Stations of the Cross at Santa Maria della Rotonda,[208] and there are 15 thousand years of indulgence.

On Saturday, there is a Stations of the Cross at San Giovanni in Laterano, and there are 15 thousand years of indulgence.

† On the Sunday in the octave of Easter, there is a Stations of the Cross at San Pancrazio, and there are 15 thousand years of indulgence and plenary remission of all sins, doubled.

The month of April

On the 2nd, the feast of Saint Mary of Egypt, plenary indulgence.

On the 3rd, at San Pancrazio, remission of sins.

On the 5th, the feast of Saint Vincent of the Order of Frati Predicatori, there is plenary remission of all **[page [75]]** sins.

On the 23rd, the feast of Saint George, there is a Stations of the Cross at his church[209] and plenary remission of all sins.

On the 25th, similarly, on the feast of Saint Mark, there is a Stations of the Cross at Saint Peter's, and there are 28 thousand years of indulgence and the same number of quarantines.

On the 29th, the feast of Saint Vitale, plenary indulgence. Similarly, on the same day there is a Stations of the Cross at San Marco and there they grant plenary remission of all sins.[210]

The month of May

Please note that on all Sundays in the month of May there is plenary remission of sins at the church of San Sebastiano.

On the 1st, the feast of Saint Philip and Saint James, there is plenary remission of all sins, as there is for every Apostle's feast day.

On the 3rd, the feast of the invention of the Holy Cross, at Santa Croce[211] in Gerusalemme there is a Stations of the Cross, plenary remission of all sins and an infinite number of other similar indulgences.

On the same day, the consecration of Santa Maria della Rotonda,[212] there is plenary remission of all sins.

On the 4th, the feast of Saint Monica, at the church of Sant'Agostino, there are infinite indulgences.

On the 6th, the feast of Saint John before the Latin Gate, there is plenary remission of all sins.

On the same day, there is a Stations of the Cross at San Giovanni in Laterano, **[page [76]]** plenary remission of all sins and the liberation of a soul from Purgatory.

On the 8th, the feast of the apparition of Saint Michael, there is a Stations of the Cross at his church[213] and plenary remission of all sins.

On the feast of the translation of Saint Jerome, there is plenary remission of all sins.

On the 12th, the feast of Saints Nereus [and] Achilleus, there is plenary remission of all sins.

On the feast of Saint Victor and Saint Corona, there is plenary remission of sins.

On the 19th, the feast of Saint Pudentiana, there is plenary remission of all sins.

On the 20th, the feast of Saint Bernardino of the Order of Saint Francis, there is a Stations of the Cross at Santa Maria in Aracoeli and plenary remission of all sins.

On the 21st, the feast of Saint Helena, plenary indulgence.

Please note that from the above-mentioned feast of Saint Bernardino until the first of August at San Giovanni in Laterano, every day there is plenary remission of all sins.

Please note that on the Monday before the Ascension of our Lord Jesus Christ, there are processions to Saint Peter's, and here there are 28 thousand years of indulgence and the same number of quarantines.

On the feast of our Lord's Ascension, **[page [77]]** there is a Stations of the Cross at Saint Peter's, and here there are 28 thousand years [of indulgence] and the same number of quarantines.

On the vigil of the feast of Pentecost, there is a Stations of the Cross at San Giovanni in Laterano, and here there are 15 thousand years [of indulgence], and plenary remission of all sins.

On the feast of Pentecost, there is a Stations of the Cross at Saint Peter's, and here there is plenary remission of all sins; thereafter there are infinite indulgences.

On Monday, there is a Stations of the Cross at San Pietro in Vincoli, and here there is plenary remission of all sins.

On Tuesday, there is a Stations of the Cross at Sant'Anastasia, and here there are 18 thousand years of indulgence.

On Wednesday, there is a Stations of the Cross at Santa Maria Maggiore, and here there are 28 thousand years of indulgence and the same number of quarantines. There is plenary remission of a third of all sins, and also plenary remission of all sins.

† On Thursday, there is a Stations of the Cross at San Lorenzo fuori le mura, and here there are 18 thousand years of indulgence and the same number of quarantines. There is plenary remission of a third of all sins, and also plenary remission of all sins, not to mention the liberation of a soul from the pains of Purgatory.

On Friday, there is a Stations of the Cross at Santi Apostoli, and here there are 18 thousand years of indulgence and plenary **[page [78]]** remission of all sins.

† On Saturday, there is a Stations of the Cross at Saint Peter's, and here there are 18 thousand years of indulgence and the same number of quarantines. There is plenary remission of all sins and the liberation of a soul from Purgatory.

On the feast of Corpus Christi, there is a Stations of the Cross at Saint Peter's, and here there is plenary remission of all sins and also for the whole of the octave.

The month of June

On the second Sunday in June, there is a Stations of the Cross at Santa Maria della Consolazione and here there is plenary remission of all sins.

On the 2nd, on the feast of Saint Marcellinus, there is plenary indulgence.

On the 11th, on the feast of Saint Barnabas, Apostle, there is plenary remission of all sins.

On the 13th, on the feast of Saint Anthony of Padua, there is a Stations of the Cross at Santa Maria in Aracoeli and there is plenary remission of all sins.

On the 15th, on the feast of Saints Vitus, Modestus and Crescentia, there is a Stations of the Cross at San Vito in Macello,[214] and here there are six thousand years of indulgence.

On the 24th, on the feast of Saint John the Baptist, there is a Stations of the Cross at San Giovanni in Laterano and plenary remission of all sins.

On the 28th, on the day before the feast of Saint Peter and Saint Paul, there is a Stations of the Cross at Saint Peter's and here there is plenary remission of all sins.

[page [79]]
On the 29th, on the feast of Saint Peter and Saint Paul, there is a Stations of the Cross at Saint Peter's and here there is plenary remission of all sins, as there is for the feast day of each of the twelve Apostles.

On the 30th, on the feast of Saint Paul, there is a Stations of the Cross at San Paolo, and there is plenary remission of all sins, not to mention infinite indulgences.

The month of July

On the 2nd, on the feast of the Visitation of the Virgin Mary, there is a Stations of the Cross at Santa Maria del Popolo and plenary remission of all sins. On the same day, there is a Stations of the Cross at Santa Maria della Pace, and here there is plenary remission of all sins. And for the octave of the above-mentioned Visitation, every day there is plenary remission of sins and innumerable and infinite other indulgences.

On the feast of Saint Bonaventure, which is on the second Sunday in July,[215] there is a Stations of the Cross at Saint Peter's and here there is plenary remission of all sins.

On the 15th, on the feast of Saint Cyricus, there is remission of sins.

On the 17th, on the feast of Saint Alexis, there is a Stations of the Cross at his church, and here there is plenary remission of all sins.

On the 20th, on the feast of Saint Margaret, plenary indulgence.

On the 21st, on the feast of Saint Praxedes, indulgence of six thousand years of pardon.

[page [80]]
On the 22nd, on the feast of Saint Mary Magdalene, there is a Stations of the Cross at her church,[216] and here there is plenary remission of all sins and infinite and innumerable other indulgences.

On the 23rd, on the feast of Saint Apollinaris, there is remission of sins.

On the 25th, on the feast of Saint James, Apostle, there is a Stations of the Cross at his church and here there is plenary remission of all sins.

On the 26th, on the feast of Saint Anne, plenary indulgence.

On the 29th, on the feast of Saint Martha, plenary indulgence.

On the 30th, on the feast of Saints Abdon and Sennen, there is a Stations of the Cross at San Marco and here there is plenary remission of all sins.

The month of August

On the 1st, on the feast of Saint Peter's Chains, there is a Stations of the Cross at that church[217] and here there is plenary remission of all sins.

On the 3rd, on the feast of the invention of the body of Saint Stephen, there is a Stations of the Cross at San Lorenzo fuori le mura (where his body lies), and here there is plenary remission of all sins.

On the 5th, on the feast of Our Lady of the Snow, there is plenary remission of all sins.

On the 5th, on the feast of Saint Dominic, there is a Stations of the Cross at Santa Maria sopra Minerva and here there is plenary remission of all sins.

On the 6th, on the feast of the Transfiguration of Jesus Christ, there is a Stations of the Cross at San Giovanni in Laterano and here there is **[page [81]]** plenary remission of all sins.

On the 8th, on the feast of Saint Chiriacco, there is plenary remission of sins.

On the 10th, on the feast of Saint Lawrence and also for the whole octave, at San Lorenzo fuori le mura, one of the seven churches in which his body lies, there is plenary remission of all sins.

On the 12th, on the feast of Saint Chiara of the Order of Saint Francis, there is a Stations of the Cross at San Silvestro and here there is plenary remission of all sins.

On the 15th, on the feast of the Assumption of the Madonna and for the whole octave, there is a Stations of the Cross at Santa Maria Maggiore and there is plenary remission of all sins. On this day there is also a Stations of the Cross at Santa Maria della Rotonda, Santa Maria del Popolo and Santa Maria in Aracoeli. At all of these churches there is plenary indulgence and remission of all sins.

On the 16th, on the feast of Saint Roch, there is plenary indulgence.

On the 21st, at Sant'Anastasia, there is remission of sins.

On the 22nd, in the octave of the Assumption mentioned above, there is a Stations of the Cross at Santa Maria in Trastevere and here there is plenary remission of all sins.

On the 26th, on the feast of Saint Louis of the French, there is plenary indulgence. Please note that beginning on the day of the feast of the Assumption of the Madonna until the Nativity, every day there are 12 thousand years of indulgence **[page [82]]** and remission of a third of all sins.

On the 19th, on the feast of Saint Louis, Bishop, who was a monk of Saint Francis, there is a Stations of the Cross at Santa Maria in Aracoeli and here there is plenary remission of all sins.

On the 25th, on the feast of Saint Bartholomew, Apostle, there is plenary remission of all sins.

On the 28th, on the feast of Saint Augustine, Doctor, there is a Stations of the Cross at his church and here there is plenary remission of all sins.

On the 29th, on the feast of the Beheading of Saint John the Baptist, there is a Stations of the Cross at San Giovanni in Laterano and here there is plenary remission of all sins.

The month of September

On the 1st, on the feast of Saint Egidio, plenary indulgence.

On the 8th, on the feast of the Nativity of the Madonna, there is a Stations of the Cross at Santa Maria Maggiore, Santa Maria della Rotonda, Santa Maria in Aracoeli, Santa Maria Inviolata, Santa Maria della Pace and Santa Maria del Popolo, and at all of these churches there is plenary remission of all sins.

On the 10th, on the feast of Saint Nicholas of Tolentino, there is a Stations of the Cross at Santa Maria del Popolo and at Sant'Agostino, and at both there is plenary remission of all sins.

On the 20th, on the feast of Saint Eustace, remission of sins.

On the 24th, on the feast of the Exaltation of the Holy Cross and also on every day in the octave, [at Santa Croce] in Gerusalemme there is plenary remission of all sins **[page [83]]** and there is plenary remission of all sins.[218]

On the Wednesday after Holy Cross in September, as for all the Ember days, there is a Stations of the Cross at Santa Maria Maggiore and there are 28 thousand years of indulgence, the same number of quarantines and remission of a third of all sins.

On the Friday, there is a Stations of the Cross at Santi Apostoli, and

there are 18 thousand years of indulgence and plenary remission of all
sins.

On the Saturday, there is a Stations of the Cross at Saint Peter's and
there are 28 thousand years of indulgence, the same number of
quarantines, and remission of a third of all sins.

On the 21st, on the feast of Saint Matthew, Apostle and Evangelist,
there is a Stations of the Cross at his church[219] and here there is plenary
remission of all sins.

On the 27th, on the feast of Saints Cosmas and Damian, plenary
indulgence.

On the 29th, on the feast of Saint Michael, there is a Stations of the
Cross at his church[220] and here there is plenary remission of sins.

On the 30th, on the feast of Saint Jerome, there is a Stations of the
Cross at Santa Maria Maggiore, where his body lies, and there is plenary
remission of all sins.

The month of October

On the 4th, on the feast of Saint Francis, Founder and Father of the
Brothers of the Lesser Order, there is a Stations of the Cross at
San Francesco in Trastevere and here there is plenary **[page [84]]**
remission of all sins, and on the day of the octave there is plenary
remission of all sins.

On the 18th, on the feast of Saint Luke, there is plenary remission of
all sins.

On the 23rd, on the feast of Saint Theodore,[221] there is infinite pardon.

On the 28th, on the feast of Saint Simon and Saint Jude, there is a
Stations of the Cross at Saint Peter's and here there is plenary remission
of all sins and other indulgences.

The month of November

On the 1st, on the feast of All Saints, there is a Stations of the Cross at
Santa Maria della Rotonda and here there are many indulgences and
plenary remission of all sins, and this is for the whole octave.

On All Souls' Day, there is a Stations of the Cross at San Gregorio and
here there is plenary remission of all sins, both on this day and for the
whole octave. Such remission can also be had for the dead.

On the 7th, on the feast of the dedication of the churches of San
Pietro and San Paolo, there is a Stations of the Cross at San Pietro and
here there is plenary remission of all sins. On that day, separately, there is

a Stations of the Cross at San Paolo and here there is plenary remission of all sins.

On the 8th, on the feast of the Santi Quattro Coronati, plenary indulgence.

On the 9th, on the feast of the Dedication of our Saviour, there is a Stations of the Cross at San Giovanni in Laterano and here there is plenary remission of all sins.

On the 10th, on the feast of Saint Trifone, there are 10 thousand years [of indulgence].

[page [85]]

On the 11th, on the feast of Saint Martin, there is a Stations of the Cross at Saint Peter's and here there is plenary remission of all sins.

On the 21st, on the feast of the Presentation of the Glorious Virgin Mary, there is a Stations of the Cross at Santa Maria Maggiore and here there is plenary remission of all sins.

On the 22nd, on the feast of Saint Cecilia, there is a Stations of the Cross at her church[222] and here there is plenary remission of all sins.

On the 23rd, on the feast of Saint Clement, Pope, there is a Stations of the Cross at his church[223] and here there is plenary remission of all sins.

On the 25th, on the feast of Saint Catherine, Virgin and Martyr, there is a Stations of the Cross at her church[224] and here there is plenary remission of all sins.

On the 26th, on the feast of Saint Chrysogonus,[225] there is plenary indulgence.

On the 30th, on the feast of Saint Andrew, Apostle, there is a Stations of the Cross at Saint Peter's and here there is plenary remission of all sins.

The month of December

The Stations of the Cross in Advent

On the first Sunday, there is a Stations of the Cross at Santa Maria Maggiore, and here there are 28 thousand years of indulgence, the same number of quarantines, and remission of a third of all sins.

On the same day there is a Stations of the Cross at Saint Peter's and here there is **[page [86]]** remission of all sins.

Likewise, there are a thousand years of indulgence for all the feasts of the Madonna.

On the second Sunday, there is a Stations of the Cross at Santa Croce in Gerusalemme and here there is plenary remission of all sins and

11 thousand years of indulgence. Saint Sylvester increased the number of the said indulgences.

On the third Sunday, there is a Stations of the Cross at Saint Peter's, and there are 28 thousand years of indulgence, the same number of quarantines and plenary remission of all sins.

On the fourth Sunday, there is a Stations of the Cross at Saint Peter's and here there is plenary indulgence and remission of all sins. On the same day, there is a Stations of the Cross at Santi Apostoli and here there are 28 thousand years of indulgence and plenary remission of all sins.

On the 2nd, on the feast of Saint Bibiana, there is a Stations of the Cross at her church[226] and there is plenary remission of all sins.

On the 4th, on the feast of Saint Barbara, there are 16 thousand years of indulgence.

On the 5th, on the feast of Saint Savo, there is remission of sins.

On the 6th, on the feast of Saint Nicholas, Bishop, there is a Stations of the Cross at San Nicola in Carcere and here there is plenary remission of all sins.

On the 7th, on the feast of Saint Ambrose, there is plenary remission of all sins.

[page [87]]

On the 8th, on the feast of the Conception of the Glorious Virgin Mary, there is a Stations of the Cross at Santa Maria Maggiore, [Santa Maria] della Rotonda, Santa Maria in Aracoeli, Santa Maria del Popolo and Santa Maria della Pace. At all these churches there is plenary indulgence and remission of all sins for the whole of the octave.

On the 13th, on the feast of Saint Lucy, Virgin and Martyr, there is plenary remission of all sins.

On the Wednesday after the feast of Saint Lucy, as for all the Ember Days, there is a Stations of the Cross at Santa Maria Maggiore, and there are 28 thousand years of indulgence, the same number of quarantines and remission of a third of all sins and plenary remission of all sins.

On the Friday, there is a Stations of the Cross at Santi Apostoli and here there are 10 thousand years of plenary indulgence and remission of all sins.

On the Saturday, there is a Stations of the Cross at Saint Peter's and here there are 28 thousand years of indulgence and the same number of quarantines.

On the 21st, on the feast of Saint Thomas, Apostle, there is plenary remission of all sins.

On the 24th, on the eve of the Nativity of our Lord Jesus Christ, there
is a Stations of the Cross at Santa Maria Maggiore, and there are
28 thousand years of indulgence, the same number of quarantines and
remission of a third of all sins.

[page [88]]

On the 25th, on the feast of the Nativity of Jesus Christ, there is a
Stations of the Cross at Santa Maria Maggiore, when they sing the first
mass and here there is plenary remission of all sins. On the same night,
there is a Stations of the Cross at Santa Maria in Aracoeli and here there
is plenary remission of all sins.

At the dawn mass, there is a Stations of the Cross at Sant'Anastasia and
here there are 28 thousand years of indulgence, the same number of
quarantines, and remission of all sins.

On the 25th, during the day, there is a Stations of the Cross at Santa
Maria in Aracoeli and there is plenary remission of all sins.

At the high mass, there is a Stations of the Cross at Santa Maria
Maggiore and here there is plenary remission of all sins.

Likewise, there is a Stations of the Cross at Santa Maria in Aracoeli.
At Santa Maria Maggiore, on the same day, in the Capella del Presepio of
our Lord Jesus Christ, there are 28 thousand years of indulgence, the
same number of quarantines and plenary remission of all sins.

On the 26th, on the feast of Saint Stephen, Protomartyr, there is a
Stations of the Cross at San Lorenzo fuori le mura, where his body lies,
and here there is plenary remission of all sins. On the same day, there is a
Stations of the Cross at Santo Stefano on the Celian Hill, and there are
28 thousand years of indulgence, the same number of quarantines and
plenary remission **[page [89]]** of all sins.

On the 27th, on the feast of Saint John, Evangelist, there is a Stations
of the Cross at Santa Maria Maggiore and here there is plenary remission
of all sins. On the same day, there is a Stations of the Cross at San
Giovanni in Laterano and here there are 28 thousand years of indulgence,
the same number of quarantines and plenary remission of all sins.

On the 28th, on the feast of the Holy Innocents, there is a Stations of
the Cross at San Paolo and here there are 15 thousand years of indulgence, the same number of quarantines and plenary remission of all sins.

On the 31st, on the feast of Saint Sylvester, there is a Stations of the
Cross at his church[227] and here there is plenary remission of all sins.

[page [90]]

In addition to those described above, the following are the special indulgences and Stations of the Cross granted by the High Pontiffs in the various churches in Rome

At Saint Peter's, every day there are six thousand years of indulgence.

At San Paolo, Apostolo, every day there are six thousand years of indulgence.

At Santo Spirito, every day there are six thousand years of indulgence.

At Santa Maria Maggiore, every day there are six thousand years of indulgence.

At San Giovanni, Apostolo e Evangelista, every day there are six thousand years of indulgence.

At San Sebastiano, every day there are six thousand years of indulgence.

At Sant'Anastasio, Martire, every day there are six thousand years of indulgence.

At Santa Croce in Gerusalemme, every day there are six thousand years of indulgence.

At San Lorenzo fuori le mura, every day there are six thousand years of indulgence.

At San Vito in Macello,[228] every day there are six thousand years of indulgence.

At Sant'Agnese, every day there are six thousand years of indulgence.

At Santa Prassede, every day there are six thousand years of **[page [91]]** indulgence.

At Santa Maria que dicitur libera nos a poenis inferni,[229] every day there are eight thousand years of indulgence at the place where Saint Silvester, Pope, bound the dragon.

At Santa Maria Scala Coeli, where ten thousand martyrs are buried, every day there are ten thousand years of indulgence.

At Santa Maria Annunciata, every day there are ten thousand years of indulgence.

At Santa Bibiana, five thousand martyrs were buried, not including the women and children. Every day there are nine thousand years of indulgence.

At the church mentioned above, on All Saints' Day, there are six hundred thousand years of true indulgence.

At Santa Prassede, every day there are one hundred and twenty thousand years of indulgence, the same number of quarantines and remission of a third of all sins.

At SS Cosma e Damiano, every day, for each time you enter the church there are a thousand years of indulgence granted by Saint Gregory, Pope.

At Sant'Eusebio, every day there are 7,800 thousand years of indulgence and the same number of quarantines.

At Santa Pudenziana, there are more than three thousand bodies of holy martyrs buried in the cemetery of Pristilo. Here, for each body there is one year of indulgence, **[page [92]]** a quarantine, and remission of a third of all our sins, granted by the Blessed Pope Simplicius.

At the church of Sant'Alessio, every day there are one hundred years of indulgence and the same number of quarantines.

At that place where Saint Peter said 'Domine, quo vadis', there are many indulgences.[230]

At the church of Santa Balbina, every day there are seven years of indulgence.

At the church called Santa Maria Imperatrice, there are 15 thousand years of indulgence each time you go there and you recite three Pater Nosters and three Ave Marias while kneeling. This was granted by Saint Gregory, Pope, because of the image of our Lady that spoke to him.

At the church of San Matteo, Apostolo, every day there are a thousand years of indulgence, the same number of quarantines and remission of a seventh of all our sins.

Please note that wherever there is a star
on the exterior, this means that here
a soul is liberated from Purgatory.

END

APPENDIX
THE LETTER TO LEO X BY RAPHAEL AND BALDASSARE CASTIGLIONE
(*c.*1519)

The letter to Pope Leo X (r.1513–21) concerning the ancient monuments of Rome is widely accepted as the joint work of Raphael and the humanist Baldassare Castiglione (1478–1529), possibly with the help of Antonio da Sangallo the Younger (1484–1546), and was probably written in 1519 and revised a year later. The following is a translation of this revised, so-called 'Munich' version.[1] The script of this Munich manuscript has been identified as the hand of the collector and

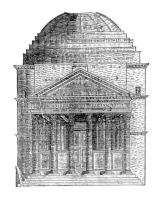

epigraphist Angelo Colocci (1474–1544), with corrections by Raphael.[2] (A woodcut of the Pantheon from *Epigrammata Antiquae Urbis* (1521), which is credited to Colocci, is illustrated here.) The complete manuscript of what is thought to be the earlier version is now lost but is known through the earliest published version of the letter, in the collected works of Baldassare Castiglione published in Padua in 1733. In

1 Held in the Bayerische Staatsbibliothek, Munich, ref: Codex Italic. 37b. Transcribed most recently in Bonelli, R., et al. (eds), *Scritti rinascimentali di architettura* (1978), pp. 461–84; Rowland, I., 'Raphael, Angelo Colocci, and the Genesis of the Architectural Orders', *Art Bulletin*, vol. 76 (March 1994), pp. 81–104; Di Teodoro, F.P., *Raffaello, Baldassar Castiglione e la Lettera a Leone X* (1994, 2003). Page numbers in our translation follow those in this manuscript, the first number indicating those in pencil in the manuscript and the second those in ink, as reproduced in Di Teodoro (1994).

2 Rowland (1994). See also Colocci, A., and J. Mazzocchi, *Epigrammata Antiquae Urbis* (1521).

addition, a draft (*minuta*) of the first parts of the text in the hand of
Castiglione has survived in the Castiglione family archives in Mantua.[3]
The Munich manuscript differs in much of its phraseology from the
printed version, and it substitutes sections on perspective and the
architectural Orders for the farewell remarks addressed to the Pope that
conclude the printed version (here translated in the endnotes). A detailed
study of the textual differences between these three versions, with
complete transcriptions and facsimiles, has now been published.[4] The
following is the first full English translation of the letter, which reveals
Renaissance interest in Rome's ancient monuments in the period leading
up to the publication of Palladio's two guidebooks.

161   Raphael and Giulio Romano, *Apparition
of the Cross*, detail showing monuments of
ancient Rome, *c.*1520, Vatican, Sala di
Costantino.

3   Held in the Archivio Castiglioni, Mantua (part of the Archivio di Stato di
Mantova, held in the former College and Convent of the Jesuits), ref: Doc.
Sciolti, a), n. 12. See Di Teodoro (1994).

4   Di Teodoro (1994). See also Bonelli et al. (1978). On two English
translations of this letter, based on these three versions, see the introduction,
above, note 70.

[83r [1r–a1]]

Most Holy Father, there are many who, on bringing their feeble judgement to bear on what is written concerning the great achievements of the Romans – the feats of arms, the city of Rome and the wondrous skill shown in the opulence, ornamentation and grandeur of their buildings – have come to the conclusion that these achievements are more likely to be fables than fact. I, however, have always seen – and still do see – things differently. Because, bearing in mind the divine quality of the ancients' intellects, as revealed in the remains still to be seen among the ruins of Rome, I do not find it unreasonable to believe that much of what we consider impossible seemed, for them, exceedingly simple. With this in mind, since I have been so completely taken up by these antiquities – not only in making every effort to consider them in great detail and measure them carefully but also in assiduously reading the best authors and comparing the built works with the writings of those authors – I think that I have managed to acquire a certain understanding of the ancient way of architecture. This is something that gives me, simultaneously, enormous pleasure – from the intellectual appreciation of such an excellent matter – and extreme pain – at the sight of what you could almost call the corpse of this great, noble city, once queen of the world, so cruelly butchered.[5] Hence, given that all men owe respect to their parents and to their native lands, I feel obliged to muster what little ability I have so that, as far as **[83v [1v]]** possible, an image may survive – barely more than a shadow – of what is in fact the universal homeland for all Christians and which at one time was so noble and powerful that the men of those times began to think that she alone of all cities on earth was above fate and, contrary to nature, not subject to death but would last forever. At that point it would appear that time, envious of the glory of mortals and yet not fully confident in its own strength alone, worked in concert with fate and the wicked, infidel barbarians who, in addition to time's gouging file and poisonous bite, brought the fierce

---

5   For similar themes, see the dedicatory letter to Pope Eugenius IV (r.1431–47) in Flavio Biondo's *Roma instaurata* (1446), and the opening of Alberti's *De pictura*. See also Di Teodoro (1994), pp. 159–67. Raphael may have acquired the books, papers and instruments of the architectural theorist Fra Giovanni Giocondo (c.1434–1515) on the latter's death in 1515, and been influenced by Fra Giocondo's Roman studies. See Müntz, E., 'Les architects de St. Pierre de Rome d'après des documents nouveaux (1447–1549)', *Gazette des Beaux-Arts*, vol. 2 (1879), pp. 506–24.

onslaught of fire and steel. Thus those celebrated buildings that would today have been in the full flower of their beauty were burnt and destroyed by the evil wrath and pitiless violence of criminal men – or should I say beasts – although the destruction is not entire, for the framework survives almost intact, but without the ornaments; you could almost describe this as the bones of a body without the flesh.[6] And yet, why are we complaining about the Goths, Vandals and other perfidious enemies of the Latin name when the very men who as fathers and guardians should have defended Rome's impoverished remains nevertheless spent a great deal of time and energy trying to destroy those relics and to expunge their memory? How many Pontiffs, Holy **[77r [2r–a2]]** Father – men who held the same office as Your Holiness but who had neither your wisdom nor your qualities or magnanimity – how many of these Pontiffs, I say again, allowed ancient temples, statues, arches and other buildings – the glory of their founders – to fall prey to ruin and spoliation? How many of them allowed the excavation of the foundations simply to get at some pozzolana, such that in a very short time those buildings collapsed? What quantity of mortar was made from the statues and other ornaments of the ancients? I would go so far as to say that this entirely new Rome that can be seen today – grand, beautiful and marvellously ornamented with palaces, churches and other buildings though it may be – is built using mortar made from ancient marbles.[7] Not without great suffering can I reflect upon the fact that during the time I have been in Rome – which is more or less twelve years now – many fine things have been ruined: for example, the Meta that was in the Via Alexandrina, the arch that was once at the entrance to the Baths of Diocletian, the Temple of Ceres in the Via Sacra and a part of the Forum Transitorium, which only a few days ago was consumed by fire, some of the marbles being made into mortar, the greater part of the basilica in the forum being ruined, [. . . . . . .][8] and in addition to this the multitude of columns being damaged or broken in two and the many architraves and **[77v [2v]]** fine friezes reduced to fragments, such that it was an outrage similarly for our times to have tolerated such a thing. Indeed you could say that such actions make Hannibal, to name but one, look God-

---

6 For bones and flesh as an architectural metaphor, see Alberti, III. vi [p. 69] and III. viii [pp. 71–3].

7 For contemporary complaints regarding the destruction of ancient works to make mortar, see Di Teodoro (1994), pp. 171–2.

8 A blank space appears here in the manuscript.

fearing.[9] Therefore, Holy Father, let it not be the lowest of Your
Holiness's priorities to ensure that – out of respect to those divine spirits,
the remembrance of whom encourages and incites to virtue the intellects
among us today – what little remains of this ancient mother of the glory
and renown of Italy is not to be completely destroyed and ruined by the
wicked and the ignorant. Unfortunately even here these people have
perpetrated evil deeds against those souls who, through their blood,
brought so much glory to the world, to this state and to us Italians.[10]
Rather, by preserving the example of the ancients, may Your Holiness
seek to equal and better them, as indeed you have done through your
magnificent buildings, by supporting and favouring the virtues,
reawakening genius, rewarding virtuous endeavours, and by sowing that
most holy seed of peace among Christian princes. Because, just as the
calamity of war engenders the destruction and ruination of all the
branches of learning and the arts, so peace and concord bring about the
happiness of peoples and the worthy leisure through which it is possible
to work in all these branches **[78r [3r-a3]]** and to reach the summit of
excellence. Everyone hopes that, through the divine wisdom and
authority of Your Holiness, this shall take place in this our age. For this is
what it means to be the Most Merciful Shepherd, indeed the Excellent
Father of the whole world.

   However, to return to the matter I mentioned briefly earlier, I record
that Your Holiness commanded me to make a drawing of ancient Rome
– at least as far as can be understood from that which can be seen today –
with those buildings that are sufficiently well preserved such that they
can be drawn out exactly as they were, without error, using true
principles, and making those members that are entirely ruined and have
completely disappeared correspond with those that are still standing and
can be seen. To this end I used all the diligence of which I was capable,
such that the mind of Your Holiness, and of all those who in future may
delight in this work of mine, might not be confused, but well satisfied.
And even though I took that which I intend to show from many Latin
authors, I nevertheless followed principally and above all P.[ublius]

---

9   This is a quotation from Francesco Petrarch's canzone 'Spirto gentil, che
quelle membra reggi', *Canzoniere*, LIII, 65. For a detailed discussion of the
buildings destroyed and the excavations undertaken in Rome between 1515 and
1520, see Lanciani, R., *The Destruction of Ancient Rome* (1901).
   10   For passages in the works of Castiglione expressing similar sentiments,
see Di Teodoro (1994), pp. 174–5.

Victor,[11] who, since he was one of the last, could give more detailed
information on the latest things while not omitting the ancient things –
indeed, it can be seen that his description of the *regiones* agrees with what
can be seen depicted on certain ancient marbles.

[78*v* [3*v*]]

And since telling the difference between ancient and modern buildings,
or between those more ancient and less ancient, might seem to some to
be difficult, and so as not to leave any doubt whatsoever in the mind of
someone who wishes to acquire this ability to discriminate, I say that this
can be done with very little effort. The fact is, there are only three styles
[*maniere*] of buildings in Rome: the first is that built by the worthy
ancients, who lasted from the first emperors up until the time when
Rome was destroyed and ruined by the Goths and other barbarians; the
second lasted for the period that Rome was dominated by the Goths and
one hundred years thereafter; the third, from that time up until our
time.[12] Taking modern buildings, they are very recognizable, both since
they are new and since they have not yet quite equalled either the
excellence or the immense expenditure that can be seen and recognized
in ancient buildings. Because, even though these days architecture may be
very clever and very closely based on the style of the ancients, as can be
seen in the many beautiful works by Bramante, nevertheless the
ornamentation is not done using raw materials of similar expense to
those used by the ancients, who, it seems, realized what they envisaged
with endless amounts of money and whose will alone surmounted every
difficulty.[13] As for the buildings of the Goth period, **[79*r* [4*r*–a4]]** they
are completely lacking in any grace [*gratia*] whatsoever, have no style and
are different from those ancient and those modern. And as for those from
the period of the emperors, they are not very difficult to recognize, for
these buildings are the most excellent, built in the best style and with the
greatest expense and artistry of all. It is only these latter that we intend to
demonstrate; but let no one be in two minds as to whether, among

11   The fictitious (perhaps deliberately invented) author of *De regionibus urbis
Romae libellus aureus*, published by Giano Aulo Parrasio in Rome in 1503.

12   On this chronology, see Di Teodoro (1994), pp. 180–1.

13   For a discussion of this passage and its links with Raphael's fresco 'The
Fire in the Borgo', see Onians, J., 'Storia dell'Architettura e Storia della
Religione: Bramante, Raffaello e Baldassare Peruzzi', in *Roma e l'antico nell'arte e
nella cultura del Cinquecento*, ed. M. Fagiolo (1985), p. 143.

ancient buildings, those less ancient were less beautiful, less well conceived [*inteso*] or in another style. The fact is, they were all of the same theory [*ragione*]. And, even though very frequently many edifices underwent rebuilding at the hands of the ancients themselves – for it is written that upon the very site where Nero's Golden House once stood, Titus's Baths, his house and amphitheatre were subsequently built[14] – nevertheless they were constructed in the same style and with the same theory as other buildings even more ancient than Nero's time as well as those contemporary with his Golden House. And, despite the fact that literature, sculpture, painting and almost all the other arts had been for a long time in decline and deteriorating up to the time of the last emperors, nonetheless architecture was respected and good theory was maintained, and building was executed in the same style as before. Of all the arts, **[79*v* [4*v*]]** it was architecture that was the last to be lost; this can be understood from many things, but most notably from the Arch of Constantine, whose composition is beautiful and well executed as regards everything concerning its architecture, while, on the other hand, the sculptures on this arch are appalling, without any skill or good design [*disegno*]. Those sculptures that are spoils from the periods of Trajan and of Antoninus Pius are excellent and in a perfect style. The same can be seen in the Baths of Diocletian. The sculptures of his time are in an awful style and badly made, and the remains of the paintings that can be seen have nothing whatsoever in common with those of the times of Trajan and of Titus, and yet the architecture is noble and well conceived. However, as a result of the fact that Rome was completely ruined, burnt and destroyed by the barbarians, it seems that, along with the buildings, this fire and wretched ruin also burnt and ruined the art of building. Hence, since the fortune of the Romans had so altered, and instead of endless victories and triumphs there had come the calamity and wretchedness of slavery, and since it was not appropriate for those who had been subjugated and been made slaves of others to live in the way and with the same grandeur as before when they had subjugated the barbarians, suddenly, along with **[80*r* [5*r*]]** their fortune, their way of building and living changed, and this new way appeared as diametrically opposed to the other as servitude is to liberty. And this building manner became reduced to a style that matched their wretchedness – one without skill, measure or any grace whatsoever. It seems that, when they

14   For a detailed discussion of these and the following monuments mentioned in the letter, see Di Teodoro (1994), pp. 182–7.

lost their empire, the men of that time also lost all their inspiration and artistry, and they became so ignorant that they appeared not even to know how to fire bricks, let alone make other sorts of ornaments. They began to strip ancient walls in order to remove the bricks, breaking the marble into small blocks, and they started to build with both, compartitioning the walls using that mixture, as can be seen today in the tower that they call 'delle Milizie'.[15] And so, for some time they continued in that ignorance that can be seen in everything dating from that period. And it would appear that this hateful and merciless storm of war and destruction also reached as far as Greece, once the homeland of the inventors and perfect masters of all the arts, since here too there arose a dreadful and completely worthless style in painting, sculpture and architecture.[16] Subsequently, almost everywhere the style of German architecture began to appear, as can still **[80v [5v]]** be seen in the ornamentation, which is far removed from the beautiful style of that of Rome and of the ancients. The ancients had, not only in the structure of the entire building but also in the very beautiful cornices, friezes and architraves, columns, capitals and bases, and in short all the other ornaments, a perfect and beautiful style.[17] And the Germans, whose style still persists in many places, often support a beam using decorative brackets composed of small hunched figures – both badly made and worse conceived – or of outlandish animals, patterns and foliage, not governed by any theory whatsoever. Yet this architecture did once have a theory because it took its origin from trees that had not yet been pruned; the Germans would bend the branches together and bind them to form their pointed arches.[18] However, despite the fact that this origin ought not entirely to be despised, the work is nevertheless weak. Because huts made with their timbers bound together and placed as columns with their ridges and coverings, as Vitruvius describes when discussing the origin of Doric work, would be much sturdier than pointed arches,

15   To 'compartition' is to divide a façade or plan into smaller, measurable units. See Alberti, I. 2 [p. 8], I. 9 [pp. 23–4]. On the 'Torre delle Milizie', see Palladio, *Antiquities*, fol. 29r. See also Krautheimer, R., *Rome, Profile of a City, 312-1308* (1980), pp. 317–19.

16   On this see Rowland (1994), p. 101, n. 6.

17   Here the Mantua *minuta* adds 'with the proportions of a man and a woman'.

18   See Vitruvius, *De architectura*, II.i.4, in reference to Gaul and the 'barbarian' fashion.

which have two centres.[19] It is for this reason that a semicircle supports much better, following mathematical theory, because all of its lines are drawn to a single **[81r [6r]]** centre. And in addition to the weakness, to our eyes a pointed arch does not have grace; the perfection of the circle is pleasing to our eyes, and it can be observed that nature almost never tends towards any other form.[20] But there is no need to talk about Roman architecture in order to compare it with barbarian architecture, because the difference is very recognizable. Nor is there any need to describe such architecture's arrangement [*ordine*] since this has already been excellently treated by Vitruvius. It is therefore enough to know that the buildings in Rome, right up to the time of the last emperors, were always built with good architectural theory; thus the later buildings always matched the ancient ones. Hence there is no difficulty in telling these apart from those that date from the time of the Goths, and also from many years after that, because the two are almost what you could call diametrically opposed extremes. Nor is there any difficulty in telling our modern buildings apart from Gothic ones, if for no other reason than their newness, by which they are very recognizable.

Thus having been sufficiently clear concerning which ancient buildings in Rome we wish to demonstrate, and also how easy it is to distinguish them from the rest, all that remains is to tell you of the way in which we decided to survey [*misurare*] and draw [*disegnare*] them, so that **[81v [6v]]** whoever wishes to work in architecture will know how to do both one and the other without making mistakes. Be well aware that in our drawing up of this work we did not allow ourselves to be governed by chance or practice alone, but we worked with excellent theory. As for the method we used – surveying with a magnetic compass [*bussola della calamita*] – since I have never seen it mentioned nor learnt of its use by any of the ancients, I think that it was invented by the moderns.[21] However, it seems to me to be worthwhile to give careful instruction in it to those who know nothing about it. You should therefore make yourself an instrument that is spherical and flat, like an astrolabe, and has a diameter of two palms – it may be more or less,

19   Vitrivius, *De architectura*, IV.i.

20   Alberti, III. xiii [pp. 81–4].

21   For this method of surveying, see Alberti's *Ludi rerum mathematicarum*, ed. C. Grayson (1973), p. 161, and his *Descriptio Urbis Romae* (see Alberti, L.B., 'Leon Battista Alberti's Delineation of the City of Rome', trans. P. Hicks, in 'Leonis Baptistae Alberti Descriptio urbis Romae', *Albertiana*, vol. 6 (2003), pp. 125–215).

following the judgement of the person who wants to use it. We will divide the circumference of this instrument into eight equal parts, and in each of those parts we will set the name of one of the eight winds, dividing these winds up into a further thirty-two smaller parts, which are to be called degrees. And so, from the first degree marking the north wind [*tramontana*], we shall draw a straight line across the centre of the instrument as far as the circumference. And this line going towards the side opposite the first degree of the north wind will make the first degree of the south wind [*austro*]. In the same way, also from the circumference, we shall draw another line that, passing through the centre, will intersect **[82r [7r]]** the line that runs from the north wind to the south wind. This will create four right angles around the centre and, on one side of the circumference, will mark the first degree of the east wind [*levante*] and on the other the first degree of the west wind [*ponente*]. And so, between these lines that make the four principal winds mentioned above, there will remain the space for the other four collateral winds, namely *greco*, *libeccio*, *maestro* and *scirocco*.[22] These are to be drawn using the same degrees and procedures mentioned for the others. Having done all this, at the centre point, where the lines intersect, we shall insert an iron 'umbillicus' – a very straight and sharp small nail – as is done with the sundials that we see every day, upon which you should place the magnetic needle [*calamita*]. Then we shall cover this place for the magnetic needle with a glass cover – it could be a piece of very thin, transparent horn – such that it does not touch the needle and hence impede its movement. This is also so that the needle is not jogged by the wind. Then across the centre of the instrument we shall place a pointer as a diameter. This will not only indicate the relevant winds but also the degrees, just like the rings on the astrolabe. And this is to be called a sight [*traguardo*] and it should be arranged such that **[82v [7v]]** it can rotate while the rest of the instrument is motionless. With this, then, we will be able to survey any sort of building, whatever shape it may have, whether circular, rectangular or with as many unusual angles or corners as you will. The method for using it is as follows: in the place that you are to survey, set the instrument such that it is completely level – thus the magnetic needle will point straight – and such that it is very close to the wall[23] you wish to survey, as far as the perimeter of the instrument

22   The north-east, south-west, north-west and south-east winds respectively.

23   Colocci had written 'parte' ('part'). Raphael corrected this to 'parete' ('wall'). See Rowland (1994).

allows. And you should continue rotating this instrument until the magnetic needle points correctly towards the wind marked *tramontana*. When it is pointing fixedly in this direction, guide the sight with a wooden or bronze ruler exactly down the line of that wall or street, or whatever else you want to survey, keeping the instrument immobile so that the magnetic needle continues to point straight towards *tramontana*. Then note with which wind that wall lies parallel and to how many degrees. Take measurements with a perch or cubit or palm up to the furthest point in a straight line determined by the sight and write down this number; that is, so many cubits at so many degrees of *austro*, *scirocco* or whatever it may be. Now, since the sight **[84r [8r]]** no longer serves, you should then follow the direction it indicates in a straight line and start again with the next line to be plotted at the point where the one you have just measured ends. Then, aligning the sight with that next line, record in the same way the degrees of the wind and the total of the measurements, carrying on until you have gone around the whole building. We are of the opinion that this is sufficient as regards the surveying; even though the heights must be determined, they can easily be calculated using a quadrant.[24] And as for circular buildings, their centres can be calculated from the smallest part of the circle, as Euclid teaches in his third book.[25]

Having surveyed in the way mentioned and noted down the measurements and directions – that is, so many rods or palms at so many degrees of such and such a wind – in order to draw the whole accurately, it is opportune to have a paper version of the magnetic compass that is in scale with it and precisely subdivided in the same way, with the same degrees of the winds, which a man can use, as I shall show. Take then the sheet of paper upon which you wish to make the drawing[26] of the building you have measured. First of all, draw a line on it. This will serve as a guide, as it were, for the direction of the *tramontana*. Then place on top of it the paper that has the copy of the compass drawn on it and that you are to use to plot, and match up the two such that the line of the

---

24   For this use of the quadrant, see Francesco di Giorgio, *Trattati di architettura, ingegneria e arte militare*, ed. C. Maltese and L. Maltese Degrassi (1967), vol. 1, pp. 120–3.

25   Euclid, *The Elements*, Book 3, prop. 1.

26   The following text down to 'which the wall or street tended' is missing in the transcription in Rowland (1994) (from '*si vol disegnare . . .* to *si vol disegnare . . .*').

tramontana drawn on the copy **[84v [8v]]** aligns with the line drawn on the sheet of paper upon which you want to draw the building. Then, for the thing that you surveyed and that is to be drawn, look up the number of feet recorded when you measured it and the degrees of the wind towards which the wall or street tended, and then find the same degree marked on the drawn copy of the compass. And keeping that copy set firmly with its *tramontana* line against the other *tramontana* line drawn on the sheet of paper, draw the line to that degree straight through the centre of the drawn copy and onto the sheet of paper upon which you wish to make your drawing. Then note how many feet were plotted along the line of that degree, and mark on the line of that degree the same number using the scale of the 'small' feet.[27] Thus, for example, if you sight down a wall that is thirty feet long and six degrees to *levante*, measure thirty feet and mark them on. And continue thus, gradually, so that with practice it will become exceedingly easy. This will then be a drawing of the plan,[28] as it were, and a record for drawing all the rest.

And since the way of drawing specific to the architect is different from that for the painter, **[85r [9r–b1]]** I shall say what I think opportune so that all the measurements can be understood and all the members of the buildings can be determined without error. The way the architect draws buildings, then, is divided into three parts. The first part is the plan – what they mean is the 'flat' drawing. The second is the 'exterior wall', with its ornaments.[29] The third is the 'interior wall', also with its ornaments.[30] The plan is what compartitions the whole of the 'flat' area of the place where one is to build – what they mean is the drawing of the base of the whole building when it is still close to the level of the ground. This area, even if it were sloping, should be rendered flat, and you should make sure that the horizontal line at the base of the slope and the area that was rendered level are parallel with all the other levels of the building. For this, you should take the horizontal line at the base of the slope and not the curve of the slope, so that all the walls of the building drop onto that line plumb and perpendicularly. This drawing is called the 'plan', as was said, because this plan encompasses the base area of the entire building, just as the sole of the foot encompasses the space that is the foundation of the whole body.

27 That is, the general scale.
28 The Italian word is 'pianta', which also means 'the footprint'.
29 That is, the elevation.
30 That is, the section.

Once the plan has been drawn **[85ν [9ν]]** and compartitioned using its members with their widths – the members can be straight, curved or any shape whatsoever – you should draw, always measuring everything with the scale, a line that equals the width of the base of the entire building. From the central point along this line, draw another straight line that makes on either side two right angles; this will be the centre line of the building. From the two extremities of the width line draw two parallel lines, perpendicular with the base line; these two lines should be as tall as the building is to be (and in this way they will make the height of the building). Between these two lines at the extremities, which make the height, you should then measure off the columns, the pilasters, the windows and other ornaments drawn on the front part of the plan of the building. And do all this always drawing the lines from every single extremity point of the columns, pilasters, openings, or whatever else, such that these lines are parallel to the lines at the extremities.[31] Then, from side to side, set the heights of the column bases, the capitals, the window architraves, the friezes, cornices and the like. All this should be done using lines that are parallel with the ground line of the building.

[86r [10r–b2]] In drawings of this sort there is never to be any diminishing at the extremities, even if the building were circular – nor even if it were rectangular and this was done in order to make the drawing show two faces – because an architect cannot get correct measurements from a foreshortened line. This is necessary for such a discipline, which demands complete accuracy of measurements and lines drawn parallel, not lines that appear to be parallel but that are not. And if sometimes the measurements taken from a circular plan are foreshortened,[32] or diminished, they can easily be found in the drawing of the plan, and those foreshortened on the plan, such as vaults, arches and triangles, are in turn perfect in their elevations. Hence it is always necessary to have the correct measurements ready and prepared in palms, feet, digits and grains, right down to their smallest parts. The third part of such drawing is the one we mentioned and called 'interior wall', with its ornaments. This is no less necessary than the other two, and it is derived in the same way as with the 'exterior wall' from the plan and parallel lines. It shows the inside of the building – half, that is, as if cut down the middle. It shows the courtyard, with the correspondence **[86ν [10ν]]** of

31   These 'lines at the extremities' refer to the end verticals.

32   For the sentence to make sense, this has to be in reference to an elevation.

the heights of the exterior cornices with those inside, and the height of the windows, doors, arches and vaults (whether barrel, cross or any other type whatsoever). In short, with these three orders [*ordini*] or styles [*modi*], it is possible to consider in minute detail all the parts of any building, inside and out.

This is the way we have pursued and maintained, as can be seen in the prosecution of the whole of this work of ours. And so that it can be understood even more easily we have set below here in a design an entire building drawn in all these three ways.[33]

[87r [11r]]

Besides the three styles [*modi*] of architecture proposed and mentioned above,[34] and in order to satisfy even more completely the desire of those who like to see and understand well all the things that are to be drawn, we have in addition drawn in perspective some buildings we thought lent themselves to it.[35] We did this so as to enable the eye to see and judge the grace [*gratia*] of that likeness,[36] which is demonstrated by the beautiful proportion and symmetry [*symmetria*] of these buildings, and which does not appear in the drawing of buildings that are measured architecturally. The fact is, the thickness of bodies cannot be shown on a plane unless the parts that are supposed to appear further away diminish in the proportions that the eye naturally sees: the eye sends rays in the form of a pyramid, setting the base of that pyramid on the object and

33   In the Munich manuscript, the rest of this page is left blank to provide space for the 'design' mentioned here. For a discussion of this passage, see Lotz, W., *Studies in Italian Renaissance Architecture* (1977). See also Di Teodoro (1994), pp. 197–8.

34   That is, plan, section and elevation.

35   This sentence and the following section is to be found only in the Munich manuscript. The printed version omits this text and substitutes the following lines: 'And we have pursued this way, as will be seen in the course of the whole of this our description. And indeed since it is high time for me to begin, I shall place beside here a design of a single edifice in all three ways mentioned above, so that what I have said can be seen quite clearly. If for the rest I were to be so fortunate as to come to be the obedient servant of Your Holiness – the first and supreme Prince of Christendom – since I could then call myself the most fortunate of all Your Holiness's most devoted servants, I would never cease to speak out in recognition of this my good fortune bestowed by the hand of Your Blessedness, whose most holy feet I kiss in deepest humility.'

36   In reference to the perspective drawing.

retaining in itself the angle at the apex related to the thing that it sees. And so, the smaller the angle, the smaller the object viewed will appear, and the same is true for higher up and lower down, more to the right and more to the left, depending upon the angle.

And in order to set on the vertical wall[37] a plane upon which things that are further away appear smaller in the appropriate proportion, you have to intersect the pyramidal rays from our eyes with a line at the same distance from that eye,[38] because that is how one sees naturally, and with the points where this line intersects the rays, you can record the correct measure for the diminishing, using that proportion and interval that makes the objects appear at a greater or lesser distance depending on the distance the painter or perspective drawer wishes to show. In this way we have followed this theory and the others necessary for perspective in the designs that lent themselves to it, reserving the architectural measurements for the three other types mentioned initially. With perspectives it would be impossible – or at least exceedingly difficult – to resolve things to their original form so that they could be measured, despite the fact that the effect of the measurements is nevertheless present. And even though this type of drawing in perspective is the preserve of the painter, it is nevertheless also useful for the architect.

Just as the painter must have knowledge of the architecture in order to be able to render the ornaments to their correct measurements and proportions, in the same way the architect needs to know perspective because through this exercise he can better imagine the whole building furnished with its ornaments.

[87v [11v]]

Of these ornaments, there is no need to say more than that they all derive from the five Orders used by the ancients – namely Doric, Ionic, Corinthian, Tuscan and Attic. Of all these, the Doric is the oldest and it was invented by Dorus, king of the Achaeans, when he was building a temple to Juno in Argos.[39] Later, when building a temple to Apollo in Ionia, he set the measurements of the Doric columns to match the proportions of a man, such that they produced symmetry [*symmetria*], firmness and beautiful dimensions, without any other ornaments. But in

37   The text has 'parete', here meaning the picture plane. See Kemp, M., *The Science of Art* (1990), p. 90.
38   That is, the same distance as the eye to the 'vertical wall'.
39   Vitruvius, *De architectura*, IV.i.3; IV.i.5–6.

the temple of Diana they changed the form, ordering [*ordinando*] the columns with the measurements and proportions of a woman, with many ornaments in the capitals, bases and over the entire shaft or scape of the column, and they composed it in imitation of the build of a woman. This they called Ionic.[40] But those that are called Corinthian are more slender and more delicate, made in imitation of the gracefulness and slenderness of a virgin. The inventor of these was Callimachus of Corinth, hence they are called Corinthian. On the origin and form of this, Vitruvius writes at great length, and we refer all those who want to know more to him.[41] As and when necessary, we shall describe the arrangements [*ordini*] for all of them, taking as a presupposition the things in Vitruvius.

There are two further works [*opere*] in addition to the three mentioned: namely Attic and Tuscan, which were not, however, much used by the ancients. The Attic has columns with four faces,[42] the Tuscan is very similar to the Doric, as will be seen in the prosecution of what we intend to do and show. And there will also be many buildings composed of different styles [*maniere*], such as Ionic with Corinthian, Doric with Corinthian, Tuscan with Doric, depending upon what seemed best to the artificer when matching these buildings appropriately to their intention, especially in the case of temples.

40　　Vitruvius, *De architectura*, IV.i.7.

41　　Vitruvius, *De architectura*, IV.i.8.

42　　Pliny, *Natural History*, XXXVI.56.179.

COMMENTARY

The Antiquities of Rome

1   The motto above reads 'Fortune favours the brave'. For Lucrino see the introduction, above; Barberi, F., 'I Dorico, tipografi a Roma nel cinquecento', *La Bibliofilia*, vol. 67, (1965), pp. 221–61; Palladio, A., *Andrea Palladio: The Churches of Rome*, trans. E.D. Howe (1991), pp. 26–9.

2   The folio numbers throughout refer to the first (1554) edition of *L'antichità*.

3   This refers to the enormously popular guide entitled 'The Marvels of Rome'; on the *Mirabilia* tradition see the introduction, above. See also Anonymous, *Mirabilia urbis Romae: The Marvels of Rome, or a Picture of the Golden City*, trans. F.M. Nichols (1889).

4   This echoes Francesco Albertini's *Opusculum de mirabilibus novæ et veteris urbis Romæ* (1510), p. 5. See the introduction, above.

5   On these ancient authors see the introduction, above. See also Cary, M., and H.H. Scullard, *A History of Rome down to the Reign of Constantine* (1975).

6   On these contemporary authors see the introduction, above.

7   On this claim see the introduction, above. See also Lewis, D., *The Drawings of Andrea Palladio* (1981), especially chapters 5–6. Noted below are the Palladio drawings held in the Vicenza City Museum and in the RIBA, London, which show Roman monuments cited in the text. On the Palladio drawings in the Vicenza City Museum see Puppi, L., *Palladio Drawings* (1990).

8   The text incorrectly has 'militaria'.

9   The legendary origins and foundation of Rome are to be found in Livy, *Ab urbe condita libri*, 1. 3. 10ff.; Dionysius of Halicarnassus, *Roman Antiquities*, 1.76.1ff.; and Plutarch's 'Life' of Romulus, *Vitae parallelae*, *Romulus*, 3ff. For Palladio's specific reference to these ancient sources, see the introduction, above. See also Cary and Scullard (1975); Bremmer, J., and N. Horsfall (eds), *Roman Myth and Mythography* (1987); Rykwert, J., *The Idea of a Town: the Anthropology of Urban Form in Rome, Italy and the Ancient World* (1988).

10   Following Roman practice, see Polybius's *The Histories*, VI. 27.2 and VI. 31.10, where the military camp is described as a perfect square. See also Rykwert (1988).

11   On the Roman's choice of commodious sites for the founding of their cities, see Vitruvius, *De architectura*, I.iv.

12   The Consualia was a festival of the Roman god of the granary, Consus,

and in fact took place on 21 August and 15 December, coinciding, respectively, with the gathering of the harvest and the onset of winter.

13   Probably from *patres* ('fathers').

14   On the *cliens* and *patronus*, see Saller, R., *Personal Patronage under the Early Empire* (1982). On these and the subsequently mentioned Plebs, the name given to the mass of Roman citizens as distinct from the privileged patricians, see Hornblower, S., and A. Spawforth (eds), *The Oxford Classical Dictionary* (2003), pp. 348, 1126–7, 1196.

15   That is, Goat's Marsh.

16   Lucius Tarquinius Superbus (534–510 BC). See Hornblower and Spawforth (2003), p. 1475. On the seven kings of Rome see Hornblower and Spawforth (2003), pp. 1322–3. The later kings are traditionally portrayed as tyrannical populists.

17   Palladio's interest in Caesar is attested by his *I Commentari di C. Giulio Cesare*, published in Venice in 1575. See the introduction, above.

18   From the Latin *pandere*, 'to open'.

19   The Porta Carmentalis was a gate in the Servian wall at the south-west corner of the Capitoline. It derived its name from the neighbouring shrine of Carmenta (which Palladio calls the 'Temple of Carmenta'; see 'On the Temple of Carmenta', below). The location of this gate was very near the intersection of the present Via della Consolazione and the Via della Bocca della Verità. It appears to have had two openings, one of which was called Porta Scelerata (from the Italian *scellerato*, meaning 'infamous') because the ill-fated Fabii marched through it into Etruscan territory in 306 BC. See Platner, S.B. (completed and revised by T. Ashby), *A Topographical Dictionary of Ancient Rome* (1929), pp. 405–6.

20   See Nash, E., *Pictorial Dictionary of Ancient Rome* (1968), vol. 2, pp. 86–103 (Muri Aureliani), 104–16 (Murus Servii Tullii); Todd, M., *The Walls of Rome* (1978); Krautheimer, R., *Rome, Profile of a City, 312–1308* (1980), pp. 6–7; Hornblower and Spawforth (2003), pp. 1616–17.

21   See, for example, Palladio's drawings in the Vicenza City Museum, of the Claudian Portico on the Celian Hill, D 1 *v*, D 3 *r* (Puppi (1990), nos. 14–15).

22   Leon Battista Alberti gives the circumference as 75 stadia in *Descriptio Urbis Romae*. See Alberti, L.B., 'Leon Battista Alberti's Delineation of the City of Rome', trans. P. Hicks, in 'Leonis Baptistae Alberti Descriptio urbis Romae', *Albertiana*, vol. 6 (2003), p. 197. The *Mirabilia Urbis Romae* gives 22 miles (that is, 101 stadia more than Alberti), but excludes Trastevere and the Borgo.

23   The *Mirabilia Urbis Romae* lists fifteen gates (not including postern gates). Many texts state that there were fourteen main gates. See Dal Maso, L.B., *Rome of the Caesars* (1975), p. 106. But Hornblower and Spawforth (2003), p. 1616, list seventeen principal gates.

24   Palladio lists, below, these eighteen gates (which serve the main highways into the city; see Krautheimer (1980), p. 55) in clockwise order, ending with the gate beside the Castel Sant'Angelo. The list in the *Mirabilia Urbis Romae* begins with the Porta Capena and finishes with the Porta Portuense in Trastevere.

25   The Porta Flaminia on the Via Flaminia consisted of a barrel vault flanked

by two towers which were heavily restored at the time of Sixtus IV (1471–84). The monumental Porta del Popolo replaced it on almost the same site, and its main features post-date Palladio's text, since the outer façade is by Nanni di Baccio Bigio (1561) and the inner by Giovanni Lorenzo Bernini (1655). On the ancient Porta Flaminia, see Nash (1968), vol. 2, pp. 210–12; Krautheimer (1980), pp. 6, 7, 9, 312, 313. Cited by Palladio, *QL*, III. iii [p. 167].

26   The fortified Porta Pinciana was constructed around AD 403 by the Emperor Honorius (395–423) from a postern gate dating from the time of Aurelian (*c.*215–75). The Via Salaria Vecchia passed through it, linking up further on with the Via Salaria. See Nash (1968), vol. 2, pp. 220–1; Krautheimer (1980), p. 313.

27   The Porta Salaria had a barrel vault with two towers of the type built by Honorius, but it was demolished in 1871. See Nash (1968), vol. 2, pp. 229–30.

28   That is, the River Anio.

29   Pope Pius IV had the ancient Porta Nomentana in the Piazza della Croce Rossa walled up, and commissioned Michelangelo to build the adjoining Porta Pia in 1561. The north tower has been preserved. See Nash (1968), vol. 2, p. 217; Krautheimer (1980), p. 9. Cited by Palladio, *QL*, III. iii [p. 167]. RIBA X 16V.

30   The Porta Tiburtina was constructed in one of the archways supporting the Aqua Marcia, Aqua Tepula and Aqua Julia aqueducts at the time of Augustus (AD 5). The arch had two circular rather than square towers, and on the attic were bronze statues of the emperors Arcadius (337–408) and Honorius. It was restored by Honorius in 403. In the Middle Ages it was also called Porta Taurina after a bull's-head decoration on the arch of the aqueduct. Today the name Porta di San Lorenzo is given to a separate structure next to the Porta Tiburtina, aligned with the Via Tiburtina. See Nash (1968), vol. 2, pp. 232–3; Krautheimer (1980), pp. 6, 9, 248, 314. Cited by Palladio, *QL*, III. iii [p. 167].

31   The Porta Prenestina, or Porta Maggiore, was built by Claudius (10 BC–AD 54) in AD 52. It was originally formed by the archways carrying the Aqua Claudia and Anio Nuovus (Aqua Aniene Nova) over the Via Prenestina and the Via Casilina (anciently the Via Labicana), becoming a gate in Aurelian's Wall. It was restored by Honorius in 405. See Nash (1968), vol. 2, pp. 225–8; Krautheimer (1980), pp. 4, 9, 258, 312. Palladio's drawings in the Vicenza City Museum show a front view and ground plan, entablature of the niche and a capital: D 1 *r*, D 3 *v* (Puppi (1990), nos. 32–3). Cited by Palladio, *QL*, III. iii [p. 167]. RIBA XII 4A.R, XII 4A.V.

32   The Porta Asinaria stood on the site of the Porta Coelimontana of the Servian Wall. It was transformed under Honorius by the construction of its towers and second door. A fire damaged it at the time of Robert the Guiscard in 1084. The present Porta San Giovanni was built in 1574 by Giacomo del Duca. See Nash (1968), vol. 2, pp. 204–5; Krautheimer (1980), p. 9.

33   The Porta Latina is an opening in the Aurelian Wall with two sixth-century towers built by Belisarius (*c.*500–65). Honorius reduced its archway for defensive reasons and added an attic. See Nash (1968), vol. 2, p. 213.

34   The Porta Appia, or Porta di San Sebastiano, was originally built by Aurelian with two archways, but Honorius and Arcadius transformed it into its pres-

ent single-arch state and heightened the towers. Belisarius restored it in the sixth century. It is the largest and best-preserved gateway in the Aurelian Wall and (as the text indicates) the traditional point of entry of Triumphs from the Appian Way. See Nash (1968), vol. 2, pp. 198–9; Dal Maso (1975), p. 107; Krautheimer (1980), pp. 6, 9, 248, 251. Cited by Palladio, *QL*, III. iii [p. 167]. See also 'On the small Senate Houses', below.

35   In Roman legend, the Horatii were male triplets who represented Rome in a battle against Alba, which was represented by the Curiatii, also triplets. After two of the Horatii had been killed, the remaining brother defeated the Curiatii.

36   The Porta Ostiense, or Porta San Paolo, originally had two archways but these were reduced to a single arch by Honorius and Arcadius. There was a postern beside it. The side towers date from the time of Maxentius (b. *c.*283). See Nash (1968), vol. 2, pp. 218–19; Dal Maso (1975), p. 108; Krautheimer (1980), pp. 6, 9, 68, 248, 266, 321.

37   The Porta Portuense dated from the time of Honorius and had two archways and two round towers. It was demolished by Pope Urban VIII (r. 1623–44) in 1643 and replaced by the present-day Porta Portese 500 yards to the north. See Nash (1968), vol. 2, pp. 222–3; Krautheimer (1980), p. 239.

38   The Porta Aurelia comprised a single archway with two square towers, and a door. It was demolished in 1644 by Pope Urban VIII during the reconstruction of the walls between the Tiber and the Janiculum and replaced by the present-day Porta San Pancrazio. See Nash (1968), vol. 2, pp. 206–7; Krautheimer (1980), pp. 6, 9, 86. Cited by Palladio, *QL*, III. iii [p. 167].

39   The Porta Settimiana in the Aurelian Wall was reconstructed in 1498 by Pope Alexander VI (r. 1492–1503). See Nash (1968), vol. 2, p. 231; Krautheimer (1980), pp. 254, 271, 290.

40   During the reign of Pius IV (Giovannangelo Medici, 1562–65), the Porta Turrionis (Torrione) or Porta Posterula was renamed Porta Cavalleggieri (the name used today, and on the Du Pérac map of Rome of 1577). Some historians place its founding date as AD 848–52, while others make it as late as the reign of Pope Nicholas V (1447–55).

41   The Porta Pertusa is commonly attributed to Pope Nicholas V, who from 1451 to 1455 began to strengthen the fortifications around the city. See Krautheimer (1980), p. 118.

42   The Porta di Santo Spirito was begun in 1540 by Antonio da Sangallo the Younger (1483–1546) and remains unfinished.

43   The Porta di Belvedere is better known by the names Porta Palatina, Porta Aurea, Porta San Petri, Porta Viridaria or Porta San Peregrini. See Biondo, F., *De Roma ristaurata, et Italia illustrata . . . Tradotte in buona lingua volgare per Lucio Fauno* (1542), fol. 9*v*. This gate was the only entrance into the Borgo for pilgrims using the Cassian Way at the time of the publication of Palladio's book. Soon afterwards, Pope Pius IV built along the edge of the Borgo not only a settlement (baptised in his name as the Borgo Pio) but also the gate into it, the Porta Angelica (similarly named after Giovannangelo), which eventually superseded the Porta Aurea.

44 Also known as the Porta di Castello Sant'Angelo, this postern gate received a noble surround designed by Francesco Peparelli in 1563 (contemporary with the creation of the Borgo Pio). The opening was blocked during the nineteenth century before the gate was finally demolished.

45 Palladio discusses Roman roads in the *Quattro libri* at III. iii [pp. 167–8]. See also Alberti, VIII. vi [pp. 261–8]. On the twenty-nine principal Roman roads (called 'consular' roads), see Chevallier, R., *Roman Roads*, trans. N.H. Field (1976). See also Dal Maso (1975), p. 112; Krautheimer (1980), pp. 55, fig. 51, 248; Hornblower and Spawforth (2003), pp. 1320, 1594–6.

46 Gnaeus Gracchus's road building is cited by Palladio, *QL*, III. iii [p. 168] (after Plutarch, *Vitae parallelae, C. Gracchus*, 7; Appian; *Civil Wars*, I. 23).

47 The Via Appia Antica (Appian Way) was the longest, widest and most important of the consular Roman roads and the Romans' principal route to south Italy. It was built by the censor Appius Claudius, called Caecus ('blind'), in 312 BC, and restored by Julius Caesar. For the first 12 miles it is lined on both sides by the tombs of Rome's patrician families, and it famously passes the tomb of Caecilia Metella. See Plutarch, *Vitae parallelae, Alexander et Caesar*, 5.9; Dal Maso (1975), pp. 112–13; Krautheimer (1980), pp. 3, 8, 9, 17, 25, 28, 83; Hornblower and Spawforth (2003), p. 1594. Cited by Palladio, *QL*, III. iii [p. 167].

48 See 'On the Gates', above.

49 On this Etruscan city see Hornblower and Spawforth (2003), p. 289.

50 So-called by Publius Papinius Statius (*c*.45–96) in his collection of poems, *Silvae*, II.ii. 12.

51 Begun in 220 BC, the Via Flaminia was named after the censor (and later consul) Gaius Flaminius (the first, d. 217 BC). It runs almost due north from Piazzale Flaminio, which adjoins the Piazza del Popolo, extending through Umbria and reaching the Adriatic at Fano, from where it continues to Rimini. See Krautheimer (1980), pp. 3, 54–5, 312, 313; Hornblower and Spawforth (2003), p. 1595. Cited by Palladio, *QL*, III. iii [p. 167].

52 See 'On the Gates', above.

53 The Via Emilia was an extension of the Via Flaminia from Rimini to Bologna, built by M. Aemilius Lepidus (d. 13–12 BC). Cited by Palladio, *QL*, III. iii [p. 167] (see also III. ii [p. 166]).

54 The Via Alta Semita ran along the ridge of the Quirinal Hill and its southwest slope. See Krautheimer (1980), pp. 9, 248.

55 See 'On the Gates', above.

56 The Via Suburra (Vicus Suburranus) ascended the Esquiline Hill. It split behind the apse of San Martino ai Monti, one branch continuing by way of San Prassede to San Vito in Macello and beyond to Porta San Lorenzo, the other turning southwards to Porta Maggiore. See Krautheimer (1980), pp. 248, 299, 314.

57 On the 'Sacred Way', at the heart of imperial Rome and part of the route of later papal processions, see Nash (1968), vol. 2, pp. 284–90; Krautheimer (1980), pp. 35, 65, 71, 75, 278; Hornblower and Spawforth (2003), p. 1595.

58   The Via Nova ran along the northern boundary of the Palatine Hill, bordering the Roman Forum. For a reconstruction see Dal Maso (1975), p. 25.

59   That is, the Palatine. See 'On the Hills', below.

60   See 'On the Tomb of Augustus, of Hadrian, and of Septimius', below.

61   See 'On the Thermae, that is Baths, and who built them', below.

62   A number of roads had this name in antiquity, one following the declivity between the Celian and Palatine hills to the Colosseum (the present-day Via di San Gregorio), another coming from the north (later the Ruga Francigena or Rue de France). See Krautheimer (1980), p. 264.

63   The Via Vitellia, about which little is known, is associated with the family of the Emperor Vitellius (15–69) and was mentioned by the Roman biographer and historian Suetonius (Gaius Suetonius Tranquillus, 75–160), in *De vita Caesarum* (*The Lives of the Caesars*), 'Vitellius', 1.

64   The Recta (the present-day Via dei Coronari and, in fact, the Via Tecta – literally 'covered way' – mentioned in Seneca's *Apocolocyntosis*, 13, and Martial's *Epigrams*, iii. 5.5; viii. 75.1, 2) originally led from the Bridge of Nero (and after the bridge's early collapse, from a short street from Ponte Sant'Angelo), through the Campus Martius to the Corso at the Column of Marcus Aurelius in Piazza Colonna. See Krautheimer (1980), pp. 244, 246.

65   In fact Palladio lists ten bridges (if the two ruined ones are included), although the Pons Aemilius is listed twice, once under this name and secondly under its medieval name of Ponte di Santa Maria. It may also have been confused with the Ponte Sisto (see notes 70 and 73, below). See in general Gazzola, P., *Ponti romani* (1963); Dal Maso (1975), pp. 94–5; Krautheimer (1980); Hornblower and Spawforth (2003), p. 260.

66   Ancus Marcius was the fourth king of Rome (traditionally 640–17 BC). See Hornblower and Spawforth (2003), p. 922. The wooden Pons Sublicius and Horatius Cocles's defence of it are cited by Palladio, *QL*, III. v [p. 171]. See also Pliny, *Natural History*, XXXVI, 100.

67   The Pons Aemilius was the first stone bridge over the Tiber. The piers date from 179 BC, and arches were built on these in 142 BC by the censors M. Fulvius Nobilior and M. Aemilius Lepidus. Since its final collapse in 1598 all that remains is a single arch in the middle of the river, known as the 'Ponte Rotto' (broken bridge) standing below the 'Isola Tiberina'. See Serlio, Book Three, p. LXXXVI [pp. 177, 442, n. 222]. See also Nash (1968), vol. 2, pp. 182–3; Krautheimer (1980), pp. 3, 76, 77, 237, 238–9, 244, 248, 250, 251, 254, 255, 266, 305. Cited by Palladio, *QL*, III. v [p. 171], III. xi [p. 183] (both mentioning Lepidus).

68   Cited by Palladio, *QL*, III. xi [p. 183], where he says that the piers can still be seen.

69   On the Ospitale di Santo Spirito in the Borgo, see Palladio, *Churches*, [p. 32] (Santo Spirito in Sassia).

70   The Ponte di Santa Maria is in fact the Pons Aemilius (see note 65, above), also known as St Mary's bridge after a picture of the Madonna in a small chapel that

stood on the bridge. See Serlio, Book Three, p. LXXXVI [p. 177]; Nash (1968), vol. 2, pp. 182–3; Krautheimer (1980), p. 238. See also Palladio, *Churches*, [p. 59]. Cited by Palladio, *QL*, III. xi [p. 183].

71   The 'bridge of the four heads' derived its latter-day name from the four-headed herms that served as the piers of the bronze balustrade on the ancient bridge. Also known as the Pons Fabricius (or Pons Judeorum), it connected the left bank of the Tiber with the 'Isola Tiberina' and was built in 62 BC by the 'Curator Viarum', L. Fabricius. On this bridge see Serlio, Book Three, p. LXXXVII [p. 176], which includes a woodcut view; *Arte Antica*, VI, p. 805, fig. 924; Nash (1968), vol. 2, pp. 189–90; Krautheimer (1980), pp. 76, 238, 244, 248, 273, fig. 209, 304, fig. 240, 305. Cited by Palladio, *QL*, III. xi [p. 183].

72   Joining the south side of the 'Isola Tiberina' to Trastevere, the Ponte Cestio was probably built by L. Cestius in 46 BC and was restored in AD 370 and in 1191–93. It was rebuilt in 1892, the central arch to its original design and measurements. See Nash (1968), vol. 2, pp. 187–8; Krautheimer (1980), pp. 198, 238, 254. Cited by Palladio, *QL*, III. xi [p. 183].

73   In fact the Ponte Sisto (the Sistine Bridge) was newly built for Pope Sixtus IV (1471–84), probably by Baccio Pontelli, to replace the ancient Pons Janiculensis (or Pons Aurelius). See Krautheimer (1980), pp. 3, 238, 254, 289. However, the ancient Pons Aemilius, called in the Middle Ages the Ponte di Santa Maria (see note 70, above), was also sometimes mistakenly called the Ponte Sisto. See Serlio, Book Three, p. LXXXVI [p. 177]. Links between the Sisto and the Aemilius are implied here because Palladio says that both were built in marble by Antoninus Pius. Cited by Palladio, *QL*, III. xi [p. 183].

74   Ponte Sant'Angelo (Aelian Bridge) was built by Hadrian (76–138) for access to his tomb in AD 134. It was repaired by Pope Nicholas V, who added two chapels. On this bridge see Serlio, Book Three, p. LXXXVII [p. 176], which includes a woodcut view; Nash (1968), vol. 2, pp. 178–81; Krautheimer (1980), pp. 3, 12, 28, 202, 238, 243, 244, 248, 261, 278. See also Alberti, VIII. vi [p. 262] and X. i [p. 346]. Cited by Palladio, *QL*, III. xi [p. 183].

75   Called the Ponte Molle since the fourteenth century, the Milvian Bridge was built in 109 BC by the censor M. Aemilius Scaurus to carry the Via Flaminia (see 'On the Roads', above). It served as the principal entrance to Rome. On this bridge see Serlio, Book Three, p. LXXXVI [p. 177], which includes a woodcut view; Nash (1968), vol. 2, pp. 191–2; Krautheimer (1980), pp. 3, 64, 312. Cited by Palladio, *QL*, III. xi [p. 183].

76   Lying on the Via Salaria and crossing the River Aniene (the classical Anio) north-east of Rome, the ancient Ponte Salario was rebuilt in 565 by Narses (c.478–573) and reconstructed in 1867. Only the two side arches are original. See Krautheimer (1980), pp. 3, 63, fig. 54.

77   This refers to the victory of Narses over the Ostrogoths in battles at Tadinum and Mons Lactarius. See Hornblower and Spawforth (2003), p. 1027.

78   Totila or Baduila (d. 552) was the last king of the Ostrogoths, ruling

between 541 and 552. By defeating the Byzantines at Faenza and Mugello (542) and by taking Naples (543) and Rome (546), he became master of central and southern Italy. Belisarius, the Byzantine commander, recovered Rome in 547 but was recalled in the following year. Rome again fell in 550, leaving only Ravenna, Ancona, Otranto and Crotona in Byzantine hands.

79   Lying on the Via Tiburtina and also crossing the River Aniene, the ancient Pons Mammeus dated from the republican era (from around 500 BC to Augustus) and was rebuilt by Julia Mamaea (c.190–235), mother of Emperor Alexander Severus (c.209–35). It was rebuilt in 1857. On Julia Avita Mamaea and Marcus Aurelius Severus Alexander see Hornblower and Spawforth (2003), pp. 222, 777.

80   On Palladio's source for the history of Rome, see 'To the Readers', above, and note 9. On the Tiber Island see Nash (1968), vol. 1, pp. 508–9; Dal Maso (1975), pp. 94–5; Krautheimer (1980), pp. 149, 150, 155–7, 241, 253–4, 305.

81   On these temples see 'On the Temples of the Ancients outside Rome', below.

82   Palladio lists nine main hills (the Pincian and the Janiculum were not counted among the seven hills). See Hornblower and Spawforth (2003), p. 1334.

83   The names 'Campidoglio' and 'Capitoline' are used to refer to both the hill and the buildings on it. On the Capitoline, the smallest of the seven hills, see Alberti, I. vi [p. 18],VII, x [p. 220]; Dal Maso (1975), pp. 30–6; Krautheimer (1980), pp. 150–3, 197–9, 285–8; Hornblower and Spawforth (2003), p. 288. See also a drawing of the mid-1530s by Maarten van Heemskerck; Filippi, E., *Maarten Van Heemskerck* (1990), no. 22, [Kupferstichkabinett, Staatliche Museen zu Berlin, 79D2 fol. 72r]. See also 'On the Campidoglio', below.

84   The text has *scalli* for *sacelli*. On the thatched shrines in the citadel next to the hut of Romulus on the Capitoline Hill, see Vitruvius, *De architectura*, II.i. 5; McEwen, I., *Vitruvius, Writing the Body of Architecture* (2003), p. 143.

85   On the Temple of Jupiter Capitolinus, see 'On the Temples', below.

86   The Palatine was the chief of the seven hills and traditionally the site of the oldest settlement in Rome, since it was the legendary home of the Arcadian demigod Evander and of Romulus. The name 'Palazzo Maggiore' probably reflected the fact that the word 'Palatine' became synonymous with the 'palace of the emperor'. Many Roman patrician palaces were located here. See 'On the Palaces', below. See Nash (1968), vol. 2, pp. 163–9; Dal Maso (1975), pp. 9–12, 24–5; Krautheimer (1980), pp. 9–11, 17, 28, 34, 67, 71, 75–6, 111, 187, 241, 258; Hornblower and Spawforth (2003), p. 1099.

87   See 'On the Building of Rome', above.

88   More correctly, Emperor Elagabalus (Aurelius Antoninus, r. 218–22). See Hornblower and Spawforth (2003), pp. 221–2.

89   On the Aventine, the southernmost hill of Rome, see Krautheimer (1980); Hornblower and Spawforth (2003), p. 225; Palladio, *Churches*, [p. 61].

90   The Celian Hill (or Mons Querquetulanus) is next to the Aventine and extends to the south and west towards the Palatine. See Krautheimer (1980); Palladio, *Churches*, [pp. 10, 59].

91   The name 'Esquiliae' denoted the eastern plateau formed by *montes* Oppius and Cispius, and was included within the republican wall (Wall of Servius). It was the site of Nero's Domus Aurea ('Golden House') and the baths of Titus and Trajan. See Krautheimer (1980); Hornblower and Spawforth (2003), p. 558; Palladio, *Churches*, [pp. 22, 52].

92   On the Viminal, which lay between the Esquiline and the Quirinal, see Krautheimer (1980); Palladio, *Churches*, [pp. 52–3, 53–4].

93   On the Quirinal, the northernmost hill of Rome (traditionally occupied by Sabines), see Krautheimer (1980); Hornblower and Spawforth (2003), p. 1291. On the 'Palazzo di Montecavallo', see Serlio, Book Three, pp. LXXX–LXXXI [pp. 170–1, 441, n. 202]. See also Santangelo, M., *Il Quirinale nell'antichità classica* (1941), Atti della Pontificia Accademia Romana di Archeologia, S. III Memorie, vol. 5, p. II. The Quirinal (Montecavallo) is cited by Palladio, *QL*, IV. iii [p. 218], IV. xii [p. 253].

94   On the Pincian Hill, the site of the Collis Hortulorum of ancient Rome (since it was covered with the monumental gardens of the Roman aristocracy and emperors), see Krautheimer (1980). On a Roman obelisk on this hill, see Dal Maso (1975), p. 43. See also Palladio, *Churches*, [p. 35].

95   On the Janiculum, the prominent rise on the west bank of the Tiber and site of the tomb of King Numa, see Krautheimer (1980); Hornblower and Spawforth (2003), p. 793; Palladio, *Churches*, [p. 31].

96   That is, the Montorio, called the 'Golden Hill' (Mons Aureus) because of its golden sand. Clearly Palladio does not make the connection between the 'Montorio' of San Pietro in Montorio (cited previously) and the Monte Auro – the latter more accurately the site of that church.

97   On the right bank of the Tiber, the Mons Vaticanus in the early empire was the site of an imperial park, the horti Agrippinae, and of entertainment structures – the naumachiae and the Vatican Circus. During the reign of Constantine I (*c.*274–337), a huge, five-aisled basilica was constructed in honour of St Peter. See Krautheimer (1980); Hornblower and Spawforth (2003), p. 1583; Palladio, *Churches*, [pp. 16ff].

98   This is Montecitorio, the very small hill on which the Italian Parliament stands today. The name 'citorio' derives from the word 'citatorium'; that is, the summoning that took place on the Montecitorio, which was part of the Campus Martius, when members of the centuria would be convoked to enter a large enclosure (called either the *ovile* or the *saepta*) for the purpose of electing magistrates (consuls, praetors and so on). On the Saepta Julia et Diribitorium (for the election of the comitia tributa) see Nash (1968), vol. 2, pp. 291–3. On the magistrates, see 'On the Magistrates', below.

99   The Pincian Hill bordered the Campus Martius. The hill is also mentioned above; see note 94.

100   The small Monte Giordano Hill was inhabited by the twelfth century and takes its name from Giordano Orsini (thirteenth century) whose legendary fortress stood here. See Krautheimer (1980), pp. 157, 253, 305, 308–9. For an isomet-

ric view of Monte Giordano showing its arrangement as a group of palaces form-ing a fortified and walled quarter with few entrances see Krautheimer (1980), p. 306, fig. 242.

101   Monte Testaccio is an isolated mound 36 metres high and covering roughly 22,000 square metres in the Emporium district of Rome, south of the Aventine, near the Tiber. It is composed of potsherds (*testae*) dumped from the Augustan period (initiated under Augustus (63 BC–AD 14)) up to the middle of the third century AD. These came from the storehouses of the republican port that lined the Tiber between Ponte Testaccio and Pons Sublicius (Ponte Aventino). See Rodríguez Almeida, E., *Il Monte Testaccio* (1984); Nash (1968), vol. 2, pp. 411–13; Hornblower and Spawforth (2003), p. 995.

102   According to Pliny, *Natural History*, XXXV, 151 ff., Boutades of Corinth was the first to make model portraits in clay and terracotta reliefs. The name 'Corebos' could be a misreading of the word 'canebos', a technical term for the frame upon which still-wet clay was fashioned. On terracottas in antiquity, see Hornblower and Spawforth (2003), p. 1486.

103   Aquae are waterways. On the aquae in general see Morton, H.V., *The Waters of Rome* (1966).

104   See 'On the Aqueducts', below.

105   See 'On the Aqueducts', below.

106   See 'On the Aqueducts', below.

107   The Aqua Tepula was built in 125 BC. It was 11 miles long and brought spring water from the Alban Hills. It ran underground for 5 miles, and then flowed for 6 miles on top of the Aqua Marcia, both waterways sharing the same arches. See Pliny, *Natural History*, XXXVI, 121; Morton (1966), pp. 29, 40.

108   In the transcription on CD-ROM in the collection entitled 'Art Theories of the Italian Renaissance' published by Chadwyck-Healey (1997), the text incorrectly has *Appia*.

109   The Aqua Julia was built in 33 BC by Agrippa (*c.*63–12 BC) and named in honour of Augustus (Gaius Julius Octavianus, 63 BC–AD 14). It was 14 miles long, running underground for half its length, the other half carried into Rome on top of the Marcia and the Tepula. See Morton (1966), pp. 29, 45, 49, 52; Nash (1968), vol. 1, p. 47, vol. 2, pp. 125–6.

110   The Aqua Anio Vetus was built in 272–69 BC. It was 40 miles long and brought water from the Anio River (now the Aniene), near Vicovaro, east of Rome. See Pliny, *Natural History*, XXXVI, 121; Morton (1966), pp. 28, 31.

111   The Aqua Anio Novus was the companion aqueduct to the Aqua Claudia and was completed by Claudius in AD 52. It was 54 miles long and travelled on arch-es for only 8 miles, entering Rome on the Porta Maggiore. See Pliny, *Natural History*, XXXVI, 122; Morton (1966), p. 31. On Sextus Julius Frontinus's *De aquis urbis Romae*, a Roman work on the aqueducts of the city dating from about AD 100, see the English translation by C.E. Bennett and M.B. McElwain, *De Aquis, The Stratagems and the Aqueducts of Rome* (1925). See also McEwen (2003), pp. 19–20, 24–5, 233; Hornblower and Spawforth (2003), p. 785.

112   The Aqua Virgo is also called the Aqua Virgine. See 'On the Aqueducts',
below. On the Aedile see 'On the Magistrates', below.

113   It is thought that the original Trevi Fountain was designed by Alberti for
Pope Nicholas V. It was restored in the seventeenth century by Pope Urban VIII. See
Morton (1966), pp. 74–87. See also 'On the Aqueducts', below.

114   The Aqua Alsietina was built in 2 BC by Augustus. It was 20 miles long
and brought water from Lake Alsietina (now Lake Martignano) to the north-west of
Rome. The water – of poor quality – was used to flood Augustus's theatre on the
Janiculum, where mock naval battles were staged. See Morton (1966), pp. 29, 31, 171,
202; Nash (1968), vol. 1, pp. 35–6.

115   The remains of the Juturna spring (the fountain of Juturna) can be seen
only a few paces from the House of the Vestal Virgins in the Roman Forum; the
Vestals are supposed to have drawn their water from it. See Morton (1966), pp. 28–9,
47, 49. On San Giorgio, see note 129, below.

116   The Aqua Trajana (Traiana; modern name, Aqua Paola because of its
reconstruction by Pope Paul V in 1605) was built by the Emperor Trajan (c. 53–117)
in AD 109. It drew its supply from springs at the north-west corner of the Lake of
Bracciano (Lacus Sabatinus), was 35 miles long and ran mostly underground. It ter-
minated on the Janiculum. Remains of the channel were found during the construction of the American Academy in 1912–14; *Mem. American Academy*, vol. 1,
(1917), pp. 59–61, and pl. 15. See Morton (1966), pp. 29, 31, 164, 165, 166, 169, 202;
Nash (1968), vol. 1, pp. 52–4.

117   Unidentified. Possibly the Aqua Antoniniana, repaired by Septimius
Severus (c. 146–211) in 196.

118   This may be a reference to the so-called 'Arco di Druso' (not the arch of
Drusus mentioned by Suetonius in the *De vita Caesarum* (*The Lives of the Caesars*),
'Claudius', 1), standing on the Via Appia near the Porta San Sebastiano. This archway
once carried the Aqua Antoniniana, built by Emperor Caracalla in 211–16 as a
branch of the Aqua Marcia. See Nash (1968), vol. 1, pp. 79–80.

119   The Aqua Alexandrina was built by the Emperor Alexander Severus
in 226. It was about 14 miles long and was fed by springs to the east of Rome in the
marshland near the Via Prenestina. The emperor built this aqueduct to supply his
baths, the Thermae Alexandrianae on the Campus Martius near the Pantheon. See
Morton (1966), pp. 31, 120, 164.

120   The Cloaca Maxima ('Great Drain') of Rome was originally a stream
draining north-east Rome from the Argiletum to the Tiber through the Roman
Forum and Velabrum. Palladio repeats the tradition that the Cloaca was completed
under the Etruscan dynasty of the Tarquins, the last kings of Rome. See 'On the
Building of Rome', above. However, while traces of early construction remain, the
main sewer is largely the result of Agrippa's overhaul in 33 BC. See Pliny, *Natural
History*, XXXVI, 104–8; Nash (1968), vol. 1, pp. 258–61; Hornblower and Spawforth
(2003), pp. 350, 1354. On the Pons Senatorius, see 'On the Bridges over the Tiber
and their Builders', above.

121   This includes such writers as Pliny; see note 120, above.

122   The text incorrectly has *Supplitio*.

123   Frontinus (see note 111, above) records that at the time of Nerva the aqueducts carrying the water to the city were: the Appia, Aniene Vecchio, Marcia, Tepula, Julia, Vergine, Alsietina, Claudia and Aniene Novo (that is, nine in total). See in general Pliny, *Natural History*, XXXVI, 121–23; Morton (1966); Dal Maso (1975), pp. 109–11; Krautheimer (1980), pp. 111, 252, 254, 259; Trevor Hodge, A., *Roman Aqueducts and Water Supply* (1992); Hornblower and Spawforth (2003), pp. 133, 1354.

124   The aqueduct carrying the Aqua Marcia was built in 144–40 BC by the praetor Quintus Marcius Rex and was about 56 miles long. It was served by a spring near Subiaco, and its waters ran for about 30 miles in an underground canal, then for the last 6 miles on arches. It served the Campidoglio, Celian, Quirinal and Aventine regions. See Pliny, *Natural History*, XXXVI, 121; Morton (1966), pp. 29, 35, 36, 56, 125; Nash (1968), vol. 1, pp. 48–51. See also Palladio, *Churches*, [pp. 24–5].

125   The aqueduct carrying the Aqua Claudia was completed by the Emperor Claudius in AD 52, with water from Subiaco. It reached the Celian Hill and was later extended to the Palatine, which borders the Aventine, serving the imperial palaces. See Pliny, *Natural History*, XXXVI, 122; Morton (1966), pp. 29, 31, 125, 126; Nash (1968), vol. 1, pp. 37–46.

126   The aqueduct carrying the Aqua Appia, the first in Rome, was built by the censor Appius Claudius Caecus (builder of the Via Appia, see 'On the Roads', above), in 312 BC. The spring from which the water originated was 10 miles east of Rome, and it was only on nearing the city that the water was carried above ground, on arches. See Pliny, *Natural History*, XXXVI, 121; Morton (1966), pp. 28, 40.

127   The aqueduct carrying the Aqua Virgine (or Aqua Virgo) was the second built by Agrippa, in 19 BC, running through the Villa Giulia and terminating at the Baths of Agrippa in the Campus Martius. It was called 'Virgo' because a young girl is said to have led the military engineers to a group of springs near the Via Collatina, to the east of Rome. The aqueduct was recommissioned by Pope Hadrian I (r. 772–95). See Pliny, *Natural History*, XXXVI, 121; Morton (1966), pp. 29, 73–116; Nash (1968), vol. 1, pp. 55–6.

128   Low ground between the Capitoline and Palatine hills.

129   San Giorgio in Velabro, known in the sixteenth century as San Giorgio alla fonte and not mentioned by Palladio in his book on the churches, perhaps because it was not a Cardinal's titular church. It was a pre-sixth-century building and was subsequently much restored.

130   Text incorrectly has *luogo* ('place') for *lago* ('lake').

131   The aqueduct carrying the Aqua Sabattina was built by Trajan and fed the mills on the Janiculum, the fountain in the atrium of St Peter's and the bath nearby. It was severed in the Longobard siege of 775, following which Pope Hadrian I rebuilt a hundred arches and repaired the pipeline. See Krautheimer (1980), pp. 111, 254.

132   For a woodcut plan of the 'Seven Halls', with a description, see Serlio, Book Three, p. XCIII [p. 183]. This cistern complex was also the subject of a sketch by Baldassare Peruzzi, Uffizi Arch. 477*v*; see Bartoli, A., *I monumenti antichi di Roma*

nei disegni degli Uffizi di Firenze (1914–22), vol. 2, fig. 322. On the Baths of Titus, see 'On the Thermae, that is Baths, and who built them', below.

133   Serlio has 'about fifteen feet'; Serlio, Book Three, p. XCIII [p. 183].

134   On the baths in general, see Vitruvius, *De architectura*, V.x; Alberti, VIII. x [pp. 287–90]; Dal Maso (1975), pp. 96–101; Fletcher, B., *A History of Architecture* (1975), pp. 295–303; Krautheimer (1980); Lewis (1981), pp. 130–40, nos. 74–81; Hornblower and Spawforth (2003), pp. 235–6. Palladio's plans, sections, and elevations of the Baths of Agrippa (no plan), Nero, Vespasian, Titus and Antoninus (Caracalla), together with seven drawings of Orders, sections and plans of the Baths of Diocletian and the Baths of Constantine were engraved and published as *Fabbriche Antiche Designate Da Andrea Palladio Vicentino E Date In Luce Da Riccardo Conte Di Burlington* (inscribed 1730, but possibly printed as late as 1740). Palladio's drawings of the Baths of Vespasian are at Chatsworth House, Derbyshire, the others in the RIBA Drawings Collection and in Vicenza (see individual notes, below). These drawings were subsequently copied – including the plan of the Baths of Agrippa – for Bartotti Scamozzi's *Terme dei Romani*, which appeared in folio edition in 1785 and in quarto in 1797.

135   The Baths of Nero were enlarged in the third century by Alexander Severus and extended from the present Piazza Navona to near the Pantheon. See Nash (1968), vol. 2, pp. 460–4; Krautheimer (1980), pp. 12, 252. RIBA III 1, III 2, III 3, III 4V, III 5, III 6, III 7, III 8, XIV 4V.

136   These were the first public baths in ancient Rome, begun by Agrippa behind the Pantheon in 25 BC, but largely destroyed by fire in AD 80. See Pliny, *Natural History*, XXXVI, 189; Nash (1968), vol. 2, pp. 429–33; Krautheimer (1980), pp. 12, 243, 252; Lewis (1981), pp. 131–2, nos. 75–6. Cited by Palladio, *QL*, IV. xx [p. 286], although the ruins to which he refers were in fact those of the Basilica of Neptune. See Palladio's drawing in the Vicenza City Museum, of a ground plan; D 33 *r* (Puppi (1990), no. 35). RIBA VII 1, VII 2R, VII 2V, VII 3, VII 4, VII 6R, VII 6V, IX 14V.

137   The Baths of Antoninus/Caracalla were built in 212–16 but finally completed under Elagabalus and Alexander Severus, and are the best preserved and most splendid of the imperial Roman baths in the city (they could accommodate some 1,600 bathers). See *Arte Antica*, I, p. 546a, II, p. 125a, III, p. 438b, VI, pp. 792a, 841b, VII, p. 718a; Nash (1968), vol. 2, pp. 434–41; Dal Maso (1975), pp. 97–100; Krautheimer (1980), pp. 17, 241; Lewis (1981), pp. 134–7, nos. 78–80. RIBA VI 1, VI 2, VI 3, VI 4, VI 5, VI 6, VI 7, VI 8, VI 9, VI 10, VI 11R, VI 11V, VII 5R, VIII 14R, XIV 3V. On these baths, see Serlio, Book Three, pp. LXXXVIII–XCI [pp. 178–81], which includes woodcut plans. See Palladio's drawings in the Vicenza City Museum, of a perspective section of an interior and a capital; D 11r, D 32 *r* (Puppi (1990), nos. 36–7).

138   It is unclear as to which baths Palladio is referring. There is no such emperor as Valerius Aurelianus, nor are there any large public baths in Trastevere, and certainly none built by Aurelian. Although Constantine's middle names were Valerius Aurelius, he did not build baths in Trastevere.

139   Built by Constantine in 326, these large baths were constructed on what
is now the site of Palazzo Pallavicini-Rospigliosi (1613–16). See Nash (1968), vol. 2,
pp. 442–7; Krautheimer (1980), pp. 28, 241; Lewis (1981), pp. 138–40, no. 81. RIBA I
1, I 3, I 5, I 6, VII 5V, VIII 8R.

140   Initiated by Maximian (c.250–310), Diocletian's co-emperor, in 298, and
dedicated in the names of both around 305–06, these were the largest of the ancient
Roman baths (they could accommodate 3,000 people at once). Standing on the
high ground to the north-east of the Viminal Hill (close to Stazione Termini – a cor-
ruption of the Italian word 'Terme'), they covered a rectangle of around 380 by 370
metres. Curiously, perhaps, Palladio omits the fact that the great central hall of the
baths had been converted into Santa Maria degli Angeli by Michelangelo. See *Arte
Antica*, I, pp. 478a, 587b, II, pp. 125a, 976b, III, p. 438a–b; Nash (1968), vol. 2, pp.
448–53. For a reconstruction model see Dal Maso (1975), pp. 100–1; Krautheimer
(1980), p. 7. Cited by Palladio, *QL*, I. ix [p. 13], IV. xii [p. 253]. RIBA V 1, V 2, V 3, V
4, V 5, V 6, V 7. On these baths, see Serlio, Book Three, pp. XCVI–XCIX [pp. 186–9],
which includes woodcut plans.

141   The name 'Baths of Domitian' was given (erroneously) to the Baths of
Trajan by early Christian writers. For the Baths of Trajan, see below. According to
the *Mirabilia* literature, Pope Dionysius (r. 259–68) built San Silvestro in Capite in
261 on the remains not of the Baths of Domitian but of what was called the
Palatium Diocletiani (the Palace of Diocletian), which became confused with the
emperor's Baths. In fact the church was built by Pope Stephen II and completed by
Paul I in 761 on the site of what may be Aurelian's Temple of the Sun. See Palladio,
Churches, [p. 37].

142   These are the Balneum Gordiani. See Steinby, E.M., *Lexicon topographicum
urbis Romae* (1993–2000), vol. 1, p. 160. According to Julius Capitolinus's text
Gordiani tres in the anonymous *Historia Augusta* (*Histoire Auguste*), ed. and trans.
J.-P. Callu, A. Gaden and O. Desbordes, (1992–), it was the villa of the Gordiani that
had two hundred pillars, and this stood on the Via Prenestina. See also Biondo
(1542), fol. 28r.

143   Santa Pudenziana is thought to have been converted around 390 from
Roman baths of the second century AD built by Novatian and Timotheus (the
brothers of Pudenziana) above the so-called house of Pudens. Parts of the baths are
evident in the Oratorium Marianum off this church. See Nash (1968), vol. 2, pp.
465–6. On Santa Pudenziana see Palladio, *Churches*, [p. 53].

144   The Baths of Septimius Severus formed part of the Domus Severiana and
the Baths of Alexander Severus (the Thermae Alexandrianae) were on the Campus
Martius, near the Pantheon, so neither of the baths were in Trastevere. See Nash
(1968), vol. 2, pp. 460–4.

145   Apollodorus of Damascus built the Baths of Trajan, after a fire in AD 104,
over part of the Domus Aurea (Golden House) of Nero on the Oppian Hill near
the Baths of Titus. Inaugurated in 109, they marked a new point in the development
of the design of thermal baths because of their arrangement, comprising a central
complex of buildings with an enclosure around the perimeter, and the addition of

gardens and 'exedrae' (open meeting places). See Nash (1968), vol. 2, pp. 472–7. RIBA IV 1, IV 2, IV 3, IV 4, IV 5. On Palladio's confusion of these baths with those of Titus, see note 147, below.

146   The Thermae Philippi – the baths of the Emperor Philip (Philip the Arab, r. 244–49) – were 'reconstructed' by Pirro Ligorio on his map of ancient Rome, dated 1561, due north of the Baths of Trajan. The very ancient church of San Matteo in Merulana (mentioned in documents dating from 499) stood on the Via Gregoriana running from Santa Maria Maggiore to St John Lateran. It was demolished during the period of Napoleonic rule in 1810.

147   The Baths of Titus were built around AD 80 on the Oppian Hill. See *Arte Antica*, I, p. 478a, III, p. 438b, IV, pp. 791a, 841a, 907b; Nash (1968), vol. 2, pp. 469–71; Lewis (1981), pp. 130–1, no. 74. Cited by Palladio, *QL*, I. xxiv [p. 60], although the ruins to which he refers were in fact those of the Baths of Trajan. RIBA I 2R, II 1, II 2, II 3, II 4, II 5, II 6R, II 6V, VIII 12V. On these baths, see Serlio, Book Three, pp. XCII–XCIII [pp. 182–3], including woodcut plans (possibly mistakenly based on the remains of the Baths of Constantine).

148   The text here concerning the Baths of Olympias is a word-for-word translation of that in the medieval 'mirabilia' text *Graphia aureae urbis*, published in Valentini, R., and G. Zucchetti, *Codice topografico della città di Roma* (1953), vol. 3, pp. 77–110. In Palladio, *Churches*, [p. 52], the text relates that the church of San Lorenzo in Panisperna 'was built by Pius I upon the ruins of the palace of the Emperor Decius', a statement repeated below in 'On Palaces'.

149   These were huge, amphitheatre-like structures containing enormous pools for staging sham naval battles. The best-known artificial pool was that excavated by Augustus in 2 BC on the right bank of the Tiber (near San Cosimato), 550 metres long and 365 metres wide, with an island in the middle, fed by a new aqueduct, the Aqua Alsietina. See 'On the Aqueducts', above. Caesar staged such naval battles in 46 BC, on the left bank of the Tiber. See Hornblower and Spawforth (2003), p. 1029.

150   On the circuses in general see Alberti, VIII. viii [pp. 278–9], Humphrey, J.H., *Roman Circuses: Arenas for Chariot Racing* (1986); Hornblower and Spawforth (2003), pp. 332–3. Concerning Palladio's design for a 'circus' for equestrian (or chariot) races in Vicenza in 1576, see also Puppi, L., *Andrea Palladio* (1975), p. 417, no. 128.

151   The Circus Maximus was the first and largest circus in Rome. According to Livy, it dates from the time of Tarquinius Priscus (*c*.600 BC), who inaugurated a display of boxing matches and races after a victory over the Latins. As the text states, in the time of Julius Caesar its length was three stadia (1,875 Roman feet) and its width one stadium. It was rounded at one end, with a spina down the middle. The circus was destroyed by fire under Nero (AD 37–68) in AD 64 and then, after rebuilding, once again in the time of Domitian (AD 51–96). It was rebuilt by Trajan. See Pliny, *Natural History*, XXXVI, 102, 162. Cited by Alberti, VIII. vii [p. 269], VIII. viii [p. 279], where the same dimensions are given; see Alberti, 'Glossary' p. 423. See also Dal Maso (1975), pp. 81–6; Nash (1968), vol. 1, pp. 236–40.

152   The Circus of Caligula and Nero, dating from the middle of the first cen-

tury AD, stood in the Ager Vaticanus just south of St Peter's. See Nash (1968), vol. 1, pp. 234–5; Dal Maso (1975), p. 87.

153 The Circus of Flaminius, built in 221 BC, stood in the Campus Martius, between Piazza Cairoli and the Theatre of Marcellus, and Via del Portico d'Ottavio and the Tiber. See Nash (1968), vol. 1, pp. 232–3; Krautheimer (1980), pp. 251, 305.

154 The Circus Agonius was the Stadium of Domitian, inaugurated in AD 92–96 with athletic games called the 'Agoni Capitolini'. The medieval name 'Campus Agonis' gradually evolved into the present appellation of Piazza Navona ('agone' → 'n'agona' → 'navona'). See Nash (1968), vol. 2, pp. 387–90; Dal Maso (1975), pp. 88–9.

155 Possibly in reference to the Circus Varianus, dating from the reign of Elagabalus. It was built on land between the church of Santa Croce in Gerusalemme and the Porta Maggiore. See also note 166, below, on the Amphitheatrum Castrense, and Nash (1968), vol. 1, pp. 241–2.

156 This refers to the hippodromus in the Horti Sallustiani – on which see 'On the Horti', below – in the valley between the Pincian and Quirinal hills, with walls and terraces extending up the slope of the latter hill. It was referred to by Renaissance antiquarians as the Circus Florae and illustrated somewhat fancifully in Domenico Rossi and Pietro Santi Bartoli, *Romanae Magnitudinis Monumenta* (1699), p. 95. On the church of the Trinità, on Monte Pincio, see Palladio, *Churches*, [p. 35].

157 Literally 'bull's head' – the Tomb of Caecilia Metella. See 'On the Mete', below.

158 This refers to the Circus of Maxentius, previously attributed to Caracalla, on the Via Appia, dedicated in 309. See Nash (1968), vol. 2, p. 159, fig. 880; Dal Maso (1975), pp. 86–7. See also 'On some Festivals and Games which they used to celebrate in Rome', below.

159 On the Roman theatres in general see Vitruvius, *De architectura*, V.iii–ix; Alberti, VIII. vii [pp. 269–78]; Dal Maso (1975), pp. 90–3; Hornblower and Spawforth (2003), p. 1495. RIBA X 4R. Palladio's interest in these buildings is attested by his production of drawings of the ancient theatre for Barbaro's edition of Vitruvius's treatise (1556), and his design for what was described by contemporaries as a 'wooden theatre . . . similar to that of the ancient Romans', erected in the Salone della Basilica in Vicenza in 1561–62. See Puppi (1975), p. 341, no. 75; see also pp. 355, no. 89, 417, no. 128.

160 The Theatre of Pompey was the first stone-built – that is, permanent – theatre in the Campus Martius, constructed in 55 BC, with a temple to Venus Victrix above the seating area and a diameter of 158 metres. It was situated between what is now Via di Grotta Pinta (which follows the semicircular line of the auditorium) and Campo dei Fiori. See Pliny, *Natural History*, XXXVI, 41, 115; Alberti, II. ii [p. 36], VIII. vii [p. 269]; Nash (1968), vol. 2, pp. 423–8; Dal Maso (1975), p. 92; Krautheimer (1980), pp. 243, 244, fig. 192, 299.

161 Marcus Claudius Marcellus (42–23 BC), the son of C. Claudius Marcellus and of Octavia (c.69–11 BC), sister of Augustus. The Theatre of Marcellus was built between 23 and 13 BC, with a capacity of 20,000 people. It was restored by the

emperors Vespasian (AD 9–79) and Alexander Severus, and (as the text indicates) in the sixteenth century it was converted into a palace for the Savelli by Baldassarre Peruzzi. See *Arte Antica*, VI, p. 837a; Nash (1968), vol. 2, pp. 418–22; Dal Maso (1975), pp. 90–3; Fletcher (1975), pp. 303–5; Krautheimer (1980), pp. 12, 17, 250, fig. 195, p. 251. On this theatre see Serlio, Book Three, pp. XLVI–XLIX [pp. 136–9], which includes a woodcut plan and elevation. Cited by Palladio, *QL*, I. xiii [p. 19], xv [p. 26]. RIBA X 20R, X 20V, XIV 3V.

162   The Theatre of Balbus was dedicated in 13 BC, with a capacity of some 6,000–7,000 people, and was adjoined to the west by a cryptoporticus known as the Crypta Balbi. The theatre is now thought to have been located on the Piazza Paganica. See Nash (1968), vol. 1, pp. 297–300 (Crypta Balbi), vol. 2, pp. 414–17 (Theatrum Balbi); Dal Maso (1975), p. 92. RIBA XI 1, XI 2R, XI 2V.

163   On the amphitheatres in general see Alberti, VIII. viii [p. 278}; Fletcher (1975), pp. 307–9; Hornblower and Spawforth (2003), p. 76.

164   See 'On the Colossi', below.

165   The Colosseum, or Flavian Amphitheatre, was begun by Vespasian in AD 70 and inaugurated by Titus in AD 80. See Nash (1968), vol. 1, pp. 17–25; Dal Maso (1975), pp. 67–79; Fletcher (1975), pp. 306–9; Krautheimer (1980), pp. 9, 11, fig. 9; Hornblower and Spawforth (2003), pp. 365–6. See Serlio, Book Three, pp. LXII-II–LXIX [pp. 154–59], which includes a woodcut plan, section and elevation. Serlio follows Andrea Fulvio in attributing the inception of this exemplar of antique architecture to Augustus. See Fulvio, A., *Antiquitates urbis*, 2nd ed. (1545), IV, fol. 26. Cited by Palladio, *QL*, I. xix [p. 55]. RIBA VIII 14R, VIII 14V, VIII 15R, VIII 15V, VIII 16, VIII 17.

166   The Amphitheatre of Statilius was erected in the Campus Martius in 29 BC, in commemoration of Titus Statilius Taurus's victory in Africa. The amphitheatre near Santa Croce in Gerusalemme was in fact the Amphitheatrum Castrense, built of brick by Elagabalus or Alexander in the second century AD. See Nash (1968), vol. 1, pp. 13–16; Dal Maso (1975), p. 80. RIBA X 17V, XI 5V.

167   In fact, eighteen fora are listed here. On the fora in general see Fletcher (1975), pp. 272–4; Krautheimer (1980); Boatwright, M.T., *Hadrian and the City of Rome* (1987), pp. 75–98; Hornblower and Spawforth (2003), pp. 606, 926 (markets and fairs). RIBA VIII 11R, VIII 11V, X 15V.

168   As the chief public square, the Roman Forum was the heart of ancient Rome. It was divided into three distinct areas: the Comitium Universale, or political centre; the religious centre of the Regia; and the Forum proper. Cited by Palladio, *QL*, I. ix [p. 15], III. xix [p. 200], IV. xviii [p. 279]. See drawings of the mid-1530s by Maarten van Heemskerck; Filippi (1990), nos. 7, 8, 24 [fols. 6r, 9r, 12r]. For reconstructions of the Roman Forum, see Nash (1968), vol. 1, pp. 446–50; Dal Maso (1975), pp. 13–29; Boatwright (1987), pp. 99–133; Hornblower and Spawforth (2003), pp. 607–8.

169   See 'On the Rostra and what they were', below.

170   The Temple of Vesta (founded in 715 BC; present structure AD 205) in the Roman Forum was where the vestals guarded the sacred fire. Vesta, goddess of the

hearth, protected the fire, which symbolized the perpetuity of the state. It is a circular structure of twenty Corinthian columns. The first temple on the site was probably made of straw and wood. It was burnt down several times, notably during
Nero's fire of AD 64 and in 191. It was rebuilt for the last time by Septimius Severus
and his wife, Julia Domna. See Dal Maso (1975), pp. 21–4; Fletcher (1975), pp. 283–4.
See also 'On the Priests, on the Vestal Virgins . . .', below.

171   The Forum of Caesar (Forum Julium) was the first of the imperial fora
and was dedicated by Caesar in 46 BC. Its focal point was the Temple of Venus
Genetrix, from whom Julius Caesar claimed descent. Palladio calls this the Temple
of Neptune; QL, IV. xxxi [pp. 340–5]. See Pliny, Natural History, XXXVI, 103; Nash
(1968), vol. 1, pp. 424–32; Bussagi, M. (ed.), Rome: Art and Architecture (1999), p. 26;
Hornblower and Spawforth (2003), p. 607. RIBA XI 20R, XIV 12.

172   The Forum of Augustus was built to commemorate the victory of
Philippi (42 BC) and dedicated to Mars Ultor (the temple to this god was dedicated
in 2 BC). See Pliny, Natural History, XXXVI, 102; Nash (1968), vol. 1, pp. 401–10;
Hornblower and Spawforth (2003), p. 607. See the plan in QL, IV. vii
[p. 226].

173   This refers to the three columns of the marble walkway built by Caligula,
mentioned above. The Forum of Nerva, or Forum Transitorium (so-called because
it led into the Forum of Vespasian), was begun by Domitian and completed in AD
97. In the east was the Temple of Minerva. This forum is illustrated by Palladio, QL,
IV, viii [pp. 233–40]. See also the drawing of the mid-1530s by Maarten van
Heemskerck; Filippi (1990), no. 9 [fol. 37r]. See Nash (1968), vol. 1, pp. 433–8;
Hornblower and Spawforth (2003), p. 607. RIBA XI 19R, XI 19V, XIV 4R.

174   Designed by Apollodorus of Damascus, the Forum of Trajan, built AD
107–12, was the last and most splendid of the imperial fora. It was approached
through the Markets of Trajan, built shortly before the forum. See Nash (1968), vol.
2, pp. 49–58. A street led towards Trajan's Column, in front of which stood the
Basilica Ulpia, dedicated to the administration of justice. See Nash (1968), vol. 1, pp.
450–6; Krautheimer (1980), pp. 10, 12, fig. 11; Hornblower and Spawforth (2003), p.
608.

175   The Forum Boarium, or cattle market, was the oldest market of ancient
Rome. Its site was bounded by the Capitoline, Palatine and Aventine hills, adjacent
to the Tiber Island and part of this site is today occupied by the Piazza della Bocca
della Verità. See Nash (1968), vol. 1, pp. 411–17; Hornblower and Spawforth (2003),
p. 607. See also 'On the Velabrum', below. See Palladio's drawing in the Vicenza City
Museum, of details of the Doric Order from the 'Boarius Forum'; D 5 v (Puppi
(1990), no. 17).

176   The Forum Holitorium was the vegetable and oil market of ancient
Rome. It extended from the Capitoline Hill to the Tiber. It was the site of temples
dedicated to Juno Sospita, Spes and Janus. See 'On the Temples of the Ancients, outside Rome', below. See Nash (1968), vol. 1, pp. 418–23.

177   The Forum Piscarium was dedicated to the commerce of fish and was

situated between the Capitoline Hill and the Tiber, in the area of the current Roman Ghetto.

178 'In Porcilibus' means next to the pigsties. See Muth, R., 'Forum suarium', *Museum Helveticum*, vol. 2 (1945), pp. 227–36.

179 The Forum Archimonium never existed. Fanciful sixteenth-century scholarship derived it (incorrectly) from Sancti Nicolai de Archemoniis, itself a garbled Latin version of the medieval church of San Niccolò degli Arcioni. See Huelsen, C., *Le chiese di Roma nel medio evo* (1927), p. 390.

180 According to Francesco Albertini in *Opusculum de mirabilibus novae et veteris urbis Romae* (1510), sig.Giiii *v* (in the chapter on fora and curias), the 'Forum Sallustianum' was on the Quirinal beyond where Santa Sabina used to stand, near to Santa Susanna. This forum was not thought to be one in which business was transacted but rather simply a decorated part of the Horti Sallustiani, on which see 'On the Horti', below.

181 The Arch of Septimius Severus was erected at the western end of the Roman Forum in AD 203. See *Arte Antica*, VI, pp. 828b–829a–b; Nash (1968), vol. 1, pp. 126–30; Fletcher (1975), pp. 320–1, 323; Dal Maso (1975), pp. 48–9; Krautheimer (1980), pp. 9–10. See also Serlio, Book Three, pp. CX–CXIII [pp. 200–3]. Cited by Palladio, *QL*, IV. xxx [p. 336]. See Palladio's drawings in the Vicenza City Museum, of a front view and ground plan, profile of entablature, profile and front view of bracket and Composite capital, various mouldings and the base of a column; D 2 *r–v*, D 13 *r–v*, (Puppi (1990), nos. 22–25). RIBA XII 6B.R, XII 6B.V. See also in general RIBA VIII 13V.

182 The Arch of Constantine was built in 312–15 to celebrate the emperor's victory over Maxentius. It used sculpture and reliefs from monuments dating from the time of Trajan, Hadrian and Marcus Aurelius (AD 121–80). See the drawings of the mid-1530s by Maarten van Heemskerck; Filippi (1990), nos. 55, 57 [fols. 69*r*, 56*v*]. See *Arte Antica*, VI, pp. 830b, 987, fig. 1094; Nash (1968), vol. 1, pp. 104–12; Fletcher (1975), pp. 322–3; Dal Maso (1975), pp. 50–1. See also Serlio, Book Three, pp. CXVI-II–CXXI [pp. 208–11]. Cited by Palladio, *QL*, I. xix [p. 55]. See Palladio's drawings in the Vicenza City Museum, of a front view and ground plan, entablature and a capital, lower pedestal, column base and various mouldings; D 14 *r*, D 15 *r–v*, (Puppi (1990), nos. 26–8). RIBA XII 5R, XII 5V.

183 The Arch of Titus was built in AD 81, after the death of Titus, and is situated at the summit of the Velia, the narrow ridge connecting the Palatine and Oppian hills at the head of the Via Sacra. See drawing of the mid-1530s by Maarten van Heemskerck; Filippi (1990), no. 56 [fol. 56*r*]. See also *Arte Antica*, VI, pp. 826a–b, 828a–b; Nash (1968), vol. 1, pp. 133–5; Fletcher (1975), pp. 318–19; Dal Maso (1975), pp. 46–7. See also Serlio, Book Three, pp. CIII–CVII [pp. 194–7]. Cited by Palladio, *QL*, I. xix [p. 55], IV. x [p. 248]. See Palladio's drawings in the Vicenza City Museum, of a front view and ground plan, cornice and Composite capital, column base, pedestal and details, pedestal of the attic story and a moulding; D 9 *r–v*, D 10 *r–v*, (Puppi (1990), nos. 18–20).

184   In the transcription on CD-ROM in the collection entitled 'Art Theories of the Italian Renaissance' published by Chadwyck-Healey (1997), the text incorrectly has *buoni* ('goods').

185   The 'Arcus Argentariorum' (or so-called 'Arco Boario'), next to the church of San Giorgio in Velabro, was erected in 204 and dedicated to Septimius Severus. See *Arte Antica*, VI, pp. 829b–830a–b; Nash (1968), vol. 1, pp. 88–91; Fletcher (1975), pp. 319, 323. See also Serlio, Book Three, pp. CVIII–CIX [pp. 198–9].

186   The Arch of Portugal (possibly of the time of Hadrian or Marcus Aurelius) bridged the Via del Corso at the corner of the Via della Vite; it was demolished by Pope Alexander VII in 1662. See Nash (1968), vol. 1, pp. 83–7. See also http://www.medici.org/news/dom/dom022001.html.

187   The Arch of Gallienus was a triple-arched gate erected in the time of Augustus but named after Emperor Gallienus and his consort Salonina by the city prefect M. Aurelius Victor in 262. To its left stood the church of SS Vito e Modesto, hence the gate's name in the text. The middle arch survives. See Nash (1968), vol. 1, pp. 115–17. RIBA XII 7.

188   Possibly in reference to the Portico of the Nations, built by Augustus and containing statues representing all the nations of the Roman world, cited by Pliny, *Natural History*, XXXVI, 39. Although current scholarship claims that its position is unknown, some have connected it with the Portico of Pompey or 'Crypta Balbi' (a long way from the Palatine). On porticoes in general see Nash (1968), vol. 2, pp. 235–58; Hornblower and Spawforth (2003), p. 1228.

189   Emperor Gordianus III (r. 225–44) intended to build – but apparently never did – the Porticus Gordiani in the Campus Martius at the foot of the Pincian Hill, 1,000 feet (304 metres) in length and therefore large enough to extend to the Via Flaminia. See Capitolinus, J., *Gordiani tres*, ed. H. Peter (1865), chapter 32.

190   In fact the monumental entrance to the Portico of Octavia (mentioned below) serves as the entrance to Sant'Angelo di Pescheria.

191   That is, the Basilica of Maxentius, or Constantine, confused in the Renaissance with the Temple of Peace, which had been completely destroyed in antiquity. See 'On the Temples', below. The Portico of Livia was built by Augustus and named after his wife, Livia Drusilla (58 BC–AD 29). Cited by Palladio, *QL*, IV. vi [p. 221].

192   The Portico of Octavia was rectangular – around 119 by 132 metres – with about three hundred columns, and enclosed two temples, dedicated to Jupiter and Juno. It was erected by Quintus Caecilius Metellus in 146 BC and was reconstructed by Augustus in honour of his sister, Octavia, in around 23 BC. It was restored by Septimius Severus in AD 203. It influenced Palladio in his design of the Villa Chieticati. RIBA VII 5V, XI 17R, XI 17V, XI 18R, XI 18V. See drawing of the mid-1530s by Maarten van Heemskerck; Filippi (1990), no. 61 [fol. 32r]. See Nash (1968), vol. 2, pp. 254–8; Krautheimer (1980), pp. 12, 248, 251, fig. 196. See Palladio's drawing in the Vicenza City Museum, of a ground plan and front elevation, with a detail of the entablature and the impost of a side doorway; D 26 r, (Puppi (1990), no. 16).

193   The Temple of Antoninus and Faustina was built in AD 141 by Antoninus

Pius in honour of his wife, Faustina, and was converted into the church of San Lorenzo in Miranda. The pronaos is composed of Corinthian monolithic columns, six in front and two on either side. Described and illustrated by Palladio, *QL*, IV. ix [pp. 241–7]. RIBA XI 11V, XI 15V, XI 16.

194   This is in fact the Temple of Saturn, by tradition inaugurated in 497 BC. This has eight surviving columns, whereas the Temple of Concord (possibly built in 218 BC, and rebuilt in 121 BC) is ruined. The temples stand either side of the Temple of Vespasian, mentioned next. For the Temple of Saturn, mistakenly identified by Palladio as Concordia (in common with his peers), see *QL*, IV. xxx [pp. 336–9, 377, n. 157]. See also Nash (1968), vol. 2, pp. 294–8. RIBA VIII 14V, XI 11R, XI 20R, XI 20V.

195   That is, the three surviving columns of the Temple of Vespasian, cited in Alberti, III. v [p. 68], and reconstructed by Palladio, *QL*, IV. xix [pp. 282–4].

196   This is the portico of the Pantheon. See especially Davies, P., et al., 'The Pantheon: Triumph of Rome or Triumph of Compromise?', *Art History*, vol. 10, no. 2 (1987), pp. 133–53, Wilson Jones, M., *The Principles of Roman Architecture*, (2000), pp. 199–213. See also Serlio, Book Three, pp. VIII–XII [pp. 102–6], and 'On the Temples', below.

197   The ruined fountain known as the 'Trofei di Mario' was built at the time of Alexander Severus. It was formerly the terminal of the Aqua Julia. See 'On the Aquae and those who built them, bringing them into Rome', above. The marble panoplies known as the 'Trophies of Marius' were removed from here to the balustrade of Piazza del Campidoglio by Pope Sixtus V (r. 1585–90). Cited by Palladio, *QL*, IV. xi [p. 251]. See Morton (1966), pp. 52, 120; Nash (1968), vol. 2, pp. 125–6; Bober, P.P., and R. Rubinstein, *Renaissance Artists and Antique Sculpture* (1986), no. 174a–b.

198   Trajan's Column stands in the Forum of Trajan and was erected in AD 113. The pedestal became his mausoleum after AD 117. See *Arte Antica*, II, pp. 756–60, and *Arte Antica*, 'Atlante dei complessi figurati', Tav. 75–107; Nash (1968), vol. 1, pp. 283–6; Dal Maso (1975), pp. 53–4; Fletcher (1975), pp. 325–6; Wilson Jones (2000), pp. 161–74; Hornblower and Spawforth (2003), p. 1544. Cited by Palladio, *QL*, I. x [p. 16], I. xxviii [p. 67]. See also Serlio, Book Three, pp. LX–LXI [pp. 150–1]. RIBA VIII 12R.

199   This is in fact the Column of Marcus Aurelius (Colonna Antonina), which was modelled on Trajan's Column and completed in AD 193. See Nash (1968), vol. 1, pp. 276–9; Dal Maso (1975), p. 55; Fletcher (1975), pp. 326–7. Cited by Palladio, *QL*, I. x [p. 16], IV. xv [p. 267]. The column of Antoninus Pius was in fact a different column that once stood in the same area, the pedestal of which now stands in the great hemicycle of the Giardino della Pigna of the Vatican.

200   The Column of Constantine (today Çemberlita), 57 metres high and taken from the Temple of Apollo in Rome, was erected in Constantinople in honour of Constantine in 330 to mark the fact that this city was then the capital of the Roman Empire. Topped by a bronze statue of Constantine dressed as Apollo, it stood in the centre of a large, oval-shaped square on top of the second hill of

Constantinople. This square, surrounded by colonnades, was called the Forum of Constantine. See Gibbon, E., *History of the Decline and Fall of the Roman Empire* (1838–39), vol. 2, chapter 17, part 2.

201   That is, 'To the father of the fatherland'. This column, inscribed in Latin *Parenti Patriae*, was erected by the mob in honour of Julius Caesar on the site where his body had been cremated at the east end of the Forum; Suetonius, *De vita Caesarum* (*The Lives of the Caesars*), 'Julius Caesar', 85. The column was soon removed by Publius Cornelius Dolabella (*c.*70–43 BC); Cicero, *Letters to Atticus*, xiv. 15.

202   The text is from Pliny, *Natural History*, XXXIV, 39, who has 500 talents.

203   That is, another colossus of Apollo (the 'Apollus Tuscanicus'): again, the text is from Pliny, *Natural History*, XXXIV, 43.

204   This was the gigantic statue of Constantine. See 'On the Campidoglio', below.

205   Pliny, *Natural History*, XXXIV, 40.

206   Emperor Commodus (161–92 BC) had the Colossus of Nero (see note 207 below) converted into a statue of himself as Hercules. See Anonymous, *Historia Augusta* (1992–), 'Commodus'. On Commodus's death, however, it was restored as god of the sun, and so it remained.

207   This was a huge gilt bronze statue of Nero as god of the sun by Zenodorus. As the text records, it was 120 feet (36 metres) high, and it was the largest bronze statue ever made – even larger than its model, the Colossus of Rhodes. The statue was given a new base when moved by Hadrian from the vestibule of the Domus Aurea ('Golden House') to near the Colosseum (which was named after it), in order to build the Temple of Venus and Roma. See Nash (1968), vol. 1, pp. 268–9. On Nero's Golden House, see 'On Nero's Golden House', below.

208   Gaius Cestius (d. *c.*12 BC) was a praetor, tribune of the Plebs, and a member of the college of the Septemviri Epulones (in charge of solemn banquets). The pyramid is of brick faced with marble, standing 27 metres high with a base of 22 metres square. It is incorporated in the city fortifications built by the Emperor Aurelian, next to the Porta Ostiensis. See Nash (1968), vol. 2, pp. 321–3.

209   Literally 'sweating meta'. A meta served as a boundary or distance post.

210   This marble-faced fountain marked the boundary of five regions of the Augustan city: I Porta Capena, II Caelimontium, III Isis et Serapis, IV Templum Pacis, and V Palatium. It received its name from its resemblance to the conical turning-post (meta) for chariot races in circuses, and from the fact that it 'sweated' water through numerous small orifices. It was erected by Domitian in AD 82, restored by Constantine, demolished in 1936 on the orders of Mussolini and excavated in 1982. See Nash (1968), vol. 2, pp. 61–3; Dal Maso (1975), p. 110.

211   This is the tomb of Caecilia Metella, dating from around 20 BC, which stands at the top of a short rise at the third mile outside Rome on the Via Appia, thereby serving as a meta. It consists of a quadrangular base, above which stands the cylindrical body of the monument. It is about 20 metres high and covered with blocks of travertine. It has a frieze of ox skulls, hence its name 'Capo di Bove' – literally 'bull's head' – and carries a tablet commemorating Caecilia Metella, daughter

of Quintus Metellus Creticus, the general who conquered the island of Crete. Caecilia married the son of the triumvir Licinius Crassus (*c.*115–53 BC), the richest man in Rome. See Dal Maso (1975), p. 112; Fletcher (1975), p. 313.

212   The smaller of these two obelisks from the Circus Maximus, that of Ramses II (thirteenth century BC), now in the Piazza del Popolo, was brought by Augustus from Heliopolis towards 10 BC. See Nash (1968), vol. 2, pp. 137–8. See also Alberti, VI. vi [pp. 164–5]; Serlio, Book Three, pp. LXII–LXIII [pp. 152–3], obelisk 'O'. The larger of the two, Obeliscus Constantii, was that of Pharaoh Totmoses III (fifteenth century BC), and was transported to Rome from Alexandria by Constantius II in 357, although it originally came from the Temple of Ammon at Thebes. See Nash (1968), vol. 2, pp. 142–3; Dal Maso (1975), p. 43.

213   Latin measure for dry goods (traditionally translated as a 'peck').

214   On how the obelisks were brought to Rome, see Pliny, *Natural History*, XXXVI, 64–74.

215   This obelisk was dedicated to Psammetichus II (sixth century BC) and later formed the gnomon for Augustus's sundial, described by Pliny, *Natural History*, XXXVI, 63–73. It was moved in 1792 to its present location in the Piazza Montecitorio. See Nash (1968), vol. 2, pp. 134–6; Dal Maso (1975), p. 43. See also Serlio, Book Three, pp. LXII–LXIII [pp. 152–3], obelisk 'R'.

216   Two obelisks had stood in front of the Mausoleum of Augustus, on which see 'On the Tomb of Augustus, of Hadrian, and of Septimius', below. They were both discovered in 1527 near the church of San Rocco. See Fulvio, A., *Antiquitates urbis* (1527), fol. 71*v*. In 1586 the obelisk that had been lying in front of the church in what is now the Via di Ripetta was taken to the Piazza dell' Esquilino, where it was erected by Domenico Fontana for Sixtus V in front of the apse of Santa Maria Maggiore. The second obelisk became buried behind San Rocco, but in 1782 it was excavated and erected in the Piazza del Quirinale. See Nash (1968), vol. 2, pp. 155–6. See also Serlio, Book Three, pp. LXII–LXIII [pp. 152–53], obelisk 'Q'.

217   This obelisk was brought from Heliopolis at the time of Caligula (AD 12–41) and placed on the spina of his circus (later the Circus of Nero), south of the basilica of St Peter's near Santa Maria della Febbre. See drawings of the mid-1530s by Maarten van Heemskerck; Filippi (1990), nos. 29, 30 [fols. 7*r*, 22*v*]. In 1586 Sixtus V ordered its removal from here to its present site in front of the basilica. See Pliny, *Natural History*, XXXVI, 74; Nash (1968), vol. 2, pp. 161–2; Dal Maso (1975), p. 43. See also Serlio, Book Three, pp. LXII–LXIII [pp. 152–3], obelisk 'P'.

218   This obelisk, 2.7 metres tall, possibly came from Heliopolis. It stood near Santa Maria in Aracoeli on the Capitoline Hill, at the foot of the steps leading to the church and convent. When Pope Paul III (r. 1534–49) was altering the Piazza del Campidoglio, he started to build a new access to the church and the obelisk was taken down in 1542. In 1582 Ciriaco Mattei, a nobleman, had it erected in the gardens of his villa on the Celian Hill, the Villa Celimontana. See drawing of the mid-1530s by Maarten van Heemskerck of Santa Maria in Aracoeli with the obelisk; Filippi (1990), no. 21 [fol. 16*r*]. See Nash (1968), vol. 2, pp. 139–41.

219   The small Obeliscus Isei Campensis – Di San Mauto – with its hieroglyphs, was discovered when the apse of Santa Maria sopra Minerva was rebuilt in 1374. In the middle of the fifteenth century it was set up in the Piazza di San Mauto. In 1711 Pope Clement XI (r. 1700–21) had the obelisk erected in front of the Pantheon. See Nash (1968), vol. 2, pp. 150–1.

220   That is, the church of Santa Maria sopra Minerva. A number of obelisks were discovered near here that had belonged to the Isaeum Campense, or Temple of Isis in the Campus Martius, which formerly stood near this church. See Nash (1968), vol. 2, pp. 148–52; Dal Maso (1975), p. 43. As for the Temple of Minerva (standing until the beginning of the seventeenth century), Palladio made drawings of it and these are held in the Vicenza City Museum, D 7 r, D 21 r, D 30 r–v, D 7 v, (Puppi (1990), nos. 7–13). See also *QL*, IV. viii [pp. 233–40].

221   The colossal equestrian statue of Marcus Aurelius, the centrepiece of Michelangelo's design for the Piazza del Campidoglio, is of gilded bronze. It is thought to date from the latter part of the emperor's reign (AD 161–80), or possibly from the year of his death. It is the only Roman equestrian statue of this period to survive. It is thought to have stood on the Lateran Hill as early as 782 (see a drawing of the mid-1530s by Maarten van Heemskerck; Filippi (1990), no. 20 [fol. 71*v*]) and was brought from there to the Capitoline Hill by order of Pope Paul III in 1538. See Nash (1968), vol. 1, pp. 391–2; Krautheimer (1980), pp. 192, 193, figs. 153–4; Bober and Rubinstein (1986), no. 176. Cited by Palladio, *QL*, IV. ix [p. 241].

222   On ancient statues in general, both Greek and Roman, see Hornblower and Spawforth (2003), pp. 1373–4, 1439–40.

223   The colossal figure known as the 'Marforio' is now thought to be of a river god. It probably dates from the second century AD and was found at the foot of the Capitoline Hill (Jupiter was regarded as the city's special protector and his temple was on the Capitoline Hill, so it was natural to associate the statue with the god). The statue is today part of a fountain by Giacomo della Porta in the inner court of the Museo Capitolino. See Bober and Rubinstein (1986), pp. 99ff. Cited by Palladio, *QL*, IV. xxi [p. 340].

224   The Equus Domitiani (AD 91) once stood in the Roman Forum. A coin of Domitian of AD 95–6 shows a rider and the horse, under whose raised right hoof is a head – a symbolic representation of the conquest of the Rhine province. See Nash (1968), vol. 1, pp. 389–90.

225   Tiridates IV received the crown of Armenia from the hands of Nero in AD 66 in Rome.

226   Long called *The Horsetamers* or *The Dioscuri*, the pair of ancient statues by the Greek sculptors Pheidias (fifth century BC) and Praxiteles (fourth century BC) gave the name Montecavallo (Horse Hill) to the Quirinal Hill during the Middle Ages and Renaissance. They are now in the Piazza del Quirinale. See Nash (1968), vol. 2, p. 444; Coffin, D., *The Villa in the Life of Renaissance Rome* (1979), pp. 181ff.; Bober and Rubinstein (1986), no. 125. These statues are mentioned by Serlio in Book Three, p. LXXX [p. 170]. Cited by Palladio, *QL*, IV. xii [p. 253].

227   On the libraries in ancient Rome in general see Hornblower and Spawforth (2003), p. 855.

228   The Greek and Latin libraries of Augustus were in the 'Domus Publica' on the Palatine Hill. They were divided by a great reading room, in the centre of which was a statue of the emperor with the attributes of Apollo. The collection included 'books' on civil law and the liberal arts. See Dal Maso (1975), p. 10.

229   The Library of the Gordians is cited in Alberti, VIII. ix [p. 286]. See also Capitolinus (1865).

230   The Bibliotheca Ulpia was in Trajan's Forum. A great civic monument, it had reading rooms covering 460 square metres (5,000 square feet).

231   Gaius Asinius Pollio (76 BC–AD 4) was a historian, although his work included poetry, tragedy and oratory in Atticist style. His *Historiae* treated the period from 60 BC to the battle of Philippi in 42 BC. A Consul in 40 BC, he celebrated a victory over the Parthini of Illyria in 39 BC and from the booty he built the first public library in Rome. See Hornblower and Spawforth (2003), p. 192.

232   Manius Valerius Maximus Corvinus Messalla was consul in 263 BC and a censor in 252 BC. In 263, alone or with his colleague M. Otacilius Crassus, he secured the surrender of several communities in eastern Sicily. According to the scholar Marcus Terentius Varro, he was the first in Rome to set up in public a (Greek) sundial. See Hornblower and Spawforth (2003), p. 1579. On timepieces in general, see Vitruvius, *De architectura*, IX.vii–viii; McEwen (2003), pp. 229–50; Hornblower and Spawforth (2003), p. 350. Valerius is cited by Palladio, *QL*, IV. xxx [p. 336].

233   According to Vitruvius (*De architectura*, IX.viii. 4), Ctesibius of Alexandria invented the water-clock in 270 BC, as Palladio would have known. See Hornblower and Spawforth (2003), p. 412. The water-clock was introduced into Greece by Plato, and into Rome by P. Cornelius Scipio Nasica, in about 157 BC. See Pliny, *Natural History*, VII, 215.

234   The text incorrectly has *Comano* for *Romano*.

235   In fact the House of Augustus was next to the Temple of Apollo on the Palatine Hill, approached from the Forum. It included the House of Livia (Augustus's wife), and dates from the first century BC. This house is distinct from the Domus Augustana, or so-called 'Palace of Augustus' – the private residence of the emperor or 'Augustus', rather than that of the Emperor Augustus – which formed part of Domitian's Palace and had a grand segmental portico and stepped terraces overlooking the Circus Maximus: RIBA XV 2, XV 11R. See Nash (1968), vol. 1, pp. 310–15 (Domus Augusti), 316–38 (Domus Augustiana); Fletcher (1975), pp. 327–38. On palaces in general, see McKay, A.G., *Houses, Villas and Palaces in the Roman World* (1975); Hornblower and Spawforth (2003), pp. 731–2, 1094; Hales, S., *The Roman House and Social Identity* (2003).

236   See 'On the Towers', below.

237   St Lawrence was martyred by Emperor Decius (*c*.200–51) in the Palace of Salustine, and the church of San Lorenzo in Panisperna was built on the spot. See Palladio, *Churches*, [p. 52], which has the same statement.

238   The Lateran Palace adjoins San Giovanni in Laterano and dates from the time of Constantine. It was almost destroyed in the fire of 1308 that devastated the basilica. See Krautheimer (1980) and, on this church, Palladio, *Churches*, [p. 10].

239   Nero's 'Golden House', or Domus Aurea, was created by him after the fire of AD 64. He turned a vast area (perhaps as much as 300 acres) of the centre of Rome into a park, with the main entrance to his palace from the Forum along the new Via Sacra, through a porticoed vestibule housing a colossal bronze statue of the emperor. The palace was a long porticoed structure covering at least two storeys with symmetrical five-sided courts either side of a domed octagonal hall. According to Suetonius, the lake was 'more like a sea than a lake'. See Pliny, *Natural History*, XXXVI, 111, 113; Alberti, VI. v [pp. 163–4]; Boethius, A., *The Golden House of Nero: Some Aspects of Roman Architecture* (1960); Nash (1968), vol. 1, pp. 339–48; Fletcher (1975), p. 329; Krautheimer (1980), pp. 17, 187, 191; Hornblower and Spawforth (2003), p. 493; Ball, L.F., *The Domus Aurea and the Roman Architectural Revolution*, (2003).

240   See 'On the Colossi', above.

241   Palladio had a special interest in the ancient house, and produced the speculative elevation and plan published in Barbaro's edition of Vitruvius's treatise (1556, and 1567) illustrating book VI, chapters iii–v. See Alberti's ninth book, on the ornamentation of private buildings, and Palladio, *QL*, II. vii [pp. 109–11]. See also McKay (1975); Hornblower and Spawforth (2003), p. 732; Hales (2003).

242   That is, the Palatine hut of Romulus. See Pensabene, P., 'Casa Romuli sul Palatino', *Pontificia Accademia Romana di Archeologia*, vol. 63 (1990–91), pp. 115–62; McEwen (2003), pp. 143, 359, n. 226.

243   Seneca (*Letters*, 86) wrote of making a visit to the villa where the great Scipio Africanus (236–c.183 BC) had spent his last days and was buried, the house having become a shrine to its famous occupant.

244   The houses of the Cornelii are cited by Palladio, *QL*, IV. xii [p. 253].

245   According to Pliny, *Natural History*, XXXVI, 7, the orator Lucius Crassus (140–91 BC) was the first to install in his house on the Palatine columns of foreign marble, and as a consequence was nicknamed the 'Palatine Venus' by the politician Marcus Brutus (c.85–42 BC).

246   Pliny, *Natural History*, XXXVI, 6 (who has 38 feet tall).

247   Pliny, *Natural History*, XXXVI, 48 (quoting Cornelius Nepos, the friend of Cicero).

248   Santa Maria della Consolazione; on this church see Palladio, *Churches*, [p. 58]. On Ovid's villa, see 'On the Temples of the Ancients outside Rome', below.

249   That is, 'curias'.

250   On the Roman curia, see Vitruvius, *De architectura*, V.ii; Alberti, VIII. xi [pp. 283–5]; Hornblower and Spawforth (2003), p. 414. On Caesar's Curia Julia, see Nash (1968), vol. 1, pp. 301–3.

251   On San Pietro in Vincoli see Palladio, *Churches*, [p. 52].

252   The curia of Hostilius, said to be the site for the so-called Temple of Peace, is cited by Palladio, *QL*, IV. vi [p. 221].

253   On the Senate, see Hornblower and Spawforth (2003), pp. 1385–8.

254   See 'On the Porticoes', above. See also *QL*, IV. xxx [p. 336]: 'In this temple public concerns and business were often discussed, and one deduces from this that it was consecrated, because the priests allowed the Senate to meet to discuss public affairs only in consecrated temples, and they consecrated only those that were built with good omens, so that temples built under those circumstances were also called Senate Chambers.'

255   See 'On the Gates', above.

256   During a battle with the Samnites and Etruscans in 296 BC Appius Claudius Caecus, so Ovid relates (*Fasti*, vi. 201–5), vowed to build the Temple of Bellona (the Roman goddess of war). It was dedicated several years later on 3 June and was built in the Campus Martius 'in the Circus Flaminius', upon part of which the Theatre of Marcellus was later built. The temple was outside the gates of the city and the earliest city boundary (*pomerium*). The Senate met there to discuss generals' claims to a Triumph and to receive ambassadors from foreign states. See Nash (1968), vol. 1, pp. 202–3 (on the history of the temple's identification with ancient remains); Hornblower and Spawforth (2003), p. 238. In front of the temple was the Colonna Bellica, where the ceremony of declaring war was performed. See 'On the Colonna Bellica', below.

257   On the seven Kings and the subsequent Consuls, see 'On the Building of Rome', above. See also Hornblower and Spawforth (2003), pp. 1240 (praetor), 1549–50 (tribuni plebis), 1287 (quaestor), 15–16 (aediles or magistrates), 307–8 (censor), 1555 (triumviri), 1238–9 (prefects), 309–10 (centumviri, a special civil court at Rome). See also Greenidge, A.H.J., *Roman Public Life* (1901); Brunt, P.A., *Social Conflicts in the Roman Republic* (1971).

258   An important aspect of the urban administration was the public games (*ludi*). The Ludi Romani and the Megalensia fell to the curules to organize, the Ludi Ceriales and Plebeii to the plebeian aediles. Augustus, however, transferred the games to the praetors. See 'On some Festivals and Games which they used to celebrate in Rome', below.

259   That is, the captain of the watch.

260   That is, *comitia*.

261   Originally the cavalry of the Roman army, the equites (literally, horsemen) were selected from the senatorial class on the basis of wealth. During the late republic they numbered 1,800, but this was to double during the empire. They wielded much influence in the state. Indeed, in the first century BC the equites were a distinct class allowed to engage in business and they allied themselves alternately with the popular and the senatorial parties. During the reign of Augustus, the equites lost their political power.

262   The Comitium Universale was the chief place of political assembly in republican Rome, situated in an area north of the Roman Forum at the foot of the Capitoline. After the mid-first century BC it ceased to exist as a recognizable monument because of Caesar's reorganization of the area. The monuments and statues that filled the Comitium Universale have perished, except for the altar, truncated

column and archaic *cippus* (a stone marker) sealed below the black marble pavement (the 'Lapis Niger'), originally dating from Caesar's alterations and subsequently incorporated into the Augustan paving. See Nash (1968), vol. 1, pp. 287–9, vol. 2, pp. 21–3 (Lapis Niger); Hornblower and Spawforth (2003), p. 373.

263   Presumably the Saepta Julia (see note 98, above, and note 318, below).

264   See 'On the Trophies and Commemorative Columns', above.

265   In early times the Roman people were supposedly divided into three tribes, namely the first three in Palladio's list. By 241 BC the number of tribes had reached thirty-five (four urban and thirty-one rustic). See Hornblower and Spawforth (2003), p. 1550.

266   On the *Rioni* or regions of Rome see Krautheimer (1980), pp. 155–6. See also: http://www.ukans.edu/history/index/europe/ancient_rome/I/ Gazetteer/Places/Europe/Italy/Lazio/Roma/Rome/churches/.Texts/Armellini/ ARMCHI*/home.html

267   That is, *monti*.

268   In the transcription on CD-ROM in the collection entitled 'Art Theories of the Italian Renaissance' published by Chadwyck-Healey (1997), the word *Parione* is missing.

269   The Basilica of Aemilius Paulus (179 BC, rebuilt in 55–4 BC) was located between the Curia Julia and the Temple of Antoninus and Faustina. It was the most famous basilica and regarded as one of the marvels of Rome. See Pliny, *Natural History*, XXXVI, 102; Plutarch, *Vitae parallelae, Alexander et Caesar*, 39.3; Palladio, *QL*, III. xix [pp. 200–1]; Nash (1968), vol. 1, pp. 174–80. The basilica later became known as the Basilica Aemilia, and its entablature was drawn by Sangallo the Younger (Uffizi 1413A *v*) and its façade – famous for its Doric Order – by his uncle, Giuliano da Sangallo, in the Codex Coner (Cod. Vat. Barb., lat. 4424, fol. 26). The Basilica Argentaria was built by Trajan in the Forum of Caesar (Forum Julium). See Nash (1968), vol. 1, p. 424; Dal Maso (1975), p. 56. According to the anonymous *Historia Augusta (Histoire Auguste)*, 'Life of Severus Alexander' (r. 222–35), 'Alexander [. . .] began the Basilica Alexandrina, situated between the Campus Martius and the Saepta of Agrippa, 100 feet broad and 1,000 long and so constructed that its weight rested wholly on columns; its completion, however, was prevented by his death.' It should be noted that the Praetor Urbanus administered justice in the Tribunal Praetorium, and trials took place in the Tribunal Aurelium, with its podium and the-atre-like accommodation for the public. See Nash (1968), vol. 2, pp. 478–83. On basilicas in general, see Vitruvius, *De architectura*, V.i; Palladio, *QL*, III. xix [pp. 200–2]; Fletcher (1975), pp. 290–5, Hornblower and Spawforth (2003), pp. 235, 827–34 (law). RIBA XIV 1, XIV 9, XV 11V.

270   That is, the Capitol, here in reference to the temple on the Capitoline Hill begun by Tarquinius Superbus in the sixth century BC. Vespasian's temple, cited below, perished in the fire of 80 AD, and the last rebuilding was undertaken by Domitian (51–96 AD). See 'On the Hills', above.

271   In fact, Suessa Pometia.

272   *Caput* is Latin for 'head', hence 'Capitolinus'.

273   Alberti also mentions the three thousand bronze tablets, restored by Vespasian, at VII. x [p. 220].

274   That is, the Palazzo Senatorio, the central palace in the Piazza del Campidoglio. An eleventh-century fortress was built by the Corsi on the remains of the ancient Tabularium (78 BC), and the Senate was probably installed here around 1150, although Palladio links the event to Boniface VIII (r. 1294–1303). See Nash (1968), vol. 2, pp. 402–8 (Tabularium); Krautheimer (1980), p. 197.

275   The reconstruction of the Capitol was planned by Michelangelo about 1546. He superintended the erection only of the approach stairway, the monumental double flight of steps of the Palazzo Senatorio and, somewhat earlier (1538), the erection of the statue of Marcus Aurelius in the centre of the piazza. See 'On the Statues', above. See Goldscheider, L., *Michelangelo, Paintings, Sculptures, Architecture* (1964), p. 21; Hibbard, H., *Michelangelo* (1978), pp. 291–6.

276   Originally on the Capitol and struck by a bolt of lightning in 65 BC that evidently broke its feet and destroyed the group of the twins (restored by Antonio del Pollaiuolo (*c.*1431–1498)), the she-wolf (the *lupa*) is thought to be an Etruscan bronze of the late sixth or early fifth century BC. It would appear to have been hidden with other sacred statues in the vaulting of the Capitol and from there brought to the Lateran Palace in the Middle Ages. It is currently in the Palazzo de'Conservatori. See Krautheimer (1980), pp. 193, 194, fig. 155.

277   The Comitium Universale. See 'On the General Assemblies and what they were for', above.

278   The Palazzo de'Conservatori on the Capitol was rebuilt by Pope Nicholas V in 1450 (and thus Palladio cites the Senate as the only surviving ancient building, above). It was remodelled after 1564 by Giacomo della Porta (*c.*1470–1555) and Guidetto Guidetti to a design by Michelangelo.

279   As the text goes on to indicate, this gilded bronze statue was found in the time of Pope Sixtus IV (Francesco della Rovere, r. 1471–84) during the demolition of the Ara Maxima, near the Forum Boarium, and is now displayed in the Sala degli Orazi e Curiazi in the Palazzo de'Conservatori. See Nash (1968), vol. 1, pp. 472–4.

280   Presumably this is the bronze statue of *The Camillus* dating from the first century BC, which previously stood in San Giovanni Laterano but which was donated to the Palazzo de'Conservatori by Sixtus IV in 1471. In Roman religious ceremonies, Camilli were acolytes. They had to have both parents living, be below the age of puberty, and (ironically given the specification here of slave dress) to be freeborn.

281   The bronze *Spinario* or *Thornpicker* dates from the first century BC and was presented to the Conservatori by Sixtus IV. It was formerly known as the *Fedele Capitolino*, because it was thought to be a portrait of Marcius, a Roman messenger who would not delay his mission even though in pain through a thorn in his foot. See Krautheimer (1980), p. 195, fig. 156.

282   Fragments of the gigantic statue of Constantine (313), including a head, hand and foot, were discovered in the west apse of the Basilica of Maxentius

('Temple of Peace') in 1487. They are still in the courtyard of the Palazzo de'Conservatori. This statue is mentioned by Serlio, Book Three, fol. XXII [p. 115], when discussing the 'Temple of Peace'.

283   Next to the staircase in the Palazzo de'Conservatori leading up to the first landing are four reliefs from triumphal arches, three of which celebrate Marcus Aurelius and his military victories in AD 176. They include a scene of the emperor sacrificing before the Temple of Jupiter Capitolinus; the fourth panel comes from an arch in Via di Pietra.

284   The fragments of the 'Fasti capitolini consolari e trionfali', records of the Roman magistrates and Triumphs of the great captains of Rome, were excavated from the Roman Forum and installed in the Palazzo de'Conservatori by Cardinal Alessandro Farnese (later Pope Paul III). They are now in the Sala della Lupa.

285   The bronze head, hand and globe (but not foot – Palladio confuses this bronze colossus with the marble one of Constantine from the 'Temple of Peace'; see note 282, above), from a colossus of Constantine or possibly Constans II, but not Commodus as cited in the text, had by the twelfth century been collected in San Giovanni Laterano along with the *Camillus* and the *Thornpicker* statues. They were moved to the Palazzo de'Conservatori by Sixtus IV in 1471. See Krautheimer (1980), p. 192. The head, hand and globe are currently in the Appartamento dei Conservatori, Sala degli Orazi e Curiazi in the Palazzo de'Conservatori.

286   This statue of Giovanni de' Medici, Pope Leo X (r. 1513–21), is no longer present in the Palazzo de'Conservatori.

287   The statue of Alessandro Farnese, Pope Paul III, once stood in what is now the Sala degli Arazzi. The statue of Charles of Anjou (1226–85), Lord Protector of Rome and King of Sicily and South Italy, was by Arnolfi di Cambio, a Florentine who settled in Rome. It was made for Santa Maria in Aracoeli around 1270. See Krautheimer (1980), pp. 158, 209, 213.

288   The Tigris/Tiber (right) and Nile (left) recline in a fountain at the foot of these stairs (set up in this position in 1565–66) and date from the second century AD. They originally adorned the Baths of Constantine. The authorities of Rome wanted to transform the Tigris into the Tiber and therefore replaced the tiger (a representation of the Tigris), which originally lay beneath the river god's right arm, with a wolf beside Romulus and Remus. See a drawing of the mid-1530s by Maarten van Heemskerck; Filippi (1990), no. 17 [fol. 61r]. See Nash (1968), vol. 2, pp. 446–7.

289   See 'On the Porticoes', above.

290   On the Treasury (the 'Aerarium') in general, see Vitruvius, *De architectura*, V.ii; Hornblower and Spawforth (2003), pp. 24–5.

291   Sant'Adriano is in the Roman Forum. It was originally the Curia Senatus – the Senate House, begun by Sulla (138–78 BC) in 80 BC, rebuilt in 44 BC by Julius Caesar after it burnt down, and completed by Augustus. The present building dates from the time of Domitian, and was converted into a church by Pope Honorius I (r. 625–38). On Sant'Adriano see Palladio, *Churches*, [p. 49]. From republican times the state treasury was the Temple of Saturn, which is mistakenly identi-

fied by Palladio with Sant'Adriano; *QL*, I. vi [p. 10]. See also Nash (1968), vol. 2, p. 294.

292   On Roman coinage see Crawford, M.H., *Roman Republican Coinage* (1974), and *Coinage and Money under the Roman Republic* (1985); Hornblower and Spawforth (2003), pp. 358–61.

293   The sixth king of Rome (578–35 BC), murdered by Tarquinius Superbus at the instigation of his daughter. See Hornblower and Spawforth (2003), p. 1558. Cited by Palladio, *QL*, IV. xiii [p. 260].

294   A sheep.

295   That is, money.

296   Legend has it that Saturnus was the first to teach people to strike bright coins from silver, gold and bronze. See Scullard, H.H., *Festivals and Ceremonies of the Roman Republic* (1981).

297   More accurately, a 'graecostasis' is a building in which foreign ambassadors awaited decisions of the Senate. James Leoni's 1742 English translation gives the title as 'Of the Ambassadors Standing-place', and embellishes that the Graecostasis 'was a place, where Foreign Ambassadors used to stand before the Rostra, or a Dwelling that was appropriate for their Use'; Palladio, A., 'The Antiquities of Rome', in *The Four Books on Architecture*, trans. J. Leoni (1742), p. 81. See also note 318, below.

298   On Santa Maria Liberatrice see Palladio, *Churches*, [p. 56].

299   See 'On the Marforio', above.

300   The Emperor's Secretariat was formed by the 'Freedmen of Caesar', a class of senior civil servants wielding considerable power. Free of influence by class interests or social prejudices, they quite literally sold public honours and privileges. See Weaver, P.R., *Familia Caesaris: A Social Study of the Emperor's Freedmen and Slaves* (1972).

301   That is, the equestrian statue of Marcus Aurelius. See 'On the Statues', above.

302   That is, place of asylum. On ancient (Greek) asylia in general, see Hornblower and Spawforth (2003), p. 199, and pp. 1415–16 on Roman slavery (mentioned below).

303   At Rome the earliest Rostra or speaker's platform lay on the south side of the Comitium Universale. It existed in 338 BC and was adorned with the prows ('rostra') of ships captured from Antium (modern Anzio), and later with statues and a sundial. Caesar replaced the republican rostra with a new curved structure (the so-called hemicycle) at the west end of the Roman Forum in 44 BC. See Alberti, VII. xvi [p. 239]; Nash (1968), pp. 272–83; Dal Maso (1975), pp. 16, 25; Cary and Scullard (1975), p. 109; Hornblower and Spawforth (2003), p. 1336, see also pp. 607–608.

304   This was the milestone set up by Augustus in the Roman Forum as the terminal point of all military roads. It served to measure the distance from Rome to the provinces of the empire.

305   In mythology Carmenta, mother of Evander, was a prophetess who had a *flamen* – a two-day festival – on 11 and 15 January, and a shrine at the foot of the Capitoline Hill near the Porta Carmentalis. On Carmenta or Carmentis see

Hornblower and Spawforth (2003), p. 293; on Evander, a minor hero or divinity of Arcadia, see Hornblower and Spawforth (2003), p. 578.

306   That is, the Forum Holitorium. On this forum, see 'On the Fora, that is, Piazzas', above.

307   See 'On the small Senate Houses', above.

308   An area immediately in front of the Temple of Bellona (the Roman goddess of war) was used by the Fetiales – the priests who carried out the procedure of declaring war – in the exercise of their rituals. When republican Rome declared a grievance against a particular state, the Roman Senate and people proceeded to declare war if satisfaction had not been offered within thirty-three days. The Fetiales would then travel to the enemy frontier, make the declaration and throw a symbolic spear into the enemy territory. See Hornblower and Spawforth (2003), p. 594. However, with the expansion of the Roman Empire, it became impossible to carry out this ceremonial, so the Fetiales would simply hurl a javelin over a column near the temple of Bellona in the direction of the enemy's territory.

309   The Columna Lactaria was placed by Paul the Deacon (an eighth-century Lombard historian) in the region of the Forum Holitorium. See Palmer, R.E.A., *Rome and Carthage at Peace. Historia Einzelschriften 113* (1997), p. 105. See also Durant, W., *Caesar and Christ: A History of Roman Civilization and of Christianity from Their Beginning to A.D. 325* (1944), p. 364.

310   The Aequimelium was an open space on the lower southern slopes of the Capitoline Hill above the Vicus Iugarius, where in Cicero's day there was a market for lambs used in household worship. On the Aequimelium see especially Livy's *Ab urbe condita libri*, where Book 38. 28 records that the censors T. Quinctius Flamininus and M. Claudius Marcellus contracted for the building of the substructure on the Capitoline Hill over the Aequimelium and also the laying down of a paved road from the Porta Capena to the Temple of Mars.

311   That is, Spurius Maelius (d. 439 BC); the text incorrectly has 'Spimelio'. In Latin, *aequata* means 'levelled to the ground'.

312   Originally pasture outside the earliest city boundary (the *pomerium*), the Campus Martius, or Plain of Mars, was first used for army musters and exercises, and it took its name from an altar to Mars that stood here. It initially included the whole area between the Capitoline Hill, the Tiber and the Quirinal and Pincian hills, but came to refer to the low-lying ground enclosed in the Tiber bend. Originally the area was said to have been the property of the Tarquins, and to have become public land after the expulsion of the kings. See Boatwright (1987), pp. 33–73; Hornblower and Spawforth (2003), p. 284. Cited by Palladio, *QL*, III. xxi [p. 206]. For Palladio's interest in military manoeuvres, see the illustrations produced by his sons Leonida and Orazio in Palladio (1575).

313   In fact Santa Maria Nuova adjoins the Temple of Peace (Basilica of Maxentius) and was called 'Basilica Nova'. On this church see Palladio, *Churches*, [p. 50].

314   When the sister of the Horatii bemoaned the death of one of the

Curiatii, who had been her lover, her brother killed her. Condemned to death, he was spared when he appealed to the people. To do penance he was led, veiled, under a yoke. Tigillum Sororium means 'sister's beam'. On the Horatii, see 'On the Gates', above. See also http://reference.allrefer.com/encyclopedia/H/ Horatii.html.

315   That is, Santi Quattro Coronati. See Palladio, *Churches*, [p. 51].

316   The Castra Peregrina (or Campi Forestieri – 'Camp for Foreigners') was on the Celian Hill. The *peregrini* were soldiers detached for special service in Rome from the provincial armies. Misenum was the northern headland of the bay of Naples and was in fact one of the Roman army's principal naval bases. They consisted principally of the Frumentarii, who were originally employed on supply service, but also used as military couriers (their institution dates perhaps from Augustus), and in the second and third centuries as a sort of special police. See Baillie Reynolds, P.K., 'The Troops Quartered in the Castra Peregrinorum', *Journal of Roman Studies*, vol. 13 (1923), pp. 168–89; Nash (1968), vol. 1, pp. 219–20. See also http://www.magellannarfe.com/virtualrome/organizations/frumentarii/

317   'Camp for Pilgrims'.

318   The Villa Publica was where the state bailiff lived and where foreign ambassadors were received. On the Saepta Julia et Diribitorium, the great voting precinct of the Campus Martius, see Nash (1968), vol. 2, pp. 291–3.

319   For the legendary foundation of Santa Maria in Trastevere, see also Palladio, *Churches*, [pp. 29–30].

320   A 'vivarium' is an enclosure for wild animals. In Rome it is thought to have consisted of a low, unfortified wall, running parallel with the Claudian aqueduct, until it joined the city wall close to the Porta Praenestina. A gate led into the enclosure from the side of the city. See Nash (1968), vol. 2, p. 516.

321   The Roman elite called its suburban garden palaces 'vegetable gardens' (horti), recalling the time when a hortus was the lot of a citizen. The horti were one of the most distinctive types of domestic space in Rome. They occupied many acres around the edge of the city, partly in the town, partly in the country. Though usually translated as 'gardens', horti were a combination of pleasure park, art gallery and residential quarters. It was in his horti, for example, that the Emperor Vespasian chose to live rather than in his central city palace. On gardens in general see Grimal, P., *Les Jardins romains* (1969); MacDougall, E. and W.F. Jashemski (eds), *Ancient Roman Gardens* (1981); Hornblower and Spawforth (2003), p. 624.

322   One of the most important and beautiful Roman gardens, the Horti Sallustiani ('The Garden of the Sallust') was laid out in 40 BC by the renowned historian C. Sallustius Crispus (known as Sallust, probably 86–35 BC), who lavished the wealth on it that he had accumulated during his governorship of Africa Nova. It was later possessed and perfected by a series of Roman emperors. See Nash (1968), vol. 1, pp. 491–9; Hartswick, K.J., *The Gardens of Sallust: A Changing Landscape* (2004). On Sallust see Hornblower and Spawforth (2003), pp. 1348–9. On Santa Susanna see Palladio, *Churches*, [pp. 56–7].

323   This obelisk (with its hieroglyphics) is now in front of Santa Trinità dei Monti and was erected there in 1789. Its antique foundations can still be seen in the vicinity of the Porta Pinciana.

324   The famous Turris Maecenatiana comprised a magnificent house and grounds on the Esquiline hill, which was bequeathed to Octavian by its owner, Gaius Maecenas (Octavian's diplomatic agent and famed patron of Virgil, Horace and Propertius, d. 8 BC). See Hornblower and Spawforth (2003), p. 907. The tower of Maecenas is cited by Palladio, QL, IV. xii [p. 253].

325   This legend is cited by Palladio, QL, IV. xii [p. 253]. On Nero and this fire, which broke out on 19 June in AD 64 in shops around the Circus Maximus, see Hornblower and Spawforth (2003), p. 1037.

326   The 'Garden Hill' or Monte Pincio (between the Porta del Popolo and the Trinità, as the text indicates) was known as the Collis Hortulorum of ancient Rome because it was covered with the monumental gardens of the Roman aristocracy and emperors. On part of the hill, for example, was the villa of L. Licinius Lucullus (c.110–57 BC), a politician and general famed for his immense wealth, built after 63 BC. On the Horti Aciliorum on the Pincio see Nash (1968), vol. 1, pp. 488–90.

327   On Santa Trinità, on Monte Pincio, see Palladio, *Churches*, [p. 35].

328   The Velabrum was an area of low ground between the Capitoline and Palatine hills. It was originally a swamp, but was drained by the Cloaca Maxima (on which see 'On the Cloaca', above). See Hornblower and Spawforth (2003), p. 1584.

329   A *velabrum* in Latin was an awning made of a sail cloth.

330   On the Forum Boarium, see 'On the Fora, that is, Piazzas', above.

331   The Latin for ox is *bos, bovis*.

332   The Carinae (Latin for 'keels') was a celebrated quarter in the region of Rome between the Celian and Esquiline hills.

333   Santa Maria della Consolazione. On this church see Palladio, *Churches*, [p. 58]. The only street in antiquity that led up to the Capitol was the Clivus Capitolinus, which was paved. It began in the Forum at the Arch of Tiberius and led in an ascending curve around the Temple of Saturn (Palladio's 'Concord', mentioned below) and then climbed in a straight line to the southern summit of the Capitol. See Nash (1968), vol. 1, pp. 250–1.

334   This is, in fact, the Temple of Saturn. See 'On the Porticoes', above.

335   That is, the steps between Santa Maria in Aracoeli and Piazza Aracoeli, comprising 124 steps and dating from 1348.

336   An area on the right bank of the Tiber, the 'Quinctian Meadows' (Prata Quinctia) were regarded as the site of Cincinnatus's 4-*iugera* farm (Livy, *Ab urbe condita libri*, 3. 26. 8). On the military hero and proto-dictator Lucius Quinctius Cincinnatus (fifth century BC), see Hornblower and Spawforth (2003), p. 1288.

337   On Gaius Mucius Scaevola (dating from Rome's earliest history) and his legendary self-mutilation of his right hand (hence the name 'Scaevola' or 'left-handed') following his failed attempt to assassinate Lars Porsenna, see Hornblower and Spawforth (2003), p. 999.

338   See Alberti, V. xiii [pp. 138–9]; Hornblower and Spawforth (2003), pp. 646–47. On the Emporium (193 BC) warehouses on the left bank of the Tiber, see Nash (1968), vol. 1, pp. 380–6.

339   On Ancus Marcius see 'On the Bridges over the Tiber and their Builders', above.

340   This story of the salt tax imposed by Marcus Livius Salinator (b. 254 BC) may be etymological fiction to explain his – in fact inherited – cognomen. See Hornblower and Spawforth (2003), p. 877.

341   The Tullianum (or Mamertine Prison) was consecrated as San Pietro in Carcere. On this prison see Palladio, *Churches*, [p. 49] (San Pietro in Carcere Tulliano). See also Vitruvius, *De architectura*, V.ii; Nash (1968), vol. 1, pp. 206–8; Hornblower and Spawforth (2003), p. 1558.

342   This was a prison of the Byzantine period situated in the Forum Boarium, next to the 'Doric Tempietto' (Temple of Piety). See Serlio [p. 438, n. 74].

343   On Roman festivals see Nash (1968), vol. 2, pp. 24–6; on the Ludus Magnus, the training school for gladiators, see Scullard (1981); Hornblower and Spawforth (2003), pp. 593 (festivals), 891 (*ludi*, or games). Palladio designed a setting for the celebration of 'the ancient Olympic games' at the Olympic Academy in Vicenza in 1558. See Puppi (1975), p. 320 no. 57.

344   The ruins of which are about a mile from the Porta Capena.

345   Also called the Temple of Romulus and Remus. See Palladio, *Churches*, [p. 49] (SS Cosma e Damiano).

346   The Mausoleum of Augustus (or Tumulus Caesarum) was erected in 28 BC for him and the principal members of his family, the gens Julia-Claudia. The last emperor to be buried here was Nerva in AD 98. It was originally surmounted by a tumulus of earth some 44 metres high, planted with cypresses and probably crowned with a statue of the emperor. The interior was subdivided into tiers of compartments, some vaulted, by a complex system of ring and radial concrete walls. Cited in Alberti, VIII. ii [p. 248]. See Nash (1968), vol. 2, pp. 38–43; Dal Maso (1975), pp. 102–3; Fletcher (1975), pp. 313, 317. See also 'On the Obelisks, or 'Needles'', above. RIBA VIII 11V.

347   This mausoleum was completed around AD 139, a year after Hadrian's death, by his successor Antoninus Pius, and is now the Castel Sant'Angelo. It consists of a square base, each side 281 metres long and 15 metres high, above which stands a drum or cylindrical body. The exterior was covered with travertine and the upper part with earth and cypress trees, surmounted by Hadrian's four-horsed chariot (*quadriga*). See Nash (1968), vol. 2, pp. 44–8; Dal Maso (1975), pp. 104–5; Fletcher (1975), pp. 313, 317; Krautheimer (1980), esp. pp. 13, 14, fig. 13, 149–51, 267–9; Boatwright (1987), pp. 161–81. See also Palladio, *Churches*, [pp. 32–3] (Sant' Angelo).

348   Belisarius was Justinian's famous general. He recaptured Ostragothic Italy, occupying Naples and Rome after much hard fighting. The surrender of King Vitigis and the Gothic capital Ravenna in 540 marked the apex of Belisarius's military career. See Hornblower and Spawforth (2003), p. 237. He features in

Trissino's epic poem *L'Italia liberata dai Gotthi* (*Italy Freed from the Goths*), published in 1547, where he is guided by an archangel named 'Palladio'. See the introduction, above.

349   The famous passageway known as the 'Passetto'. In 1378 the castle had been severely damaged by the citizens of Rome, resentful of foreign domination. Rebuilding in fact began under Pope Boniface IX (r. 1389–1404), and Pope Alexander VI had Antonio da Sangallo the Elder (*c.*1455–1534) complete the four bastions of the square inner ward begun by Pope Nicholas V. Paul III built the north loggia and decorated the interior with frescoes.

350   The Sepulcrum Severi is known from only one passage in the anonymous *Historia Augusta* (1992–), Get. 7: 'inlatusque est maiorum sepulcro, hoc est Severi, quod est in via Appia euntibus ad portam dextra, specie Septizonii extructum' ('He was buried in the sepulchre of his ancestors, namely that of the Severi which is on the Via Appia on the right for those going towards the gate, built in the form of a septizonium.') Severus, Caracalla and Geta were, however, all buried in the Mausoleum of Hadrian, and the passage is interpolated. See http://www.ukans.edu/history/index/europe/ancient_rome/E/Roman/Texts/secondary/SMIGRA*/Ovatio.html.

351   The famous Septizonium of Septimius Severus was in the Domus Severiana on the south-east corner of the Palatine. A three-storeyed Corinthian colonnade and nymphaeum (although see note 350, above), the Septizonium was dedicated in AD 203 and demolished by Sixtus V in 1588–89. See drawing of the mid-1530s by Marten van Heemskerck; Filippi (1990), no. 15 [fol. 87]. See also Huelsen, C., 'Septizonium', *Zeitschrift für Geschichte der Architektur*, vol. 5 (1911–12), pp. 1–24; Dombart, T., *Das palatinische Septizonium zu Rom* (1922); Nash (1968), vol. 2, pp. 302–5; Dal Maso (1975), pp. 110–11; Hornblower and Spawforth (2003), p. 1391. See also Serlio, Book Three, p. LXXXII [p. 172]. RIBA I 2V, IX 17V.

352   The Temple of Jupiter Optimus Maximus Capitolinus was the most venerated temple in Rome, since Jupiter was seen as the city's special protector. Tradition has it that it was founded by Tarquinius Priscus, completed by Tarquinius Superbus and dedicated in 509 BC. It was destroyed by fire in 83 BC during the civil wars, rebuilt by Sulla, destroyed again in AD 69 and rebuilt by Vespasian and again by Domitian. See Vitruvius, *De architectura*, III. iii. 5; Pliny, *Natural History*, XXXV, 157, XXXVI, 187; Alberti, VII. ii [p. 193]. See also Nash (1968), vol. 1, pp. 530–3; McEwen (2003), pp. 24, 28–30, 81–2, 191–2.

353   The 'Templum Pacis' was actually completely destroyed in antiquity. In the Renaissance it was thought to be what is in fact the ruined Basilica of Maxentius/Constantine in the Roman Forum, begun by Maxentius in AD 306–12 and finished by Constantine. Pliny praises it (*Natural History*, XXXVI, 58, 102). For a woodcut plan and section see Serlio, Book Three, pp. XXII–XXIIII [pp. 115–16]. Described and illustrated by Palladio, *QL*, IV. vi [pp. 221–5]. RIBA I 4, XV 3.

354   Pliny, *Natural History*, XXXVI, 4. Vespasian constructed the actual Temple of Peace between AD 71 and 75 to commemorate his victory over the Jews and to house the plundered treasures from the Temple in Jerusalem. It stood near the

Forum of Augustus, was burnt in AD 192 and was reconstructed by Septimius Severus. The Basilica of Maxentius was constructed nearby on the Velia. Commodus and the burning of the temple are cited by Palladio, *QL*, IV. vi [p. 221].

355   The original temple was built in 27 BC during the third consulate of Agrippa, son-in-law of Augustus, to commemorate the victory of Actium over Antony and Cleopatra. See Pliny, *Natural History*, XXXIV, 13, XXXVI, 38. In spite of the dedicatory inscription on the pediment, the existing temple is not that of Agrippa but a new one built by Hadrian. This second temple was begun in AD 118 or 119 and finished AD 125–28. See Nash (1968), vol. 2, pp. 170–5; Boatwright (1987), esp. pp. 43–51; Davies et al. (1987), pp. 133–53; Wilson Jones (2000), pp. 177–213. See also Alberti, VII, x [p. 219], Fulvio (1545), IV. fol. 358. See Palladio's drawings in the Vicenza City Museum, of a cornice and detail of a Corinthian capital and the upper entablature of the tabernacles, with Corinthian capital; D 8 *v*, D 16 *r* (Puppi (1990), nos. 5–6). RIBA VI 11V, VIII 9R, VIII 9V. The Pantheon is cited by Palladio, *QL*, I. vi [pp. 10–11], I. ix [p. 13], I. xvii [p. 41], I. xxviii [p. 70], IV. xi [p. 251], IV. xv [p. 267], IV. xix [p. 282], and described and illustrated at IV. xx [pp. 285–96]. For woodcut plan, section, elevation and details, see Serlio, Book Three, pp. V–XVII [pp. 99–111].

356   See *QL*, I. vi [pp. 10–11].

357   On this see Palladio, *Churches*, [p. 40] (Santa Maria della Rotonda).

358   The roof of the Pantheon was thought to be covered with a sheeting of metal. A bronze roof is referred to by Paul the Deacon (*Historia Langobardorum*, ed. R. Cassanelli (1985), Book V, ch. 11) and in the Liber Pontificalis (*Le 'Liber Pontificalis': Texts, Introduction et Commentaire*, ed. L. Duchesne (1886–92), vol. 1, p. 246). However, a silver covering is cited by Andrea Fulvio (Fulvio (1545), V. fols. 360–1), Pomponio Leto (in *Excerpta a Pomponio dum inter ambulandum cuidam domino ultramontano reliquias ac ruinas urbis ostenderet*, MS Venice, Biblioteca Marciana, classe lat. X, 195ff. 15–31, and in *De vetustate urbis* (1510, –15, –23)), and by Francesco Albertini (Albertini (1510)). All these texts appear in Valentini and Zucchetti (1953).

359   St Gregory the Great (590–604). See Krautheimer (1980), esp. pp. 78–80, 110–13. For citations of his works see Palladio, *Churches*, [p. 59] (San Gregorio), [pp. 32–3] (Sant'Angelo).

360   Alberti states that 'in the portico of Agrippa there remain to this day trusses composed of bronze beams 40 feet in length'; VI. xi [p. 179, see p. 389, n. 94]. These trusses were replaced by those of wood at the time of Pope Urban VIII. Serlio refers to bronzes in the portico; Serlio, Book Three, p. VIII [p. 102]. In fact there are sixteen free-standing columns. See 'On the Porticoes', above.

361   These two lions were placed either side of a sarcophagus, and they are evident (together with a vase or basin) in a drawing of the mid-1530s of the Pantheon façade by Maarten van Heemskerck; Filippi (1990), no. 10 [fol. 10r]. See Nash (1968), vol. 2, p. 174, fig. 900. Puppi points out that the sarcophagus was similar to the funeral monument to Bishop Girolamo da Schio in Vicenza cathedral, when discussing two porphyry sarcophagi that Palladio drew and recorded as

'in Santa Maria Rotonda', in Puppi (1990), no. 39 (Vicenza City Museum, D 8 *r*).

362   On Numa Pompilius, the legendary second king of Rome (traditionally 715–673 BC), see Hornblower and Spawforth (2003), pp. 1217–18. Cited by Palladio, *QL*, IV. xiv [p. 264].

363   See 'On the Fora, that is, Piazzas', above.

364   On the vestal virgins and their cult see Dal Maso (1975), pp. 24–5; Hornblower and Spawforth (2003), p. 1591.

365   The Palladium, or statue of Pallas Athena, was supposedly taken from Troy by Aeneas. It was an object of great veneration, as the safety of Rome was thought to depend on its preservation. When the Emperor Elagabalus tried to steal it, the vestals are supposed to have substituted it with another statue. See Hornblower and Spawforth (2003), pp. 1100–1.

366   'The Field of the Wicked.'

367   The three major flamines were the *flamen Dialis*, *Martialis* and *Quirinalis* – Jupiter, Mars and Quirinus (sometimes identified as the god of the first furrow and thereby associated with Romulus). They were always patricians and were chosen by the members of the pontifical college, never elected. See Vanggaard, J.H., *The Flamen: A Study in the History and Sociology of Roman Religion* (1988); Hornblower and Spawforth (2003), pp. 599–600.

368   The pontifex was one of the four major colleges of the Roman priesthood, and the leading member of the college was the pontifex maximus. See Hornblower and Spawforth (2003), pp. 1219–20.

369   The salian priests are cited by Palladio, *QL*, IV. ix [p. 241, p. 366, n. 76]. See also the anonymous *Historia Augusta (Histoire Auguste)*, 'Life of Antoninus Pius'. XIII.

370   On the Augurs see Rykwert (1988); Hornblower and Spawforth (2003), p. 214.

371   This and the following technical terms for liturgical items appear to come from the *De verborum significatione* written in the second century AD by the grammarian Sextus Pompeius Festus, whose work was summarized by Paul the Deacon. See Festus (Sextus Pompeius Festus), *S. P. Festi de verborum significatione quæ supersunt, cum Pauli epitome*, ed. K.O. Müller, (1839) p. 248.

372   Festus (1839), p. 113.

373   Festus (1839), p. 18.

374   Festus (1839), pp. 11, 51.

375   Festus (1839), pp. 348, 349.

376   Festus (1839), p. 313.

377   Festus (1839), pp. 348, 349.

378   There was an armamentarium in the Castra Praetoria. On the armaries of the public games and the gladiators, see Steinby (1993–2000), p. 126.

379   Appian of Alexandria. See 'To the Readers', above. See also Hornblower and Spawforth (2003), pp. 172–3 (armies), 1030 (navies).

380   On Triumphs in general see Versnel, H.S., *Triumphus: an Inquiry into the*

Origin, Development and Meaning of the Roman Triumph (1970); Hornblower and Spawforth (2003), p. 1554.

381   See Hornblower and Spawforth (2003), pp. 411, 1084.

382   On Aulus Postumius Tubertus (fl. 430 BC) see Hornblower and Spawforth (2003), p. 1235.

383   On Marcus Claudius Marcellus see 'On the Theatres, what they were for, and who built them', above.

384   On Lucius Quinctius Cincinnatus see 'On the Meadows', above.

385   On crowns in general see Maxfield, V.A., *The Military Decorations of the Roman Army* (1981); Hornblower and Spawforth (2003), p. 411.

386   See 'On the Treasury', above.

387   On Roman population in general see Hornblower and Spawforth (2003), p. 1223.

388   On Roman wealth in general see Shatzman, I., *Senatorial Wealth and Roman Politics* (1975); Finley, M.I. (ed.), *Studies in Roman Property* (1976).

389   On Roman marriages in general see Treggiari, S., *Roman Marriage: Iusti Coniuges from the Time of Cicero to the Time of Ulpian* (1991); Hornblower and Spawforth (2003), pp. 928–9.

390   On children in general see Wiedemann, T., *Adults and Children in the Roman Empire* (1989); Evans, J.K., *War, Women and Children in Ancient Rome* (1991); Rawson, B. (ed.), *Marriage, Divorce, and Children in Ancient Rome* (1991).

391   On Roman divorce in general see Rawson (1991); Treggiari (1991); Hornblower and Spawforth (2003), pp. 928–9.

392   On Spurius Carvilius (fl. 290–70 BC) see Hornblower and Spawforth (2003), p. 297.

393   On Quintus Antistius Adventus Postumius Aquilinus (fl. 160) see Hornblower and Spawforth (2003), p. 112.

394   On Publius Sempronius Tuditanus (fl. 129 BC) see Hornblower and Spawforth (2003), p. 1385.

395   On Gaius Iulius Caesar and the Bona Dea scandal see Hornblower and Spawforth (2003), p. 780. On Caesar in general see Palladio (1575), and *QL*, III. xxi [p. 206]. The Bona Dea ('Good Goddess') was an Italian goddess worshipped especially in Rome and Latium. Her annual nocturnal ceremony, from which men were excluded, was a state ritual performed in secret for the welfare of the Roman people.

396   On Pompeia (fl. 67 BC) see Hornblower and Spawforth (2003), p. 1214.

397   On Publius Clodius Pulcher (b. *c.*92 BC) and the Bona Dea scandal see Hornblower and Spawforth (2003), p. 350. See also note 395, above.

398   On Roman funeral ceremonies in general see Toynbee, J., *Death and Burial in the Roman World* (1971); Reece, R. (ed.), *Burial in the Roman World* (1977); Hornblower and Spawforth (2003), pp. 33–4, 431–2.

399   On Numa Pompilius see 'On the Priests, on the Vestal Virgins . . .', above.

400   The Tor de' Conti was in fact erected after 1198 by Riccardo de' Conti, brother of Pope Innocent III (r. 1198–1216). It was damaged in an earthquake in

1348 and reduced to its present ruined state by Urban VIII in the seventeenth century. See Krautheimer (1980), pp. 202–3, 204, fig. 162.

401   The Torre delle Milizie, behind the Markets of Trajan, is a brick tower (originally of three storeys) apparently built over the remains of much older, possibly Byzantine, fortifications. In 1179 it was held by the Frangipani, but it fell to the Annibaldi in 1250 and the Caetani in 1301. The present tower is possibly a thirteenth-century construction. See Krautheimer (1980), pp. 317–19, fig. 254. See also 'The Letter to Leo X by Raphael and Baldassare Castiglione (c.1519)' in the appendix, below.

402   On the Tiber in general see Hornblower and Spawforth (2003), p. 1522.

403   That is, the Palatine. See 'On the Hills', above.

404   In the transcription on CD-ROM in the collection entitled 'Art Theories of the Italian Renaissance' published by Chadwyck-Healey (1997), the words *Roma, allargò* are missing.

405   On Belisarius see 'On the Tomb of Augustus, of Hadrian, and of Septimius', above.

406   A house was constructed beside the first basilica of St Peter's (see Palladio, *Churches*, [pp. 16ff]) during the pontificate of St Symmachus (498–514). It was used for state occasions, and the pope lived in the Lateran Palace. In 1208 Innocent III built a fortified residence on the site, and when Pope Gregory XI (r. 1370–78) returned from Avignon in 1378 he took up residence there. Nicholas V rebuilt the house as a palace, centred on the Cortile dei Pappagalli. Pope Sixtus IV added the Sistine Chapel in 1473. Innocent VIII (r. 1484–92) had Giacomo da Pietrasanta build the Belvedere Pavilion on the north summit of the Vatican Hill. Julius II (r. 1503–13) began the famous collection of sculptures set up in the courtyard of the Belvedere Pavilion, and united this pavilion with the main palace of Nicholas V through the arcades designed by Bramante (see note 411, below).

407   On this work in particular see Westfall, C.W., *In this Most Perfect Paradise: Alberti, Nicholas V, and the Invention of Conscious Urban Planning in Rome, 1447–55* (1974).

408   The Sistine Chapel.

409   The tribunal of the Sacred Roman Rota.

410   On this work in particular see Coffin (1979), p. 81. See a drawing of the mid-1530s by Maarten van Heemskerck of the vista from the Belvedere; Filippi (1990), no. 37 [fol. 36r].

411   This is Bramante's 'Cortile del Belvedere', begun in 1505. On this work see Ackerman, J., 'The Belvedere as a Classical Villa', *Journal of the Warburg and Courtauld Institutes*, vol. 14 (1951), pp. 70–91, and *The Cortile del Belvedere*, Studi e documenti par la storia del Palazzo Apostolico Vaticano, vol. 2 (1954); Brummer, H.H., *The Statue Court in the Vatican Belvedere* (1970); Bruschi, A., *Bramante* (1973); Coffin (1979), pp. 81–2. For woodcut elevations of the upper and lower arcades, see Serlio, Book Three, pp. CXLII–CXLVII [pp. 232–7]. Cited by Palladio, *QL*, I. xxviii [p. 70].

412   The famous statues of the river gods were found on Montecavallo (as

Serlio, for example, reports in Book Three, p. LXXX [p. 170]; see also p. CXLVI [p. 236]), and put in the Statue Court of the Belvedere in 1513 by Leo X. See Coffin (1979), p. 85.

413   The famous *Apollo Belvedere* – a second-century copy of a bronze original probably by Leochares (fourth century BC). It was brought to the Vatican in 1503, and was mentioned by Serlio in Book Three, p. CXLVI [p. 236].

414   That is, Athenodorus.

415   The famous sculpture of Laocoön and his two sons in the coils of serpents (*c.*50 BC), ascribed, as the text states, to Agesander, Polydorus and Athenodorus, was discovered on the Esquiline Hill on 14 January 1506. Pliny records that this 'outstanding' statue stood in the house of Emperor Titus; *Natural History* XXXVI, 37. See Coffin (1979), pp. 82, 83, fig. 50. It is mentioned by Serlio in Book Three, p. CXLVI [p. 236].

416   This was added by Pope Paul III, who had niches prepared for a statue of Venus in 1536. See Coffin (1979), p. 85.

417   Mentioned by Serlio in Book Three, p. CXLVI [p. 236].

418   The statue of Antinous was also added by Paul III in 1544 and set up in its own niche in the Statue Court. See Coffin (1979), p. 85.

419   Michelangelo began the *Last Judgement* in the Sistine Chapel in 1534 and the *Conversion of St Paul* in the Pauline Chapel in 1542. On this work see Goldscheider (1964), pp. 7–8; Hibbard (1978), pp. 99–147, 239–54, 273–80. See also Seymour, C., *Michelangelo: Sistine Chapel Ceiling* (1972).

420   See the engraving by Antonio Lafreri (1512–77) of the Belvedere Court in the *Speculum Romanae magnificentiae, omni fere quaecunque in urbe monumenta extant* (1540–92), illustrated by Coffin (1979), p. 82, fig. 49. See also Serlio, Book Three, p. CXLII [p. 232].

421   The area 'across the Tiber' ('trans Tiberim'), has, since the Middle Ages, been the popular district of Rome. From Roman times it was distinguished, as the text says, by numerous artisans' houses and workshops. On Trastevere in general see Krautheimer (1980), esp. pp. 155–7, 305–7.

422   That is, Santa Maria in Trastevere.

423   See 'On Naumachias, where they staged Naval Battles, and what they were for', above.

424   The text incorrectly has *otto* ('eight').

425   Suetonius stated that Augustus 'could justly boast that he found [Rome] built of brick and left it in marble', in *De vita Caesarum* (*The Lives of the Caesars*), 'Augustus', 28. Vitruvius, in his opening dedication of Book One of *De architectura*, praised Augustus's building works. On the extravagant building programme financed and administered by Agrippa under Augustus's rule, see Favro, D., *Image of Augustan Rome* (1996); McEwen (2003), esp. pp. 10–12, 280–98.

426   See 'On the Wards, that is, the *Rioni* and their Symbols', above.

427   This refers to the Temple of Mars, said to be 4 miles outside Rome, which Palladio has already cited. See 'On some Festivals and Games that they used to celebrate in Rome', above. On Palladio and the siting of temples see *QL*, IV. i

[p. 215], where the ancient Tuscans are acknowledged as building the temples to Venus, Mars and Vulcan outside the city.

428   Built in 181 BC.

429   That is, the Porta Salaria. See 'On the Gates', above.

430   In imperial times Venus was worshipped as Venus Genetrix, mother of Aeneas; Venus Felix, the bringer of good fortune; Venus Victrix, bringer of victory; and Venus Verticordia, protector of feminine chastity.

431   That is, the Porta Sant'Agnese. See 'On the Gates', above.

432   Nenia, Latin for 'funeral song', also goddess of funeral songs. On Nenia (and citation of her temple) see Hornblower and Spawforth (2003), p. 1034. See also Wissowa, G., *Religion and Kultus der Römer* (1912).

433   The Fanum Quietis (Temple of Quiet) is mentioned by Livy, *Ab urbe condita libri*, 4. 41. 8. and St Augustine, *City of God*, IV. 16.

434   The Templum Fortunae Muliebris, founded at the fourth milestone outside the city, was built in honour of Coriolanus's wife and mother – Veturia and Volumnia, respectively – for saving Rome from Coriolanus when he planned to attack the city. See Livy, *Ab urbe condita libri*, 2. 40; St Augustine, *City of God*, IV. 19; [Aurelius Victor], *De viris illustribus urbis Romae*, ed. F. Pichlmayr (1911), 19. 3–5.

435   In 211, in an attempt to relieve the siege of Capua, begun the previous year, Hannibal marched on Rome but failed to force the Romans to withdraw troops from Capua, and so returned to the south. Soon afterwards Capua fell to the Romans. See Livy, *Ab urbe condita libri*, Book 21. For an encounter with this temple by Jules Cloquet in 1837 see http://www.bium.univ-paris5.fr/cloquet/pages/128/debut.htm.

436   See 'On some Festivals and Games that they used to celebrate in Rome', above.

437   One of the three original gates, situated at the foot of the Capitoline Hill. See 'On the Circumference of Rome', above.

438   A temple of Janus stood in the Forum Holitorium, close to the Theatre of Marcellus and the Porta Carmentalis. It was built by C. Duilius after victory over the Carthaginians at Mylae (260 BC). The day of dedication was the Portunalia, on 17 August. The restoration of this temple was begun by Augustus and completed by Tiberius in AD 17. According to Pliny (*Natural History* XXXVI, 28), Augustus dedicated in this temple a statue to Janus that was brought from Egypt – the work either of Scopas or Praxiteles. See Platner (1929), pp. 277–8; Nash (1968), vol. 1, pp. 500–1.

439   The Temple of Aesculapius was dedicated on the Tiber Island in 291 BC, after a plague in 293 BC, and the island became associated with healing. On San Giovanni Calibita on the island, attached to the Hospital of the Brothers of San Giovanni di Dio (the Fatebenefratelli), see Palladio, *Churches*, [p. 28]. The Temple of Faunus was dedicated in 193 BC and was built with money from a fine imposed on the *pecuarii* ('drovers'). The Sanctuary of Jupiter was also on the island. See Nash (1968), vol. 1, p. 508.

440   That is, the Fanum Fors Fortuna or Temple to the Goddess Fors Fortuna.

Several (possibly four) temples of this name stood outside the city on the right bank of the Tiber – that is, in Trastevere. See Platner (1929), pp. 212–14.

441   On the Liber Pater, god of fertility and especially of wine, see Hornblower and Spawforth (2003), p. 854.

442   Commonly defined as the household gods or guardians of the house. On the two possible origins of the Lares see Hornblower and Spawforth (2003), pp. 815–86.

443   Cicero's *On the Laws*, Book II. 8: 'let the people maintain the sacred groves in the country, and the abodes of the Lares'.

444   These were the gardens of the poet Terence, on the Via Appia near the temple of Mars; Suetonius, *On the Poets*, 'Terence', 5. See Suetonius, *De poetis e biografi minori*, ed. A. Rostagni (1944).

445   The villa of Ovid was long lost until its remains were discovered on the banks of the Tiber in 2000. See *London Times*, 23 September 2000. The poet says in his letters that from his villa he could see people streaming across the Milvian Bridge and then dividing to go along the Via Flaminia, which ran along the river, or up the Via Cassia, which heads north at right angles to it; Ovid, *Ex ponto*, I, 8, 44. See Ovid, *Tristia. Ex Ponto*, ed. A. E. Wheeler (1988). At the height of his fame Ovid was exiled by Augustus to the Black Sea and was never allowed to return to his beloved villa. In 'On other Houses, notably those for Citizens', above, Palladio says that Ovid owned a house near Santa Maria della Consolazione.

446   The 'villa suburbana' is defined as a retreat near the city but not designed for agriculture. See Ackerman, J., *The Villa: Form and Ideology of Country Houses* (1990), p. 42. Lucullanum was the villa of Marcus Lucullus, the praetor of Macedonia; see Ackerman (1990) p. 42. Cicero's favourite villa was the Tusculanum, which he bought in 68 BC; see *Arte Antica*, II p. 579b. Cicero is also known to have built a villa, the Formianum, at Formiae, the region now known as Mole di Gaeta.

447   That is, Hadrian's villa at Tivoli (the classical 'Tibur'). Palladio studied the villa and drew (probably in 1554) a plan of the Island Enclosure and Circular Hall, the Reverse-Curve Pavilion, Fountain Court West and other Villa structures. See RIBA VII 6R, IX 12R, IX 12V, IX 13R, XV 10. See also IX 13V and X 16R (Temple of Hercules at Tivoli). On these, and Hadrian's villa in general, see MacDonald, W., and J. Pinto, *Hadrian's Villa and its Legacy* (1995), esp. p. 214.

448   Prytaneum means 'council house'; Canopus was connected to Alexandria by a notorious canal; Poecile was a celebrated portico in the agora in Athens; and Tempe was a valley in Thessaly, famed in antiquity for its beauty. Palladio's sources on this aspect of Hadrian's villa are the imperial biographies (from 117 through to 284) anonymously written in about the fourth century and entitled the *Historia Augusta (Histoire Auguste)*, on which see MacDonald and Pinto (1995), pp. 6–7.

449   See descriptions of agricultural villas by Pliny the Younger, Varro (*De re rustica*), Columella (*De re rustica*) and Vitruvius, *De architectura*, VI.vi. 1–4. See also *QL*, II. xvi [pp. 147–8]. RIBA XI 4R, XI 4V.

450   Brennus was a Gallic chieftain who by tradition captured and destroyed Rome around 390 BC. See Hornblower and Spawforth (2003), p. 259.

451   A gothic tribe, like the Ostrogoths. See in general Hornblower and Spawforth (2003), pp. 643–4. For reference to Roman conflicts with the Goths, see 'On the Bridges over the Tiber and their Builders' and 'On the Tomb of Augustus, of Hadrian, and of Septimius', above. See also *QL*, 'Letter' p. 3, and I, Foreword, p. 5 [pp. 3–5]; 'The Letter to Leo X by Raphael and Baldassare Castiglione (*c.*1519)' in the appendix, below.

452   See in general Hornblower and Spawforth (2003), p. 1581.

453   A gothic tribe, see note 451 on the Visigoths, above.

454   On Totila see 'On the Bridges over the Tiber and their Builders', above.

455   That is, the Sack of Rome by Charles V and his German mercenaries during the 'Italian wars'. See the introduction, above.

Description of the Churches

1   The motto above reads 'Fortune favours the brave'. On Lucrino see the introduction, above.

2   The 1554 edition is unpaginated. The page numbers throughout appear in the transcription on CD-ROM in the collection entitled 'Art Theories of the Italian Renaissance' published by Chadwyck-Healey (1997).

3   The following preface is omitted in later, anonymous versions, when Palladio's text was reissued without his name on the title page. See the introduction, above, p. xviii.

4   That is, all one route.

5   There are in fact four routes. See the introduction, above.

6   Palladio's sources for this history, often word for word, are *Le cose maravigliose di Roma* and *Le Indulgentie e Reliquie de le chiese de Roma*, both published in many editions between 1540 and 1550. See the introduction.

7   The text from 'After him . . .' to here is identical to that in Palladio, *Antiquities*, fols. 2*r*–*v*.

8   Palladio's source for the story of Constantine (*c.*274–337) and Sylvester (r. 314–35) is the *Legenda Aurea, Historia de Sancto Silvestro* of Jacobus de Voragine (1230–98). See Jacobus de Voragine, *The Golden Legend*, trans. W.G. Ryan (1995). The information on Constantine and Helena repeats the text in the 1550 edition of *Le cose maravigliose*. See also Eusebius's 'Life' of Constantine in Eusebius, H.E., *The Ecclesiastical History*, trans. H. Jackson Lawlor and J. Oulton (1927).

9   On the seven principal churches in Rome as pilgrimage centres in the Middle Ages, see Krautheimer, R., *Rome, Profile of a City, 312–1308* (1980), pp. 248–9 (for Lafréry's 1575 engraving of these churches, see here, fig. 115).

10   San Giovanni in Laterano is the Cathedral of Rome and of the world. It was founded by Constantine and, as the first Christian basilica to be constructed in Rome, served as a model for all subsequent Christian churches. The original five-aisled church with an apse, on a basilican plan, was probably built between 314 and

318. It was dedicated to the Redeemer and later to saints John the Baptist and John the Evangelist. Partly ruined by the Vandals, it was restored by popes St Leo the Great (r. 440–61) and Hadrian I (r. 772–95) and, after the earthquake of 896, by Pope Sergius III (r. 904–11). The church was enlarged and embellished by Pope Nicholas IV (r. 1288–92) to such an extent that it was considered the wonder of the age. Destroyed by fire in 1308, it was rebuilt by Pope Clement V (r. 1305–14) and decorated by Giotto (1301–37). It was burnt down once more in 1360 and under popes Urban V (r. 1362–70) and Gregory XI (r. 1370–78) it was entirely rebuilt by the Sienese Giovanni di Stefano (fl. 366–91). In 1646–49 Pope Innocent X (r. 1644–55) commissioned Francesco Borromini (1599–1667) to rebuild the church yet again, and in 1734 Pope Clement XII (r. 1730–40) added the east façade. See a drawing of the mid-1530s by Maarten van Heemskerck; Filippi, E., *Maarten Van Heemskerck* (1990), no. 19 [Kupferstichkabinett, Staatliche Museen zu Berlin, fol. 12r]. Sebastiano Serlio refers to an ancient throne in this church; Serlio, Book Four, p. LXIII*v* [p. 368]. See Huelsen, C., *Le chiese di Roma nel medio evo* (1927), p. 272; Armellini, M., *Le chiese di Roma dal secolo IV al XIX* (1942), p. 91; Krautheimer (1980), esp. pp. 21–4, 54, 56–8. See also Palladio, *Antiquities*, fol. 14r, and *QL*, I. vi [p. 10], [p. 273].

11   An eight-day period of celebration following, but including, the day of a major festival or saint's day.

12   That is, the dedication day of this church (9 November).

13   A quarantine is an ecclesiastical term frequently used in grants of indulgence and it signifies a strict ecclesiastical penance of forty consecutive days. A quarantine indulgence implies the remission of as much time in purgatory as a forty-day penance.

14   The heads of Peter and Paul are still held in this altar.

15   That is, St John the Evangelist prayed at this spot when he was brought to Rome.

16   This is based on Virgil's *Georgics*, 3.28–9. In the *Quattro libri* (*QL*, I. vi [p. 10]), Palladio notes: 'In St. John Lateran in Rome can be seen four bronze columns of which only one has a capital; Augustus had them made from the metal prows of the ships which he captured from Mark Anthony in Egypt.' These columns are now in the transept.

17   The church was the seat of five general councils: in 1123, 1139, 1179, 1215 and 1512.

18   This refers to Pope Joan (by tradition either r. 855–57 or *c.*1100). See [page [50]], below. The legend that the pope was so examined is thought to originate from the 'Visions' of the Dominican Robert D'Usez, who died in 1290. See Brewyn, W., *A XVth-Century Guide-book to the Principal Churches of Rome*, trans. C.E. Woodruff (1933), p. 33.

19   The *Hystoria de vitis Pontificum periuncunda* by Bartolomeo Platina (1421–81), which ran to many editions. E.D. Howe believes that this reference does not necessarily mean that Palladio actually studied Platina, but rather that he copied other references to him; Palladio (1991) p. 36.

20   This chapel, the only part to survive of the old Lateran Palace, was rebuilt on the walls of an earlier ground floor between 1278 and 1280. See Krautheimer (1980), p. 211.

21   This ancient painting on wood of Christ possibly dates from as early as the fifth century and still survives, although it has been many times repainted.

22   That is, near San Giovanni in Laterano.

23   The Baptistery of St John, or San Giovanni in Fonte, was built by Constantine around 315−24, though not, as legend has it, on the site of his baptism. It is octagonal and was remodelled by Pope Sixtus III (r. 432−40) and restored by Hadrian III (r. 884−85) in 884. See Krautheimer (1980), p. 50. Described and illustrated by Palladio, *QL*, IV. xvi [pp. 273−5]. RIBA XII 3, XIV 2R, XV 9R.

24   The Chapel of the Holy Cross, Santa Croce, founded by Pope St Hilary (r. 461−68) and demolished in 1588. See Krautheimer (1980), pp. 50−1.

25   As the text relates, this chapel was founded by St Hilary and it retains its original doors, once thought to come from the Baths of Caracalla, which resound musically when opened.

26   This chapel was dedicated by St Hilary and has bronze doors dating from 1196.

27   On the Confraternity of the Ospedale di San Giovanni in Laterano during the Middle Ages see Krautheimer (1980), pp. 300−1.

28   According to the *Liber Pontificalis*, the official chronicle of the papacy, Pope St Anacletus (r. *c*.76−*c*.90) built an oratory over the tomb of St Peter around AD 90, close to the Circus of Nero, near which the Apostle had been martyred. There may have been a confusion of names, however, and Pope St Anicetus (r. 155−66) was probably responsible for the oratory. Constantine, at the request of Pope St Sylvester I, began a basilica on this site between 319 and 322, which was consecrated on 18 November (as the text indicates) in 326. The basilica was preceded by a great quadrangular colonnaded portico, and the nave and double aisles were divided by eighty-six marble columns. In the middle of the fifteenth century the old basilica showed signs of collapse and Pope Nicholas V (r. 1447−55) decided to rebuild it. The work was entrusted to Bernardo Rossellino (1409−64), Leon Battista Alberti (1404−72), and Giuliano da Sangallo (1445−1516), but on the death of Nicholas the rebuilding came to a virtual halt. Pope Julius II (r. 1503−13) decided on a complete reconstruction, and Donato Bramante (1444−1514) started work in 1506. The new basilica was on a Greek-cross plan surmounted by a central dome. On Bramante's death in 1514, the four central piers and the arches of the dome had been completed. Pope Leo X (r. 1513−21) employed Raphael (1483−1520) to continue the building on a Latin-cross plan in collaboration with Fra Giovanni Giocondo (*c*.1434−1515) and Giuliano da Sangallo. Following the Sack of Rome in 1527, the work received fresh impetus under Paul III (r. 1534−49) from Antonio da Sangallo the Younger (1494−1546) and later Michelangelo (1475−1564), who continued to direct the work until his death. Michelangelo substituted Bramante's piers with stronger ones, built the dome and developed a plan for the façade based on the Pantheon (eventually

substituted by Carlo Maderno's façade, which stands today). This is the point the work had reached at the time of Palladio's text, which fails to mention any of this rebuilding, or its famous architects, preferring to imply that the building had stood as a 'finished' and coherent entity from its foundation. Its incomplete state about this time is recorded in drawings of the mid-1530s by Maarten van Heemskerck; Filippi (1990), nos. 25, 26, 27, 28, 29, 31, 32, 33, 34, 35 [fols. 51r, 13r, 8r, 15r, 7r, 52r, 54r, 1r, 60r–v]. Palladio is thought to have visited Rome in November–December 1549 with a view to giving advice concerning the basilica (see Puppi, L., *Andrea Palladio* (1975), p. 276, no. 30). The cloth of St Veronica with the image of Christ, and the lance of St Longinus, both mentioned below, are still held in the church. See *Le 'Liber Pontificalis': Texts, Introduction et Commentaire*, ed. L. Duchesne, (1886–92), translated as *The Book of Pontiffs (Liber pontificalis). The Ancient Biographies of the First Ninety Roman Bishops to AD 715*, trans. R. Davis (2000). Cited by Alberti at I. viii [p. 22], I. x [p. 26], II. vi [p. 43], VI. xi [p. 179], X. xvii [p. 362]. See also Huelsen (1927), pp. 417–18; Armellini (1942), p. 695; Krautheimer (1980), pp. 26–8, 112 (on opulent ornaments of the type mentioned below), 113–17, 123–4, 139–41, 204–11.

29   Ember days are the days of fasting and abstinence ordered by the Church for the beginning of the four liturgical seasons.

30   This story appears in Jacobus de Voragine's *Legenda Aurea, Historia de Sancto Silvestro*. For the life of Sylvester see also the *Liber Pontificalis*.

31   These twisting columns were (wrongly) believed to have been imported by Constantine from the Holy of Holies in the Temple of Solomon. Eight were reused by Giovanni Lorenzo Bernini (1598–1680) in the tabernacles facing his baldacchino in St Peter's, within the angled inner corners of the piers of the crossing. See Krautheimer (1980), pp. 27–8.

32   The historian Giovanni Ciampini in *De sacris aedificiis* (1693) noted the presence of bronze tiles in the central nave and transepts. In 1575 Etienne Du Pérac identified the origins of these tiles as possibly the Temple of Jupiter Capitolinus or Santa Maria della Rotonda (the Pantheon), and noted their restoration by Pope Benedict II (r. 684–5). See Ashby, T. (ed.), *Topographical Study in Rome in 1581; A Series of Views with Fragmentary Text by Etienne Du Pérac* (1916), p. 31.

33   That is, Filarete (*c*.1400–69). On these doors commissioned by Eugenius IV, signed and dated 1445 by Filarete, see Giordano, L., 'On Filarete's *Libro architettonico*', in Hart, V., and P. Hicks (eds), *Paper Palaces: the Rise of the Renaissance Architectural Treatise* (1998).

34   The pine cone, together with two of the peacocks mentioned in the next sentence, remain in the semicircular niche of the upper Belvedere (the so-called Garden of the Pine). Palladio followed medieval tradition, most notably repeated in the *Mirabilia urbis Romae*, in attributing the first location of the pine cone to the dome of the Pantheon (Santa Maria della Rotonda). Legend held that when the Devil hurled the pine cone at St Peter's, it landed in the courtyard. See Brewyn (1933), p. 34. A more current theory, substituted in the 1563 anonymous version of *Le chiese*, was that the pine cone originated from the Tomb of Hadrian. Du Pérac

and Antonio Labacco suggested that it came from the Circus of Nero. See Labacco, A., *Libro appartenente a l'architettura* (1552), pl.vi; Ashby (1916), pp. 35–6. In fact the pine cone had belonged to a fountain near to the Serapeum (a complex of temples dedicated to the Egyptian god Serapis) in Campus Martius, and was subsequently installed under a canopy in front of the early Christian church of St Peter's.

35 One of the four great patriarchal basilicas, San Paolo fuori le mura commemorates the martyrdom of St Paul and is believed to contain the Apostle's tomb. According to Christian tradition the Roman matron Lucina buried the body of Paul in a vineyard on this site. In 384 a large basilica was financed by the emperors Valentinian II (r. 371–92) and Theodosius the Great (*c.*346–95) at the request of Pope Damasus (r. 366–84) (a contradictory account of a rich Constantinian foundation, which Palladio mentions here, had been inserted in the *Liber Pontificalis*). It was englarged by Theodosius's son, Honorius (384–423), and decorated with mosaics by Galla Placidia (sister of Honorius). In the eighth century Leo III (r. 795–816) further embellished it, and it became the largest church in Rome. Having been pillaged by the Saracens in the ninth century, it was restored by Abbot Hildebrand (later Pope Gregory VII, r. 1073–85) around 1070. The present basilica replaced the ancient one, which was virtually destroyed by fire in 1823. See Huelsen (1927), pp. 415–16; Armellini (1942), p. 928; Krautheimer (1980), pp. 42–3, 119–20, 175, 177, 180.

36 Once also called the Basilica Liberiana, Santa Maria Maggiore retains more completely than any of the other four patriarchal basilicas its original interior magnificence. A basilica was built on the site, occupied by a Roman edifice, by Pope Liberius (r. 352–66) following, as legend has it, the vision described by Palladio here. This basilica was reconstructed by Pope Damasus (r. 366–84) and again by Sixtus III. The present church dates from Sixtus's time. Nicholas IV added the transepts and polygonal apse, which was rebuilt under Clement X (r. 1670–76). The relic of the Santa Culla or Holy Crib that Palladio mentions is still displayed on the high altar on Christmas morning. See Huelsen (1927), p. 342; Armellini (1942), p. 226; Krautheimer (1980), pp. 46–9, 90, 175, 191.

37 Although Palladio credits the building of this church to Constantine, in fact the large basilica of San Lorenzo fuori le mura was laid out at the end of the twelfth century by Cencius Camerarius, later Pope Honorius III (r. 1216–27), and completed in the first quarter of the thirteenth century. At this time the basilica built by Pope Pelagius II in 579 was deprived of its apse and turned into the sanctuary of the new church, its ground floor half-buried except for a small crypt, and the resulting sanctuary floor level was nine steps above the new nave. The parallel covered cemetery is of Constantinian date. The bodies of saints Lawrence and Stephen mentioned in the text are still preserved in the church. See a drawing of the mid-1530s by Maarten van Heemskerck; Filippi (1990), no. 23 [fol. 21*r*]. See Huelsen (1927), pp. 285–6; Armellini (1942), p. 865; Krautheimer (1980), pp. 83–5, 172–3, 175.

38 The catacombs of St Cyriaca, where the body of St Lawrence is said to have been placed after his death in 258.

39 The basilica of San Sebastiano was originally dedicated to saints Peter and

Paul and called the Basilica Apostolorum. It was built in the first half of the fourth century over the cemetery of Calisto (see note 40, below). At a later date St Sebastian was buried here and after the ninth century the association with the Apostles was forgotten and the church was renamed San Sebastiano. The church originally had a nave and two aisles, the aisles being walled up in the thirteenth century. It was rebuilt in 1612 for Cardinal Scipio Borghese by Flaminio Ponzio (c.1559–1613). The stone that was once believed to bear the imprint of Christ's feet, mentioned below, is still present in the church, in the Chapel of the Relics. See Huelsen (1927), p. 460; Armellini (1942), p. 249; Krautheimer (1980), pp. 19, 24–5. Cited by Palladio, QL, IV. xxii [p. 300].

40   The catacombs, into which, as Palladio's text indicates, the bodies of saints Peter and Paul were temporarily moved from their tombs in St Peter's and San Paolo fuori le mura during the persecution of Valerian in 258. See Krautheimer (1980), p. 19.

41   The Chiesa (or Capella) di 'Domine quo vadis?' (Lord, where are you going?), at the crossroads where the Via Appia and the Via Ardeatina meet, was so-called because it was on the site where Peter, when fleeing Rome, had a vision of Christ. The Apostle asked Jesus where he was going. Peter heard a voice saying 'I am going to be crucified once again', at which he retraced his steps to meet his fate. Cardinal Francesco Barberini had the façade renovated in 1637. See Armellini (1942), p. 900; Zeppegno, L., and R. Mattonelli, Le chiese di Roma (2000), pp. 221, 223. Photographs of the church are at http://www.romacivica.net/tarcaf/img/quo_vad.jpg

42   According to tradition, Santa Croce in Gerusalemme was founded by Constantine's mother, St Helena (c.225–c.330), but it was probably built some time after 326 within the large imperial palace erected for her in the early third century. It was rebuilt in 1144–45 by Pope Lucius II (r. 1144–45) and remodelled again by Benedict XIV (r. 1740–58) in 1743–44. The pieces of the True Cross that Palladio goes on to mention were held to have been saved in Jerusalem by St Helena (hence the name of the church) and are still preserved in the Chapel of the Relics. See Huelsen (1927), p. 243; Armellini (1942), p. 795; Krautheimer (1980), pp. 24, 58, 175, 258, 324–5.

43   The traditional date in the Church calendar for this celebration is 22 March.

44   On the titular churches see Krautheimer (1980), pp. 18, 112.

45   The text incorrectly has anzi ('in fact' or 'before') for anni ('years').

46   San Giovanni Calibita, as San Giovanni nell'Isola is properly known, was first recorded in existence in 1018, and was reconstructed in the first half of the twelfth century and again in 1640. It is now attached to the Hospital of the Brothers of San Giovanni di Dio (the Fatebenefratelli). See Ashby (1925); Huelsen (1927), pp. 275–6; Armellini (1942), p. 618; Krautheimer (1980), p. 273.

47   Standing on the site of the temple of the pagan god Aesculapius, this large basilica dedicated originally to SS Adalberto and Paolino was built before 1000. See

Huelsen (1927), p. 206; Armellini (1942), p. 619; Krautheimer (1980), pp. 170, 273. It was restored most notably by the architect Orazio Torriani (fl. 1602–30) in 1624. The tower is Romanesque.

48   This attribution to Pope Gelasius II (r. 1118–19) is incorrect, although it is also found in accounts by Andrea Fulvio and Etienne Du Pérac; see Ashby (1916). The church was in fact founded by the German emperor Otto III (980–1002); see Krautheimer (1980), pp. 254, 273.

49   This church, on the Via Anicia, was founded in 1488–89. See Huelsen (1927), p. 537; Armellini (1942), p. 668. The church on the site today was built around 1566 by Guidetto Guidetti (d. 1564), with a façade attributed to Giacomo Barozzi da Vignola.

50   The house of St Cecilia and her husband, St Valerian, whom she converted to Christianity, was adapted to Christian use probably in the fifth century. A basilica was erected here by Pope Paschal I (r. 817–24), and the church (radically altered from the sixteenth century onwards) was partly restored to its original form in 1899–1901. For internal details, including the ninth-century mosaics, see Huelsen (1927), p. 229; Armellini (1942), p. 669; Krautheimer (1980), pp. 18, 127, 137, 176, 209, 214–17, 222–3, 254, 274.

51   Pope Julius I (r. 337–52) first laid out a church on the site, although some kind of Christian foundation is known to have existed here under St Calixtus (pope from 217 to 222). Julius's basilica was rebuilt from the 1120s and completed by Pope Innocent II (r. 1130–43) in 1140. See Huelsen (1927), p. 371; Armellini (1942), p. 637; Krautheimer (1980), pp. 33, 34, 163, 168, 173, 279. On the Taberna Meritoria and the miraculous founding of this church see Palladio, *Antiquities*, fol. 20r.

52   This is incorrect, since Gregory III was pope from 731 to 741 and the church was a fourth- and ninth-century structure at the time of its rebuilding by Innocent II. See Krautheimer (1980), p. 163.

53   Founded in the fifth century and rebuilt by John of Crema between 1123 and 1130, this church was reconstructed by Giovanni Battista Soria in 1623. See Huelsen (1927), p. 238; Armellini (1942), p. 686; Krautheimer (1980), pp. 168–70.

54   San Francesco a Ripa, built in 1231 to replace the old hospice of San Biagio, where St Francis stayed in 1219. Huelsen (1927), p. 253, however, dates the foundation to 1229. See also Armellini (1942), p. 667.

55   Lodovica Albertoni was a Franciscan who had been a Roman noblewoman and had taken her vows after being widowed. She worked for the poor of Trastevere under the direction of the fathers of this church, where she was buried in 1533. Her tomb was the object of one of Bernini's greatest sculptures.

56   The church dates from the tenth century but was rebuilt in 1475. It was within the convent (now the Hospice of Regina Margherita) that replaced the monastery of SS Cosma e Damiano in Mica Aurea. See Huelsen (1927), pp. 240–1; Krautheimer (1980), p. 254. Not mentioned in Armellini (1942).

57   Mentioned in the ninth century, the church was rebuilt in the late fifteenth century at the expense of Ferdinand of Aragon (1452–1516) and Isabella of Castile (1451–1504). See Huelsen (1927), p. 418; Armellini (1942), p. 660.

58   The altarpiece above the high altar (the 'Transfiguration') was painted by Raphael (as given in the later, 1561 anonymous version of *Le chiese*) and installed in 1523. It was removed in 1809 and is now in the Vatican. The 'Scourging of Christ at the Pillar' mentioned here (one of the stations of the cross) was painted by Sebastiano Luciani (del Piombo, *c.*1485–1547) in 1518 for the chapel of Pier Francesco Borgherini.

59   The Tempietto (1502–10) by Bramante. In Palladio (1991), E.D. Howe sees the curious omission of Bramante's name (and of Raphael's above) as 'indicative of Palladio's circumscribed objectives'; p. 156, n. 20; see also p. 40. For woodcut plans and sections, see Serlio, Book Three, pp. XLI–XLIIII [pp. 131–4]. See also Palladio's drawing in the Vicenza City Museum, of the elevation, D 26 *v* (Puppi, L., *Palladio Drawings* (1990), no. 42). Discussed and illustrated by Palladio, *QL*, IV. xvii [pp. 276–8]. This is the only modern building discussed and illustrated in the *Quattro libri* apart from Palladio's own works.

60   In the Chapel of San Paolo inside the church, designed by Giorgio Vasari (1511–74) and completed in 1552, the tombs of Cardinal Antonio del Monte (d. 1533) and Vincenzo del Monte (d. 1504) were sculpted by Bartolomeo Ammanati (1511–92).

61   This large basilica was built by Pope Honorius I (r. 625–38) in 630 to replace an oratory built by Pope St Symmachus (r. 498–514). It was remodelled in the seventeenth century. The apse, part of the transept and the annular crypt of the seventh-century church survive. See Huelsen (1927), p. 409; Armellini (1942), p. 951; Krautheimer (1980), pp. 86–7.

62   Another name for the Porta Aurelia. See the anonymous, *Mirabilia urbis Romae: The Marvels of Rome, or a Picture of the Golden City*, trans. F.M. Nichols (1889), 'De portis urbis'. See also Palladio, *Antiquities*, fol. 3*v*.

63   Probably the feast of St Peter and St Paul, held on 29 June when it falls upon a Sunday.

64   The catacombs, which date from the fourth century.

65   This church was founded by Blessed Nicolò da Forca Palena in 1419, and restored in 1857. It houses the tomb of the famous poet Torquato Tasso. Huelsen (1927), p. 541, however, dates the foundation to 1434. See also Armellini (1942), p. 658.

66   The text has *Setignana*.

67   The church of Santa Maria in Saxia, or Sassia as it was known during the Middle Ages, was founded around 728 by the saintly king Ina of Wessex (r. 688–728) for Anglo-Saxon pilgrims and rebuilt by Antonio da Sangallo the Younger from 1538 to 1544. Palladio is thought to have designed the ciborium here in 1546–47, and the altar tabernacle in the central chapel of the Corsia Sistina. See Puppi (1975), pp. 27, 265 no. 24, 266 no. 25; Palladio (1991), pp. 11–12. See also Palladio's drawing for a tabernacle, RIBA XVII 18V, attributed to this church (Puppi (1975), p. 266, no. 25). The façade was executed in 1585 by Ottavio Mascherino (1536–1606). On the early church, see Krautheimer (1980), p. 82.

68   That is, the church at the huge Ospedale di Santo Spirito, a hospital and

hostel founded by Pope Innocent III (r. 1198–1216) around 1198 and rebuilt for
Sixtus IV (r. 1471–84) around 1473–82. See Huelsen (1927), pp. 363–4; Armellini
(1942), p. 772; Howe, E.D., *The Hospital of Santo Spirito and Pope Sixtus IV* (1978);
Krautheimer (1980), p. 267; Onians, J., *Bearers of Meaning: The Classical Orders in
Antiquity, the Middle Ages, and the Renaissance* (1988), pp. 197, 199.

69   That is, Santo Spirito in Sassia. See note 68, above.

70   It is clear from Palladio's account that the church referred to here is the
small chapel built on the very top of Castel Sant'Angelo, Sant'Angelo de Castro S.
Angeli (also called the Chapel of St Michael), founded in the seventh century. While
Palladio attributes it to Gregory I (r. 590–604), other authors cite a certain Boniface
– probably Pope Boniface IV (r. 608–15). In Palladio (1991), E.D. Howe suggests that
the church referred to here might equally be S. Angeli prope Castellum S. Angeli or
Sant'Angelo prope S. Petrum in civitate Leonina; p. 156 n. 23. However, neither
church has a founding myth dating back to the seventh century; Sant'Angelo prope
S. Petrum was founded in 1552 and the earliest known citation of S. Angeli prope
Castellum S. Angeli dates from 1492. See Huelsen (1927), p. 196; Armellini (1942),
pp. 774, 791, 958; Krautheimer (1980), p. 75.

71   Legend has it that Pope Gregory I (r. 590–604), while crossing the Pons
Aelius at the head of a procession to pray for end of the plague of 590, witnessed
the Archangel Michael with his sword on top of the fortress of Sant'Angelo. The
vision accurately announced the end of the plague and gave the church its present
name. See Krautheimer (1980), p. 75.

72   Close to each other stand a church and an oratory, both of which are
known by the fuller name Santa Maria della Pietà in Campo Santo ('campo santo'
meaning cemetery). The church is situated on the south side of St Peter's and was
built by Pope Leo IV (r. 847–55). See Titi, F., *Descrizione delle Pitture, Sculture e
Architetture esposte in Roma* (1763). The oratory (now named Santa Elisabetta)
belonged to the confraternity of the same name and was situated within the Campo
Santo Teutonico – a cemetery (adjoining the Ospizio Teutonico) where, as Palladio
says, pilgrims who died during their visit to Rome were buried. On the Campo
Santo Teutonico, see Krautheimer (1980), p. 261. Not identified by Huelsen (1927)
or Armellini (1942).

73   Today called Santo Stefano degli Abissini, this church is situated behind
the apse of St Peter's and was originally built in the ninth century. See Krautheimer
(1980), pp. 134, 267. The church was rebuilt by Clement XI (r. 1700–21) in the eighteenth century. See also Huelsen (1927), pp. 477–8; Armellini (1942), p. 750.

74   Known in modern times as Sant'Egidio, this church is placed by Huelsen
(1927), p. 164, and Armellini (1942), p. 788, outside the Porta Angelica and not, as
Palladio says, the Porta di San Pietro in Vaticano. The earliest known reference to the
church is dated 1278. It was united with St Peter's by a bull of Pope Boniface VIII
(r. 1294–1303) dated 27 April 1300. The celebrations of 1 September referred to here
included bonfires and races in the streets.

75   The earliest known citation of this church, which is located on Via
Trionfale and was formerly called Santa Maria Maddalena, dates from the 1270s.

E.D. Howe notes that Palladio's text is the earliest known reference to this church under its new name of San Lazzaro (degli leprosi): Palladio (1991), p. 156, n. 25. See also Huelsen (1927), p. 378; Armellini (1942), p. 842. On 22 July is the feast of Mary Magdalene.

76   The disease of Lazarus – that is, leprosy (made clear in later, anonymous versions).

77   Once situated near the entrance to St Peter's, this church and monastery, founded at the beginning of the fourteenth century, was demolished under Pope Alexander VII (r. 1655–67) in 1659. See Huelsen (1927), pp. 235–6; Armellini (1942), p. 782. On Alexander VII's replanning of the Piazza di San Pietro, see Krautheimer (1985), pp. 63–9.

78   Known as San Giacomo a Scossacavalli in Borgo, this church was situated in what used to be Piazza San Giacomo a Scossacavalli and was referred to in the fourteenth and fifteenth centuries as San Giacomo de Porticu. In the twelfth century it had been called San Salvatore a Scossacavallo after a bull of Hadrian IV on 10 February 1158. Some also think that this church was known as San Salvatore de Bordonia. The Confraternity of the Sacrament established itself in the church in 1520 and commissioned Antonio da Sangallo the Younger to provide a complete refacing. Work on the single nave ended in 1590–92, as can be seen on the Large Cartaro Map of Rome of 1576; see Krautheimer (1980), p. 260. See also Huelsen (1927), pp. 267–8; Armellini (1942), p. 776. The church was demolished under Benito Mussolini in 1936–37 for the creation of the Via della Conciliazione.

79   The first known citation of this church, also known as Santa Maria in Traspadina, occurs in the *Liber Pontificalis* in the 'Life' of Pope Hadrian I. The church was, however, demolished in 1564 to make way for the extended fortifications of Castel Sant'Angelo commissioned by Pope Pius IV (r. 1559–65). This church is recorded in Giovanni Antonio Dosio's bird's-eye view of the city of 1562. It was reconstructed between 1566 and 1587 in the middle of the Borgo Nuovo, a street destroyed in opening up the approach to St Peter's in 1937. See Huelsen (1927), pp. 370–1; Armellini (1942), p. 773.

80   This is a rectangular structure with an oval (not circular) cupola, designed by Giacomo Vignola (1507–73) for Pope Julius III (r. 1550–55) in 1551–53 to commemorate his deliverance from the soldiers of the Holy Roman Emperor, Charles V, while he was a cardinal. See Huelsen (1927), p. 527; Armellini (1942), p. 848; Palladio (1991), pp. 15–16.

81   The origins of this church are obscure. Fifteenth-century sources claim that Pope Paschal II (r. 1099–1118) built a chapel on the site in 1099, over the tombs of the Domitia family, believed to be haunted by demons because Nero was buried there, as Palladio reports. The church was rebuilt in 1227 and again under Sixtus IV. The façade is attributed to Andrea Bregno (1421–1506). See Huelsen (1927), p. 358; Armellini (1942), p. 319. See also the introduction, above.

82   Also known as the Oratorio di San Giacomo, this small church was founded by the Confraternity of San Giacomo degli Incurabili in 1525. See Huelsen (1927), pp. 537–8; Armellini (1942), p. 323. The icon from the Oratorio was moved

to the new church by Bernini and Carlo Fontana (1638–1714), a twin with Santa Maria in Montesanto.

83   That is, Santa Trinità dei Monti. The church was in fact founded by Louis's son, King Charles VIII. The first record of the church was in 1492. See Huelsen (1927), p. 543; Armellini (1942), p. 339.

84   There is some doubt as to the site of this church. Huelsen, p. 265 (following Panciroli, O., *I tesori nascosti nell'alma citta di Roma, raccolti e posti in luce* (1600)), dates this church to after 1339 and places it on the same site as Santa Maria Porta Paradisi, which stood close to the Ripetta port, not far from Augustus's mausoleum, hence the name 'in Augusta'. Others, notably Armellini (1942), p. 324, think that San Giacomo in Augusta was in fact San Giacomo degli Incurabili on the Via del Corso, rebuilt in 1584 by Cardinal Salviati, although that church is not particularly close to the mausoleum.

85   Sant'Ambrogio dei Lombardi was founded by Sixtus IV in 1471 and replaced the former San Nicolò de Tufis. The church was rebuilt as Sant'Ambrogio e Carlo al Corso (named after the great Milanese saints Ambrogio and Carlo Borromeo) by Onorio Longhi (*c.*1569–1619) between 1612 and 1619. See Huelsen (1927), p. 407; Armellini (1942), p. 337.

86   According to seventeenth-century sources, this church near the Ripetta port was built by the Borgia pope Alexander VI (r. 1492–1503), for the Confraternity of San Rocco. See Huelsen (1927), p. 541; Armellini (1942) p. 328. E.D. Howe notes that this is the earliest known reference to this church; Palladio (1991), p. 157, n. 32. See also Schudt, L., *Le Guide di Roma; Materialien zu einer Geschichte der römischen Topographie* (1930), p. 28. The church now has a neoclassical façade made in 1834 by Giuseppe Valadier.

87   This church is situated on the site of the mausoleum, in the south-west corner.

88   Mentioned in the eleventh century, the church that previously occupied this site on the banks of the Tiber, today on the Via Ripetta, was variously called Santa Marina de Posterula, Santa Maria de Posterula, Santa Martina in Monte Augusto and Santa Marine de Campo Martio. In the fifteenth century this building fell into disrepair, whereupon Pope Nicholas V promulgated a bull in 1543 giving the site to the Compagnia degli Schiavoni (Company of Slavs) – exiles from the Balkans, recently conquered by the Turks. In place of the dilapidated church, the company built the church of San Girolamo degli Schiavoni, which itself was completely rebuilt to a design by Martino Longhi the Elder in 1585–90. Also known as San Girolamo dei Croati and San Girolamo degli Illirici, it still stands today. See Huelsen (1927), pp. 380–1; Armellini (1942), p. 326; Zeppegno and Mattonelli (2000), p. 200.

89   Mentioned in a document dated 366, the basilica here was restored and enlarged by Sixtus III on land granted by the Emperor Valentinian III (419–55). It was again rebuilt in the twelfth century and in 1650, although the campanile, the portico (with six Ionic columns) and the doorway all survive from the twelfth-century church. The gridiron that Palladio mentions below is contained in the first

chapel on the south side. See Huelsen (1927), p. 288; Armellini (1942), p. 291; Krautheimer (1980), pp. 34, 57, 173, 312.

90   San Silvestro in Capite was in fact originally built by Pope Stephen II (r. 752–57) and completed by Paul I (r. 757–67) in 761 on the site of a Roman building, possibly Aurelian's Temple of the Sun. On the legend that in 261 Pope Dionysius built this church on the remains of what was called the Palatium Diocletiani, see Palladio, *Antiquities*, fol. 8*v*. The addition to the title of the words *in capite* ('of the head') is encountered in sources for the first time in 1194; the relic of John the Baptist's head had been transferred to the monastery here in the time of Innocent II. See Huelsen (1927) pp. 465–7; Armellini (1942), p. 296; Krautheimer (1980), pp. 103, 113, 124, 139.

91   Built after 1520 by the Compagnia della Carità per le donne convertite (that is, ex-prostitutes), this church, variously known as Santa Maria Maddelena and Santa Lucia delle Convertite, stood on the site of Santa Lucia de Columna (or 'de Confino'), itself dating back to at least 1233. Le Convertite was destroyed in the eighteenth century. See Huelsen (1927), p. 302; Armellini (1942), p. 293.

92   Begun around 560 during the pontificate of Pope Pelagius I (r. 556–61) and completed during that of John III (r. 561–74), possibly by the Byzantine viceroy Narses (*c.*478–573) to commemorate his defeat and expulsion of the Goths, this church was originally dedicated to the Apostles Philip and James. It was restored in the fifteenth and sixteenth centuries and almost completely rebuilt by Carlo and Francesco Fontana in 1702–14. See Huelsen (1927), pp. 201–2; Armellini (1942), p. 249; Krautheimer (1980), pp. 68, 70, 97. Cited by Palladio, *QL*, I. xxvii [p. 70].

93   The text incorrectly has *papa* ('pope').

94   The fifth-century church of San Marcello was rebuilt on a design by Jacopo Sansovino (1486–1570) after a fire in 1519. Its façade is by Carlo Fontana (1683). See Huelsen (1927), p. 308; Armellini (1942), p. 459.

95   Of seventh- and eleventh-century origins, this church was rebuilt in the fifteenth century. The façade was completed by Pietro da Cortona (1596–1669) in 1660. See Huelsen (1927), p. 376; Armellini (1942), p. 471; Krautheimer (1980), p. 77.

96   This church was founded in 336 by Pope St Mark (r. 336), restored in the eighth century and in 833, and rebuilt in the fifteenth century by Pope Paul II (r. 1464–71). It was restored in the seventeenth century and again in 1744. See Huelsen (1927), p. 308; Armellini (1942), p. 459; Krautheimer (1980), pp. 33, 34, 137.

97   Known as Santa Maria di Loreto al Foro Traiano, this church was built by Antonio da Sangallo the Younger for the Confraternity de' Fornari in 1507. A lantern was added by Giacomo del Duca (*c.*1520–1604) in 1582. See Huelsen (1927), p. 537; Armellini (1942), p. 252.

98   In fact, near Trajan's Column; corrected in later, anonymous versions.

99   Founded around 1550 by Ignatius Loyola (1495–1556), the present church of Santa Marta (which during the nineteenth century became a Masonic lodge and a military magazine but now serves as an exhibition centre) stands near the Collegio Romano and was designed by Carlo Fontana. See Huelsen (1927), p. 540; Armellini (1942), p. 471.

100   The 1566 catalogue of Pope Pius V (r. 1566–72) lists the Convent of the Malmaritate as containing a closed order. See Huelsen (1927), p. 540; Armellini (1942), p. 471.

101   This church was known originally as Santa Maria de Astariis (from documents dated 1337), a name that became corrupted in the vernacular to Santa Maria della Strada. Other names include Santa Maria Alteriorum, from the piazza upon which the church stood. It was demolished during the reign of Pius V to make way for the Jesuits' headquarters church, the Gesù. See Huelsen (1927), p. 313; Armellini (1942), p. 465.

102   This church stands on the site of a small oratory probably built here before 800 on the ruins of a temple to Minerva. It was rebuilt in the 1280s, by Florentine Dominicans according to Vasari, in emulation of the order's church in Florence, Santa Maria Novella. It was altered beyond recognition in 1848–55. See Huelsen (1927), pp. 346–7; Armellini (1942), p. 485; Krautheimer (1980), pp. 211–12, 275.

103   That is, the Pantheon, as the next sentence makes clear. Dedicated by Boniface IV in 609, it was the first temple in Rome to be christianized, and before 1000 it was called Santa Maria ad Martiri. On its role as a church see Huelsen (1927), p. 363; Armellini (1942), p. 483; Krautheimer (1980), p. 72. The Pantheon is cited by Palladio, *QL*, I. vi [pp. 10–11], I. ix [p. 13], I. xvii [p. 41], I. xxviii [p. 70], IV. xi [p. 251], IV. xv [p. 267], IV. xix [p. 282], and described and illustrated at IV. xx [pp. 285–96]. See also Palladio, *Antiquities*, fols. 23r–v ('On the Temples').

104   Also listed in Santa Croce in Gerusalemme.

105   The earliest known mention of Santa Maria Maddalena dates from 1403. During the fifteenth and sixteenth centuries it was owned by the Arciconfraternità del Gonfalone. Pope Gregory XV (1621–23) handed the church over to the Ministri degli Inferni, and it was entirely rebuilt and rededicated in 1727. The present Rococo façade was designed in 1735 by Giuseppe Sardi. See Huelsen (1927), p. 379; Armellini (1942), p. 318.

106   A nunnery was installed at Santa Maria de Campo Marzo before the tenth century and perhaps as early as 806; see Krautheimer (1980), pp. 252, 275. The present church was rebuilt in 1563–64 and remodelled in 1685 by Giovanni Antonio de'Rossi (1616–95). See Huelsen (1927), pp. 320–1; Armellini (1942), p. 334.

107   Unidentified. The only church in this piazza is Santa Maria in Aquiro, possibly linked to a diaconia as early as around 600; see Krautheimer (1980), pp. 81, 252. See also Huelsen (1927), pp. 310–11; Armellini (1942), p. 315. Given that Palladio goes on to say that the children are 'tutored in letters and virtues', this may be a reference to the Collegio Capranica in the piazza, although its chapel is dedicated to St Agnese.

108   The earliest known reference to San Mauto (also Mauro or Macuto) in Via del Seminario is dated 1192 and the church was restored in 1254. It was completely rebuilt in 1577–79 to a design by Francesco da Volterra and still stands today. From 1538 to 1729 the church belonged to a confraternity of men from Bergamo who rechristened the building after their patron saints, Bartholomew and Alexander.

When the confraternity moved to inhabit their own church in 1729, the old name San Mauto was once again used. See Huelsen (1927), p. 307; Armellini (1942), p. 317.

109   While this church is of earlier origins than the time of Pope Caelestinus III (r. 1191–98), mentioned in the text, it was nevertheless rebuilt by him and the campanile dates from this period. On the diaconia of Sant'Eustachio, founded well before 715, see Krautheimer (1980), pp. 81, 252, 271. See also Huelsen (1927), p. 251; Armellini (1942), p. 429.

110   San Luigi dei Francesi is the French national church and was built next door to Santa Maria de Cellis during the reign of Sixtus IV, sometime shortly before 1492 (the date it first appears in a catalogue of churches). A new church replacing both was consecrated on 8 October 1589. The façade is attributed to Giacomo della Porta (1539–1602). See Huelsen (1927), p. 534; Armellini (1942), p. 436.

111   This church was built between 1479 and 1483 (the façade records 1483) for Guillaume d'Estouteville (1403–83), Cardinal of Rouen, by Giacomo da Pietrasanta. On a view of Rome of 1495 including Sant'Agostino, see Krautheimer (1980), p. 264. See also Huelsen (1927), p. 528; Armellini (1942), p. 441.

112   See note 113, below.

113   The church and hostel dedicated to San Trifone was rebuilt behind the present site of Sant'Agostino in 1006; see Krautheimer (1980), p. 252. Enlargement of the convent of Sant'Agostino led to the church's demolition in the eighteenth century. See Huelsen (1927), pp. 494–5; Armellini (1942), p. 350.

114   The hospital of this name, mentioned in the text, existed in the fourteenth century, while the church was built in 1445 by Cardinal Antonio Martinez di Chaves. The 'Scrofa' is a street in Rome. The present church was built in the seventeenth century. See Huelsen (1927), p. 528; Armellini (1942), p. 333.

115   This church is mentioned in the *Liber Pontificalis* in the biographies of popes Hadrian I and Leo III. It survives largely intact on the same site. See Huelsen (1927), p. 200; Armellini (1942), p. 345; Krautheimer (1980), p. 253.

116   Originally known as the church of the Sacro Cuore di Gesù, it was built on the eastern side of the Piazza Navona in 1450 by Alfonso de Paradinas (d. 1485), canon of Seville Cathedral and later bishop of Ciudad Rodrigo, and restored in 1879. The chapel off the north side is by Antonio da Sangallo the Younger. See Huelsen (1927), p. 533; Armellini (1942), p. 380.

117   Begun around 1450, this is the German national church and was completed during the pontificate of Alexander VI. Its façade is possibly by Giuliano da Sangallo. See Huelsen (1927), p. 535; Armellini (1942), p. 386.

118   Initially called Santa Maria della Virtù, this church was built by Sixtus IV around 1480–84 on the site of Sant'Andrea degli Acquararii to celebrate the successful outcome of the Pazzi conspiracy and victory over the Turks. The architect is thought to be Baccio Pontelli (1450–92). The church was partly rebuilt in 1611 and again by Pope Alexander VII. See Huelsen (1927), pp. 538–9; Armellini (1942), p. 370.

119   The feast of Our Lady of the Snow ('Dedicatio Sanctae Mariae ad Nives') was celebrated on 5 August to commemorate the dedication of the church of Santa Maria Maggiore on the Esquiline Hill in Rome. See [page [23]] above.

120   Founded on 21 December 1139 as the text indicates, based on an inscription in the church, this is a modest basilica retaining its original plan, although much restored. See Huelsen (1927), p. 492; Armellini (1942), p. 470; Krautheimer (1980), pp. 271, 272 (here the Piazza di Parione is identified as today's Piazza San Pantaleo, although this is not on the route between the previous church, Santa Maria della Pace, and the following, San Salvatore in Lauro).

121   Alessandro Farnese, Pope from 1534 to 1549; see Palladio (1991), pp. 3–4.

122   This church was standing at the start of Urban III's pontificate in 1186; see Krautheimer (1980), p. 271. The interior was remodelled by Ottaviano Mascherino (1536–1606) in 1594 after a fire. The façade was rebuilt in 1857–62. The cloister and refectory of the monastery survive. See Huelsen (1927), p. 444; Armellini (1942), p. 366.

123   In 1519 Pope Leo X entrusted the church of San Pantaleone (a daughter church of San Lorenzo in Damaso and mentioned in a bull of Pope Urban III (r. 1185–87) in 1186) to the Compagnia della Pietà dei Fiorentini. The company demolished this small old church and on the same site began building the imposing basilica of San Giovanni dei Fiorentini. See Huelsen (1927), pp. 410–11; Armellini (1942), p. 354. A competition was held for the design, which included Raphael and Baldassare Peruzzi as contestants, but it was won by Jacopo Sansovino. The work was continued by Antonio da Sangallo the Younger. Palladio's reference to 'haste' refers to these early stages of the rebuilding, in 1520–21, after which work came to a halt. It was resumed by Giacomo della Porta between 1583–1602.

124   According to an inscription in the church, San Biagio a Gatta Secuta, as it was then known, was restored in 1072 under Pope Alexander II (r. 1061–73). It is regularly mentioned under varying names in documents from the twelfth to fourteenth centuries. During the fifteenth century it became known as San Biagio della Pagnotta ('pagnotta' meaning 'bread bun') from the blessed buns distributed to the poor from this church on 3 January, the patronal festival. Bramante began rebuilding the church in 1508. See Huelsen (1927), pp. 214–16; Armellini (1942), p. 355. See also Palladio's drawing in the Vicenza City Museum showing a section, D 11 *v* (Puppi (1990), no. 43).

125   This is a reference to Bramante's unfinished Palazzo dei Tribunali, begun on a plot between the new Via Giulia and the Via Papalis at a point where the two roads come closest together.

126   Also known as Santa Lucia Nuova (and in the sixteenth century, the Oratorio di Santa Lucia del Gonfalone, although 'La Chiavica' means 'The Sewer'), this church was built in the middle of the fourteenth century, before 1352. It still stands on the Via dei Banchi Vecchi. See Huelsen (1927), pp. 302–3; Armellini (1942), p. 421.

127   Referred to as subservient to S. Lorenzo in Damaso in 1186, the small church of San Giovanni in Agina was a parish in its own right by 1395. It still stands in Via di Monserrato but was deconsecrated at the beginning of the twentieth century. In the medieval period the Corte Savella was an area known for its prisons. See Huelsen (1927), p. 269; Armellini (1942), p. 419.

128   Situated at the beginning of Via di Monserrato, this church is known today as San Girolamo della Carità – literally 'St Jerome of Alms-giving', an activity emphasized by Palladio. St Jerome is said to have lived here in 382 and St Filippo Neri lived in the house next door between 1551 and 1583. The church was largely rebuilt in 1654 by Domenico Castelli (d. 1657) and Carlo Rainaldi (1611–91). See Huelsen (1927), pp. 532–3; Armellini (1942), p. 414; Zeppegno and Mattonelli (2000), p. 162.

129   'Casa Santa' simply means monastic house, and it is unclear as to which religious establishment Palladio is referring. However, Santa Brigida in Piazza Farnese (founded in 1513; Huelsen (1927), p. 529; Armellini (1942), p. 414), with the adjoining house of Santa Brigida, is a strong candidate, given that this is the only church that stood on the route leading from the previous church, San Girolamo, to the following one, San Lorenzo in Damaso.

130   The ancient basilica was founded by Pope St Damasus I (r. 366–84) in the fourth century. Cardinal Raffaelle Riario (d. 1521) began the church's reconstruction on part of the old site in 1486, incorporating it into the Palazzo della Cancellaria. It was restored in 1868–82 and again in the twentieth century after a fire. See Huelsen (1927), p. 284; Armellini (1942), p. 373; Krautheimer (1980), pp. 33, 34, 271.

131   Today known as Santa Barbara e San Tommaso d'Aquina dei Librai, this church was built on the ruins of the Portico of Pompey sometime before the eleventh century. See Huelsen (1927), pp. 204–5; Armellini (1942), p. 410.

132   Also known as San Martino ai Pelamantelli, this is a daughter church of San Lorenzo in Damaso and was mentioned in a bull of Pope Urban III in 1186. This small building – 'Martinello' means 'little martin' – which stood near the Ponte Sisto, was demolished in September 1747. See Huelsen (1927), p. 383; Armellini (1942), p. 402.

133   The text incorrectly has '30'. Tradition has it that Gualtiero performed this deed in 1220.

134   A daughter church of San Lorenzo in Damaso and mentioned in a bull of Pope Urban III in 1186, this was originally called San Salvatore in Domno Campo. The church was demolished in 1639 to make way for the Palazzo del Monte di Pietà. The modern church of the same name was not built on the same site. See Huelsen (1927), p. 434; Armellini (1942), p. 407.

135   Although radically restored in 1860, the ancient church of Santa Maria in Monticelli (founded between 1099 and 1118 but consecrated in 1143) has a campanile and a mosaic head of Christ in the apse both dating from the twelfth century. See Huelsen (1927), pp. 349–50; Armellini (1942), p. 404; Krautheimer (1980), p. 272.

136   This small church of San Biagio dell'Anello (previously San Biagio dell'Oliva) was ceded to the Barnabite Order in 1575 and then demolished to make way for the Theatine church of Sant'Andrea della Valle. The Barnabites transferred the order to the church they built nearby, San Carlo ai Catinari, begun in 1612 by Rosario Rosati (c.1560–1622), which stands in the present-day Piazza B. Cairoli. See

Huelsen (1927), p. 220; Armellini (1942), pp. 368, 444; Zeppegno and Mattonelli (2000), pp. 161, 267.

137   Previously San Salvatore in Cacabariis, this church is a sister church of San Lorenzo in Damaso. It dates from pre-1186 and stands on the corner of Via dei Calderari and Via del Progresso. The name 'Our Lady of Weeping' comes from a picture of the Virgin that wept when a bloody incident took place in front of it on 10 January, 1546. The interior as it appears today is by Nicola Sebregondi, dating from the early seventeenth century. See Huelsen (1927), p. 433; Armellini (1942), p. 570; Zeppegno and Mattonelli (2000), p. 175.

138   According to a bull of Caelestinus III in 1192, the first monastery with a church on this site stood here before 1000 and was called Sancta Maria Domna Rosa. The name was changed to Sancta Maria in Castro Aureo, and Paul III granted it to Ignatius Loyola, who not only founded the conservatory for poor girls mentioned by Palladio but also had brought from Germany a peal of bells that caused great amazement. The present church with its fine façade was built by Guidetto Guidetti in 1560–64 for Cardinal Donato Cesi. See Huelsen (1927), p. 331; Armellini (1942), p. 567.

139   Sant'Angelo in Pescheria was founded in 755 (or 770) by Theodotus, uncle of Pope Hadrian I, inside the Roman Portico of Octavia, which housed two temples, dedicated to Jupiter and Juno (mentioned here). See Huelsen (1927), p. 196; Armellini (1942), p. 561; Krautheimer (1980), pp. 12, 81, 105, 251. According to the Vatican report on the state of the churches in Rome for the year 1660, entitled *Stato temporale delle chiese di Roma*, the church was rebuilt in 1611.

140   This church was consecrated in 1128, although probably standing on the site of an older sanctuary, and remodelled in 1599 by Giacomo della Porta. It occupies the site of three republican temples in the Forum Holitorium, thought to have been dedicated to Janus, Juno Sospita and Spes. See Huelsen (1927), p. 392; Armellini (1942), p. 623; Krautheimer (1980), pp. 12, 157, 273.

141   A brick building dating from before the seventh century, when it was already considered ancient, this church occupies the site of the Roman citadel on the highest point of the Capitoline Hill, hence its name, 'Altar of Heaven'. In the tenth century the church belonged to the Benedictines, but in 1250 Pope Innocent IV (r. 1243–54) handed it over to the Franciscans, who rebuilt it in the Romanesque style. The south elevation of the church was drawn in the mid-1530s by Maarten van Heemskerck; (Filippi (1990), no. 21 [fol. 16r]. See Huelsen (1927), pp. 323–4; Armellini (1942), p. 540; Krautheimer (1980), pp. 175, 202, 211, 285–8.

142   The staircase was built in 1348, ascending from the Piazza Aracoeli, as an offering for deliverance from the plague. For a plan reconstructing a Roman palace and staircase on Montecavallo see Serlio, Book Three, p. LXXX [p. 170, see also p. 441, n. 202].

143   Now underneath the church of San Giuseppe dei Falegnami (1598) in the Forum, the Tullianum was called the Mamertine Prison in the Middle Ages, and was later consecrated as San Pietro in Carcere. It is thought originally to have been

a cistern, like those in Tusculum and other Etruscan cities. The building was used as a dungeon in Roman times for criminals awaiting execution. As Palladio notes, according to Christian tradition St Peter and St Paul were imprisoned here. However, the church could not have been consecrated by Sylvester since the prison was still being used as such in 368, over thirty years after his death; see Ammianus Marcellinus, *History*, ed. M.-A. Marié (1984), Book XXVIII, I, 57. The fountain referred to by Palladio was not here but rather on the Janiculum or the Vatican, and no mention is made of San Pietro in Carcere Tulliano before 1450. See Huelsen (1927), pp. 421–2; Armellini (1942), p. 539.

144   Situated at the north end of the Comitium Universale, this church (also referred to as Sant'Adriano in Tribus Fatis/Foris) was originally the Curia Senatus – the Senate House begun by Sulla (138–78 BC) in 80 BC, rebuilt by Julius Caesar (*c.*101–44 BC) in 44 BC after it burnt down, and completed by Augustus (63 BC–AD 14). The present building dates from the time of Domitian (51–96), and was converted into a church by Pope Honorius I between 625 and 638. Hadrian I raised the church to the status of a diaconia, and Pope Gregory IX (r. 1227–41) restored it in 1228. In addition to the relics mentioned by Palladio there were also deposited in 1215 relics of the bodies of the martyrs Nereus and Achilleus. The church was restored to its ancient Roman form in 1935–38. See Huelsen (1927), pp. 260–1; Armellini (1942), p. 157; Krautheimer (1980), pp. 72, 75, 76.

145   See Palladio, *Antiquities*, fol. 18r.

146   This church occupies a large rectangular hall, thought to have been the audience hall of the city prefect, on the Via Sacra, which Pope St Felix IV (r. 526–30) adapted, adding mosaics to the apse. The so-called temple of Romulus (also called the Temple of Castor and Pollux) once served as a vestibule to the church. See Palladio's references, *QL*, I, vi, [pp. 10–11], III, xix [p. 200]). The church was largely remodelled in 1632 under Urban VIII (r. 1623–44) following a design by Bernini's pupil, Luigi Arrigucci. Details from the church are referred to in Serlio's Book Four (pp. VIII*v*, XIIII*v*, [pp. 264, 276]). See Huelsen (1927), p. 242; Armellini (1942), p. 152; Krautheimer (1980), pp. 28, 71, 75.

147   Also now called Santa Francesca Romana, this church incorporates the Oratory of Saints Peter and Paul, built by Pope Paul I in the west portico of the Temple of Venus and Rome. In 847, after structural damage to the church of Santa Maria Antiqua in the Forum, the diaconate of that church was transferred to the Oratory, which became Santa Maria Nuova. The church was enlarged and the apse mosaic and campanile added before it was consecrated anew in 1161. As Palladio records, the church burnt down during the reign of Honorius III (to be rebuilt by the same pope in 1216). See Huelsen (1927), p. 352; Armellini (1942), p. 150; Krautheimer (1980), pp. 71, 136, 170. The present façade was designed by Carlo Lombardi (*c.*1554–1620) as part of his reconstruction work on the church in 1615. The body of St Francesca Romana (Francesca Buzza de' Buxis de' Leoni, 1384–1440), mentioned by Palladio, is now in the crypt. Although Palladio maintains that she was canonized by Alexander VI, modern historians date her accession to

sainthood to 1608, under Pope Paul V (r. 1605–21). Cited by Palladio, *QL*, I. xix [p. 55], IV. vi [p. 221], IV. x [p. 248].

148   In 996 Gregory V (r. 996–99) is said to have placed here the bodies of saints Nemesio, Lucilla, Olimpio, Stefano, Teodulo and Sempronio. Palladio's unusual saint *Essemperio* could be a misreading for *Sempronio*.

149   An exceedingly early church, mentioned in chapter 15 of St Jerome's *De viris illustribus*, a work completed in 385, San Clemente is one of the best-preserved of the medieval basilicas in Rome, although it is in effect two churches superimposed. The upper church was built by Pope Paschal II over the lower one, completely obscuring it, in 1110 and restored in the eighteenth century. The lower church was discovered and excavated in 1857 by Father Giuseppe Mullooly. See Huelsen (1927), p. 238; Armellini (1942), p. 124; Nash, E., *Pictorial Dictionary of Ancient Rome* (1968), vol. 2, pp. 75–8; Krautheimer (1980), pp. 161–3.

150   This refers to Pope Joan.

151   The pope thereby avoids the site of the profanity. See Palladio, *Antiquities*, fol. 7*v*.

152   A very small church containing an image of the Virgin, situated between Via Maggiori and Via dei SS Quattro Coronati, Santa Maria Imperatrice was in fact an aedicule, the door to which was built by the sculptor and architect Giacomo del Duca. An inscription noted that the indulgences would only be obtained if those praying were kneeling. The church was destroyed around 1890. See Titi (1763), under 'Santi Quattro Coronati', p. 230; Armellini (1942), p. 497. Not mentioned in Huelsen (1927).

153   See [page [92]] below.

154   The original seventh-century foundation, established, as Palladio notes, by Pope Honorius I, was rebuilt in the ninth century in basilica form under Leo IV but burnt down in 1084 by the Normans. The present church was dedicated by Paschal II in 1116, incorporating surviving ninth-century fabric. See Huelsen (1927), pp. 427–8; Armellini (1942), p. 497; Krautheimer (1980), pp. 87, 134, 138, 164–6, 321–2.

155   That is, Symphorian.

156   The four preceding names, the Quattro Coronati of the church's title, are soldiers who refused to worship a statue of the pagan god Aesculapius.

157   This church was built on the site of an early community centre dedicated to two martyrs during the period of Diocletian (285–305) – Marcellino, priest, and Peter, exorcist (Damasus, epigram 29, in *Damasi Epigrammata*, ed. M. Ihm (1895)), hence Palladio's attribution to Constantine is apocryphal. It was standing by around 500. It was restored first during the pontificate of Gregory III in the eighth century and again during that of Alexander IV in the thirteenth, when it was dedicated on 10 April, as Palladio's text relates, but in the year 1256, not 1260 as he has it. The façade was remodelled under Pope Benedict XIV (r. 1740–58) in 1751. See Huelsen (1927), pp. 419–20; Armellini (1942), p. 221; Krautheimer (1980), pp. 32, 258.

158   Situated on the Via Merulana, as its name and Palladio's text makes clear, this church was mentioned at the Synod of Rome of 499. During the sixth

century it lost its titular status, and the title was passed on to SS Marcellino e Pietro. Restored during the reign of Paschal II in 1110 and again during the reign of Innocent III in 1212, the church was destroyed during the French period in 1810. A new church was built on this site in 1883. See Huelsen (1927), pp. 386–7; Armellini (1942), p. 244; Krautheimer (1980), pp. 32, 258.

159 Also called the Basilica Eudoxiana and the Basilica Apostolorum, the church was in existence by 431. It was restored during the reign of Pope Sixtus III with the participation of the Empress Eudoxia, wife of Valentinian III, as a shrine for the chains of St Peter. The church was again restored in 1475 under Sixtus IV by Meo del Caprina (1430–1501), who designed the façade with its colonnaded portico. See Huelsen (1927), pp. 418–19; Armellini (1942), p. 208; Krautheimer (1980), pp. 34, 66 (Krautheimer dates the church to around 400, consistent with Palladio's dating; see note 160, below).

160 In fact Arcadius (378–408) preceded Eudoxia (see note 159, above). On the Curia Vecchia, see Palladio, *Antiquities*, fol. 15r.

161 In 1876, on opening the crypt below the altar, a fourth-century sarcophagus divided internally into seven parts was discovered. In each of the compartments lay the mortal remains of the seven Maccabaeus brothers (Old Testament martyrs, c.168 BC) and a lead plaque identifying them.

162 The tomb of Julius II (still present in the church, although Julius II lies uncommemorated in St Peter's) is the famous unfinished masterpiece of Michelangelo, who was so hindered by his quarrels with Julius and by the jealousy of the pope's successors that he finally abandoned work on the tomb. Together with the surviving figure of Moses, some forty statues were to have decorated the tomb, including the two slaves now in the Louvre and the four unfinished slaves now in the Accademia gallery in Florence.

163 According to tradition (the Golden Legend), a church was erected here on the site of Lawrence's martyrdom as early as 313. The almost mythical Pius I (r. c.140–54) all but certainly did not found the church as Palladio states. Restored by Hadrian I, it was rebuilt in 894 by Pope Formosus (r. 891–96), hence it was occasionally called San Lorenzo in Formoso. The façade dates from 1574. For reference to the relics in this church in the seventh century, including St Lawrence's grill, see Huelsen (1927), pp. 292–3; Armellini (1942), p. 199; Krautheimer (1980), p. 83.

164 This exceedingly early church was built or restored by the Roman patrician Flavio Ricimero (d. 472) around 470. Though initially called Sant'Agata super Subura, after the medieval period it came to be called Sant'Agata dei Goti because when Rome was occupied by the Goths, Sant'Agata was their national church. Pope Gregory I restored it, removing all evidence of its Arian past. It retains its Byzantine plan. See Huelsen (1927), pp. 166–7; Armellini (1942), p. 201; Krautheimer (1980), p. 56.

165 These include antique columns and capitals with pulvins. On the fifth-century apse mosaic, see Krautheimer (1980), p. 127.

166 Built upon the ruins of a third-century house in the Via Urbana, this small medieval church with one nave and three side chapels was rebuilt by Pope Paul

III in 1543. Of the present-day façade, only the door dates from the sixteenth century. See Huelsen (1927), pp. 286–7; Armellini (1942), p. 223; Zeppegno and Mattonelli (2000), p. 191 (with an anonymous woodcut image dated 1632 of the wellspring the church is named after – 'in Fonte').

167   One of the oldest churches in Rome, Santa Pudenziana is thought to have been converted around 390 from Roman baths of the second century AD built by Novatian and Timotheus, brothers of Pudenziana, above the so-called House of Pudens. Parts of the baths are evident in the Oratorium Marianum off this church. See Palladio, *Antiquities*, fol. 8*v*. Pudenziana was the daughter of the Roman senator Pudens, a legendary figure who is supposed to have given hospitality to St Peter in this house. The church was rebuilt several times, most notably in 1589. See Huelsen (1927), pp. 424–5; Armellini (1942), p. 192; Krautheimer (1980), pp. 33–4, 40–1.

168   Known as St Vitus in the Abbatoir (*macello*) because it was near the Macellum Liviae (Abbatoir of Livia), this church in Via Carlo Alberto was also called SS Vito e Modesto. It existed as a titulus before around 500, became a diaconia after 750, and was rebuilt in 1477 by Sixtus IV a short way from the original site. Artworks include a painting attributed to the school of Antoniazzo Romano, *Madonna with Child and Saints*. See Huelsen (1927), pp. 499–500; Armellini (1942), p. 811; Krautheimer (1980), pp. 32, 74; Zeppegno and Mattonelli (2000), p. 188.

A photograph of the church is at http://www.romaspqr.it/ROMA/Foto/ss_vito_e_modesto.htm.

169   This stone was known as the 'pietra scelerata' and people believed that filings scraped from it would cure the bite of rabid dogs.

170   Apparently founded in 1220, this church was initially inhabited by Carmelites. The Vatican report on the state of the churches in Rome for the year 1662, the *Stato temporale delle chiese di Roma*, describes it as follows: 'The church has a choir, a campanile with a single bell and a sacristy. It has only one altar and the said church serves as a cemetery for the said religious community.' The church was destroyed in 1874 to make way for the Piazza Vittorio Emanuele. See Huelsen (1927), p. 279; Armellini (1942), p. 810.

171   That is, the Trophies of Mario. These are not in fact mentioned above in the text on churches (an error corrected in later, anonymous versions), but are mentioned in Palladio, *Antiquities*, fol. 11*v*.

172   Founded in the fourth century, this church was reconsecrated to SS Eusebius and Vincentio by Gregory IX in 1238. It was given to the Celestines in the fifteenth century and rebuilt in 1711 and 1750. During the reign of Sixtus IV one of the first printing presses in Rome was set up here, printing the works of John Chrysostom with a commentary by Francesco Aretino. The fifteenth-century carved top of the tomb of St Eusebius survives in the sacristy of the present church. See Huelsen (1927), p. 251; Armellini (1942), p. 807.

173   This fifth-century titulus, dedicated by Pope Simplicius (r. 468–83), as Palladio notes, was replaced by a thirteenth-century basilica, which was in turn remodelled by Bernini in 1624 during the reign of Urban VIII. See Huelsen (1927), p. 213; Armellini (1942), p. 804; Krautheimer (1980), pp. 58, 111, 314.

174   The church of the Carmelites from the fourteenth century, San Martino ai Monti was built around 500 by St Symmachus to replace an older church dedicated to St Sylvester of the fourth century. It was restored in the eighth century by Pope Hadrian I and rebuilt in the ninth by Pope Sergius II. In the medieval period its name of SS Sylvestri e Martino was shortened to San Martino. It was remodelled in around 1650 by Filippo Gagliardi (d. 1659). See Huelsen (1927), pp. 382–3; Armellini (1942), p. 214; Krautheimer (1980), pp. 136, 313, 326.

175   The oldest inscription in this church is dated 491. The church was restored by Pope Hadrian I and later by Pope Paschal I (r. 817–24), who is mentioned in the text. It was restored again in 1450, 1564 and in the nineteenth century. Fragments of a column brought from Jerusalem in 1228 after the sixth Crusade and said to be that at which Christ was scourged, as Palladio mentions, survive in the present church in the Chapel of St Zeno (formerly the Horto del Paradiso), above which is mounted the casket that until 1699 contained the bones of the saints Valentine and Zeno. See Huelsen (1927), p. 423; Armellini (1942), p. 237; Krautheimer (1980), pp. 113, 123–4, 128, 134, 173, 313–14.

176   'The Garden of Paradise'.

177   Known in full as SS Quirico e Giulitta. While many, including Krautheimer, date this church to between 537 and 545, Huelsen (1927), pp. 428–9, doubts this, noting that the earliest written reference is in the twelfth-century *Mirabilia urbis Romae*. This church, with its trifoil chancel and a polygonal apse, was rebuilt in 1606 by Pope Paul V and the orientation reversed, with the entrance placed where the medieval apse once stood. See Armellini (1942), p. 172; Krautheimer (1980), pp. 67, 68, 74, 75, 97, 320.

178   This church was remodelled by Pope Leo III, apparently from a fourth-century reception hall with galleries, in 798–99, and restored several times, latterly by Cardinal Rusticucci (1595–1603). The façade of 1603 is by Carlo Maderno (c.1556–1629). See Huelsen (1927), pp. 486–7; Armellini (1942), p. 268; Krautheimer (1980), pp. 85, 105.

179   Built from a bequest left by the widow Vestina during the reign of Pope Innocent I (r. 402–17), this little church, known initially as SS Gervasio e Protasio, was dedicated in 416 and several times restored. The restoration by Sixtus IV, mentioned in Palladio's text, and one by Pope Clement VIII (r. 1592–1605) in 1595, just after the publication of Palladio's book, left little of the original building. See Huelsen (1927), pp. 498–9; Armellini (1942), p. 187; Krautheimer (1980), pp. 32, 33, 34–5 (with a reconstruction of the narthex and interior).

180   This structure was built around 320 as a mausoleum for Constantine's daughter, Costanza. Shortly afterwards it was changed into a baptistery and then transformed into a church in the thirteenth century. Mosaics dating from the fourth century are in the vaulting, with scenes of grape harvesting and Bacchic motifs, giving rise to the structure's attribution as a temple of Bacchus, as mentioned by Palladio here and in the *Quattro libri* (see reference below) and by Serlio. See Serlio, Book Three, pp. XVIII–XXI [pp. 112–14], which includes a a woodcut plan and section. See Huelsen (1927), pp. 238–9; Armellini (1942), p. 860; Krautheimer (1980),

pp. 25, 26, 28, 50. Described and illustrated by Palladio, *QL*, IV.xxi [pp. 297–300]. RIBA VIII 12R.

181   Begun by Constantine and dedicated by his daughter Constantina, the basilica of Sant'Agnese fuori le mura, with its galleries, was beginning to fall into ruin in the seventh century and was rebuilt by Pope Honorius I around 630. It was restored three times: in 1479 by Giuliano della Rovere (later Pope Julius II), by Cardinal Varallo after the Sack of 1527, and in 1856 by Pope Pius IX (r. 1846–78). The nave and aisles are separated by fourteen ancient Roman columns of breccia and pavonazzetto – perhaps the 'diverse stones' mentioned by Palladio. See Huelsen (1927), p. 170; Armellini (1942), p. 857; Krautheimer (1980), pp. 85, 87 (on the rich decoration), 177, 191, 248. Cited by Palladio, *QL*, I. vi [p. 11].

182   This small church, also called S. Maria Libera nos a Poenis Inferni, had a structure dating from before the fourteenth century, but was destroyed in 1901–02 because of the excavation of Santa Maria Antiqua. See Huelsen (1927), p. 339; Armellini (1942), p. 527.

183   The church and hospital of Santa Maria della Consolazione were built shortly before 1460 and the church was consecrated on 3 November 1472. See Huelsen (1927), p. 536; Armellini (1942), p. 317; Krautheimer (1980), p. 312. The façade is by Martino Longhi the Elder (1583–1606).

184   The story of this image of the Virgin Mary, which performed many miracles in 1460 and later, is recounted in Fanucci, C., *Trattato di tutte le opere pie dell'alma città di Roma* (1601), Book II, p. 2.

185   Possibly founded in the first half of the fourth century – according to an inscription, Pope Damasus I commissioned some of the early decoration during his reign from 366 to 384 – Sant'Anastasia was subsequently restored twice: by Leo III and by Gregory IV (r. 827–44). Although the façade was rebuilt in 1636 by Arrigucci, the present front dates from 1722. See Huelsen (1927), pp. 172–3; Armellini (1942), p. 532; Krautheimer (1980), pp. 14, 34, 139, 312.

186   Reconsecrated by Gregory VII on 8 July 1073 under the patronage (or so it is thought) of the prestigious Pierleoni family, this small church sheltered a venerated image of the Virgin. On 14 January 1662 this image was transferred to the nearby large church of Santa Maria in Campitelli, which as a result became known as Santa Maria in Porticu in Campitelli. Santa Maria in Porticu was shortly afterwards completely refurbished by the architect Mattia de Rossi (1637–95) and renamed Santa Galla. See Huelsen (1927), pp. 318–19; Armellini (1942), p. 552; Krautheimer (1980), pp. 157, 267 (on the eighth-century diaconia), 272. If Palladio did in fact visit this church it is remarkable that he does not record the presence of relics mentioned in an inscription on the high altar (the True Cross, the sponge from the Crucifixion, the cross and bones of St Andrew and the bones of the martyrs Stephen, Lawrence, Mark, James, Sebastian, Cromatius, Mennes, Valentine, Boniface, Anastasius, Leudicius, Donatus, Hippolitus, John the Priest, Agnes, Cecilia, Agatha, Concordia, Cirilla and Vebrobia).

187   The Ponte di Santa Maria, also known as the Pons Aemilius or Ponte Rotto (illustrated by Serlio in his Third book, p. LXXXVI [p. 177]), was the oldest

bridge crossing the Tiber. See Palladio, *Antiquities*, fol. 4*v*. Palladio here describes a temple of Vesta (Pudicitia watched over the chastity of matrons), now identified as the Temple of Hercules Victor. The first known reference to this building as a church, with the title Santo Stefano Rotondo, was in a bull by Innocent II of 27 October 1140. Not surprisingly, authors such as Flavio Biondo, Andrea Fulvio and Bartolomeo Marliani, writing in the late fourteenth and early fifteenth centuries, confused the building here with Santo Stefano Rotondo on the Celian Hill (for this church, see Palladio's text below on [page [60]]). In the second half of the sixteenth century the church became known as Santo Stefano delle Carrozze, changing to Santa Maria del Sole in the seventeenth century, only to be deconsecrated in the nineteenth century. See the 1593 view of Rome by A. Tempesta in Krautheimer (1980), p. 67, fig.58. See also Huelsen (1927), p. 484; Armellini (1942), p. 611. Described and illustrated by Palladio, *QL*, IV, xiv, [pp. 264−7]. RIBA VIII 1B/R.

188   Known in full as San Gregorio Magno, this medieval church was altered and restored in 1633 by Cardinal Scipio Borghese (1576−1633), and stood next to a monastery founded by Pope Gregory I on the site of his father's house and dedicated to St Andrew. This was demolished in 1573 except for two chapels. See Huelsen (1927), pp. 256−7; Armellini (1942), p. 513; Krautheimer (1980), pp. 59, 173, 321.

189   This church occupies a site traditionally connected with the house of John and Paul, two court dignitaries under Constantine II (316−40), who were martyred by Julian the Apostate (emperor 361−63). The original sanctuary was founded before 410 by the senator Pammachius (d. 409), a friend of St Jerome, and demolished in 1084. Rebuilding was begun by Pope Paschal II and continued by Hadrian IV (r. 1154−59). The church has a twelfth-century portico of the Ionic Order comprising eight antique columns. See Huelsen (1927), p. 277; Armellini (1942), p. 506; Krautheimer (1980), pp. 33, 34, 52, 173, 176, 177 fig.133, 325.

190   Previously called Santa Maria in Domnica, this ancient church was rebuilt with three apses by Pope Paschal I and again practically rebuilt by Cardinal Giovanni de' Medici (later Pope Leo X) from the designs of Andrea Sansovino (*c.*1470−1529) in the sixteenth century, when the five-bayed front portico was added. The navicella ('small ship') of the title refers to the Roman stone ship − probably a votive offering from the Castra Peregrina − that Leo X had made into a fountain in front of the church. See Huelsen (1927), pp. 331−2; Armellini (1942), p. 501; Krautheimer (1980), pp. 105, 122, 259.

191   Known in the medieval period as Santo Stefano in Monte Celio (the church known as Santo Stefano Rotondo was the small circular edifice near the Ponte di Santa Maria mentioned by Palladio on [page [59]]; see note 187, above), this church was founded by Pope Simplicius. The marble and mosaic decoration was continued by Pope John I (r. 523−26) and completed by Felix IV. Pope Theodore (r. 642−49) rededicated the church after having brought the bodies of saints Primus and Felician there. The building was again restored by Hadrian I and enriched by popes Leo III, Gregory IV and Leo IV. The five-bayed front portico was added in the twelfth century. The original plan, comprising three concentric rings intersected by the four arms of a Greek Cross, was almost certainly based on eastern models, per-

haps the church of the Holy Sepulchre in Jerusalem, and on Roman buildings. In 1450 Nicholas V demolished the outer ring and three of the arms, 'greatly ruining it' as Francesco di Giorgio remarked at the time. See Huelsen (1927), p. 474; Armellini (1942), p. 119; Krautheimer (1980), pp. 52, 90 (on the bodies of saints Primus and Felician), 325.

192   Recorded as existing as early as 595, San Sisto Vecchio (later known as San Sisto in Piscina or Santa Maria in Tempore) was granted benefices by Leo III. It was the residence in Rome of St Dominic (1170–1221). Although the church is much rebuilt, the campanile dates from the thirteenth century and the façade and interior were designed by Filippo Raguzzini (c.1680–1771) in 1727–35. See Huelsen (1927), pp. 470–1; Armellini (1942), p. 518.

193   This sentence is erroneously repeated in the 1554 edition and in later, anonymous versions.

194   This church was begun during the reign of Pope Caelestinus I (r. 422–32) by Peter the Illyrian, a priest from Dalmatia, and finished under Sixtus III on the site of a Roman mansion that, according to legend, belonged to the sainted Roman matron Sabina and was near the temple of Juno. It was restored by Pope Leo III and the work was completed by Pope Eugenius II (r. 824–27). In 1219 Pope Honorius III gave it to St Dominic for his new Dominican order, as the text indicates, although with the wrong date. The building was again restored in 1441 and 1481 (it has a small fifteenth-century portico), then completely renovated in 1587 by Domenico Fontana (1543–1607) and again by Borromini in 1643. See Huelsen (1927), pp. 430–1; Armellini (1942), p. 581; Krautheimer (1980), pp. 18, 34, 44–5, 51, 70, 173.

195   Etienne Du Pérac describes the stone at the altar as 'of Lucullan marble . . . an ancient weight of the Romans'; see Ashby (1916), p. 3.

196   Although rumours dating the founding of this church to the fourth century are unfounded, the building is nevertheless ancient and was originally dedicated to St Boniface. The name of St Alexis was added to that of Boniface in the tenth century, and he later became the sole dedicatee. In 977 Pope Benedict VII (r. 974–83) handed the church, which retains its Romanesque campanile, over to the Greek metropolitan Sergius, and it became a monastery of Latin Benedictines and Greek Basilians. In 1221 Gregory IX gave the monastery to the Premonstratensians. In 1426 Martin V (r. 1417–31) gave it to the Gerolomitani or Hermits of San Girolamo, as related in later, anonymous versions. Du Pérac relates the legend that Alexis married the emperor's daughter, fled to Palestine on his wedding day and returned in disguise as a beggar to live until his death under the stairs mentioned by Palladio, some of which are still present in the church. See Ashby (1916), p. 3; Huelsen (1927), pp. 171–2; Armellini (1942), p. 585. The image of the Virgin mentioned by Palladio also survives.

197   The earliest known reference to this church, which was said to occupy the site of the house of saints Aquila and Prisca, who entertained St Peter, is a fifth-century inscription at San Paolo fuori le mura. Pope Hadrian I added a new roof, and Leo III offered gifts in 806. Around 1600 Cardinal Benedetto Giustiniani from

Genoa (1554–1621) had the church repaired following designs by Carlo Lombardo di Arezzo (c.1554–1620); notable alterations included the façade and the renovation of the confessional and the crypt altar, supposedly consecrated to St Peter. See Huelsen (1927), p. 424; Armellini (1942), p. 577; Nash (1968), vol. 2, pp. 79–84.

198   These details concerning the Temple of Hercules and Calixtus's restoration are from an inscription in the church, to the left-hand side of the main altar.

199   The ancient church once standing on this site, which twelfth-century documents related to the Cella Nova of Sylvia, mother of Pope Gregory I, and which was occupied by Greek monks, was probably destroyed by the Normans in 1084. The present church was built by Cluniac monks and the accompanying monastery was granted to them by Pope Lucius II in 1145. Cistercians took over in 1503. The loggia was added above the portico in 1463. The present building was restored in 1943. See Huelsen (1927), pp. 429–30; Armellini (1942), p. 589; Krautheimer (1980), p. 173.

200   The first known mention of the titulus of this church was in 595, almost contemporary with its consecration (St Gregory, mentioned in the text, was pope from 590 to 604). From the fourteenth to the sixteenth centuries the church became known as San Salvatore e Santa Balbina because of a miraculous picture of Christ held there. The church was restored twice in the nineteenth century (1813 and 1825) and once in the twentieth (1930). On the fourth-century reception hall on this site, see Huelsen (1927), pp. 203–4; Armellini (1942), p. 590; Krautheimer (1980), p. 35.

201   While Armellini (1942), p. 520, dates this church to the reign of Pope Gelasius I (492–96) and others date it to around 550, all that can be learnt from the earliest documentary evidence is that it was rebuilt by Hadrian I. Subsequently restored several times, although the interior retains its eleventh-century basilican form, it was reconsecrated on 10 May 1191 by Pope Caelestinus III, as an inscription in the church relates. See Huelsen (1927), p. 274; Krautheimer (1980), pp. 68, 97, 167–8.

202   An inventory in San Giovanni a Porta Latina made during the reign of Pope Boniface VIII (1294–1303) records the existence of this chapel, called San Giovanni in Oleo. As can be read in an inscription in the architrave above the door (see photograph at: http://www.ukans.edu/history/index/europe/ancient_rome/Images/Gazetteer/Places/Europe/Italy/Lazio/Roma/Rome/churches/S.Giovanni_in_Oleo/exterior/2.jpg), it was rebuilt in 1509 during the pontificate of Julius II to a design attributed to Bramante (or to Antonio da Sangallo the Younger and his school) and funded by a French cleric called 'Adam'. The chapel was further restored in 1658 by Borromini. See Huelsen (1927), p. 274; Armellini (1942), p. 521.

203   The first basilica of what is now known as SS Vicenzo e Anastasio was founded in the eighth or ninth centuries and the current building was begun in 1131. This church is the abbey in the three-church monastical complex of L'Abbazia delle Tre Fontane on the Via Laurentina, which branches from the Via Ostiense. The other two churches are Santa Maria Scala Coeli (by Giacomo della Porta, 1582–84) and San Paolo alle Tre Fontane (also by della Porta, 1599–1607). The

church contains an important mural by an anonymous master contemporary with Giotto. Honorius I, mentioned by Palladio, was pope from 625 to 638 and therefore could not have consecrated the church in 1201. It is recorded that Honorius built the abbey to house monks from Cilicia (modern south-eastern Turkey), who came to Rome bearing the head of St Anastasius. Relics of St Vincent were brought to the abbey around 1370, and that saint's name was added at that time to the church's title. The abbey as it appears today was built by Innocent II. It was consecrated in 1221 (not 1201). The pillar upon which Paul was executed, mentioned by Palladio, is in fact in the small church San Paolo alle Tre Fontane. The story concerning St Paul's head comes from the apochryphal fifth-century Greek text *Acta Petri et Pauli* (*The Acts of Peter and Paul*) by Pseudo-Marcellus. See Huelsen (1927), p. 173; Armellini (1942), p. 940; Krautheimer (1980), pp. 90, 210; Zeppegno and Mattonelli (2000) pp. 181–2 (with a woodcut of the monastical complex by Girolamo Maggi). Photographs of the church are at http://www.medievale.it/new_site/artic_content.asp?target=demarco_005

204   A sanctuary on the Via Ardeatina, known in the vernacular as the 'Nunziatella', the Chiesa dell'Annunciata existed already at the beginning of the thirteenth century, as the inscription recorded by Palladio shows. (Huelsen, however, gives 12 August as the date of consecration.) From the seventeenth century this church belonged to the Confraternità del Gonfalone. See Huelsen (1927), pp. 309; Armellini (1942), p. 913; Zeppegno and Mattonelli (2000), pp. 221, 223 (with a woodcut illustration by Girolamo Maggi).

205   The Latin reads 'at the oil fountains': for the history of the founding of this church see [page [29]] above.

206   The text could also mean 'at the church of San Giuliano'.

207   The text on the Annunciata [page [64]] has ten thousand years.

208   The Pantheon.

209   San Giorgio.

210   This sentence would make more sense in the previous entry on the feast of Saint Mark, given the reference to the plenary remission of sins at San Marco on the 25th in the text above on that church [page [39]].

211   The text incorrectly omits 'At Santa Croce'.

212   The Pantheon.

213   Sant'Angelo.

214   The text has 'Santo Vito & Marcello'; also known as SS Vito e Modesto.

215   Here a moveable feast but normally fixed on 14 July.

216   Le Convertite. See note 91, above.

217   San Pietro in Vincoli.

218   The text is repeated here.

219   San Matteo in Merulana.

220   Sant'Angelo.

221   The text could also mean 'at the church of San Teodoro'.

222   Santa Cecilia.

223   San Clemente.

224   Santa Caterina.

225   The text could also mean 'at the church of San Crisogono'.

226   Santa Bibiana.

227   San Silvestro.

228   Here again the text has 'Santo Vito & Marcello'; also known as SS Vito e Modesto.

229   Santa Maria Liberatrice. See [page [57]] above.

230   The Chiesa (or Capella) di 'Domine quo vadis?'. See note 41, above.

BIBLIOGRAPHY

Ackerman, J., 'The Belvedere as a Classical Villa', *Journal of the Warburg and Courtauld Institutes*, vol. 14 (1951), pp. 70–91.

—— *The Cortile del Belvedere*, Studi e documenti per la storia del Palazzo Apostolico Vaticano, vol. 3, Vatican City (1954).

—— *Palladio*, Baltimore (1966).

—— *The Villa: Form and Ideology of Country Houses*, London (1990).

Alberti, L. B., *Ludi rerum mathematicarum*, ed. C. Grayson, Bari (1973).

—— *On the Art of Building in Ten Books*, trans. J. Rykwert, N. Leach and R. Tavernor, Cambridge, Mass. (1988).

—— 'Descriptio Urbis Romae', *Albertiana*, vol. 6 (2003), pp. 125–215.

—— 'Leon Battista Alberti's Delineation of the City of Rome', trans. P. Hicks, *Albertiana*, vol. 6 (2003), pp. 197–200.

Albertini, F., *Opusculum de mirabilibus novae et veteris urbis Romae*, Rome (1510).

Ammianus Marcellinus, *History*, ed. M.-A. Marié, Paris (1984).

Armellini, M., *Le chiese di Roma dal secolo IV al XIX*, 2 vols, Vatican City (1891; corrected and augmented by Carlo Cecchelli, 1942). See: http://www.ukans.edu/history/index/europe/ancient_rome/I/Gazetter /Places/Europe/Italy/Lazio/Roma/Rome/churches/.Texts/Armellini/A RMCHI★/home.html

Ascarelli, F., *La tipografia cinquecentina italiana*, Florence (1953).

—— *Le cinquecentine romane; censimento delle edizioni romani del XVI secolo possedute dalle biblioteche di Roma*, Milan (1972).

Ashby, T. (ed.), *Topographical Study in Rome in 1581; A Series of Views with Fragmentary Text by Etienne Du Pérac*, London (1916).

—— 'Note sulle varie guide di Roma che contengono xilografie di Girolamo Franzini', *Roma*, vol. 1 (1923), pp. 345–52.

—— 'Nuove note su varie guide di Roma', *Roma*, vol. 2 (1925), pp. 201–9.

[Aurelius Victor], *De viris illustribus urbis Romae*, ed. F. Pichlmayr, Leipzig (1911).

Baillie Reynolds, P. K., 'The Troops Quartered in the Castra Peregrinorum', *Journal of Roman Studies*, vol. 13 (1923), pp. 168–89.

Ball, L. F., *The Domus Aurea and the Roman Architectural Revolution*, Cambridge (2003).

Barberi, F., 'I Dorico, tipografi a Roma nel cinquecento', *La Bibliofilia*, vol. 67, (1965), pp. 221–61.

Barbaro, D., *I dieci libri dell'architettura di M. Vitruvio tradotti e commentati da Monsig. Daniele Barbaro*, Venice (1556).

Barbier de Montault, X., *L'année liturgique à Rome*, Rome (1870) (An inventory of the principal relics in the churches in Rome).

Bartoli, A., *I monumenti antichi di Roma nei disegni degli Uffizi di Firenze*, Rome (1914–22).

Bates, E., *Touring in 1600*, Boston (1911).

Bianchi Bandinelli, R. (ed.), *Enciclopedia dell'arte antica, classica e orientale*. 7 vols., Rome: Istituto della Enciclopedia Italiana (1958–66).

Biondo, F., *De Roma ristaurata, et Italia illustrata . . . Tradotte in buona lingua volgare per Lucio Fauno*, Venice (1542).

Boatwright, M. T., *Hadrian and the City of Rome*, Princeton (1987).

Bober, P. P., and R. Rubinstein, *Renaissance Artists and Antique Sculpture*, London (1986).

Boethius, A., *The Golden House of Nero: Some Aspects of Roman Architecture*, Ann Arbor (1960).

Bonelli, R., A. Bruschi, C. Maltese and M. Tafuri (eds), *Scritti rinascimentali di architettura*, Milan (1978), pp. 461–84.

Boucher, B., *Andrea Palladio, The Architect in his Time*, New York (1994).

Bremmer, J. and N. Horsfall (eds), *Roman Myth and Mythography*, London (1987).

Brewyn, W., *A XVth-Century Guide-book to the Principal Churches of Rome*, trans. C. E. Woodruff, London (1933).

Brown, P. F., *Venice and Antiquity*, New Haven and London (1996).

Brummer, H. H., *The Statue Court in the Vatican Belvedere*, Stockholm (1970).

Brunt, P. A., *Social Conflicts in the Roman Republic*, New York (1971).

Bruschi, A., *Bramante*, London (1973).

Burns, H., L. Fairbairn and B. Boucher, *Andrea Palladio 1508–1580: The Portico and the Farmyard*, London (1975).

Burns, H., and A. Nesselrath, 'Raffaello e l'antico', in *Raffaello architetto*, ed. C. Frommel, S. Ray and M. Tafuri, Milan (1984), pp. 379–452.

Bussagi, M. (ed.), *Rome: Art and Architecture*, Cologne (1999).

Calvo, M. F., *Antiquae urbis Romae simulachrum*, Rome (1527).

Capgrave, J., *Ye Solace of Pilgrims*, ed. C.A. Mills, London (1911).

Capitolinus, J., *Gordiani tres*, ed. H. Peter, Leipzig (1865).

Cary, M., and H. H. Scullard, *A History of Rome down to the Reign of Constantine*, London (1975).

Castellani, G., 'La tipografia del Collegio Romano', *Archivum Historicum Societatis Iesu*, vol. 2 (1933), pp. 11–16.

Castiglione, B., *Opere volgari, e latine del Conte Baldassar Castiglione*, Padua (1733).

Cevese, R. (ed.), *Mostra del Palladio: Vicenza, Basilica Palladiana*, Milan and Venice (n.d., 1973?).

Chevallier, R., *Roman Roads*, trans. N.H. Field, Berkeley, Calif. (1976).

Ciampini, G., *De sacris aedificiis*, Rome (1693).

Cicero, *Letters to Atticus*, Harmondsworth (1978).

Coffin, D., *The Villa in the Life of Renaissance Rome*, Princeton (1979).

Colocci, A., and J. Mazzocchi, *Epigrammata Antiquae Urbis*, Rome (1521).

Constant, C., *The Palladio Guide*, New York (1985).

Cooper, T. E., *Palladio's Venice: Architecture and Society in a Renaissance Republic*, London (2005).

Crawford, M. H., *Roman Republican Coinage*, Cambridge (1974).

—— *Coinage and Money under the Roman Republic*, London (1985).

Dal Maso, L. B., *Rome of the Caesars*, Florence (1975).

Damasus, *Damasi Epigrammata*, ed. M. Ihm, Leipzig (1895).

Davies, P., D. Hemsoll and M. Wilson Jones, 'The Pantheon: Triumph of Rome or Triumph of Compromise?', *Art History*, vol. 10, no.2 (1987), pp. 133–53.

De Beer, E. S., 'Francois Schott's *Itinerario d'Italia*', *The Library*, vol. 23 (1942), pp. 57–83.

—— 'The Development of the Guide-Book until the Early Nineteenth Century', *Journal of the British Archaeological Association*, 3rd series, vol. 15 (1952), pp. 35–46.

Di Teodoro, F. P., *Raffaello, Baldassar Castiglione e la Lettera a Leone X*, Bologna (1994; 2nd ed. 2003, augmented with new introduction by C. Thones and studies of Albertian echoes in the letter).

Dickinson, G., *Du Bellay in Rome*, Leiden (1969).

Dombart, T., *Das palatinische Septizonium zu Rom*, Rome (1922).

D'Onofrio, C., *Roma dal Cielo: Itinerari antichi della città moderna: Laterano – Borgo – Vaticano*, Rome (1982).

Dorez, L., *La Cour du Pape Paul III*, 3 vols, Paris (1932).

Du Bellay, J., *Le premier livre des antiquitez de Rome*, Paris (1562).

Du Pérac, E., *I vestigi dell'antichità di Roma*, Rome (1575) (see Ashby (1916)).

Durant, W., *Caesar and Christ: A History of Roman Civilization and of Christianity from Their Beginning to A.D. 325*, New York (1944).

Eusebius, H. E., *The Ecclesiastical History*, trans. H. Jackson Lawlor and J. Oulton, London (1927).

Evans, J. K., *War, Women and Children in Ancient Rome*, London (1991).

Fanucci, C., *Trattato di tutte le opere pie dell'alma città di Roma*, Rome (1601).

Farmer, D., *Oxford Dictionary of Saints*, Oxford (1978).

Fauno, L., *Delle antichità della città di Roma raccolte e scritte da M. Lucio Fauno con somma brevità e ordine, con quanto gli antichi or moderni scritto ne hanno. Libri V*, Venice (1548).

—— *De antiquitatibus urbis Romae ab antiquis novisque auctoribus exceptis & summa brevitate ordineque dispositis per Lucium Faunum*, Venice (1549).

—— *Delle antichità della città di Roma raccolte e scritte da M. Lucio Fauno con somma brevità e ordine, con quanto gli antichi or moderni scritto ne hanno. Libri V: Revisti hora, e corretti dal medesimo autore in molti luoghi, con aggiungervi per tutto infinite cose degne: E con un compendio di Roma antica nel fine, dove con somma brevità si vede quanto in tutti questi libri si dice,* Venice (1552).

Favro, D., *Image of Augustan Rome*, Cambridge (1996).

Festus (Sextus Pompeius Festus), *S. P. Festi de verborum significatione quae supersunt, cum Pauli epitome*, ed. K. O. Müller, Leipzig (1839).

Filippi, E., *Maarten Van Heemskerck*, Milan (1990).

Finley, M. I. (ed.), *Studies in Roman Property*, Cambridge (1976).

Fletcher, B., *A History of Architecture*, London (1975),

Francesco di Giorgio, *Trattati di architettura, ingegneria e arte militare*, ed. C. Maltese and L. Maltese Degrassi, 2 vols., Milan (1967).

Frank, T., 'Elizabethan Travellers in Rome', *English Miscellany*, vol. 6 (1953), pp. 95–132.

Frommel, C., 'Palladio e la chiesa di S. Pietro a Roma', *Bollettino del Centro Internazionale di Studi di Architettura A. Palladio*, vol. 19 (1977), pp. 107–24.

Frontinus, S. J., *De Aquis, The Stratagems and the Aqueducts of Rome*, trans. C.E. Bennett and M.B. McElwain, London (1925).

Fulvio, A., *Antiquitates urbis*, Rome (1527); 2nd ed. (1545).

Gamucci, B., *Libri quattro dell'antichità della città di Roma*, Venice (1565).

Gazzola, P., *Ponti romani*, 2 vols., Florence (1963).

Ghezzi, B., *The Times Book of Saints*, London (2001).

Gibbon, E., *History of the Decline and Fall of the Roman Empire*, London (1838–39 ed.).

Gnoli, U., *Topografia toponomastica di Roma medioevale e moderna*, Foligno (1984).

Goldscheider, L., *Michalangelo, Paintings, Sculptures, Architecture*, London (1964).

Golzio, V., *Raffaello, nei documenti e nelle testimonianze del suo secolo*, Vatican City (1936).

Greenidge, A. H. J., *Roman Public Life*, London (1901).

Gregorovius, F., *History of the City of Rome in the Middle Ages*, trans. A. Hamilton, 6 vols, London (1894–98).

Grimal, P., *Les Jardins romains*, Paris (1969).

Gualdo, P., 'La vita di Andrea Palladio', *Saggi e Memorie di Storia dell'Arte*, vol. 2, ed. G.G. Zorzi (1958–59), pp. 91–104.

Hale, J. R., 'Andrea Palladio, Polybius and Julius Caesar', *Journal of the Warburg and Courtauld Institutes*, vol. 40 (1977), pp. 240–55.

Hales, S., *The Roman House and Social Identity*, Cambridge (2003).

Hart, V., *Paper Palaces: Architectural Works from the Collections of Cambridge University Library*, Cambridge (1997).

Hart, V., and P. Hicks (eds), *Paper Palaces: the Rise of the Renaissance Architectural Treatise*, New Haven and London (1998).

Hartswick, K.J., *The Gardens of Sallust: A Changing Landscape*, Texas (2004).

Heinz, M., *San Giacomo in Augusta in Rom und der Hospitalbau der Renaissance*, Bonn (1977).

Hibbard, H., *Michelangelo*, Harmondsworth (1978).

Holt, E., 'A Report to Pope Leo X on Ancient Rome', *A Documentary History of Art*, vol. 1 (1957), pp. 289–96.

Hornblower, S., and A. Spawforth (eds), *The Oxford Classical Dictionary*, Oxford (2003).

Howe, E. D., *The Hospital of Santo Spirito and Pope Sixtus IV*, New York (1978).

Huelsen, C., 'Septizonium', *Zeitschrift für Geschichte der Architektur*, vol. 5 (1911–12), pp. 1–24.

—— *Römische Antikengarten des XVI Jahrhunderts*, Heidelburg (1917).

—— *Le chiese di Roma nel medio evo*, Florence (1927). See: http://www.ukans.edu/history/index/europe/ancient_rome/I/Gazetter /Places/Europe/Italy/Lazio/Roma/Rome/churches/.Texts/Huelsen/H UECHI★/2/M.html

Hulbert, J. R., 'Some Medieval Advertisements of Rome', *Modern Philology*, vol. 20 (1922–23), pp. 403–24.

Humphrey, J. H., *Roman Circuses: Arenas for Chariot Racing*, Berkeley, Calif. (1986).

Isermeyer, C. A., 'I Commentari di G. Cesare nell'edizione palladiana del 1575 e i suoi precedenti', *Bollettino del Centro Internazionale di Studi di Architettura A. Palladio*, vol. 21 (1979), pp. 253–71.

Kemp, M., *The Science of Art*, New Haven and London (1990).

Krautheimer, R., *Rome, Profile of a City, 312–1308*, Princeton (1980).

—— *The Rome of Alexander VII, 1655–1667*, Princeton (1985).

Labacco, A., *Libro appartenente a l'architettura*, Rome (1552).

Lafreri, A., *Speculum Romanae magnificentiae, omni fere quaecunque in urbe monumenta extant*, Rome (1540–92).

Lanciani, R., 'Maps, Plans and Views of the City of Rome with Especial Reference to a Drawing of the Sixteenth Century in the Burlington-Devonshire Collection', *Journal of the Royal Institute of British Architects*, 3rd series, vol. 2 (1895), pp. 645–50.

—— *The Destruction of Ancient Rome*, London (1901).

—— *Storia degli scavi di Roma*, 3 vols, Rome (1902–07).

Lauro, G., *Antiquae urbis splendor*, Rome (1612–15).

Lavagnino, E., *La chiesa di Santo Spirito in Sassia*, Rome (1962).

Lea, H. C., *A History of Auricular Confession and Indulgences in the Latin Church*, 3 vols, Philadelphia (1896).

Leto, G. P., 'Excerpta a Pomponio dum inter ambulandum cuidam domino ultramontano reliquias ac ruinas urbis ostenderet', Biblioteca Marciana, Venice, classe lat. X, 195ff. 15–31.

—— *De vetustate urbis*, Rome (1510).

Lewis, D., *The Drawings of Andrea Palladio*, Washington, D.C. (1981).

Ligorio, P., *Libro di M. Pyrrho Ligori napolitano, delle antichità di Roma, nel quale si tratta de' circi, theatri, & anfitheatri*, Venice (1553).

Lotz, W., *Studies in Italian Renaissance Architecture*, Boston (1977).

Lugano, P., *Le Sacre Stazioni Romane*, Vatican City (1960).

MacDonald, W., and J. Pinto, *Hadrian's Villa and its Legacy*, New Haven and London (1995).

MacDougall, E., and W. F. Jashemski (eds), *Ancient Roman Gardens*, Washington, D.C. (1981).

Mandowsky, E., and C. Mitchell, *Pirro Ligorio's Roman Antiquities*, London (1963).

Marliani, B., *Antiquae Romae topographia, libri septem*, Rome (1534).

—— *L'antichità di Roma*, trans. Hercole Barbarasa, Rome (1548).

Martin, G., *Roma Sancta (1581)*, ed. G.B. Parks, Rome (1969).

Masetti-Zannini, G. L., *Stampatori e librai a Roma nella seconda metà del cinquecento*, Rome (1980).

Mauro, L., *Le antichità della città di Roma*, Venice (1557).

Maxfield, V. A., *The Military Decorations of the Roman Army*, London (1981).

Mazzolari, G. M., *Diario Sagro*, revised by G. Marini Fuertez, Rome (1819–20).

McEwen, I., *Vitruvius, Writing the Body of Architecture*, Cambridge, Mass., and London (2003).

McKay, A. G., *Houses, Villas and Palaces in the Roman World*, London (1975).

Mitrovic, B., 'Palladio's Canonical Corinthian Entablature and the Archaeological Surveys in the Fourth Book of *I quattro libri dell'architettura*', *Architectural History*, vol. 45 (2002), pp. 113–27.

—— *Learning from Palladio*, London (2004).

Montaigne, M. de, *The Diary of Montaigne's Journey to Italy in 1580 and 1581*, trans. E. J. Trechmann, New York (1929).

Morton, H.V., *The Waters of Rome*, London (1966).

Moryson, F., *An Itinerary Containing His Ten Years Travel*, vol. 1, Glasgow (1907).

Munday, A., *The English Romayne Lyfe 1582*, ed. G.B. Harrison, Edinburgh (1966).

Murray, P., 'introduction' to *Five Early Guides to Rome and Florence*, Farnborough (1972).

Müntz, E., 'Les architects de St. Pierre de Rome d'après des documents nouveaux (1447–1549)', *Gazette des Beaux-Arts*, vol. 2 (1879), pp. 506–24.

Muth, R., 'Forum suarium', *Museum Helveticum*, vol. 2 (1945), pp. 227–36.

Nash, E., *Pictorial Dictionary of Ancient Rome*, 2 vols, London (1968).

Nova, A., *The Artistic Patronage of Pope Julius III (1550–55): Profane Imagery and Buildings for the Del Monte Family in Rome*, New York (1988).

Olivieri, A., *Palladio, le corte e le famiglie*, Vicenza (1981).

Onians, J., 'Storia dell'architettura e storia della religione: Bramante, Raffaello e

Baldassare Peruzzi', in *Roma e l'antico nell'arte e nella cultura del Cinquecento*, ed. M. Fagiolo, Rome (1985).

—— *Bearers of Meaning: The Classical Orders in Antiquity, the Middle Ages, and the Renaissance*, Cambridge (1988).

Ovid, *Tristia. Ex Ponto*, ed. A. E. Wheeler, Harvard (1988).

Palladio, A., *L'antichità di Roma di M. Andrea Palladio, raccolta brevemente da gli auttori antichi, & moderni*, Rome (1554).

—— *Descritione de le chiese, stationi, indulgenze & reliquie de Corpi Sancti, che sono in la città de Roma*, Rome (1554).

—— *I quattro libri dell'architettura*, Venice (1570).

—— *I Commentari di C. Giulio Cesare*, Venice (1575).

—— *Fabbriche Antiche Designate Da Andrea Palladio Vicentino E Date In Luce Da Riccardo Conte Di Burlington*, London (1730).

—— 'The Antiquities of Rome', in *The Four Books on Architecture*, trans. Giacomo (James) Leoni, 3rd ed., London (1742).

—— *Andrea Palladio: The Churches of Rome*, trans. E. D. Howe, Binghamton, N.Y. (1991).

—— *The Four Books on Architecture*, trans. R. Tavernor and R. Schofield, Cambridge, Mass. (1997).

Palmer, R. E. A., *Rome and Carthage at Peace. Historia Einzelschriften 113*, Stuttgart (1997).

Panciroli, O., *I tesori nascosti nell'alma citta di Roma, raccolti e posti in luce*, Rome (1600).

Pane, R., 'Palladio artista e trattatista', *Palladio*, vol. 6, no. 1, (1942), pp. 16–24.

—— *Andrea Palladio*, Turin (1961).

Panvinio, O., *Le sette chiese di Roma*, Rome (1575).

Parks, G. B., *The English Traveller to Italy*, vol. 1, *The Middle Ages (to 1525)*, Rome (1954).

Pastor, L. von, *The History of the Popes*, vol. 16, ed. F. I. Antrobus et al., London (1949).

Paul the Deacon, *Historia Langobardorum*, ed. R. Cassanelli, Milan (1985).

Pedretti, C., *A Chronology of Leonardo Da Vinci's Architectural Studies After 1500: In Appendix: A Letter to Pope Leo X on the Architecture of Ancient Rome*, Geneva (1962), pp. 157–71.

Pensabene, P., 'Casa Romuli sul Palatino', *Pontificia Accademia Romana di Archeologia*, vol. 63, (1990–91), pp. 115–62.

Pescarzoli, A., *I libri di viaggio e le guide della Raccolta Luigi Vittorio Fossati Bellani*, 3 vols, Rome (1957).

Platner, S. B., *A Topographical Dictionary of Ancient Rome*, completed and revised by T. Ashby, London (1929).

Pliny the Elder, *Natural History*, trans. D. E. Eichholz, Cambridge, Mass. (1962).

Publius Victor, *De regionibus urbis Romae libellus aureus*, Rome (1503)

Puppi, L., *Scrittori vicentini di architettura del secolo XVI*, Vicenza (1973).

—— 'Bibliografia e letteratura palladiana', in *Palladio: Catalogo della Mostra*, Vicenza (1973), pp. 171–90.

—— *Andrea Palladio*, London (1975).

—— *Andrea Palladio: Scritti sull'architettura (1554-1579)*, Vicenza (1988) (including a transcription of the guidebooks, without commentary).

—— *Palladio Drawings*, New York (1990).

—— (ed.), *Andrea Palladio; Il testo, l'immagine, la città*, Vicenza (1980).

Quilici Gigli, S., *Roma fuori le mura*, Rome (1986).

Raphael, *Tutti gli Scritti*, ed. E. Camesasca, Milan (1956).

Rawson, B. (ed.), *Marriage, Divorce, and Children in Ancient Rome*, Oxford (1991).

Reece, R. (ed.), *Burial in the Roman World*, London (1977).

Rinaldi, E., *La fondazione del Collegio Romano*, Arezzo (1914).

Rodríguez Almeida, E., *Il Monte Testaccio*, Rome (1984).

Rossi, D., and P. S. Bartoli, *Romanae Magnitudinis Monumenta*, Rome (1699).

Rossi, G. G. de, *Disegni di Vari Altari e Cappelle nelle chiese di Roma con le loro facciate fianchi piante e misure de piu celebri architetti*, Rome (1685).

Rowland, I., 'Raphael, Angelo Colocci, and the Genesis of the Architectural Orders', *Art Bulletin*, vol. 76 (March 1994), pp. 81–104.

Rybczynski, W., *The Perfect House: A Journey with the Renaissance Master Andrea Palladio*, New York (2002).

Rykwert, J., *The Idea of a Town: the Anthropology of Urban Form in Rome, Italy and the Ancient World*, Cambridge, Mass., and London (1988).

Saller, R., *Personal Patronage under the Early Empire*, Cambridge (1982).

Salvetti, C. B., 'Il sottosuolo delle terme di Diocleziano nel secolo XVI nei disegni della Biblioteca d'Arte nel Museo di Stato di Berlino', *Studi romani*, vol. 28, no. 1 (1970), pp. 462–66.

Santangelo, M., 'Il Quirinale nell'antichità classica', in '*Atti della Pontificia Accademia Romana di Archeologia*', S. III Memorie, vol. 5, Rome (1941), p. 11.

Scaglia, G., 'The Origin of an Archaeological Plan of Rome by Alessandro Strozzi', *Journal of the Warburg and Courtauld Institutes*, vol. 27 (1964), pp. 137–63.

Schroeder, H. J., *Canons and Decrees of the Council of Trent*, St Louis, Miss. (1941).

Schudt, L., *Le Guide di Roma; Materialien zu einer Geschichte der römischen Topographie*, Vienna (1930; reprint 1971).

Scullard, H. H., *Festivals and Ceremonies of the Roman Republic*, London (1981).

Seymour, C., *Michelangelo: Sistine Chapel Ceiling*, London (1972).

Serlio, S., *Il Terzo libro di Sabastiano Serlio Bolognese*, Venice (1540).

—— *Sebastiano Serlio on Architecture*, vol. 1: Books I–V of *Tutte l'opere d'architettura et prospetiva*, trans. V. Hart and P. Hicks, New Haven and London (1996).

Shatzman, I., *Senatorial Wealth and Roman Politics*, Brussels (1975).

Sicari, G., *Bibliografia delle guide di Roma in lingua italiana dal 1480 al 1850*, Rome (1991).

—— *Reliquie Insigni e 'Corpi Santi' a Roma*, Monografie Romane, Rome (1998).

Sparrow, J., *Visible Words*, Cambridge (1969).

Steinby, E. M., *Lexicon topographicum urbis Romae*, 6 vols, Rome (1993–2000).

Stinger, C., Humanism and the Church Fathers: Ambrogio Traversari (1386–1439) and Christian Antiquity in the Italian Renaissance, Albany, NY (1977).

—— *The Renaissance in Rome*, Bloomington, Ind. (1984).

—— 'Italian Renaissance Learning and the Church Fathers', in *The Reception of the Church Fathers in the West: From the Carolingians to the Maurists*, ed. I. Backus, Leiden (1997).

Suetonius, *De poetis e biografi minori*, ed. A. Rostagni, Turin (1944).

—— *De vita Caesarum* (*Lives of the Caesars*), Harvard (1977).

Tamenza, T., *Vita di Andrea Palladio*, Venice (1762).

Tavernor, R., *Palladio and Palladianism*, London (1991).

—— *On Alberti and the Art of Building*, New Haven and London (1998).

—— 'Palladio's "Corpus": *I quattro libri dell'architettura*', in *Paper Palaces: The Rise of the Renaissance Architectural Treatise*, ed. V. Hart and P. Hicks, New Haven and London (1998), pp. 233–46.

Thoenes, C., 'La "Lettera" a Leone X', in *Raffaello a Roma, il convegno del 1983*, ed. C. L. Frommel and M. Winner, Rome (1986), pp. 373–81.

Titi, F., *Studio di pittura, scultura ed architettura nelle chiese di Roma*, Rome (1674).

—— *Descrizione delle Pitture, Sculture e Architetture esposte in Roma*, Rome (1763).

Todd, M., *The Walls of Rome*, London (1978).

Toynbee, J., *Death and Burial in the Roman World*, Ithaca (1971).

Treggiari, S., *Roman Marriage: Iusti Coniuges from the Time of Cicero to the Time of Ulpian*, Oxford (1991).

Trenkler, E., *Le guide di Roma in der Österreichischen Nationalbibliothek*, Vienna (1976).

Trettenero, V., *Andrea Palladio scrittore*, Milan (1938).

Trevor Hodge, A., *Roman Aqueducts and Water Supply*, London (1992).

Valentini, R., and G. Zucchetti, *Codice topografico della città di Roma*, 4 vols, Rome (1953).

Van Eck, C., ' "The Splendid Effects of Architecture, and its Power to Affect the Mind": the Workings of Picturesque Association', in *Landscapes of Memory and Experience*, ed. J. Birksted, London (2000), pp. 245–58.

—— *British Architectural Theory 1540-1750*, Aldershot (2003).

Vanggaard, J. H., *The Flamen: A Study in the History and Sociology of Roman Religion*, Copenhagen (1988).

Vasari, G., *Lives of the Painters, Sculptors and Architects*, trans. G du C. de Vere, 2 vols, London (1996).

Versnel, H. S., *Triumphus: an Inquiry into the Origin, Development and Meaning of the Roman Triumph*, Leiden (1970).

Vitruvius, *De architectura*, trans. I. D. Roland, Cambridge (1999).

Vogel, J., *Bramante und Raffael*, Leipzig (1910).

Voragine, Jacobus de, *The Golden Legend*, trans. W. G. Ryan, Princeton (1995).

Weaver, P. R., *Familia Caesaris: A Social Study of the Emperor's Freedmen and Slaves*, Cambridge (1972).

Westfall, C. W., *In this Most Perfect Paradise: Alberti, Nicholas V, and the Invention of Conscious Urban Planning in Rome, 1447–55*, University Park, Pa. (1974).

Wiedemann, T., *Adults and Children in the Roman Empire*, London (1989).

Wilson Jones, M., *The Principles of Roman Architecture*, New Haven and London (2000).

Wissowa, G., *Religion and Kultus der Römer*, Munich (1912).

Wittkower, R., *Architectural Principles in the Age of Humanism*, London (1949).

Zeppegno, L., and R. Mattonelli, *Le chiese di Roma*, Rome (8th ed., 2000).

Zorzi, G. G., *La vera origine e la giovenezza di Andrea Palladio*, Venice (1922).

——*I disegni delle antichità di Andrea Palladio*, Venice (1959).

——*Le Chiese e i ponti di Andrea Palladio*, Venice (1967).

Anonymous Works

The Book of Pontiffs (Liber pontificalis). The Ancient Biographies of the First Ninety Roman Bishops to A.D. 715, trans. R. Davies, Translated Texts for Historians, vol. 6, Liverpool (2000).

Diario Romano, Vatican City (1926) (a booklet published annually giving the routine of feasts and fasts to be observed in Rome and the ecclesiastical functions to be performed in the city, in this case for the year 1926).

Historia Augusta (Histoire Auguste), ed. and trans. J.-P. Callu, A. Gaden and O. Desbordes, Paris (1992–).

Le cose maravigliose della citta di Roma, Rome (1544).

Le 'Liber Pontificalis': Texts, Introduction et Commentaire, ed. L. Duchesne, Paris (1886–92; reprint 1955–57).

Martirologio Romano, Vatican City (1964).

Martyrologium Hieronimianum, ed. J. B. de Rossi and L. Duchesne, Brussels (1894; reprint 1971).

Mirabilia urbis Romae: The Marvels of Rome, or a Picture of the Golden City, trans. F. M. Nichols, London (1889)).

Mirabilia vel potius historia et descriptio urbis Romae, Rome (1485). See: http://www.thelatinlibrary.com/mirabilia.html

'A Sixteenth-Century Guidebook', *Connoisseur*, vol. 2 (1902), p. 204.

Stato temporale delle chiese di Roma (Vatican reports on the state of the churches in Rome, for the years 1660, 1662 and 1666).

INDEX